PENGUIN BOOKS

ANGLER

Barton Gellman is a special projects reporter at *The Washington Post*, follow-ing tours that covered diplomacy, the Middle East, the Pentagon, and the D.C. superior court. His Cheney series, with partner Jo Becker, won a 2008 Pulitzer Prize, a George Polk Award, and the Goldsmith Prize for Investiga-tive Reporting. Gellman also shared a Pulitzer for national reporting in 2002, and his work has been honored by the Overseas Press Club, the Society of Professional Journalists, and the American Society of Newspaper Editors. Gellman graduated with highest honors from Princeton University and earned a master's degree in politics at University College, Oxford, as a Rhodes scholar. He is the author of *Contending with Kennan: Toward a Phi-losophy of American Power*. Gellman lives in New York City with Dafna Linzer and four children: Abigail, Michael, Lily, and Benjamin.

Praise for Barton Gellman's *Angler*

"Jaw-dropping . . . It reads like a thriller."
—Nicholas D. Kristof, *The New York Times*

"*Angler* could well turn out to be the most revealing account of Cheney's activities as vice president that ever gets written. . . . Full of fresh information and insights about the vice president in particular and the Bush administra-tion in general . . . Again and again, *Angler* deftly proves the logic of Cheney's actions. . . . There will almost certainly be no vice president as powerful as Cheney for decades and no account of what he has wrought that is as compel-ling as this book." —James Mann, *The Washington Post*

"A forceful new study . . . connecting the dots to give the reader a visceral understanding of just how Mr. Cheney maneuvered within the administra-tion." —Michiko Kakutani, *The New York Times*

"Gellman's narrative deserves to be read in full, in all its dismaying detail. It is a triumph of reporting on a figure who, in a public life that reaches back some forty years, has demonstrated unparalleled skills at remaining un-known and unknowable. . . . Gellman's book may well be the fullest account we will ever get of its subject." —Sam Tanenhaus, *The New Republic*

"[Gellman] has interviewed numerous associates and antagonists of the vice president, offering the most penetrating portrait of him yet. The result is that Cheney doesn't seem as bad as you might think. He's even worse."
—Jacob Heilbrunn, *The New York Times*

"[*Angler*] is simply one of the scariest stories ever written about contemporary America . . . an indispensable volume without which the Bush presidency can't be understood." —Steve Clemons, *The American Conservative*

"Again and again, Mr. Gellman shows how, through guile and sheer stubborn resolve, the vice president moved the country."
—Jeremy Lott, *The Washington Times*

"*Angler* . . . is the best account so far of the vice president's drive for 'power without limit.' It is an absorbing if depressing book."
—Clive Crook, *Financial Times*

"This look at this second most powerful office in the land couldn't be timelier."
—Gilbert Cruz, *Time*

"Carefully reported and vigorously written."
—Tim Rutten, *Los Angeles Times*

"The picture of stealth presented in the book is at times staggering. . . . Cheney emerges as a savvy, sometimes vengeful master of the Washington game—a man who used his influence to redefine the U.S. presidency, giving it powers that most constitutional experts denied it had."
—Celestine Bohlen, Bloomberg News

"There can be no doubt after reading this fair but quietly withering book that Cheney's role in shaping Bush's presidency—governing from the right, not the center; skirting procedures to achieve his goals on taxes and the environment; and above all setting an extremist course in the war against al-Qaida—has been overwhelmingly malign."
—David Greenberg, *Slate*

"[Gellman] lets fact and anecdote build to a persuasive case that Cheney controlled the Bush administration at least until the Justice Department debacle."
—Richard Oppel, *Austin American-Statesman*

"Fascinating, appalling, compulsively readable."
—Adam Begley, *The New York Observer*

"Barton Gellman . . . lays out the veep's unprecedented tenure action by action. As Gellman makes clear, Cheney's power is due as much to the nature of President George W. Bush as it is to his own forceful, uncompromising personality."
—Bob Hoover, *Pittsburgh Post-Gazette*

"In his meticulously researched, highly readable new biography . . . Barton Gellman tells the story of a man who has left a powerful imprint on American government."
—Theo Lippman Jr., *The Christian Science Monitor*

"A must-read to understand how Cheney wielded power in the White House."
—*Political Wire*

Angler

THE CHENEY VICE PRESIDENCY

Barton Gellman

PENGUIN BOOKS

PENGUIN BOOKS
Published by the Penguin Group
Penguin Group (USA) Inc., 375 Hudson Street, New York, New York 10014, U.S.A. •
Penguin Group (Canada), 90 Eglinton Avenue East, Suite 700, Toronto, Ontario, Canada
M4P 2Y3 (a division of Pearson Penguin Canada Inc.) • Penguin Books Ltd, 80 Strand,
London WC2R 0RL, England • Penguin Ireland, 25 St. Stephen's Green, Dublin 2, Ireland
(a division of Penguin Books Ltd) • Penguin Books Australia Ltd, 250 Camberwell Road,
Camberwell, Victoria 3124, Australia (a division of Pearson Australia Group Pty Ltd) •
Penguin Books India Pvt Ltd, 11 Community Centre, Panchsheel Park, New Delhi–110 017,
India • Penguin Group (NZ), 67 Apollo Drive, Rosedale, North Shore 0632, New Zealand
(a division of Pearson New Zealand Ltd) • Penguin Books (South Africa) (Pty) Ltd,
24 Sturdee Avenue, Rosebank, Johannesburg 2196, South Africa

Penguin Books Ltd, Registered Offices: 80 Strand, London WC2R 0RL, England

First published in the United States of America by The Penguin Press,
a member of Penguin Group (USA) Inc. 2008
Published in Penguin Books 2009

1 3 5 7 9 10 8 6 4 2

Photograph credits
Insert page 1 (both): David Burnett/Contact Press Images; 2 (above): AP Photo/Jerry Laizure;
2 (below), 3, 5 (below): Eric Draper/White House; 4 (above): White House; 4 (below): AP Photo/
J. Scott Applewhite; 5 (above): AP Photo/*The Herald and News,* Ron Winn; 6 (above): Charles
Ommanney/Contact Press Images; 6 (below left): Brendan Smialowski/Getty Images; 6 (below right):
Stefan Ruiz; 7 (above): AP Photo/Haraz Ghanbari; 7 (below): Charles Ommanney/Getty Images; 8:
David Bohrer/White House

While the author has made every effort to provide accurate Internet addresses at the time of
publication, neither the publisher nor the author assumes any responsibility for errors or for changes
that occur after publication. Further, the publisher does not have any control over and does not
assume any responsibility for author or third-party Web sites or their content.

THE LIBRARY OF CONGRESS HAS CATALOGED THE HARDCOVER EDITION AS FOLLOWS:

Gellman, Barton 1960–
Angler : the Cheney vice presidency / Barton Gellman.
p. cm.
Includes bibliographical references and index.
ISBN 978-1-59420-186-8 (hc.)
ISBN 978-0-14-311616-5 (pbk.)
1. Cheney, Richard B.   2. Vice Presidents—United States—Biography.   3. Cheney, Richard B.—
Political and social views.   4. United States—Politics and government—2001–   I. Title.
E840.8.C43G45   2008
973.931092—dc22   [B]   2008030128

Printed in the United States of America
Designed by Claire Naylon Vaccaro

For Dafna, my soul mate

Contents

Chapter One

A Very Short List

F rank Keating reached for the telephone on a desk the size of a Cadillac sedan. He was the picture of a governor in command, the first Republican to break the Oklahoma jinx on reelection. Working oil rigs outside his window—drilled right there on the capitol grounds—pumped cash into a booming state economy. Keating had big plans for the second term, not least the construction of a grand new dome atop the statehouse. And now here came Dick Cheney on the line. Truth was, Keating had been half expecting the call.

The week before, a "Dear Frank" note had arrived from George W. Bush. Keating's Texas neighbor had locked up the Republican presidential nomination on Super Tuesday, besting John McCain in six of ten states. Now Bush wanted advice on a running mate, "one of the most important decisions I will make this year," he wrote on May 18, 2000. A form letter, Keating knew. The newspapers said Bush sent one to every big name in the GOP.

And yet . . . Keating could not help but tally his prospects. He was fifty-six years old, telegenic and tough and going places. Bush admired the way Keating handled himself in 1995, when homegrown terrorists in a Ryder van blew up the Alfred P. Murrah Federal Building across town. The two men had a friendly football rivalry, liked to bet on Sooners-Longhorns games, and watched each other's back in national politics. Bush supported Keating to chair the Republican governors; Keating endorsed Bush for president early on. More than endorsed him: Keating vouched for Bush with right-to-lifers, who needed the reassurance, and he delivered his Oklahoma political machine. All that and the right kind of résumé—special agent in the FBI, U.S. attorney, senior posts in Washington at Treasury, Justice, and Housing. True, Keating did not offer a whole lot of balance to the ticket. He was an oil-state fiscal conservative, hawkish on the death penalty and union-busting "right-to-work" laws. Too much like Bush, most probably. Still, a person might wonder.

Cheney dialed the call himself. A lot of people liked that in a man of his rank, the sense that he refused to take on airs. The habit had other aspects. Cheney was chairman of a Fortune 500 company and had been a war-winning secretary of defense. Phoning unannounced had a way of catching people off balance, depriving them of that "Hold, please" moment to collect their thoughts. Aides said Cheney liked a glimpse at an unstudied interlocutor on the other end of the line. When Keating picked up, Cheney said his piece without preamble.

"The governor would like to have you be considered as running mate," he said.

Cheney let the statement hang, in that disconcerting way of his, stopping before the other person quite expects. Keating found nothing to read in the man's flat, clipped tone. He waited a beat, then probed.

"Dick, I don't really do anything for you-all," Keating said, thinking Cheney might add a word or two.

Cheney chose to take that as a question of geography.

"No, it doesn't matter," Cheney said. "Oklahoma and Texas, you may be joined by a border, but that is not a factor to us. Would you be willing to fill out all the paperwork?"

Indirection was getting Keating nowhere. He decided to ask flat out. Was this just a friendly gesture, or was Bush serious? Before running for governor, Keating had been through FBI background checks and four Senate confirmation hearings. He knew, or thought he did, what it meant to hand cool-eyed strangers the keys to every lockbox in his life. He did not care to go through that again without good cause.

"I want you to know the list is a very short list," Cheney replied.

People would talk about all kinds of names, Cheney said matter-of-factly, but most of them would be decoys. Three, maybe four, were genuine. Keating's was one of those, Cheney said. The next day a thick envelope arrived. Inside was the most demanding question-naire the Oklahoma governor had ever seen.

Keating knew Cheney, trusted him. He had helped recruit Cheney five years before to chair the memorial committee for Oklahoma City bombing victims. Later, Cheney headlined a fund-raiser for Keating's reelection campaign. "My relationship with Cheney was a good one, a correct one, and one that I thought was aboveboard and transparent," Keating recalled. "It turned into a very unpleasant association."

What happened after that was prologue to the play of Cheney's two terms as vice president. Amid stealth and misdirection, with visible formalities obscuring the action offstage, Cheney served as producer for Bush's first presidential decision. Somewhere along the way he stepped aside as head of casting, taking the part of Bush's running mate before anyone really auditioned. And he dodged most of the paperwork, bypassing the extraordinary scrutiny he devised for other candidates.

Keating filled out the questionnaire, handed over volumes of his most confidential files. In time he would have cause to regret that.

Two states east, in Tennessee, Lamar Alexander got word that Cheney was looking for him, too. He waited a couple of days to return the call. The campaign had come and gone for Alexander, and he had made up his mind to skip the GOP convention in July.

"You're hard to reach," Cheney began, the Wednesday before Memorial Day.

"Oh, not so hard, I don't think," Alexander said. "I'm sitting right here in front of our picture of the cabinet with President Bush."

Bush senior, he meant. Alexander had been education secretary from 1991 to 1993, when Cheney ran the Pentagon.

"Governor Bush would like to consider you as vice president," Cheney said.

Again the words hung, unembellished.

"I don't know what to say," Alexander replied. "I've changed my life. I've put politics behind me."

Not for nothing. Alexander had mounted two drives for the presidency himself, neither a juggernaut. His 2000 campaign did not last out 1999, dying with a sixth-place finish in the Iowa straw poll—behind Gary Bauer and Pat Buchanan, for heaven's sake. He was weary and disappointed and ready for his first long vacation in years.

"Surely there are other, better people," Alexander said.

"The governor has told me to put race and gender and geography aside and go for the person who would make the best president."

"There must be a long list," Alexander said.

"*You* try to make a long list," Cheney said. "When you make a list of Republicans, using that criterion, it is a short list."

"How about Fred Thompson?"

"He might," Cheney said.

Another silence.

"There are plenty of people who'd like the notoriety of being on the vice-presidential list, and I'm not one of them," Alexander said.

"I'm not talking about that kind of list. This is a short list," Cheney repeated.

"How short?"

"A handful."

"How big is a handful?"

"I've got five fingers on my hand," Cheney said, amused or impatient or maybe neither, Alexander couldn't tell. "How many have you got on yours?"

Alexander tacked again.

"Why don't *you* do it?" he asked.

"It's not for me. He's asked me to find someone else to do it."

Enough. Alexander owed the nominee a yes or no. He would have to think on the offer, talk things over with Honey. She wasn't going to like it. Five days later, May 29, Alexander called Cheney in Texas. Send the forms, he said.

Alexander did have one question. What should he tell reporters?

Cheney knows, if anyone does, how to keep a secret. His reply might have raised an eyebrow on a more suspicious man. "Of course we want to keep this private," Cheney said. But he added: Confirm that you're a candidate. Tell them you're filling out the questionnaire.

Bill Frist and Tom Ridge, John Engler and John Kasich, Chuck Hagel and John Danforth and Jon Kyl—they all got similar calls and similar instructions. Speculation in the media was intense. With the nomination decided, the race for running mate was front and center. Feed the beast, Bush's Austin campaign staff insisted, or the press pack will come up with its own story line. Alexander and Keating and the rest gave the talking heads something to chew on.

"I'll send you the papers," Cheney told Alexander, signing off. "Fill them out and send them back to me. Late in the month we'll get together."

Alexander headed to Nantucket for what would have been four weeks of biking alongside cranberry bogs and strolling the beaches of Siasconset. He spent half of it with his accountant and lawyer, on the phone and on a plane, assembling a comprehensive record of his life. He sent the package to Cheney in the second week of June, boxed in a heavy carton best left to younger backs. No easy task, but he understood that a campaign had to run all the traps.

"The only thing was," Alexander recalled, "I never heard from him again."

Secrecy was part of the bargain Cheney struck in the first week of April, when he agreed to run Bush's vice-presidential search. Worked best out of the limelight, he said. Fewer involved, fewer the leaks, fewer the egos to stroke. For Cheney, the low profile was a means to an end, the way to get things done without obstruction. Bush did not worry about losing control—the final word was his anyway—but he enjoyed the cloak-and-dagger by temperament. Old hands had long observed the pure pleasure he took in ambushing know-it-alls in the press, subverting expectations of critics and rivals. Aides who followed Bush and Cheney to Washington would see the pattern again and again, not only in their mutual secrecy but in the way the two men reached a meeting of minds for different reasons entirely. "Cheney was pushing on an open door," recalled Dan Bartlett, who became White House communications director, even if Bush took a different path to meet him.

Not even Bush's closest aides were allowed inside the machine that Cheney built to sift the vice-presidential contenders. Not Dan Bartlett, not Karen Hughes, not Karl Rove, and not Joe Allbaugh, Bush's former chief of staff and campaign manager. Sometimes Bush would tell his people about a candidate or a piece of advice he heard, like the letter from Dan Quayle on behalf of Lamar Alexander. (Quayle pitched Alexander as the kind of right-to-lifer who doesn't scare off swing voters. Rove cared a lot more about the base than the swing, but he phoned Quayle to let him know that Bush had shared his note.) There were plenty of things Bush could not have told his retinue, though, because he did not know all the fine points himself. He was a big-picture man, comfortable with broad objectives, broadly declared. He had given Cheney marching orders, described the qualities he wanted in his Number Two. He left most of the legwork to the older man, taking briefings when his vetter had something new to say. Cheney lived in a different world. He had spent his professional life in places where ends and means collide, where the choices are often zero-sum and outcomes ride on the details.

Only three people were privy to the dossiers that Cheney assembled. One was his older daughter, Liz Cheney, thirty-three, a politically active lawyer who had left the State Department for private practice. Another was David J. Gribbin III, a loyal retainer since high school who had followed Cheney to Congress, the Pentagon, and Halliburton. The third was David Addington, the gifted and ferocious attorney who had been Cheney's intellectual alter ego since the Iran-Contra hearings of 1987.

Addington and Liz Cheney wrote an exhaustive questionnaire, the language honed to pierce attempts at evasion. In precise legal prose, it asked about things a person might not tell his best friend—addictions, infidelities, crimes proved and unproved, plagiarism, bad debt, mental illness, embarrassing failures to pass a licensing test. Even by the bare-it-all standards of American politics after Watergate, the questions from the Cheney team were strikingly intrusive. For a Top Secret clearance in the U.S. government, which entrusts the holder with information that could do "exceptionally grave damage to the national security," an applicant must answer thirty questions, generally limited to events of the previous seven years. The Cheney form had close to two hundred questions under seventy-nine headings, requiring answers that covered the whole span of adulthood. "By definition, this is a process that looks very deeply into the lives of public figures," Gribbin recalled. "It's an extraordinarily sensitive process."

Some of Cheney's inquiries were more or less standard in the vetting of potential running mates. Presidential campaigns had accumulated lengthy checklists over the years, adding fresh queries in each election to guard against the scandals of the last. Mental health became fair game when a history of electric shock therapy drove Thomas Eagleton off the Democratic ticket in 1972. Spouses came in for scrutiny after Geraldine Ferraro, Walter Mondale's 1984 running mate, was dogged by questions about her husband's tax returns. Two years later, William Rehnquist made a contribution to the checklist when his confirmation as chief justice of the United States was imperiled by news that he once owned property under a deed forbidding sale to Jews. Clarence Thomas's confirmation hearing in 1991 revealed the political risk of a sexual harassment charge. Beginning in 1993, when Zoe Baird was forced to withdraw as nominee for attorney general, candidates for high office had to answer for the green cards and tax returns of their domestic employees. Other political scandals, great and small, lent precedent to Cheney's questions about defaults on child support or student loans, controversial business clients, and links to foreign governments or donors.

Even so, the structure of Cheney's questionnaire bespoke unusual distrust of those who filled it out, with a corresponding demand for access to primary evidence. Cheney and his team were not prepared to accept a doctor's summary of the candidate's present health and medical history, which traditionally focused on fitness for the rigors of office. They asked for copies of all medical records, complete with clinical notes and laboratory results. Unlike investigators for U.S. security clearances, who tell applicants they may withhold information about "marital, family, or grief counseling, not related to violence by you," the Cheney team also sought details of any visit, for any reason, to a "psychiatrist, psychologist, therapist or counselor."

Another distinguishing feature of Cheney's review was its expansion of the usual scope of inquiry. Cheney asked about the military service records, the criminal histories, and other intimate details of parents, children, siblings, spouses, and in-laws as well as the vice-presidential contenders themselves. He asked about not only professional sanctions and allegations of malpractice but also "misconduct in school"; not only whether the candidate had been charged with a crime but also whether he had been identified as a suspect or witness; not only about recorded civil judgments and admissions of wrongdoing but also about no-fault settlements and cases sealed by a court.

A catchall question near the end asked each contender to specify in writing—it was just as bald as this—any event or proclivity that might leave him "vulnerable to blackmail or coercion."

To guard against omissions, Cheney ensured he had a free hand to tap directly into sources of information that are ordinarily guarded by privacy law. The vetting forms required each candidate to sign a notarized authorization for "Richard B. Cheney or . . . any person designated by him" to obtain from hospitals, doctors, and insurance companies "without limitation, any medical records" covering "any time period." Candidates were obliged to sign a similar form permitting the Internal Revenue Service to release their tax returns and schedules, and another for credit reports. They were further asked to request, on Cheney's behalf, the contents of their FBI files. One of the forms conferred on Cheney and his team, along with anyone who answered their questions, a blanket waiver of "any liability with regard to seeking, furnishing or use of" the confidential information. No expiration date was specified.

Cheney hired lawyers at Latham & Watkins to sift the thousands of pages thus produced on each of the candidates. The supervising partner was Philip J. Perry, Liz Cheney's husband.

On June 8, after two weeks of labor, Keating delivered an eight-inch stack of documents, spilling out of triple-hinged binders that proved unequal to the mass.

"Dear Dick," he wrote. "I enclose responses to the questionnaire, with supporting material. The Freedom of Information request to the FBI has been transmitted and I will forward the resulting material as soon as I receive it."

Arrayed for Cheney's inspection were photographs, Social Security numbers, education and employment histories of his wife, Catherine; his daughter, Carrie, then twenty-six; and sons Kelly and Chip, respectively twenty-four and twenty years old. Keating listed each address since 1962 and each job since 1969. As requested, he attached copies of every speech and every article he had written; interviews and transcripts of testimony; every published story in his files about the ups and downs and controversies of his career. He enumerated assets of $2,587,208.41, breaking down twenty-seven investments to the penny. (Most were mutual funds from Fidelity, Templeton, Janus, Vanguard, and T. Rowe Price.)

Keating's medical summary described a man of normal weight and robust health, based on annual physicals and his doctor's assessment of diagnostic tests. He took no prescription drug but Lipitor, which controlled a tendency to high cholesterol. He worked fifteen-hour days without ill effect. An ordinary candidate screening would have stopped about there. Keating's submission, as specified by Cheney, attached scores of pages more—examination records, electrocardiograms, a scheduled sigmoidoscopy, laboratory results. The files said Keating's neck and shoulder made it hard to sleep comfortably sometimes; an orthopedist saw signs of wear and tear that might be early arthritis. He recommended ibuprofen and cleared Keating to resume a daily three-mile run. The governor confessed to his doctors that he drank too much coffee, eight to ten cups a day, and did not eat as well as he ought to on the road. He took Geritol. He had a forty-one-inch chest and thirty-four-inch waist. His blood pressure, at 150/90, would bear watching. There was a sick visit on October 26, 1998, when Keating complained of sore throat, fever, and fatigue. (He had been self-medicating, the doctor noted, with hot tea and honey.) An unfortunate meal of catfish in 1996 left him nauseated and weak. Another exam turned up a slight enlargement of Keating's prostate, but the standard assay for cancer-related antigens found nothing untoward. Elsewhere the files recorded the usual indignities of the human animal under modern medicine, from the shape of Keating's testicles to the sphincter tone observed in rectal exams. As a physical specimen, Keating stood altogether naked before Cheney's team.

These were not the disclosures that Keating came to regret. Nor did he have trouble with the small points in his file that might open a national candidate to attack—draft deferments during the Vietnam War and tempests over ill-chosen words that inspired opponents to dub him "Governor Pop-off." Keating ascribed the latter to his "sense of humor—a saving grace in life, if occasionally a liability in politics."

What brought him low, in the bitter aftermath of his screening by Cheney, were the answers at tabs 69 and 73. The first asked about any potential question of ethics, regardless of merit. The second sought information on any other matter, whether part of the public record or not, that might embarrass the campaign.

Keating decided, in what he called "an abundance of caution," to describe a history of gifts to his family from an eccentric New York philanthropist. Keating had met Jack Dreyfus, founder of the eponymous mutual funds, in late 1988. Keating was then the third-ranking Justice Department official in the waning days of the Reagan administration. Dreyfus had suffered depression as a young man and made a spectacular recovery after taking the prescription drug Dilantin, which is government approved primarily for seizure disorders. He became convinced that Dilantin was a miracle medicine, capable of curing ailments across a broad medical landscape, from car sickness to Tourette's syndrome. Dreyfus had no known financial interest in Dilantin or the company that makes it, but he wrote two books and sank much of his fortune into a foundation to tell its story. When the two men met, Dreyfus bent Keating's ear on a proposal to promote the rehabilitation of criminals by distributing Dilantin in federal prisons. Keating deflected Dreyfus to the U.S. Bureau of Prisons, which lacked enthusiasm. When Keating left government, he turned down an offer to join the Dreyfus foundation, but the two men became friends nonetheless. "Somebody who thinks celery is a miracle fruit, you know, a lot of people might say, 'This guy's strange,'" Keating said. "But Jack is a wonderful guy."

By the spring of 1990, Keating was back in government as general counsel to Jack Kemp's Department of Housing and Urban Development. One evening over dinner Dreyfus announced that he was a wealthy man, could do as he liked, and wanted to pay the college costs of Keating's three children. A jaw-dropping temptation, no doubt. Keating, the G-man turned prosecutor, succumbed. After all, he reasoned, there was no question of personal corruption—nothing Dreyfus wanted in return, and nothing Keating could do for the man, anyway, in the Housing Department. Those rationales would come to seem naive, even vaguely untoward, in a man who had built his career on uprightness. But he decided to treat the matter as a narrow question of law: Was he allowed to accept the money or not?

Government documents back Keating's recollection that he asked for a ruling from the Housing Department's ethics staff. The lawyers had no objection so long as Keating declared the gifts on standard annual disclosure forms and recused himself from business affecting his friend. Gary Davis, general counsel of the Office of Government Ethics, seconded the departmental opinion, finding that the gifts were neither prohibited nor improper in appearance. It is undisputed that Keating reported them every year during his federal employment. Even so, Keating decided that Cheney ought to know.

"What did you do that for?" demanded Catherine Keating, his wife, when he told her what he had written in the Cheney questionnaire. A note of grievance came through seven years later, as Keating recounted the story by telephone. A woman's voice, soft but insistent, became audible in the background. Keating laughed ruefully and said, "As a matter of fact my Cathy is standing here," reminding him that she "and my chief of staff and everybody was saying, 'Why would you put this down? Because it's not what they're after.'" The governor believed he was as square as they come, but asked himself, "You know, could an issue be raised? Possibly so." And with the vice presidency at stake, he ought to be "purely Caesar's wife."

How Cheney counseled Bush as the weeks went by, and by what subtle shifts he crossed the line from adviser to running mate, are questions likely to frustrate categorical answer. Too much of the action took place without witnesses, on the back porch of the big house on Bush's Crawford ranch or in telephone calls that, according to aides, Bush would leave the room to take. But some of Cheney's advice, then and later, did make its way to Bush's confidants, because the Texas governor was not half as committed as Cheney to silence. Sometimes Bush's inner circle could see the boss reframing the older man's observations as his own, adding new thoughts and new turns of phrase to his lexicon.

As First Son, Bush had witnessed tensions between his father's White House staff and the hard-charging operators who looked out for the political future of Vice President Quayle. Cheney reinforced the lesson that ambition in a vice president leads inexorably to conflict with the man in the Oval Office, especially as the next election nears. Anyone could see it happening that summer between Bill Clinton and Al Gore, he said. Cheney told Bush how much Gerald Ford, a man accustomed to leadership, hated his brief tenure as Richard Nixon's Number Two. He recounted inside stories of his own subsequent battles, as Ford's White House chief of staff, with Vice President Nelson Rockefeller. (Cheney helped persuade Ford to throw Rockefeller off the ticket in 1976.) Bush, for sure, wanted none of that kind of nonsense. He sought a trustworthy adviser, conversant in the ways of Washington—but most of all loyal, content to remain backstage. What Bush seemed to picture, the author Jacob Weisberg has proposed, was the constitutional equivalent of his wife, Laura.

Federal Reserve chairman Alan Greenspan, an old friend, chatted with Cheney about the vice-presidential search that summer. Cheney ran down the wish list—a person capable of commanding the presidency should need arise, yet satisfied to wait quietly in the wings; a confidant of sound judgment with experience in foreign affairs, in Congress, or in the corridors of the executive branch. Greenspan was struck by Cheney's poker face. In a few economical phrases, the man had just sketched as neat a self-portrait as Greenspan could imagine. Was it possible that Cheney did not know it? Cheney appeared to be organizing a nationwide search for himself. If so, Greenspan said privately, he approved. Greenspan had worked with or for every president since 1968. Only Nixon and Clinton—an odd couple, Greenspan allowed—matched Cheney's intellect. None was his equal at turning a strategic goal into operational plans.

Critics who cast Cheney as Svengali, luring Bush into a choice that was not his own, tend to slight the plentiful evidence that Bush took an early shine to his father's secretary of defense. By both men's accounts, confirmed by aides who bear no love for Cheney, Bush made the first approach. At a dinner in November 1999, he asked the Halliburton CEO to chair his national campaign. Then, in March 2000, Bush dispatched Allbaugh, his chief of staff, to sound out Cheney's interest in being considered for running mate. In an interview with his authorized biographer, Cheney said he declined both overtures. "It was a firm no," he said of his reply to Allbaugh. Bush depicted himself as a suitor who slowly broke down Cheney's resistance. "It became apparent to me that Cheney was the kind of guy that would be a good fit for a two-term governor from Texas who, while he had a pretty good political pedigree, didn't have a lot of what they call 'Washington experience,'" he said. Bush's biographer, who likewise spoke to both men, said the president emphasized the virtue of a partner "whose own political ambitions would not supersede his loyalty to Bush."

And yet the story is not so simple, because ambition's link to disloyalty was exactly what Cheney impressed upon Bush with his parables of Rockefeller and Ford. In that context, Cheney's denial of interest—the very act of spurning a shot at the ticket—proclaimed him as a man who posed no threat. Bush made clear, in his most revealing interview, how much that appealed to him. "He's a thoughtful guy, he has the respect of the people around the table, and what he said made sense," Bush said. "And plus, *he didn't want it.*" There was a logic in that, from Bush's point of view. Even so, equating ambition with latent mutiny pointed Bush toward an unusual idea: that he ought to choose a running mate who had no particular interest in reaching the White House. Historically, that was anomalous. Beginning with its first two occupants, John Adams and Thomas Jefferson, the vice presidency was at once the most frustrating job in government and the surest route to the top. Former vice presidents accounted for fully one-third of all presidents by the year 2000; still more had sought or won their party nominations. If that was not a good thing, as Cheney intimated, then candidates for Bush's ticket acquired a hint of suspicion the moment they agreed to apply. Most of them, unlike Cheney, were in their political primes, young enough to think of elections to come.

No one but Cheney can say when he began to see a vice president in the mirror. By agreeing to manage the search, however, Cheney did something he does as well as anyone in Washington. He placed himself in the only vantage point that could show him how much time he had left to decide. Had Bush displayed signs of settling on someone else, Cheney would have been the first to know.

What Cheney did not choose to do, more than what he did, offers the strongest evidence of intent to keep his options open. Cheney is among the most careful of men with words, and every experienced executive knows how to say no with finality. In politics the classic formula was William Tecumseh Sherman's in 1884: "If drafted I will not run; if nominated I will not accept; if elected I will not serve." Florida's Connie Mack offered an updated model in 2000, saying he would never speak to Cheney again if Cheney placed him on the list. Cheney, by contrast, took no unequivocal stand. When Bush announced at a campaign stop in Dayton, Ohio, that Cheney would lead the search for a running mate—that was April 24, 2000, three weeks after Cheney actually began—the first point Bush added was that the role did not rule out Cheney's own selection. Some weeks later, Colin Powell asked for and obtained a public announcement from Bush that he did not wish to be, and would not be, a candidate for the job. Cheney never did that. He therefore left a future president at risk of the embarrassment that comes with extending still another invitation and receiving still another rebuff. Such a breach of protocol would have been gratuitous had Cheney been determined to refuse.

Close inspection of the record, bolstered by recent interviews with senior figures in the Bush campaign, shows that Cheney in fact advanced no commanding reason to keep him off the ticket. Every objection was either curable or framed in terms that Bush might easily think unimportant, even ignoble. The official story, in accounts the two men gave in 2000 and more recently to their authorized biographers, describes the Twelfth Amendment as a thorny problem, with Cheney pointing out more than once that the Constitution does not permit a president and vice president from the same state. (As chairman of the Dallas-based Halliburton, Cheney lived in Texas.) When the time came, he plucked that thorn with a day trip to register to vote at his second home in Jackson Hole, Wyoming. Cheney told Bush, moreover, that he had been arrested twice in the 1960s for driving under the influence of alcohol. The nominee, with a DUI of his own, could hardly be expected to blanch. Much the same went for Cheney's argument that his oil-industry background might prove controversial, another point in common. As a son of Wyoming, whose paltry three electoral votes were reliably Republican anyway, Cheney said he had nothing to offer Bush in battleground states. But Bush had already declared himself indifferent, in his choice of running mate, to short-term electoral advantage. Cheney protested that he was happy in private life. That may have been the flimsiest excuse, the converse of the usual evasion of departing officials who talk about leaving their jobs for more time with the family.

On its face, Cheney's strongest argument against himself was a history of heart disease. He put the point reservedly. Cheney did not profess concern that running for vice president might damage his health or pose a risk to his life. Bush would have had little choice but to accept a firm refusal on those grounds. Cheney portrayed his heart, instead, as a threat to Bush's *political* health, protection of which was properly for the nominee to decide. Cheney explained that he had not suffered a cardiac event for twelve years, and that his present health was good. In one of the few such meetings attended by the campaign's inner circle, Cheney said "he was active and vigorous," Karen Hughes recalled, "and ran a big worldwide business." He warned that if he should suffer chest pains, he would have to go to a hospital for an exam. The potential problem was the "impact it might have on the campaign," not on Cheney's fitness for office. When asked whether his heart would impede his service as vice president, Cheney told the group he "didn't think it would, since he had run an international business and been through lots of stress and intensity as secretary of defense during the Gulf War," according to Hughes. Cheney was advising Bush to worry about himself, not Cheney—and about appearances, not reality. Bush had to decide, by that rubric, whether he had the spine to stand up to an empty political attack.

The public record on David Addington, after three decades in Washington, turned up exactly one hearing in Congress, one grand jury transcript, and one on-the-record interview in print. The interview was largely unremarkable, save for its allusion to an intriguing moment in the early days of the vice-presidential search. As they designed the screening process, Addington recounted, he "joked that if Cheney did a good job on the search, Bush might ask him to be his running mate." According to both men, Cheney "dismissed the comment with a laugh."

Acquaintances said Addington and Cheney shared a dry sense of humor, but neither was given to idle chat. Their wit tended more toward the topical than the trifling. One point of context for that exchange was a history they shared on the Cheney for President exploratory committee in 1994, before Cheney abandoned his brief flirtation with a campaign of his own.

For all the talk of desired qualities—judgment, experience, gravitas—the search for Bush's running mate looked harder at vice than virtue. What unpleasant surprise awaited if this or that contender joined the ticket? Which predictable lines of attack? Where were the hidden defects, the offenses against valuable interest groups? Such are the preoccupations of any national campaign, protecting itself against risk. Cheney had been through the exercise before, when he helped Ford choose Robert Dole as Rockefeller's replacement. Much later, he told his biographer that the 2000 screening bore out his "experience over the years . . . that you usually end up with the least worst option." Dan Quayle, who once passed through the wringer himself and consulted with the Bush campaign from afar, compared the process to enactment of a law. "It's a lot easier to kill legislation than pass legislation," he said. "So it's a lot easier to knock off V.P. candidates than to actually get one through the mill."

It was Addington who oversaw the disassembly, cataloging blemishes and mounting them for inspection. Admirers and critics alike called him a paperwork prodigy, slashing through great volumes of text and carving out points of interest with uncanny speed. Bearded and barrel-chested and standing more than six feet tall, Addington was prone to strong opinions and a pugilistic tone in advancing them. After compiling the records on Keating, Alexander, Frist, Hagel, and the rest, Addington prepared a com-prehensive memo on each. "That's the way presidential and vice-presidential processes go," Alexander said in a conversation in early 2008, as the Democratic and Republican fields were winnowed down to two contenders each. "We can see it going on right now. You take very good people and you begin to poke holes in them."

Two things stood out in retrospect about Cheney's selection for the 2000 ticket, neither understood at the time.

The hardest one to explain was that Bush—who put so much stock in his instinct for people, that knack for decoding a handshake or the quality of a gaze—did not interview a single candidate before he settled on Cheney. Bush was acquainted with most of them, to one degree or another. But those interactions came "in a very different context," as Keating put it, in his case "on issues of importance to governors." Bush never sat the contenders down, never laid eyes on them as they answered points of doubt, never heard out their worldviews or their visions of a White House partnership. Bush and Cheney concealed that omission by maintaining a false suspense in the weeks before the Republican convention began in Philadelphia on July 31. Timing the news for best advantage is routine in any political campaign. In this case the tactic did not so much postpone the news as rewrite it, promoting a tale of scrutiny by Bush that included personal interviews with top contenders.

The calendar told the story. July 3 was the decisive day, when Bush asked Cheney to join the ticket and Cheney replied for the first time that he was willing. (Cheney told his biographer it was only then, in the sweltering heat of Bush's back porch, that he reached the reluctant conclusion that the "least worst option" was himself.) Cheney told Bush he would decide how to divest from Halliburton and gather the required assurances from his doctors.

For the next three weeks, campaign spinners fed news stories touting Ridge, Keating, and Danforth as front-runners. Only after the Independence Day weekend did Bush and Cheney begin to schedule interviews for a vacancy that no longer existed. Cheney phoned Ridge on July 5 to make one such appointment. The Pennsylvania governor replied instead that he no longer wished to be considered. Cheney asked him not to say so in public. Four days later, on July 9, CNN found Ridge in State College, Pennsylvania, where he was host of a summer gathering of fellow governors. Correspondent Gary Tuchman introduced Ridge as "the leader of an important swing state" and "a top-tier possibility" to join the ticket with Bush. "Are you nervous about waiting for this decision?" he asked. "No," Ridge replied gamely. "I believe ultimately it's a matter of trust, and let the chips fall where they may."

Two days after that, July 11, Cheney flew to Washington. On his public agenda was a meeting with Frist, in fact Cheney's first substantial interview with a contender. Not disclosed, the same day, was Cheney's appointment with his doctor to arrange a summary health report for Bush. On July 14, Bush conducted his own first audition—with New York governor George Pataki, who had filled out Cheney's questionnaire. Campaign officials said Pataki was "in the mix." Pataki did not dispute the report at the time. In truth, the New York governor chatted briefly with Bush "about their families, about politics and whatnot," David Catalfamo, Pataki's communications director, recalled recently. Bush "never brought up the issue of the vice presidency."

Back in Texas the next day, July 15, Bush disclosed for the first time to Hughes, Rove, and Allbaugh that Cheney was his man. (He heard out their best efforts as devil's advocates, but none of them had access to Cheney's files.) Three days after that, on July 18, Bush scheduled his second and last interview with a candidate, generating news coverage of a meeting with Danforth and his wife. Retired senator Alan Simpson, one of Cheney's oldest political friends, said Cheney had recommended Danforth for the job and set up the meeting, saying "Here's one for you. This guy's great." If Cheney told that to Simpson, it was not true. The deal was already done.

Only after this final feint, on July 21, did Cheney register to vote in Wyoming, a fact he had to know would become public. The same day, satisfying a requirement of his contract with Halliburton, he notified the board of directors that he might be about to depart the job. On July 25, Bush announced his decision to face Al Gore in the general election with Cheney at his side. Neither Bush nor Cheney held a face-to-face interview for the job with Keating, Alexander, Ridge, Hagel, Kasich, Engler, or any of the other ersatz finalists.

Some campaign officials disputed that, pointing to Bush's late-June campaign stop in Wayne, Michigan, alongside Engler. Bush was quoted as saying Engler is "on the list," adding, "What do you expect me to say? He's standing right here." Years later, Engler said Bush spent his downtime on a treadmill that day. The two men spoke for a few minutes about Michigan politics and their children—Bush's twin girls, Engler's triplets. As for becoming Bush's running mate, "I never had that conversation," Engler said.

The precedent Bush and Cheney set, establishing a forum of

two for the most sensitive deliberations, would follow them to Washington. Equally meaningful in light of events to come was Cheney's deft avoidance of the scrutiny he had conducted on the other candidates. "He went down through everybody's negatives," Quayle recalled. "And everybody has negatives. . . . And nobody really vetted him on what his negatives were." Gribbin, for example, was a trusted friend who maintained his own records of work with Cheney across the years. When the author asked him whether anyone requested that he produce those files, or review them, he replied, "No. Heaven and good grief, no." Gribbin, who had full access to the other dossiers, added, "I don't have knowledge of who vetted the vetter. I don't know who vetted Cheney or what process they used. It was not something I was involved in or that anybody ever told me. At some point there was a decision that all these names were going to be set aside, and they were going to select Cheney. It was a shock to me."

Cheney did not fill out his own questionnaire, a fact obscured in the days after Bush's announcement. "Secretary Cheney told me he subjected himself to the same kind of scrutiny" as everyone else, campaign spokeswoman Karen Hughes said in a briefing for reporters. Hughes said Allbaugh scrutinized the record of Cheney's service in the executive and legislative branches, while only Bush himself—a man known even then for aversion to detail—inspected Cheney's financial and medical history. Gradually it emerged that all this took place in the space of just over a week. The story left untold was that no one had access to Cheney's tax or corporate records, and no one but his own doctor read a word of his medical files. Cheney, who had employed a man named James Steen for many years as a personal archivist, did not submit even his public speeches, interviews, testimony, and voting record to Allbaugh, who ostensibly was combing them for red flags.

Dan Bartlett, then and later a top communications strategist for Bush, said the campaign was "utterly unprepared" for Cheney and that weeks after the announcement he was still scrambling to uncover basic facts about Bush's running mate. "We were caught flatfooted," unable to respond to Democratic attacks on Cheney's voting record against Head Start, school lunch programs, and the Martin Luther King Jr. national holiday. "Literally our in-house research team, myself and others, were just poring through—I mean, boxes were kind of just dumped, there was no road map, there were no concise answers," Bartlett said. "Like I said, we were on our heels." A member of Halliburton's public relations shop, designated by Cheney to answer corporate questions, proved unhelpful. When the campaign asked questions, Bartlett said, Halliburton replied that the records were in storage or "'That lawyer doesn't work for us anymore.'" Cheney set his heels against opening the books at Halliburton, saying "We're not going to drag them in." Bartlett went to Bush and said, "We're getting our asses kicked in the media because we're not prepared."

Cheney rode it out, and Bush went along. "To his standard he probably thinks he's an open book," Bartlett said. "To his standard—trust me. It really goes to this whole mind-set of how he entered this job. He entered this job less in his mind as a politician than as a public servant. He made his decision not to run for president in '96, and I think he viewed this as 'I was in private life, this guy has convinced me to come back, I'm going to help him, [but] I'm not going to completely tear my private life apart to do this.' When it came to things that touched home, his thing was 'I'm not going through that.' I'm not saying it's logical, I'm just saying that was the Cheney worldview."

And as for Cheney's ailing heart? Hughes told reporters after the announcement that Bush had commissioned an independent review of his running mate's medical fitness. Bush's father, the former president, suggested a second opinion from Denton A. Cooley, a man of sterling authority. Cooley was founder of the Texas Heart Institute and recipient of a Medal of Freedom from President Ronald Reagan. According to the Bush campaign, Cooley took his own careful look and vouched for Cheney's health.

That was not quite half true. Cooley thought he was doing the former president a quiet favor, and did not expect his involvement to be cited as an independent medical review. Reached at the soaring glass building named for him at St. Luke's Episcopal Hospital in Houston, he said Bush's father asked him to sound out Cheney's personal physician in Washington, Jonathan S. Reiner. Cooley did not know the man but found him open and persuasive. In a brief conversation, Cheney's doctor offered a "personal assurance that his cardiac status was sound." Cooley did not look at Cheney's films, electrocardiac data, or any other records, nor did he make the wide-ranging medical inquiries conducted on the other candidates for Bush's running mate.

Four months later, Cooley saw the news that Cheney had been rushed to the hospital for insertion of a stent in a coronary artery. "It wasn't a real surprise at all," he said, because Cheney clearly had chronic heart problems. In retrospect, Cooley said, he had "some misgivings to pass on his condition" without examining Cheney or seeing the records for himself. In any case, he said, he is a surgeon, not a cardiologist. For a thorough review of Cheney's health, another doctor would have been a better choice.

As it happened, Keating had scheduled his own news conference on the day Bush announced that Cheney would join the 2000 ticket. Keating went ahead with the unveiling of his Oklahoma Capitol

Dome, a big and popular project. That evening, he accepted an invitation to sing Cheney's praises on television. "There are really only two people in public life in America, at least on our team, that certainly are stratospheric characters, and that's Colin Powell and Dick Cheney," he said on CNN's *Crossfire* program. "The rest of us are down with the cumulus clouds. And when Dick Cheney was selected by George, I was enthusiastic about it. This guy has a distinguished record in the Congress, in the administration, he led the country, he certainly led the Department of Defense, was Colin Powell's boss in the Persian Gulf War, did a great job. A matter of pride for all of us as Americans. He's been an extraordinarily successful business guy. I was thrilled. I wasn't disappointed at all, because I never thought I would get it."

There would be other fish to fry if Bush reached the White House. Bush liked familiar faces around him. Keating had served barbecue with the man at a high school on the Oklahoma-Texas border. By late November, Keating found himself in Palm Beach, counting chads with the other VIP volunteers as the Florida recount ground on. When the Supreme Court called the election for Bush, Keating was on everybody's lips for a senior cabinet post. *Newsweek* said he "was on the supershort veep list and could be attorney general or FBI chief."

Cheney, who was running the transition, had other plans. The law—its interpretation, its enforcement—was critical to the exercise of White House power. As Cheney saw things, the attorney general, like every other member of the cabinet, ought to be subordinate to the president. There was only one executive authority in the Constitution. You might hardly know it from the way some attorneys general behaved. To Cheney's way of thinking, independence and Justice Department experience might not be virtues. In any case, Cheney had another person in mind. John Ashcroft, the former Missouri senator, had just been defeated for reelection by a dead man. That was a rude way of saying it, but euphemism did not capture the chagrin. Ashcroft's opponent, Democratic governor Mel Carnahan, had perished in a plane crash three weeks before election day, too late to have his name removed from the ballot. He won anyway. (Jean Carnahan, his wife, was appointed in his place.) Ashcroft would be grateful for the Justice post, and he would have a steep learning curve to climb. Ashcroft was accustomed, as well, to minding the party leadership. Or so went the thinking at the time. Later, Ashcroft would surprise the vice president on that point.

Keating wanted the job, and he enjoyed vocal support. That needed watching. Not many constituencies mattered more than the Federalist Society, which had brought its influence to bear on government and legal education since its birth at the dawn of the Reagan revolution. "Most of the conservatives were backing either Keating or Ashcroft," recalled Leonard Leo, the society's executive vice president. "I and a number of other Catholics had kind of put our weight behind Governor Keating." The Oklahoman's track record in the Justice Department lent confidence that he would be not only conservative but effective. Still, as Leo added in an e-mail: "Frank Keating is a straight shooter. He doesn't mince words. He would have believed in the unitary executive, but, as AG, certainly would have told the WH what he thought and would have pushed back when there were differences of opinion." A conservative with comparable views said, "Maybe that's not what they were looking for."

Keating's incautious wit, which had drawn him into hot water before, may have sealed his fate. Shortly before election day 2000, someone asked Keating, a bit naughtily, whether he planned a bid for the vacancy left by Cheney at Halliburton. "No," Keating replied, smiling. "But I would like to chair the next selection committee." Years later, a joke like that would become permissible. Cheney told it on himself in February of his final year in office. "My close association with the President goes back to the year 2000, when he asked me to lead the search for a vice presidential nominee," he deadpanned. The friendly audience at the Omni Shoreham Hotel was laughing already. Cheney didn't need the punch line, but he delivered it with nice comic timing: "That worked out pretty well." The audience roared. The next month, a reporter asked Bush how he would advise John McCain to choose a running mate for 2008. "I'd tell him to be careful about who he names to be the head of the selection committee," Bush cracked.

Back in the fall of 2000, with the general election looking close, Keating's jibe had some sting. It got back to Bush-Cheney campaign headquarters. "I was told that my friends in the new administration were not amused," Keating said.

Keating had risen with *Newsweek,* and *Newsweek* brought him down. The magazine's investigative bulldog, Michael Isikoff, was fresh from a series of scoops in the long-running Clinton-Lewinsky impeachment scandal. Keating was celebrating the Oklahoma Sooners' Orange Bowl victory in a cottage in the Florida Keys when he got word that Isikoff was looking for him. Now, that could not be anything good. Keating returned the call. Isikoff, as it turned out, had come across a fragment of Keating's vice-presidential file.

"We have information that the reason you weren't selected as attorney general is because of these questionable gifts to your kids," Isikoff said, as Keating recalled the conversation. "From the highest sources, I've heard that you didn't disclose any of this."

"What?" Keating said. "The only reason you know about it, Mike, is because I disclosed it, and the only person who had the information is Dick Cheney."

"Well, I can't tell you how I got this, but what's your answer?"

And so Keating explained his history with Dreyfus. Isikoff's story did him no favors. The Oklahoma governor, *Newsweek* wrote, lacked the "skeleton-free closet" that Bush demanded of his nominees. "The man who wanted to be the country's top cop quietly took cash gifts totaling about $250,000—largely unreported but legal—from one of his top political fundraisers," Isikoff wrote. In fact, as the story acknowledged, Keating had reported the gifts and cleared them with federal ethics officers. But the gifts had not become public knowledge in Oklahoma, which has no such disclosure requirement. The *Newsweek* story touched off an explosion in Keating's home state. The legislature launched an investigation. Scores of local stories spoke of Keating's abandonment even by his great friend George W. Bush. To stanch the bleeding, Keating decided to return all the money to Dreyfus, "a terrible burden on me financially." By the time reporters examined the federal ethics rulings, the biggest man in Oklahoma was political roadkill, crushed under wheels he never heard coming. No one caught a clear view of the driver.

There was a clue, Keating recalled. In December or early January, he said, long after the campaign returned his disclosure files, Cheney had phoned from transition headquarters. Refresh my memory, he asked, about those college gifts from your friend?

"It obviously came from Dick Cheney or one of his people," Keating said, referring to the *Newsweek* piece. "To say that it was chickenshit, excuse the expression, is an understatement. It was gratuitous, and it was petty, and it appeared vindictive to me, and it was utterly beneath the dignity of a person of Cheney's achievement. . . . I mean, Dick Cheney coming into my life has been like a black cloud."

Liz Cheney, in an e-mail, denied the charge. A fellow governor, John Engler—a Bush supporter from day one of the campaign—said he had reluctantly come to agree with Keating. "There's only one way that it could have emerged," he said. "I've always felt it was somebody other than Cheney himself, but Cheney as impresario of the process—someone in that process breached the confidentiality that had been promised."

The story did not go unnoticed in Washington. Keating made no public accusation—not until his interview for this book—but he hinted at his suspicion among friends. The rumor spread, and Keating thereby did the vice president a favor he did not intend. He propagated the message, educational and just deniable enough: Don't cross Cheney. The town was full of important people who had handed the vice president their most personal files—John Kasich, the House Budget Committee chairman; Tom Ridge, the future secretary of homeland security; Bill Frist, the future Senate majority leader; John Danforth, the future UN ambassador; Jon Kyl, chairman of the Senate Republican Policy Committee and the subcommittee on taxation; Chuck Hagel, a senator inclined to cast dissenting votes on some of the Bush administration's more controversial requests. "Dick Cheney knows more about me than my mother, father, and wife," Frist told the *Washington Post*. Not, he added, that he was complaining or anything.

Keating's bright future fell behind him. He phoned the White House, asked to speak to the president. It fell to Andrew Card, the new chief of staff, to return the call. Card absorbed Keating's rage with soothing words of surprise and concern, assuring him of the president's highest regard. "The president and I had an excellent relationship as governors," Keating said, from his postpolitical perch as an insurance lobbyist. "And of course when this issue occurred, then the doors were closed and the lights were turned off, and I never talked to him again."

Chapter Two

A Different Understanding

Dick Cheney picked himself up from an armchair in his Four Seasons suite on San Jacinto Boulevard. As dawn approached on November 8, 2000, election night had given way to burlesque. The cable news began to hint of an ugly brawl in Florida. Cheney, exhausted, walked the few steps to his bedroom, leaving old friends and aides to keep vigil at the living room TV. By the time he awoke, it was war. James A. Baker III, one of half a dozen Republican Party lions who spent the night with Cheney in Austin, soon decamped to take command of the troops in Tallahassee. The official tally had George Bush ahead by 537 votes out of more than 5.9 million cast. For the next thirty-six days the two sides fought the recount precinct by precinct, chad by hanging chad, until Bush persuaded the Supreme Court to halt it for good. By then the greater part of the GOP talent pool—senators and governors, cabinet secretaries emeriti and aspiring—had enlisted one way or another in the Battle of Florida.

Not Cheney. The recount had generals enough. After napping a few hours, he joined Bush at the governor's mansion on Eleventh and

Colorado, a mile north. Cheney had another mission in mind. Assume we win, he told Bush. There will be thousands of jobs to fill, not only in the cabinet but across the upper ranks of the federal government. Without appointments in waiting, Bush would limp out of the gate as president. And the Florida recount might take a week, a month, no way to tell.

Somebody had to start assembling a team to take control at noon on January 20, 2001. Cheney volunteered. This was exactly the kind of inside job that Bush had in mind for his running mate. He appointed Cheney on the spot as chairman of the shadow transition for a presidency that might or might not come to be.

With no official winner and thus no government office space, Cheney set up operations at 6613 Madison McLean Drive in the affluent Washington suburb of McLean, Virginia. He and Lynne had bought the three-bedroom town house in the Reagan years, when she chaired the National Endowment for the Humanities and he was climbing the GOP leadership in Congress. Now their round kitchen table became the nerve center of a government in waiting.

Three cell phones formed a makeshift switchboard for Cheney—his own, his daughter Liz's, and the one assigned to Brian V. McCormack, the "body man" who kept Cheney supplied and connected wherever he went. A rotating cast of aides fielded telephone calls, beginning with the trio who had run the vice-presidential screening the summer before: Liz Cheney, counsel David Addington, and troubleshooter David Gribbin. Joining them from time to time were Mary Cheney, the younger daughter, and senior visitors from the Bush campaign. Cheney did much of the work alone. He had extensive networks in Washington, beginning with a database of his own former aides. The kitchen television, volume down, tracked developments in Florida—usually Fox News, sometimes the Don Imus show on MSNBC. Jim Baker, the former secretary of state and treasury and political operator par excellence, called with updates from behind the scenes. But Cheney focused steadily on the four years ahead. Referring to the recount, McCormack said Cheney's view was that "we need to prepare in the event this war comes out in our favor."

Those were turbulent weeks, all adrenaline and foreboding. Nobody could say how it all would end—who would be president, how we would know, whether a fractured electorate could unite. Could anyone even guarantee there would *be* a president when Bill Clinton walked out the door? Juleanna Glover, Cheney's newly arrived press secretary, observed that Cheney "had a calming effect" on Bush and the staff. "When things got especially tumultuous his decision was to get more involved."

Amid so many anomalies, it was easy to miss the peculiarity of what Cheney was doing in McLean. Vice presidents do not run transition teams. They do not hire cabinet chiefs and assistant directors and deputy assistant secretaries. A vice president breaks tie Senate votes and tries to keep on breathing in case the president happens to stop. In ordinary times the White House chief of staff, or someone else with real authority, looks for a delicate way to box the fellow in. Cheney had done exactly that with Nelson Rockefeller.

At an academic conference in 1986 he described the headaches.

"The problem when you try to put a vice president in roles, you're always trying to fit him somehow in staff operations inside the White House," he said. "And the fact of the matter is you've got a different set of criteria for selecting a vice president than you do staff. And by virtue of the fact that he is a constitutional officer, that he isn't subject to the same kinds of—"

Cheney stopped and rewound the sentence. Point was, even the president could not fire the vice.

"—that it's a different relationship, that other staff people oftentimes will defer to him as vice president, rather than treat him as a staff person and argue and debate with him and so forth. There are just some very basic fundamental problems there in trying to make that work."

From his new perspective, Cheney saw things differently. If vice-presidential autonomy was a problem, it was no longer his. John Marsh, one of Cheney's closest associates since their work in side-by-side offices in the Ford White House, said his "major concern, one of them was, and I agree, that there needs to be a greater and more effective role for the Vice President." Cheney now "holds the view, as do I . . . that everything should run through his office. You'll notice that he's never said it. But he's demonstrated it by action, by the accretion of power."

It is true that Cheney does not speak in those terms in public. Not, at least, about the vice presidency. But just before reaching that office, he gave a precise taxonomy of power in the White House. At a Washington conference in October 2000, Cheney described James Baker's division of labor with Edwin Meese when Baker was White House chief of staff and Meese was counselor to Ronald Reagan. "So, Jim had laid down on one side of the piece of paper things like personnel, process, schedule, speech writing, legislative relations," Cheney said. "That was his side of the chart. On the other side of the chart were all the policy areas that Ed Meese was responsible for. I wanted Jim's side of the ledger! He knew exactly what he was doing when he went in and he was an effective chief of staff, because those were the items that he had that let him control and preside over the White House."

As vice president, Cheney would dip into each of those bailiwicks, and more.

"Once he's taken a position, I think that's it," Baker said in an interview. "He has been pretty damn good at accumulating power, extraordinarily effective and adept at exercising power."

In one-on-one talks with Bush, according to accounts Bush gave his senior aides afterward, Cheney was explicit about his conception of the vice presidency. Before agreeing to join the Republican ticket, in the pivotal conversation on the back porch in Crawford over Independence Day weekend, Cheney made clear he was not interested in the traditional portfolio of political fund-raisers and ceremonial trips. "He said from the outset, 'If I'm going to do this I'm going to do this differently. . . . I'm not going to be the guy going to funerals. I want to be a real partner in helping you make decisions with regard to domestic and foreign policy,'" recalled Dan Bartlett, who served as counselor to Bush in Austin and for most of two terms in the White House. That negotiation, Bartlett said, had already been sealed by July.

So here Cheney was at his kitchen table in November, populating the federal government. In those crucial six weeks before the Supreme Court called the election on December 12, he was by any measure the dominant force in creating the Bush administration to be.

He did not steal the role or sneak up on it. He asked for it openly, and Bush said yes. Nor was it unknown for an incoming vice president to suggest a friend or two for the cabinet. Al Gore sponsored Les Aspin for Defense and Carole Browner for the Environmental Protection Agency. But Cheney's commanding role on major appointments was without precedent.

Cheney lived by the Reagan-era slogan "personnel is policy," a battle cry for conservatives who regarded the permanent bureaucracy with unease. It started before Reagan, if Lynne Cheney's novel is any reflection of his views. Her fictional president "made a mental check list of what he should be worrying about. It was all people, he realized."

Cheney told associates that the career civil service, resistant to change and invested in years of liberal excess, would be no friend of George W. Bush. The president, he said, would need a cadre of tough-minded enforcers to carry out his agenda. McCormack, his twenty-six-year-old personal aide, said Cheney spent those days in the kitchen making up lists on a lined yellow pad and sounding out potential nominees. He began with the four power posts: State, Treasury, Justice, and Defense. Cheney recruited candidates, preinterviewed them, and escorted them for Bush's approval in Austin. All promises, of necessity, were provisional. But Cheney behaved as if there were no doubt that he and Bush were headed for the White House. "He was moving forward with 'How do we prepare to govern?'" McCormack recalled. By the time the young aide arrived each morning, usually by 6:30, "the cell phones were going. He had his lists. The guy never stopped." One day, the Secret Service detail stopped McCormack on his way in.

"Is he okay?" one agent asked. "Because the light went on at 4:30 in the morning."

"He was probably reading," McCormack replied.

There is no way to understand what happened when Bush took office without a brief tour of how his government came to be. For the State Department, Bush had already set his sights on Colin Powell. Cheney had handpicked Powell as chairman of the Joint Chiefs of Staff ten years earlier, elevating him over more-senior generals. Their relationship, forged in the crucible of the Persian Gulf War, was correct and professional but not warm. Cheney suspected the man of too much fondness for his own press clips, a cardinal defect by Cheney's lights. Still, Cheney believed Bush could make good use of Powell's popularity. And if it came to a policy struggle, according to aides, Cheney seemed to have a pugilist's confidence that Powell would be the one to hit the canvas. In late November, Cheney escorted the third-most-admired man in America to Bush's dusty east Texas ranch to seal the deal. Later, Cheney would see to it that allies, including his daughter Liz, found influential posts in Powell's State Department. "You could help yourself a lot," he told Powell in December, by finding a senior job for John R. Bolton, a vocal advocate of unilateral U.S. intervention against "rogue regimes."

On the day of Powell's coming out, December 16, 2000, he appeared with Bush at a news conference that reinforced Cheney's determination to limit his authority. Powell made the mistake of giving a bravura tour of the global horizon, at length, with an expressionless Cheney and a fidgeting president-elect standing behind him. Bush pursed his lips and glanced from side to side as the minutes passed. Powell spoke fluently about a broad range of foreign policy issues—and strayed, as well, into military affairs. He would need a counterweight, according to Cheney's aides, and the vice president–elect had just the man for the job.

Donald Rumsfeld, Cheney's mentor since the Nixon administration and probably his closest friend, got the nod for defense secretary. That came in the face of a pointed reminder from Jim Baker of Rumsfeld's toxic history with George H. W. Bush, whose political ambitions Rumsfeld tried to crush in the 1970s. "All I'm going to say to you is, you know what he did to your daddy," Baker told the younger Bush. Cheney brought Bush one other option, former senator Daniel Coats, but Coats was ambivalent about the job and had no executive experience. Rumsfeld was a force of nature. He appealed to Bush's fondness for "transformation," "game changers," big ideas. It was not a hard choice, as Cheney framed it.

To fill the Treasury job, Cheney would hear of no one but Paul O'Neill, a Ford administration comrade who had since turned the once-sleepy Alcoa company into a leviathan. O'Neill was competent, conservative, and deferential to the president's prerogatives, a quality that augured well for Cheney's plans to centralize economic policy in the White House. For attorney general, Cheney tapped John Ashcroft, who had just suffered his humiliating reelection defeat and was all the more grateful for a face-saving exit from the Senate. Spencer Abraham, too, had just lost his Senate seat. Abraham impressed Cheney in the first Bush administration as deputy chief of staff to Vice President Quayle. Cheney placed him at Energy, a department that Abraham had proposed to abolish. Cheney also hired Christine Todd Whitman, who once worked for him in Nixon's Office of Economic Opportunity, to run the Environmental Protection Agency. Robert Zoellick, Jim Baker's right-hand man at State and Treasury in the 1990s, was Cheney's pick for U.S. trade representative.

Cheney took care to defer to Bush, leaving the final yea or nay on each prospective nominee to the man at the top of the ticket. Bush ratified each choice.

Cheney had a westerner's gut hostility to regulation, and he asked a like-minded friend from his House days, former congressman Robert Smith, to identify candidates for Interior and Agriculture. Cheney was looking for "the aggressive establishment of another philosophy of government," Smith recalled. He wanted nominees who would bring "accountability, finally, that the government wasn't there to put people out of business." For Interior, Cheney settled on Gale Norton, who spent much of her legal career representing oil, lumber, and mining interests. She was an advocate of "market-oriented, property rights–based, locally controlled" decisions on the environment. For Agriculture it was Ann Veneman, a former Number Two in that department who went on to work for a trade group funded by agribusiness giants Nestlé, Kraft, and Archer Daniels Midland.

The cabinet mattered, but Cheney did not stop there. Second- and third-ranking officials could be vital allies. He sponsored Sean O'Keefe, his old Pentagon comptroller and Navy secretary, for deputy director of the Office of Management and Budget—among the least glamorous and most powerful of positions. The OMB not only allocated every dollar spent by the federal government, but spoke for the executive branch, thumbs-up or thumbs-down, on legislation pending before Congress.

Stephen J. Hadley, who landed the deputy national security adviser job under Condoleezza Rice, was another of Cheney's "Defense Dogs," an informal group of Pentagon alumni. The Dogs held reunions now and then—soft drinks at the Army-Navy Club, in deference to pack leader David Gribbin, a Mormon. Like a lot of Cheney's employees, then and since, Hadley admired the man and found him unnerving in roughly equal measure. One day at the Pentagon, where Hadley served as an assistant secretary in the early 1990s, he emerged from Cheney's office and ran into Gribbin. Once again he had briefed his boss and received little more than an inscrutable nod in return.

"You know, Cheney somehow intimidates me," Hadley told Gribbin. "He's not *trying* to intimidate me, but when I'm sitting there briefing him, I'm talking a little fast and my voice is a little high."

Gribbin, who described that encounter, said Cheney "doesn't lavish praise. It's not the way he leads. Nevertheless I have heard him say of Hadley, 'He's a good hand.'"

In the policy fields that Cheney cared about, he found places for allies even deeper in the bureaucracy. He did it gently, by way of suggestions, not commands, to those who did the hiring. Most of the government's work, Cheney knew, never reached the altitude of Senate-confirmed appointees. Reliable people in midlevel posts would have the last word on numberless decisions about where to spend or not spend money, whom to regulate, how to enforce. Thus did Paul Hoffman, the former state director of Cheney's congressional office in Casper, Wyoming, become deputy assistant secretary of the interior for fish and wildlife. That position, which oversees the listing and delisting of endangered species, went to Hoffman after Cheney "penned a short letter" on his behalf, Hoffman said.

"What he knows as well as anyone is you can't run all of government from the seat of the vice president's office," Hoffman said. "You cannot insert yourself into every branch and agency. His genius is"— here Hoffman laughed modestly—"with the exception of me, he picks brilliant people, he builds networks and puts the right people in the right places, and then trusts them to make well-informed decisions that comport with his overall vision."

Gribbin spoke of Cheney's "web of contacts—it's the people he knows, and the people they know."

The web had its limits. It did not include most of the Friends of George from the Republican Governors Association. Bush had cast himself as a Washington outsider and promised to bring outside talent with him. John Engler of Michigan, Tom Ridge of Pennsylvania, Marc Racicot of Montana, Frank Keating of Oklahoma, George Pataki of New York—all of them were touted as top prospects. When the dust cleared in January, none of them had found a place in the cabinet.

Cheney's first two hires were for his own staff. The men he appointed, possessed of far more experience and force of will than their counterparts on Bush's staff, would have outsized influence on the course of events to come.

David Addington, Cheney's longtime lawyer and a ferocious advocate of presidential authority, was the obvious choice as counsel to the vice president. He had a prodigious capacity for work and a résumé that taught him how the change of a sentence in the right place could shift the nation's path. At forty-three, he had already served as staff attorney to three House committees, assistant general counsel of the CIA, a deputy assistant to the president under Ronald Reagan, and general counsel of Cheney's Pentagon. The son of an Army general, Addington had aspired to a military career but dropped out of the Naval Academy as a freshman. He was a gun enthusiast and liked to join Cheney on hunting trips. In several jobs, he had served as Cheney's enforcer in the bureaucracy.

"Addington was brutally effective and efficient at that," Gribbin said. "Gatekeepers like that who are remarkably talented also have a capacity to bend things in their direction," though Gribbin said he never saw Addington do so for personal advantage.

There was nothing of the cynic in Addington, none of the expedience that often comes with power. Addington displayed an immoderate zeal for principle in matters great and small. Colleagues came to expect eccentric bursts of passion, including a campaign to forbid the personal use of frequent-flier miles earned on government business.

The new leader of Cheney's retinue was I. Lewis Libby, fifty, a compact man of angular features confined under taut control. He, too, had served under Cheney at the Defense Department, but he did not reach the innermost circle. A late arrival to the presidential campaign, Libby soon made himself indispensable as "Cheney's Cheney," the consummate operator and adviser. Libby oversaw months of preparation for Cheney's most important campaign event, the vice-presidential debate. Warm and charming among friends, Libby hewed to a punctilious formality at work. He probed deeply and spoke with precision, revealing little. In photographs, smiling or not, he compressed his lips. Allies and rivals described Libby as an implacable negotiator, gifted, like his boss, in the uses of silence and an unbroken gaze.

With all this came an incongruous nickname, "Scooter," acquired in infancy. Pete Williams, who brought a mischievous streak to his work as Cheney's chief spokesman at the Pentagon in the early 1990s, once heard a puzzled general ask, "Who is 'Skippy'?" Delighted at the misfire, Williams allowed himself to repeat it around the building. One day Libby summoned Williams to his office, sat him down, and closed the door. "My name is Scooter," he said, locking eyes. "Not 'Skippy.'"

At Yale, years before, Libby had studied political science under Paul Wolfowitz, then followed him on an ideological exodus from their liberal Jewish roots. As an undergraduate, Libby was vice president of the campus Democrats, a young man who could call the roll of all seventy-nine original episodes of *Star Trek*. (Some of those old episode titles, in light of Libby's subsequent path, invite double takes now: "Journey to Babel," "Balance of Terror," "A Private Little War," "The Doomsday Machine," "The Enemy Within.") Like Wolfowitz and other neoconservatives, Libby grew disenchanted with the government's expansion at home but more inclined to endorse a muscular role abroad. Wolfowitz left academic life for the State Department in 1972, and Libby joined him in 1981. Eight years after that, Cheney appointed Wolfowitz undersecretary of defense for policy, the Pentagon's third-ranking job. Libby signed on as principal deputy. The two men were among the few to dissent in 1991, when George H. W. Bush cut short the Persian Gulf War without toppling Iraqi president Saddam Hussein.

Libby had a literary bent and a dark imagination, romantic and violent. Off and on for more than twenty years, he wrote a novel set in turn-of-the-century Japan amid a smallpox outbreak and intimations of war. In *The Apprentice,* a nameless youth bears witness to murder, stumbles upon a wooden box of unknown but urgent import, and is tortured with hot coals and tongs for a secret he does not possess. Silent, lethal men appear and disappear in a snow-blinded landscape, carrying out intrigues in service of . . . the reader learns not what.

"What great truth would you know?" scoffs a member of the mysterious elite toward the end of the novel, when the youth looks for answers about his ordeal. "What would make a difference for you? At stake were the plans for war with the Russe or the emperor's secret goals in Manchuria. There was a list of conspirators that threatened the lords of the land, or a list of the lords of the land who are conspirators. You helped us keep from others the lay of our defenses. Or our offenses. They are all nothing to you."

"They meant something to you," the youth replies.

"Yes, to us. Much."

Friends and colleagues said Libby identified with strong men who labor in shadows to protect a public that grasps little of their work. He alluded to that frame of mind in 2002, three months after *The Apprentice* came out in paperback and less than a year before the invasion of Iraq. When Wolfowitz recruited him to government, Libby recalled, he happened to be reading *A Man Called Intrepid,* the rousing account of a British spy's secret exploits against the Nazis. The central character, sometimes cited as a model for the fictional James Bond, led a life of purpose and excitement that Libby could not hope to find in a Philadelphia law firm. That realization, he said, drew him to Washington.

In November 2000, Cheney asked Libby to become his national security adviser. That was a canny move in light of Libby's history with Condi Rice, the Stanford University provost who was likely to take the corresponding job for Bush. Rice had been a director on the National Security Council staff under Bush's father. To outsiders that sounds like a powerful post, but directors live on the bottom rung of the White House ladder, below senior directors, deputy assistants to the president, and—most exalted—assistants to the president. Libby's job at the Defense Department, in the same period, made him Rice's senior when they met in interagency debates. Steve Hadley, the mild-mannered lawyer who would become Rice's deputy, had served beneath Libby at Defense.

Libby did not accept Cheney's offer, not at first. He played a gambit that Cheney might have tried in his place. Libby proposed to hold two jobs—chief of staff *and* national security adviser. That would give him command of every employee in the office of the vice president, or OVP, and a portfolio that spanned domestic as well as foreign affairs. It was an audacious bid, but Cheney saw something he liked. Libby got what he asked for, and more. Cheney arranged for Libby, whom Bush knew only slightly, to hold a third title as assistant to the president. Like so many apparent technicalities to come, this meant something.

The presidential appointment placed Libby atop two separate and parallel hierarchies in the White House. He would work for Cheney, but also outrank nearly everyone who worked for Bush in the Executive Office of the President. Among his few peers would be Rice, White House chief of staff Andrew Card, and political adviser Karl Rove. No one save Cheney and Bush themselves were his superiors. Like every assistant to the president, Libby would see and have the right to challenge any speech, legislation, or executive order before it reached the Oval Office. No reciprocal right came with Card's job, or Rove's, when documents flowed to or from the vice president.

Two weeks into the Florida recount, on November 22, Cheney awoke in the night with a radiating pain in his chest and shoulder. The Secret Service sped him through nearly deserted streets, arriving at 4:30 a.m. in the emergency room at George Washington University Hospital.

The votes were all cast, if not all counted, but as a matter of electoral politics Cheney's ailing heart was unwelcome news. A weak-ened candidate would not change the arithmetic in Florida, but the Bush campaign feared the episode could tip the subtle psychology of national acceptance. Bush would arrive at the White House, if at all, with the slenderest of mandates. He could ill afford any intimation of frailty. Campaign strategists held a conference call and settled on a plan: they would manage the news to dampen its shock, then rap-idly rebuild Cheney's image of strength and calm.

Bush came out early that morning, announcing in Austin that Cheney had gone to the hospital "as a precautionary measure." Bush added, "He had no heart attack. I'm pleased to report that." Soon after, Cheney's doctors gave a matter-of-fact account of Cheney's treatment. They told reporters they had used a balloon on a catheter to open the patient's blocked coronary artery, then inserted a stent— a tiny coil, resembling a Slinky—to shore up the arterial walls. What all that obscured, and what the doctors did not mention, was that Cheney in fact had suffered a heart attack, his fourth since the age of thirty-seven. Several hours passed, and the story had been defined as a minor event, before Dr. Alan Wasserman returned to the cameras with news that there was "a very slight heart attack."

In chronic coronary disease, damage to the heart muscle is cumu-lative. Cheney appeared to rebound quickly, but the public had no way to judge his underlying health. He declined, then and after, to release the results of diagnostic tests.

That night, at a few minutes past nine, CNN's *Larry King Live* prepared to showcase a debate between lawyers from the Gore and Bush campaigns. By then the Florida recount was tangled in twenty-two county lawsuits and had reached the state supreme court. The lawyers were just getting started when a producer transmitted some-thing into Larry King's ear.

"Let me interrupt—let me hold you right there," King told the lawyers. "Dick Cheney from his hospital bed at George Washington University Hospital is joining us. How are you feeling, Dick?"

"Well, I feel pretty good, Larry."

Not for nothing was the avuncular King the television host of choice for politicians and celebrities in trouble.

"Well, you sound great," he declared.

"Well, it's—you've been through this procedure yourself, I'm sure," Cheney said. They had spoken once, off camera, of their respective adventures in coronary care.

"Yes," King agreed.

"But no, I feel good and everything's looking good. We did a stent today. But everything's fine, and the catheterization looked good, so I should be out of here in a day or two."

"How about the stress?" King asked.

"Well, I—frankly, it may sound hard to believe, but I have not found this last couple of weeks as stressful, for example, as, say, the Gulf War."

Did Cheney have any doubt he could do the job if elected?

"No doubt about my serving," Cheney said.

Settled that.

By the next day, Thanksgiving, Cheney's reassuring tones were accounted a public relations coup. Colin Powell's wife, Alma, delivered a roast turkey and trimmings to Cheney's hospital room. Cheney sat half upright in bed with the TV remote, surfing through channels for news from Florida. The family set up tables, brought out the bird and the cranberry sauce, and invited Cheney's Secret Service detail to sit down. It was "a regular Thanksgiving feast, except for the fact that you're sitting in a sterile room," recalled McCormack, his personal aide.

A few days after leaving the hospital, Cheney transferred operations to a privately funded office suite at 1616 Anderson Road, a six-minute drive from his town house in McLean. The election was still up for grabs in court, but Cheney declared the transition formally open for business. He gave out official-sounding titles, such as director of congressional relations. Applicants for presidential appointments were directed to forms at www.bushcheneytransition.com. The General Services Administration still declined to release federal transition funds, Cheney said, but "my job is to get an organization stood up, and I've got a job to do, and I'll let others worry about the degree of cooperation we have or haven't received."

Bush remained at his Crawford ranch.

Three doors greeted visitors to the transition office. The one on the left said "Mr. Rove." The middle one said "Mr. Libby." The door on the right said "Secretary Cheney."

Ron Christie, a Republican congressional aide, arrived on January 9, 2001, nearly a month after the final election result. Scooter Libby had recruited him for Cheney's domestic policy staff, and now it was time to meet the vice president–elect. "There was nothing on his desk," Christie said. "Nothing. Nothing." Cheney stood, shook hands, and proceeded to tell the young man the story of his own life.

"You grew up in California," Cheney said. "Went to Haverford. Worked for John Kasich."

Cheney kept going.

Where was the file? Christie asked himself. Under the desk?

Cheney was not putting on a show. This was how he worked. He read a great deal and remembered what he read. When he talked with someone he wanted to learn something new.

The television was on. Cheney was expecting something. Pretty soon it came.

"I want to watch this," he said, turning away from Christie.

The picture cut to Linda Chavez, Bush's designee to run the Labor Department. She was not one of Cheney's picks, and she was in trouble. For three days Chavez had tried to defend her payments to an undocumented immigrant who once lived with her, offering domestic help in return. Chavez called the money "emergency assistance," not a breach of employment law, but the controversy refused to die.

Now she had called a press conference and the cable news carried it live. Chavez scolded reporters for making too much of the story. She deplored the "game of search-and-destroy" aimed at "good people out there who want to serve their government." But in the circumstances, she said, "I have asked President Bush to withdraw my name for secretary of labor." No one instructed her to pull out, she said late the same night, "but I've also been around this town long enough to know that when nobody is calling you and saying 'Hang in there,' that that isn't a great signal either."

Cheney turned away from the screen.

"What do you think?" he asked Christie.

"It's the start of a new administration, and if someone is a distraction, that's a problem," Christie said.

"Right answer," Cheney said.

Christie got the job. At thirty, he would soon find himself participating as a peer in daily meetings of the president's Domestic Policy Council. Nancy Dorn, who became Cheney's chief lobbyist on the Hill, would function as coequal to Nick Calio, who spoke for the president. In gatherings at the White House counsel's office, Addington would not only attend but routinely dominate the conversation. None of this remotely resembled the ways of White Houses past.

Some of Cheney's staffers followed the Libby precedent, acquiring presidential as well as vice-presidential appointments. Mary Matalin, who became Cheney's counselor, had the same rank—and office space—as her West Wing counterparts, Karen Hughes and Dan Bartlett. Stephen E. Schmidt, another Cheney counselor, likewise wore a second hat as deputy assistant to the president.

Cheney aides often emphasized that they worked in tandem with the main White House staff, on behalf of a single client. Matalin, for example, said Cheney chose a structure that was "not separate and contributing, but integrated with the West Wing in ways I know were a radical departure from previous White Houses." There was no competition, she said. "It wasn't, 'Here's Cheney's view' and 'Let's overlay it on Bush's view,' and add red and blue and come out with purple. It wasn't like that." In the first days of the administration, Cheney's office offered rare access to a news magazine to emphasize that Cheney had no agenda of his own because he did not see himself as "a future presidential candidate" and was not "tending the gardens of politics" on his own behalf.

This was a variation of Cheney's message, in the summer just past, about the disadvantages of an ambitious running mate. True to his implicit promise, Cheney seldom let slip any public hint of disagreement with Bush.

In a can't-make-this-up moment in the second term, Cheney said his favorite movie was *Red River,* an epic power struggle between a rancher and the right-hand man who displaces him. But Cheney, unlike Montgomery Clift, offered no challenge to his John Wayne. He simply took care of business that the boss was too busy to attend.

Matalin and others liked to blur the line, but "no ambition" and "no agenda" were not quite the same thing. Cheney "gave himself permission not to run for president," as one old friend put it, but he had strong views in abundance on the course his country should take. If anything, Cheney's awareness of reaching the end of the line spurred his pursuit of policy goals that had eluded him before. Not only would this be his last chance, but Cheney was more impervious than ever to public opinion.

Through the next eight years, the vice president fell loyally in line behind Bush's decisions, whether or not he approved. But the first MBA president soon emerged as a manager who left a great deal to his subordinates, and who allowed disputes among his advisers to fester for months and years. The vice president–elect believed vital national interests were at stake. Until and unless Bush settled an argument, Cheney felt free—and even obliged—to use every advantage of his office to prevail.

That is why Cheney raised the status of his aides and inserted them into West Wing policy roles. The vice president was equipping his lieutenants to fight above their weight. Cheney was Number Two, but his office would bear no sign of secondary importance. In meetings of the president's cabinet-rank foreign policy advisers, "Scooter would be with Condi" and the other principals, said William Kristol, who was chief of staff to Dan Quayle in the first Bush administration. "His deputy attended the deputies meetings. Everyone is up a step from my day."

In late December 2000, Joshua Bolten sat down with Scooter Libby. He wanted to know what kind of job the vice president–elect had in mind. It was an odd question on its face, but prescient. The Constitution specified no executive duties for a vice president, and each administration invented the job anew. Bolten, who learned his way around the White House under Bush's father, had moved to London in the Clinton years and made a lot of money at Goldman Sachs. Now he was returning as deputy White House chief of staff, looking to establish some kind of order.

"I remember at the outset, during the transition, thinking, 'What do vice presidents do?'" Bolten recalled. "And so Scooter Libby had some thoughts, and we looked at what other vice presidents do."

Bolten noticed a pattern. Vice presidents did not govern, exactly, but kept an eye on how the rest of the government worked. They advised the president as the president saw fit. Sometimes they had niche projects, like Gore's focus on the environment. They chaired commissions and laid out proposals for reform. "Quayle had the 'Council on Competitiveness,'" Bolten said. "Gore was 'Reinventing Government.' So we looked at portfolios that we thought might be appropriate for the vice president, but that was more staff-driven than anything else, because we were adopting the old template."

Somebody—probably Libby, maybe Andy Card—briefed Cheney on what they had in mind.

"The vice president," Bolten said drily, "didn't particularly warm to that."

Word came back that Cheney would engage in "whatever area the vice president feels he wants to be active in," Bolten said. And Bush backed him up. "The president made it clear from the outset that the vice president is welcome at every table and at every meeting," said Bolten, speaking in 2006 after succeeding Andy Card as chief of staff. "That's just a standing rule. I don't know if that's been true of other vice presidents. Probably mostly has, as a formal matter. But it's been true as a practical matter and as a real matter of atmosphere here at the White House."

Which was not to say that Cheney "put an oar in," a favorite expression, on everything. Bush came to office with big plans for education reform and "faith-based initiatives" to enlist religious groups in providing social services. Cheney had voted in Congress against establishing a Department of Education and was skeptical of federal intervention in local schools. He resolutely avoided discussions of faith. Social issues had seldom engaged him, and concern for his daughter Mary's privacy led Cheney to avoid the subject of gay and lesbian rights. Some social conservatives blamed "Cheney's influence" for Bush's failure to push a federal ban on gay marriage. Jan LaRue, chief counsel of the Concerned Women for America, took note that Lynne Cheney once wrote a novel "celebrating lesbian lifestyles."

According to Matalin, Cheney arrived in office with a "preordained policy portfolio" that spanned "the economic issues, the security issues—even before 9/11 we had homeland security—and the energy issues." There was a lull in the conversation as Matalin searched for the right word. "The iron issues, I don't know what else to call them. The steely issues." Apart from those, "we had the go-to guy on the Hill" because of Cheney's Senate duties and experience in the House.

That was a remarkable list: war and peace, the economy, natural resources, and negotiations with Congress. Nor was Matalin's description complete. It omitted, among other things, a preeminent role for Cheney in nominations and appointments, which did not stop with the transition. Cheney's brief, all in all, encompassed most of the core concerns of any president.

White House aides quickly tired of the cartoon that Cheney was the president in all but name. He was not. Whenever Bush chose to be, he was exactly the Decider he proclaimed. But Bush's style of leadership, said Bradford Berenson, an associate White House counsel in the first term, involved "guiding the ship of state from high up on the mast. It seemed to me that the vice president was more willing to get down in the wheelhouse below the decks." Cheney, he said, "has probably tasted from the cup of presidential power more than any other vice president in modern history. But remember, if the president and the vice president disagree, the president gets to decide."

Nothing engaged Cheney more than worst-case scenarios. "Whatever stuff was scariest, the vice president was directly grappling with it," Berenson said.

Cheney gave an early public hint that he would take a strong hand on the economy as well. On NBC's *Meet the Press* on December 3, 2000, Cheney said, "We may well be on the front edge of a recession here." High-ranking officials seldom cast economic gloom for fear their words may help fulfill themselves. Cheney's prediction, which proved accurate, served two purposes. It laid the groundwork to blame Bill Clinton for bad news that might emerge on Bush's watch. More important, it set the stage for tax cuts of the type, scale, and timing that Cheney had in mind.

Early on, Libby floated the idea that Cheney would chair meetings of Bush's foreign policy team. When the president attends, that gathering is called the National Security Council. When he does not, it is called the Principals Committee and includes the attorney general, the director of central intelligence (a title that later changed), and the secretaries of state, defense, and treasury. By decades of tradition, Principals Committee meetings were chaired by the national security adviser. That agenda-setting and coordination role, in fact, was half the job. Rice was alarmed. Hadley, who knew Cheney better than Rice did, made the approach.

"Mr. Vice President, a number of people are saying you want to chair the Principals Committee," Hadley said. "That doesn't sound like you to me, Mr. Vice President."

Cheney disclaimed the idea, to Hadley's relief. Then he reframed it.

"I want to participate, obviously. Be heard."

When Hadley told that anecdote in early 2007, he offered it, unsolicited, in rebuttal to what he described as a common Cheney myth. "A lot of vice presidents, if they had their own agenda and wanted to be the 'president for foreign affairs,' would make a different decision," Hadley said. "He didn't want to be the 'president of foreign affairs.' He wanted to be an adviser to the president and to help the president get the best information."

That was a puzzling statement. There were not, in fact, a lot of vice presidents who could have tried to grab the helm of the Principals Committee. No other vice president had even attended those meetings, as a rule, since the committee's creation in 1947. Cheney would join nearly every one, filling the first chair on the right in the Situation Room or patching in by video link from out of town. In the years to come, scores of major policy choices were cued up at that table or died there. Rice, and later Hadley, chaired the meetings, but they did so as peers of the other participants. When Cheney entered the room, everyone stood. After each meeting, Rice briefed Bush. But so did Cheney, often separately and alone.

Richard Haass, who would quit his post as the State Department's director of policy planning after many defeats by the vice president and his allies, said Cheney's methods gave him "three bites at the apple" on every decision. "There's the one with the president, when they're alone. That's the most interesting one, and we know the least about it. There's his participation in the Principals Committee meetings. And there's the staff role, from the deputies on down."

As White House chief of staff in the 1970s, Cheney drew what he called "staffing loops" to establish attendance at key policy meetings and "who sees paper before it goes in" to the president. Bolten's question for Libby in December amounted to asking where Cheney and his staff would appear on that kind of map. The answer turned out to include a lot of venues in which vice presidents were seldom seen.

Vice presidents traditionally joined the president at "policy time," if the president so desired. Cheney intended to get involved sooner, long before the moment of decision. By "reaching down," a term that recurs often in interviews with his aides, Cheney set himself up to shift the course of events while deferring to Bush's prerogatives at the top. Cheney would exert a quiet dominance over meetings in which advisers framed their goals, narrowed options, and decided when—or whether—to bring them to the president. Cheney's presence unavoidably changed the tone, and often the outcome.

There was a regular Wednesday lunch of the president's economic team in the Ward Room, a dark-paneled adjunct to the White House mess where Navy stewards served amid nautical decor. This, too, was virgin territory for a vice president. Most administrations had something like it, a regular occasion to float ideas—frankly and informally—in private. It was as casual as this kind of gathering could be: no aides, no prepared agenda, no PowerPoint slides. Now it was blocked out weekly as a vice-presidential event. Cheney joined the treasury, labor, and commerce secretaries, the budget director, and other top advisers as they previewed policy initiatives and hashed out differences.

Cheney probed hard and displayed a depth of technical knowledge that impressed the professional economists. He came prepared and usually had a strong point of view. Bolten said Cheney cast himself as an exponent of conservative "first principles," which made him "a pretty vigorous voice for holding the line on spending and for holding the line on tax cuts."

It required a healthy dose of boldness for anyone at the table to press a disagreement very far. Cheney became "a big time-saver for us in that he takes off the table a lot of things that he knows are going to go nowhere," said Ed Lazear, who chaired the Council of Economic Advisers. Lazear, who ordinarily carried himself with the confidence of a man at the pinnacle of his profession, said he could not name a time when "I have thought I was right and that the vice president was wrong." Sometimes, he said, "I might fight for ten minutes or so, and you know, kind of try to argue it out with him. He's a very open guy. . . . He tries to avoid using his position to cut off conversation. But it's clear, by the time we've talked something through, I agree with him. He's persuaded me. I can't think of a case where he hasn't persuaded me."

Thus was formed a consensus, far more often than not.

Cheney also decided to join the National Economic Council, which coordinates day-to-day policy in the White House. Lawrence Lindsey, who chaired that panel in the first two years, said its members tried to reach consensus and served as honest brokers for the president if differences remained. Cheney had a somewhat different role: "He'd form his own judgments and bring those to the president." By the time Cheney had Bush's ear, he was intimately familiar with opposing views.

Nearly every Tuesday, just before noon, Cheney's six-car motorcade carried him sixteen blocks southeast on Pennsylvania Avenue to the Capitol. The vice president strode through the Ohio Clock corridor and into a members-only passage between a bust of Richard Nixon and a portrait of the nineteenth-century vice president John C. Calhoun. There Cheney joined Senate Republicans at their weekly caucus, the only regular forum in which the senators gathered as a group behind closed doors. Lyndon Johnson, the last vice president who tried to attend his party's Senate caucus, found himself barred at the door. Majority Leader Mike Mansfield lined up the votes to exclude him back then, describing Johnson's request as an affront to Senate autonomy. Arlen Specter, the Pennsylvania Republican, said the same question was raised in Cheney's case, with different results. "He's very pointed in his defense," Specter said, "saying he's the president of the Senate and he's paid by the Senate."

The effect of Cheney's presence in the caucus itself was hard to measure, though it certainly raised the stakes of speaking out. In the White House, Cheney's privileged access to the senators made him Bush's principal source of information about what would and would not work on Capitol Hill. Jon Kyl, the Arizona Republican, said, "It's not always easy to speak directly with the president about an idea or concern, and sometimes you want to kind of filter them through the ear of a wise man like the vice president."

Shortly after Cheney took his oath of office on January 20, 2001, Dan Quayle paid him a courtesy call in the West Wing. Government officials of a certain rank have the privilege of borrowing from the National Gallery. Cheney had chosen portraits of John Adams and Thomas Jefferson, the first and second vice presidents. He called them "Number One" and "Number Two."

Quayle, Number Forty-four, brought advice from one vice president to another. Cheney had a right to know what he was in for. Hundreds of thousands of miles in the air, to begin with. Quayle had flown to forty-seven countries for George H. W. Bush. Something like a full year, a quarter of his term, overseas. At home, there was the space committee and the competitiveness council. Good to have projects like that.

Cheney listened politely. Quayle felt as though he could not quite connect.

"Dick, you know, you're going to be doing a lot of this international traveling, you're going to be doing all this political fundraising," Quayle repeated. "I mean, this is what vice presidents do. We've all done it. You go back and look at what I did, or what Gore did."

Cheney did that thing he does with one raised eyebrow, a smile on just the left side of his face.

"I have a different understanding with the president," he said.

"Well, did you get that directly from Bush?"

"Yes."

Quayle drew him out as best he could. The conversation took a while.

"Look, you know Cheney," Quayle recalled, recounting the story from a Park Avenue suite at Cerberus Global Investments. "He doesn't say a lot. He wasn't going into it." Even so, a picture emerged. "He had the understanding with President Bush that he would be— I'm just going to use the word 'surrogate chief of staff.' He didn't want to do that much international travel. He wanted to be there all the time. And this was the deal he had."

Quayle stopped, shook his head. "He just said he had a different understanding about how it was going to function. And he did."

The two men had a history that made Cheney's words all the more remarkable to Quayle. On November 30, 1989, the first President Bush had been airborne for Malta, headed to a meeting with the Soviet premier, when a coup attempt broke out in the Philippines.

Quayle rushed to the Situation Room and convened a meeting of the National Security Council. In person and by teleconference, Quayle pulled together the chairman of the Joint Chiefs of Staff, the attorney general, the White House counsel, and the highest-ranking officials in town from State and CIA. Cheney was secretary of defense. He refused to attend. There was no such thing as an NSC meeting without the president, Cheney said. As Quayle chaired the Situation Room debate, Cheney bypassed it with a stream of calls to Air Force One and to Colin Powell at the Pentagon. Powell, Cheney's direct subordinate, had to keep on ducking away from the video link with Quayle.

"I could see every now and then that Colin would put it on mute and I'd see him pick up the phone," Quayle recalled. Finally, Quayle phoned Cheney to inform him that Bush had approved his plan to launch fighters over the Philippine capital in support of the lawful government. Cheney replied that he would have to hear that order from the president. The following week, the defense secretary asked to see Bush one on one. Cheney "thought the vice president had overstepped his bounds," Quayle said. "He wanted to make sure the president understood that he was in the chain of command and I was not."

As he sat with Cheney in the West Wing in 2001, Quayle was reminded of Ronald Reagan and Gerald Ford. They were bitter rivals, but when Reagan clinched the GOP nomination in 1980 he tried to recruit Ford for a "dream ticket" to unite the party. Cheney took part in the talks. At a conference in 2000, Cheney recalled intense negotiations on how to expand the vice presidency enough to lure a former commander in chief. Ford "made a number of requests in terms of his influence over the budget, personnel, foreign policy, et cetera," Cheney said. "I can remember sitting in a session with Bill

Casey, who later became CIA director. Bill had a list of items that in fact the Reagan people were prepared to discuss. They went a long way toward trying to accommodate President Ford."

The dream ticket never happened, and Cheney said afterward that he concluded that a presidency cannot be shared. But Quayle thought maybe Cheney had re-created elements of that model.

"He wouldn't like the term 'deputy president,' because that's what Ford tried to do with Reagan," he said. "Remember that? Have a sort of copresidency. But you know, Cheney's a Ford guy. And he saw it with Reagan, and I'm wondering now if that was part of it."

In a way, it made sense. Andy Card, Condi Rice, Steve Hadley, Colin Powell, Christie Whitman, Bob Zoellick, Spencer Abraham, Paul O'Neill—all of them had worked for Cheney once, or served alongside him at lesser rank. That kind of relationship—patron and protégé, principal and aide—has a way of persisting in whatever part of the hindbrain measures status. "These guys were all subordinates to him in the past," Quayle said. "He walks in, start of a new administration, and says, 'Oh, same relationship. I talk to the president, and you work for both of us.'"

Quayle took it all in. He left Cheney that afternoon on a cautionary note.

"Well, let me tell you one other thing. It changes. You know, the role of the vice president is what the president wants, and the president can change his mind," he said.

"I know," Cheney replied.

Quayle had no way to tell whether Cheney believed it.

Chapter Three

PIVOT POINTS

On December 13, 2000, the day after the Supreme Court ruled, Dick Cheney drove to Capitol Hill for lunch with a little band of Republican nonconformists. They were not exactly Cheney's crowd, nor he theirs. Wasn't that just like the man, turning up in some unlikely spot when all eyes were looking somewhere else? This was his first full day as certified vice president–elect. No end of demands on his time. But Cheney spotted strategic ground, and there he marched.

Arlen Specter, the senior senator from Pennsylvania, assembled four like-minded colleagues in his Capitol hideaway, an unlisted annex he used when he wanted to stay out of sight. Specter and his friends had devoted some thought to the aftermath of a bitter election contest. So had Cheney.

The bare fact was that George W. Bush reached the White House with half a million fewer votes than his opponent. The last time the Electoral College reversed a popular ballot, in 1888, had belonged to another age. Those were the latter days of the frontier, when the West was still half wild and the fate of the Dakota territories swung the vote. Not as many people thought it scandalous then for appointed electors to choose a president. Modern sensibilities, a century later, equated the popular vote with the people's will. Bush faced a challenge of legitimacy, and he knew it. In the first days after victory, he spoke often of bipartisanship and healing. Democrats were invited, back then, when the president met with leaders in Congress.

As early as November, Cheney counseled Bush against taking such gestures too far. The president is the president, he said. The chief of the executive branch cannot govern from weakness or share powers that belong to him alone. There might come a time to concede a point, but it was a bad idea to telegraph compromise.

"We don't negotiate with ourselves," Cheney said.

Later, that became a mantra for the president and his staff.

In public, Cheney took Bush's lead, adopting the language of unity. But even as he spoke the words, he repositioned their meaning. On his favorite Sunday talk show, in the first week of December, Cheney offered a fresh take on the commonplace view that Bush would rally the nation around its center. Cheney began, much as Bush had done, by professing a wish "to build bridges to the opposition." Tim Russert, the host of NBC's *Meet the Press,* leaned into his next question with a tone suggesting that Bush and Cheney had no choice.

"In reality, with a fifty-fifty Senate, and a close, close—small majority in the House, you're going to have to have a moderate, mainstream, centrist governance, aren't you?"

"Oh, I think so," Cheney said, agreeably.

Almost as an afterthought, he added: "But I think there's no reason in the world why we can't do exactly what Governor Bush campaigned on."

It was ten days later that Cheney made his way to lunch in Specter's hideaway, a high-ceilinged chamber just off the Senate floor. The other guests, New Englanders all, were swimming against a twenty-year tide that had swept most of their fellow moderates from the GOP. Jim Jeffords of Vermont, Lincoln Chafee of Rhode Island, Olympia Snowe and Susan Collins of Maine—they cared about things like urban blight, global warming, campaign finance reform, balanced budgets, and a patient's bill of rights. They were open to compromise with Democrats on gun control and birth control and the minimum wage.

Conservative ideologists had taken to calling them RINOs, Republicans in name only, or the "Mod Squad." Yet just as the moderates neared extinction, their moment appeared to arrive. With the Senate exactly in balance, this nameless little caucus of five sat on the pivot point. And pivot points were just where Cheney liked to work.

Chafee was the junior senator present, green enough to imagine that the vice president–elect had come "to sell us rather than tell us." The model Chafee had in mind was his home state legislature, dominated by rival Democratic factions. The balance of power in Rhode Island rested on the tiny Republican caucus. "I thought that we at that table could have been the same thing," Chafee recalled, smiling a little bit sadly at his lack of guile.

The conversation started warmly enough. Laconic on most subjects, Cheney spoke with fondness of a trip he once took on horseback with Chafee's late father, John. Magnificent country. Up the headwaters of the Yellowstone, about as far from a road as you can get in the lower forty-eight states. After a while, Cheney recomposed his face and said what he came to say. In the election just past, the Bush-Cheney ticket stood for a trillion-dollar tax cut and a sharp increase in military spending. It stood against the Kyoto environmental agreement, against the International Criminal Court, and against any treaty that interfered with ballistic missile defense. Retreat from that agenda, Cheney said, was not on the table.

"It was just matter-of-fact," Chafee recalled. "'This is it.' There was no explanation or solicitation of comments."

Chafee could not quite credit what he heard. Out in Texas, Bush kept talking about national reconciliation. In foreign affairs, Bush had said only three months before that he aimed to lead "a humble nation" that won friends with self-restraint. Yet here Cheney sat, interpreting Bush's platform, as Chafee saw it, in the most aggressive of terms. "It was not going to be humble," Chafee said. "It was going to be the opposite."

The Rhode Island freshman had not planned to do much talking. He was forty-seven years old and barely thirteen months in office, an accidental senator whose seat was a legacy from his dad. He came from privilege, boarding at Phillips Andover Academy and immersing himself in Greek and Latin classics at Brown. Chafee looked the part: aquiline features, silk four-in-hands with whimsical designs of seahorses and the like. But the Rhode Island senator projected something closer to patrician modesty than hauteur. He had worked seven years as a blacksmith and served enough time on the Warwick City Council to learn how to listen.

No one else seemed inclined to speak up. Chafee decided to say the obvious.

"It's a fifty-fifty Senate," Chafee told the vice president–elect. "Our votes are going to be important."

Cheney looked at him mildly. In his days as House Republican whip, he had been a deft enforcer. Cheney knew how to count, and he knew how to make the numbers move.

"All votes are going to be important," he said.

Left it at that.

Don't be too sure who's in the driver's seat.

Most of the senators in the room would take up the challenge, one way or another. Usually that proved unwise. Two would quit the party; one would lose his seat; another would be humbled in his own committee. None of that was easy to foresee as the Bush administration arrived.

Two days after the hideaway lunch, Chafee addressed a letter to the Honorable Richard Cheney.

"In my view," he wrote, "one of the most popular refrains expressed by Governor Bush during the Presidential campaign was 'I am a uniter, not a divider.' I believe moderate Republicans can help the new administration develop a unifying agenda in the next session of Congress." Bush and Cheney, Chafee wrote, could "maintain discipline" in the scale of their tax cut and pay down the national debt. They could support a Democratic substitute, from the previous Congress, that went a long way toward the Republican bill on estate taxes and the so-called marriage penalty. They could emphasize mass transit and conservation of energy. A little compromise on the minimum wage, or on unregulated sales of firearms at gun shows, could do wonders for the atmosphere in Congress. "I look forward to working with you to help shape an approach," Chafee wrote.

To Cheney the letter must have seemed a little dense. He had just finished explaining, at lunch, the way things were going to be. The vice president–elect sent no reply. It was nothing personal, one aide said. Cheney simply saw no point in redundancy. Later, in weekly lunches with the Republican caucus, he and Chafee shared a table now and then, calling each other Linc and Mr. Vice President. Not an unpleasant word passed between them. But Cheney had no use for Chafee's program, and he was not the man to pretend.

Having delivered his message in private, Cheney broadcast it emphatically later that week. A foolish proposition, in his view, was taking hold in Washington, even among some of Bush's advisers. Too many people were asking the president-elect to buy his way out of some purported debt to the electorate, remaking himself as half a Democrat. Tom Daschle, the Senate Democratic leader, had gone so far as to demand equal seating on Senate committees. Cheney was not looking to split their differences. Scaling back the president's goals would serve the country poorly and please no one, he said. He and Bush would hit Washington like a landslide.

On CBS's *Face the Nation* on December 17, Cheney took a strong vanguard position and attributed it to Bush. At a news conference that morning from Austin, Bush defended his campaign proposals while emphasizing his intention to work with Democrats.

"It doesn't seem to make much sense for people to be drawing lines in the sands until we've had a chance to discuss things," Bush said.

Hours later, Cheney drew a line in cement.

"As President-elect Bush has made very clear, he ran on a particular platform that was very carefully developed," Cheney said. "It's his program. It's his agenda. And we have no intention at all of backing off of it. . . . Now the suggestion that somehow because this was a close election we should fundamentally change our beliefs, I just think it's—is silly."

Had Bush and Cheney planned things this way, the old good-cop, bad-cop routine? Was it the president's idea for his vice to press a harder line? Had Cheney even cleared what he said with the boss? Questions like these kept coming back. Even close aides did not always know.

Gloria Borger, the cohost of *Face the Nation,* interrupted the vice president–elect.

"Mr. Cheney, with—with all due respect, the Democrats are saying that this administration cannot proceed as the Reagan administration did, for example, with a large tax bill, because you don't have the mandate that a Ronald Reagan had."

Cheney raised an eyebrow.

"I simply don't buy the notion that somehow we come to office now as a, quote, 'weakened president,'" he said, with a rare lapse into the first-person plural. He added, "We've got a good program, and we're going to pursue it."

Which program, exactly?

"If you had interviewed Bush candidly within the first two or three months after he took office, and asked him what he thought the single sentence that would define and summarize his agenda was, he would have talked about 'compassionate conservatism,'" recalled David Frum, who was a senior White House speechwriter at the time. Bush wanted to recast the party's image, realign national politics around a new set of common ideals. There was political power in that concept, but "it wasn't a governing philosophy in terms of actual policy," Frum said. "So there was kind of an aimless quality within the first year to the president's domestic policy agenda."

There was nothing aimless, then or ever, about Cheney. Nor was he much inclined to visionary themes. Cheney read history, not philosophy. In the Bush administration, Frum said, Cheney was "a force for achieving achievable ends."

Force was not a bad metaphor. Cheney's approach to government was well established by the time he became defense secretary in 1989, but the military offered a vocabulary to describe it. Identify a threat or an objective. Analyze its "center of gravity" and your own resources and constraints. Attack. Cheney drove policy the way commanders are taught to drive operations in the field, calculating the "mission, enemy, troops, terrain and time available." During Cheney's tenure at the Pentagon, Army doctrine was rewritten to emphasize that "each operation must contribute to the ultimate strategic aim," that "intermediate objectives must directly, quickly, and economically contribute to the operation," and that resources must be expended on nothing else.

This was Cheney's discipline exactly: to define a problem, study options, make a choice, ignore distractions, and execute. There would be many reasons for Cheney's dominance in the Bush administration, some of them subtle. One was as simple as could be. The vice president knew what he wanted. Unlike most of his rivals, and even the president he served, Cheney seldom indulged in ambivalence. Either he had a direction in mind or he regarded the choice as unimportant and stepped aside.

Education reform held little interest for the vice president, though it was Bush's top legislative priority and the subject of his greatest campaign passion. Nina Shokraii Rees, then a member of Cheney's domestic policy staff, said he "had given most of that to the president"—an intriguing turn of phrase, though not meant literally. The same went for Bush's second priority, which press secretary Ari Fleischer identified as "getting prescription drugs to seniors." Members of his staff said Cheney doubted either subject's fitness for federal attention.

Cheney knew how to hold his tongue, and he betrayed no outward sign of disagreement. But Phil Gramm, a friend since his 1982 defection from the Democratic Party to join Cheney's House GOP caucus, said, "Dick once told me that our president is a 'big government conservative.' Now, Dick keeps his own opinions to himself whenever he disagrees with the administration, as he should. But I believe that Dick is a small government conservative."

The vice president had an instinct for power and unrivaled knowledge of its junctions around the government. One of his first assignments to his staff was a fast-track review of Bill Clinton's departing executive orders. That would have been a routine step, sooner or later, but Cheney had the savvy to call a halt to operations at the Government Printing Office. Not many aides would have thought of it. Cheney knew regulations have no legal force until they are published in the *Federal Register.* Some of Clinton's orders, signed in his closing hours as president, never made it. The same went for end-of-term appointments to government jobs. At Cheney's suggestion, Bush ordered a hiring freeze that covered everyone whose paperwork was incomplete.

Cheney's top legislative priority was a tax and budget package. In Washington, money was not only money. Tax and spending bills, to those who knew how to read them, told the story of what government would and would not do. When Scooter Libby hired Cesar Conda as Cheney's chief domestic adviser, he told Conda, "Focus on the economy, because that's what the client wants."

Early that spring, Cheney approached California Republican Bill Thomas for a favor.

"He wanted to know if I would help him get an office on the House side" of the Capitol, recalled Thomas, an old friend.

As chairman of the House Ways and Means Committee, Thomas happened to control a prime piece of real estate: room H-208, with a big table and private bathroom, adjacent to the House floor. Cheney could borrow the space, Thomas said. There was collateral: a signed photo of the two men, inscribed, "Bill, thanks for the loan of the office." Thomas specified that Cheney should underline the word "loan."

This was another strategic outpost for Cheney, who already had a Senate-side office as vice president.

"He understands Article I, Section 7, of the Constitution," Thomas said. "Unfortunately, some senators aren't familiar with it. All revenue bills originate in the House, which means all tax policy." Cheney planned to shape legislation at its point of entry. A House office gave him an added edge, too, in managing the rivalry implied in Thomas's remark.

The relationship with Thomas proved pivotal. So too, albeit more briefly, did the vice president's old friendship with Alan Greenspan. From the Federal Reserve, the nation's central bank, Greenspan began to visit the White House at a markedly increased pace. "He used to go monthly under Clinton," primarily for meetings of the Council of Economic Advisers, according to Wharton School economist Ken Thomas, who analyzed the visitor logs. "In January 2001, he started going weekly."

The Fed chairman was not usually there to see Bush or his economic team. Most of the time he came for Cheney alone. This was more than unusual; it was unique. As vice president, Al Gore never met with Greenspan alone, according to Gore's chief of staff, Ron Klain. Even Clinton knew, Klain said, that the treasury secretary "owned the relationship with Greenspan."

Cheney was far too sophisticated to lobby the Fed chairman on interest rates or money supply, the central bank's exclusive bailiwicks. The vice president listened more than he talked, according to accounts Greenspan gave privately afterward. But there was something Cheney wanted. Close votes loomed in Congress on Bush's ten-year, $1.6 trillion tax cut. Greenspan had spoken out against a tax cut less than half that size toward the end of the Clinton administration. Cheney did not need an endorsement, aides said, but it was vital to keep Greenspan from lining up squarely against the White House.

In their conversations, the two men discussed the slowing economy and the unaccustomed federal budget surplus. Greenspan did not believe the surplus would last. Human nature said politicians would spend it. But he trusted Cheney, simple as that. The man had sense, and discipline. In his memoir, years later, Greenspan wrote that Cheney's return to government, along with Paul O'Neill's at Treasury, looked like "a golden opportunity to advance the ideals of effective, fiscally conservative government." Level heads were bound to bring a reality check to Bush's trillion-dollar-plus campaign promise— negotiations with Congress would scale back the tax cut, especially if the surplus began to shrink. Cheney understood economics as well as any politician Greenspan had met, and he'd met them all. The vice president spoke the language, read the reports. Greenspan left their conversations, he said privately, believing that Cheney, like O'Neill, shared his outlook.

From a distance, Ken Thomas, the Wharton professor, saw something untoward in the relationship, given their positions. "I teach monetary economics," he said. "You always preach that the central bank should be independent of the political apparatus." When Greenspan spoke, was he "influenced by frequent visits to the White House"?

On January 25, 2001, Greenspan arrived at the Senate Budget Committee to talk about the hottest subject in town. Would he support the Bush-Cheney plan? Not for nothing was the Fed chairman known as the Sphinx. He read aloud a statement that doubled back on itself, tangled in modifiers and subjunctives. But there was enough there, Senator Fritz Hollings declared, "to start a stampede." Greenspan acknowledged a place for some degree of tax reduction if surpluses persisted, and a tax cut could do "noticeable good" if the economy turned out to be weaker than he expected.

Greenspan later wrote that he thought he was hedging his remarks, but the "nuanced position misjudged the emotions of the moment." Others accused him of tipping the political scales by design.

As it happened, nuance was all Cheney needed. Greenspan had removed himself as an obstacle.

The vice president meanwhile consolidated his influence over tax and spending policy inside the White House. He convened a kitchen cabinet of outside economists, with varied if largely conservative views, and encouraged them to disagree at will among themselves— or with him. He wanted to hear the strongest arguments on every side. "He looks you right in the eye, with his crystal clear blue eyes, and he catches everything," said Allen Sinai, chief global economist at Decision Economics Inc. "He's a very subtle decision maker, takes account of risks as well as opportunities, weighs a lot of factors and then makes a conditioned judgment."

There was one odd thing, Sinai noticed.

"Treasury wasn't participating much, if at all, in these policy discussions," he said. "It looked to me that these decisions were made by a very small group of people."

John Makin, a visiting scholar at the American Enterprise Institute, also found Cheney impressive, but wondered why the vice president was "taking up the slack that otherwise would have gone to the assistant secretary for economic policy at the Treasury." This White House, Makin came to see, was "the locus of all the major policy initiatives," something that was not true under Reagan or the first President Bush. Within the White House, he said, "the day-to-day responsibility of following the economy has fallen more to the vice president."

Bush had the instincts of a populist, talking about people who "work 40, 50 hours a week, and still have trouble paying the electric bill and the grocery bill at the same time." He felt the pain of the waitress raising two kids on $25,000 a year. He told his staff, speechwriter David Frum said, "I want to be compassionate." What about doubling the child tax credit, from $500 to $1,000? How about making it refundable if a person doesn't owe any tax? Michael Boskin, an economist who advised both Bush and Cheney, said "that was what candidate Bush got most animated about."

Cheney thought like a CEO. His approach was "to ask, 'To what problem was the increase in the child tax credit a solution?'" Frum said. "Maybe Americans aren't having enough children? But no one ever said that. They didn't give a rationale. Maybe the problem is worsening poverty and [Bush] wants to use the tax code to address that." But an extra $500 for the waitress—not even ten bucks a week—will not change her life or drive economic growth.

Cheney, by contrast, brought "very targeted solutions to precisely defined problems." He had turned away from the consumer-driven theories of growth associated with John Kenneth Galbraith and other liberal economists of the 1960s. Cheney wanted to boost production, not consumption—the fundamental goal of "supply side" advocates. That meant looking for incentives for productive behavior. Investment, construction, entrepreneurial risk. Those were the provinces of the rich, not the paycheck-to-paycheck workers on Bush's mind.

There can be hundreds of pages in a tax bill. It's one thing to cut a trillion dollars, another to spell out the distribution of benefits. Cheney lived and breathed that kind of detail, knew how to find his way to the places that mattered in the numbing expanse of the Internal Revenue Code. Bush found the fine print aggravating, repellent. He was delighted to give the vice president the lead on negotiations with Capitol Hill.

Bill Thomas, who had lent the vice president an office, loved the man's decisiveness.

"I can pitch the specific structural modification, and he can give immediate assurance that the administration is supportive of what I want to do," Thomas said. Cheney was careful to say the final call belonged to Bush, Thomas said, but he promised "he'll do everything he can to sell it to the president." It was hard to recall a time when Cheney failed. Phil Gramm, on the Senate side, said the difference between Cheney and other White House lobbyists was that "Dick could make a deal. He didn't have to check with the president, not as far as I could tell. I'm sure at the end of the day, he would fill the president in on what had happened. But Dick had the agency of the president."

Candida Wolff, who was Cheney's chief legislative assistant and later the president's, said Cheney used to tell her, "All you have in Washington is your reputation." Once he committed himself, she said, "the V.P. said, 'I've given my word. . . . You need to watch and make sure it happens the way I said it needs to happen.'"

Memories diverge, but it may have been Democrat John Breaux who first called Cheney's Senate office "the Star Chamber," a reference to the court that heard treason cases in medieval England. After a while "a lot of people" started using the name, according to Wolff. "Like it was some torture thing. It was this feeling of, when the vice president was sitting off the floor, if you have to go see him you must have been bad."

Lincoln Chafee qualified. In the spring of 2001, the Rhode Island Republican was lining up with Democrats against the White House tax cut. More than $1.5 trillion. Trillion! He wouldn't do it. The plan was radical, unaffordable, unbelievable.

A full-court press began. Chief of Staff Andy Card invited Chafee to the White House on March 26. Chafee wouldn't budge. One week later, April 2, a polite retainer approached Chafee after a vote.

"The vice president would like to talk to you."

Now?

Now.

Chafee followed. Cheney was waiting. Offered a chair.

"The president and I feel strongly about this one," he said.

What about what I feel? Chafee wondered. Will he ask what I have on my mind?

He would not.

"Cheney did all the talking," Chafee said.

Cheney did not raise his voice. He made no threats. There was just something about him, hard to pin down, the undercurrent that spooked Steve Hadley at the Pentagon.

"Did he try to squeeze their vote out of them?" said Wolff, the legislative assistant. "Yeah, it's his job. But he didn't do it in a way that was aggressive."

Two days later, on April 4, the Republican Party began targeting Democrats with radio spots in their home states. The president believes "working families deserve a tax cut, and our economy needs a boost," the announcer said. "But what about our senator?" Fill in name here.

Chafee was a Republican. The ad did not play in his state. But Andy Card gave an interview to the *Providence Journal-Bulletin,* talking about the state's 385,000 taxpayers and saying, "I'm surprised that Senator Chafee doesn't want tax relief for them." Then Card picked up the phone and called Rhode Island's top-rated conservative talk show.

"I asked around," Card told Steve Kass of WPRO radio, and everyone said Kass was the go-to host if you wanted to "lobby Senator Chafee in his backyard." The White House chief of staff had a guest to offer.

"How would you like the vice president?"

"And I said, 'Of course,'" Kass recalled.

At half past ten on April 4, Cheney patched into *The Steve Kass Show* from the White House. As far as any listener could tell, it was Kass who turned the conversation to the tax bill.

"I think you may be aware that there's a senator from Rhode Island" who is not with the program, Kass said. "What's your relationship with Senator Chafee right now?"

The vice president began softly, his tone suggesting a reservation of judgment. Cheney had only just met the senator. His late father? Different story. Cheney had known John Chafee very well, worked with him closely. Nothing but respect for the man. "Linc is of course new to the Senate," Cheney said. "Working hard, I'm sure.

"I didn't get on the show this morning to criticize him," the vice president continued.

Almost too gradually to notice, he unsheathed a knife.

"I do, ah, disagree with him, because I think what the Senate did last week is a classic example of what's going to happen with the surplus if we don't give it back to the American taxpayer."

Kass said nothing for two full minutes. Cheney held to his pleasant cadence, as though he were discussing the weather. People like Chafee were promoting "the idea that somehow the government is going to be starved" by the president's tax cut. "The budget that they're complaining about involves a *one* . . . *hundred* . . . *billion*-dollar increase in spending, next year over this year." Senators had gotten used to "spending money like drunken sailors down here, and there needs to be some kind of restraint."

"Mr. Vice President, thank you very much for being here with us," Kass said. "I imagine you would not be averse to our listeners giving Senator Chafee's office a call?"

"I wouldn't want to discourage anybody from contacting their senator," Cheney said.

WPRO rebroadcast the interview four or five times. By the end of the week, an estimated one hundred thousand listeners had tuned in—one in ten Rhode Islanders, if you count every man, woman, and child. Chafee heard from a lot of them, "and they were all mad at me. 'Why aren't you supporting the president?'"

Jim Jeffords, another moderate from that Specter lunch, was giving Cheney even more trouble than Chafee. He was chairman of the Education Committee, determined to claim a slice of the budget surplus for a cause he had supported for some years. Decades earlier, the federal government had made a promise. Congress imposed a mandate on every school district to offer special education for the disabled. Washington would pay 70 percent of the cost. The money never came. Jeffords demanded that Bush divert $450 million from his tax cut into schooling for the least advantaged. Jeffords was a Navy veteran, son of a chief justice of the Vermont Supreme Court, and a black belt in tae kwon do. Stubborn as a mule on this one: no special-education funds, no yea vote on the tax bill.

The whole Republican leadership came down on him. Cheney hovered in the background. A Senate aide walked into the cloakroom one day and found Jeffords negotiating his amendment with Pete Domenici, the Budget chairman. "And Domenici is on the phone with Vice President Cheney, going over these nitty-gritty details," the aide recalled.

Finally, Jeffords took out his big gun. Maybe it was time to switch sides, leave the Republican Party and caucus with Democrats. The 50–50 Senate would go 51–49.

Here it was, the ultimate test of Chafee's Mod Squad Theorem— the one from the December lunch that said Cheney would have to take heed of the centrist vote. This was a stickup. Would the president hand over the cash, or take his chances?

The Jeffords threat placed the White House on red alert. Bush's top advisers conferred. Trent Lott, the Senate majority leader, counseled compromise. Other senior Republicans, worried for their committee chairmanships, urged the same. Karl Rove, one participant said, was all for fucking Jeffords over—that was the way he talked—but not for driving him out of the party. Make him pay for his disloyalty, embarrass him, cancel something he cares about. But wait for a better moment. Control of the Senate was too important to lose. "It was a spirited discussion that went on for a couple of days," recalled Sean O'Keefe, who was then deputy director of the Office of Management and Budget. Nobody took a vote as such, but there seemed to be more voices for deflecting the fight than for pressing it to the bitter end.

Bush took his time, waiting for advice from his commanders on the ground.

"Even though he knew what hung in the balance," O'Keefe said, Cheney was "very forceful in the view that . . . this was not the way you make these kinds of choices." Blackmail could not be permitted to drive "significant decisions about public policy as it pertains to education, with huge budget implications." Phil Gramm, who spoke to Cheney about the choice, said, "It was about both the money and the principle. The principle was, 'Hell, we can't go around funding programs based on what some individual might do.' . . . If we make one change, we'll have a thousand changes and pretty soon we're going to lose more than we get."

Some of Bush's lieutenants feared that Cheney was walking the president off a cliff. How hard would it be for the self-described education president to give Jeffords what he wanted and declare victory?

It seemed inexplicable that Cheney, so close a student of institutional power, would throw away control of the Senate in the president's first hundred days. But this missed something fundamental about Cheney's worldview. Acquiescence to Jeffords, as Cheney saw it, would mean the White House had *already* lost the Senate. Negotiation, in this context, was akin to surrender. This was not a conventional view of the give-and-take of lawmaking in Washington. But Cheney wanted nothing to do with government by least common denominator. This would not be an administration, he said, that sacrificed principle to expedience.

One by one, those of the senior staff who held other views stood down. Cheney's position "prevailed at that meeting, and thereafter," O'Keefe said.

Building consensus was crucial in the Bush White House. By temperament the president was very nearly the reverse of his description by spokesman Ari Fleischer. "He likes to have strong people who have a lot of opinions to share, and he will put them in the room and listen to them, and he wants to hear a cacophony of ideas," Fleischer said as Bush prepared to take office. Actually, Bush generally hated it when advisers disagreed, demanding that they get their acts together. At decision time, according to Cheney aide Ron Christie, Bush wanted to hear that "your senior advisers believe X." Political scientist Charles E. Walcott, who has studied every White House since Nixon's, said Bush valued not only consensus but finality. "Once he's made up his mind, controversy ceases, so getting to him at just the right time is extremely important," Walcott said.

That was what happened on the Jeffords question. The president wanted unanimity, and unanimity was what Cheney brought.

Stand firm.

On May 24, 2001, Jeffords resigned from the GOP. Trent Lott became minority leader; Democrat Tom Daschle ascended to the gavel and the spoils of the majority. It was a political earthquake, the only thing anyone in Washington could talk about. To Cheney, the aftermath was noise. The decision had been made weeks before, the die cast. It was time to move on.

A Princeton professor named Aaron Friedberg came to the White House that day, invited by Scooter Libby to brief the vice president on recent trends in Asia. Friedberg had to run a gauntlet of cameras at the Northwest Gate, the reporters broadcasting live about the Jeffords meltdown. Inside the vice president's office, all was serene. Cheney engaged Friedberg in a wide-ranging discussion of Chinese economic and military prospects, divisions in the senior leadership, implications for U.S. interests in the Far East.

"He spent an hour-plus, overtime, as if none of this was going on," said Friedberg, who later joined Cheney's foreign policy staff. "He was completely focused."

Chapter Four

ENERGY IN THE EXECUTIVE

The spring of 2001 brought Cheney a fresh confrontation with the legislative branch. On the surface, the dispute was about pedestrian details of process. The true stakes were the constitutional balance of power.

Bush set events in motion at 11:35 a.m. on January 29, 2001, inviting a media pool to the Cabinet Room for what the press office called a camera spray, photos but no questions. Television footage panned across the mahogany and leather table where Cheney chaired the first meeting of a new task force on "our nation's energy situation." Cheney had asked for the assignment. Some commentators compared it to the niche projects that had been handed off to vice presidents before. That was a mistake.

Cheney took his appointment as a mandate to redefine two boundaries: one between the executive branch and its competitors, the other between regulation and the marketplace.

The four-month energy assignment would have a transformative impact on the environment in coming years, if not so much on the nation's power grid. Sometimes openly and more often not, Cheney recast rules that governed air and water quality, the preservation of endangered species, and the status of millions of square miles of public land. Much of it happened later, but the task force marked the new direction.

Cheney's overriding goal was enlargement of presidential authority. Since the mid-1970s, he believed, power grabs by Congress and courts had intruded on the dominion of the executive. There was also a disturbing trend toward independence in federal agencies and commissions, which belonged under White House control. The first directive he gave to general counsel David Addington, Cheney told his authorized biographer, was to "restore the powers of the presidency."

Global warming and its implications posed a challenge. Cheney made it his mission to brake the growing political momentum for a government response. Those who were most alarmed by global warming called for painful shifts of practice in heavy industry, entirely at cross-purposes with Cheney beliefs. That kind of thinking, the instinct to dream up a new set of rules every time someone identified a risk, was altogether alien to Cheney.

The vice president had to tread carefully here. One of the people thinking those thoughts, and speaking them aloud, was George W. Bush. Candidate Bush had accepted that industrial emissions produce a "greenhouse effect," trapping the sun's heat in the atmosphere and posing a threat of dangerous climate change. In his energy speech of September 29, 2000, positioned to blunt Al Gore's environmental appeal, Bush said he would "require all power plants to meet clean air standards in order to reduce emissions of sulfur dioxide, nitrogen oxide, mercury and carbon dioxide." A campaign position paper, released the same day, mirrored the scientific consensus by describing those emissions as the "four main pollutants." Inclusion of carbon dioxide was significant: it was generally thought to be the most important greenhouse gas, but also the costliest to control. Equally significant was the reference to "all power plants," because older plants were grandfathered under existing rules. Bush's position paper said he would "establish mandatory reduction targets" on old and new plants alike.

Once in office, Cheney set about arranging a retraction. Carbon dioxide caps were anathema to the fossil fuel industries at the center of Cheney's thinking on energy.

As always, Cheney avoided a frontal challenge to Bush. He had no time to intercede before Christie Whitman, administrator of the Environmental Protection Agency, set off for a climate change summit in Trieste, Italy. Whitman confirmed in advance with White House chief of staff Andy Card that Bush stood by his promise on carbon emissions. She delivered that message to the Group of Eight industrial allies on March 4, 2001. Aboard the flight home, Whitman composed a memo for Bush: "I would strongly recommend that you continue to recognize that global warming is a real and serious issue. Mr. President, this is a credibility issue for the U.S. in the international community."

Unseen as yet, a Cheney-led insurgency was already gathering force. Haley Barbour, who had left the chairmanship of the Republican National Committee to lobby for fossil fuel companies, sent the vice president a trenchant memo on March 1, describing a "moment of truth" for the new administration. Did Bush really plan to associate himself with the "eco-extremism" of those who sought to "regulate and/or tax CO_2 as a pollutant"?

Some debates go on for months. Some fade away without result. Cheney had a knack for creating decision points. He found his opportunity on March 6, the same day Whitman sent her plea to the president. Four Republican senators wrote to Bush to ask for "clarification of your Administration's policy on climate change."

Two days later, on March 8, three members of Cheney's staff—domestic advisers Cesar Conda and Karen Knutson, and energy task force chief of staff Andrew Lundquist—produced a four-page plan to walk the president away from his promise.

The Cheney document was a case study in management of an errant boss. Addressed to White House domestic policy adviser John Bridgeland, the March 8 memo acknowledged that Bush had taken an unequivocal stand on carbon emissions. The September promise had not been made off-the-cuff; it was a major speech, accompanied by a printed policy analysis. The declared intent of the Cheney staff memo was to sell the president and the public on a substitute policy that "may appear to differ with our campaign statement." The vice president's aides, none of them scientists, said Bush should be nudged toward the position that "the current state of scientific knowledge about causes of and solutions to global warming is inconclusive. . . . Therefore, it would be *premature* at this time for the President to propose *any* specific policy or approach aimed at addressing global warming." The tack to take, they wrote, was that "the President believes . . . more scientific inquiry" is required. Any contrary statement in the campaign—including the inconvenient September speech—"did not fully reflect the President's position." The man just did not know what he was saying.

As an alternative, Bush should declare "a new, innovative, and pro-active approach" to protecting air quality, with no method or deadline specified.

What Cheney and his staff proposed would put the White House on record against the collective judgment of the world's climate scientists. Two authoritative studies had just drawn to a close: one from the Intergovernmental Panel on Climate Change, the other from the U.S. government's own National Assessment Synthesis Team, a decade in the making. Both studies reported with high confidence that human activity was giving rise to worrisome shifts in temperature on a planetary scale. Domestic consequences in the coming century were likely to include floods, drought, costly damage to coastal cities, "heavy and extreme precipitation events," loss of habitat, and the extinction of one or more ecosystems on the North American continent. Elsewhere, the impact would likely be graver. Career U.S. officials, in a memo for Cheney's task force, called the two studies "as close to a global scientific consensus as can be achieved." Failure to embrace them, the officials warned, "would be portrayed as a fundamental assault on the science."

Whitman did not see the Cheney staff memo or the one from Haley Barbour—those were circulated only among friends—but she sensed trouble. Bush had said when he hired her, "If you ever need to talk to me directly, just blow away the palace guard." On Friday, March 9, five weeks into the job, Whitman phoned for an appointment.

Bush's schedulers slotted Whitman for 10 a.m. the following Tuesday. She knew the president had no patience for lengthy briefings, and she spent the weekend honing a set of short, sharp talking points. Cheney, who saw the president's calendar in advance, had plenty of time to preempt her. Shortly before Whitman arrived on March 13, National Security Adviser Condi Rice learned that Cheney had brought Bush a ready-to-sign reply to the senators. In it Bush would announce a reversal of course on carbon emissions. The EPA, the State Department, and the Treasury Department, each of which had a big stake in the decision, had not seen the text.

Throughout his long government career, Cheney counseled against exactly that kind of policy surprise. Unvetted decisions, he often warned, lead presidents to costly mistakes. When James A. Baker III was named White House chief of staff in 1980, he interviewed many of his living predecessors. Advice from Cheney filled four pages of a yellow legal pad. Only once, to signify Cheney's greatest emphasis, did Baker write in all capital letters:

BE AN HONEST BROKER

DON'T USE THE PROCESS TO IMPOSE YOUR POLICY VIEWS ON PRES.

Cheney told Baker, according to the truncated notes, that an "orderly paper flow is way you protect the Pres.," ensuring that any proposal has been tested against other views. Cheney added: "It's not in anyone's interest to get an 'oh by the way decision'—& all have to understand that. Can hurt the Pres. Bring it up at a Cab. mtg. Make sure everyone understands this." In 1999, not long before he became Bush's running mate, Cheney warned again about "oh by the way decisions" in an interview with presidential scholar Martha Joynt Kumar.

"If you don't trust the process, you're going to start looking for a way around it, try to find a friendly congressman who has a good relationship with the president," Cheney said. "All of a sudden you have people freelancing, trying to get around the decision-making process because they feel the process lacks integrity. So it's very, very important when you set up shop to make certain that you have a guaranteed flow—you know what's going in; you know what's coming out. You know when it goes in that it's complete, that everybody's got their shot at the decision memo. You know if there's going to be a meeting, the right people are going to be in the meeting, that the president has a chance to listen to all of that and then make a decision."

In the Bush administration, Cheney paid no apparent heed to those values. One explanation is that his role was altogether different from the ones he had filled as cabinet officer and chief of staff. Though Cheney often described the president as his boss, repeated references to his constitutional role made clear that Cheney understood a fundamental fact of the job: he could not be fired. He styled himself no more than an adviser to Bush, but unlike every other adviser, he did not serve at the pleasure of the president. Cheney had sworn an independent oath of office, had an independent obligation to advance the national interest. He no longer felt bound by a neutral process when it conflicted with the course he believed to be right. Only once, as far as the author could discover, did he come close to spelling this out. "I'm not a staffer, I'm the vice president, a constitutional officer, *elected same as he is,*" Cheney told his biographer.

Even as White House chief of staff, Cheney was no enthusiast for endless debate.

"Ford was someone who, when making a difficult decision, wanted to see a lot of people and hear from them," said Terry O'Donnell, who served with Cheney then and is now his personal lawyer. "Cheney made sure that the president's style was taken into account. That took time. Cheney respected it but at times I think he found it to be inefficient."

According to the prevailing metaphor in the Ford White House, the president wanted to be the hub of the wheel, supported by many spokes. Cheney gradually tightened access. When he left the White House, one official said, "his staff gave him a bicycle wheel with all the spokes busted out except for one—his. That's the way he works now." In those days, recalled Stuart Spencer, the plainspoken political adviser to decades of GOP candidates, "he could disagree with you but your view would get to the president. I think that's why people say [the vice president is] not the Cheney I know. Well, his role was different then. Now he doesn't have to filter anything." Cheney's demand for a disciplined process, under Ford, coincided with his own role as processor-in-chief. The late political scientist Nelson Polsby, who became friendly with Cheney when his daughter served an internship in Cheney's office, put his finger on that: "I think he's been fairly consistent over the years in wanting to maximize power wherever he was sitting at the moment. So, for example, if you'd asked him twenty years ago, 'How do you think power should be distributed between chief of staff at the White House and the vice president?' he wouldn't have had any trouble figuring that out. But now he's on the other side. So he does change sides. He plays for his team."

How Cheney brought the president around on global warming was a mystery to most of Bush's lieutenants. It did not hurt, officials said, that Cheney and the energy task force staff portrayed the scientific debate as complex, unresolved. Bush hated wading into that sort of thing, and usually told experts to come back when they had hammered out their facts. Bush and Cheney also enjoyed a joke now and then at the expense of Al Gore, a man for whom they shared no small distaste. Carbon caps and global warming were "Saint Al's" big issue. Maybe, one staff aide said, Bush regretted the September speech, fearing it had positioned him too close for comfort to the Kyoto climate accord, which a unanimous Senate rejected for its lenience toward developing states. Some of Bush's longest-serving aides saw the appeal of Cheney's call for a paradigm shift—using smarter policy and technology to avoid the old choice between less energy and more pollution. Bush liked game changers, not small ball.

To Condi Rice, it looked as though the president was about to pull out the Sharpie in his breast pocket and sign. Like Whitman, Rice believed the carbon turnabout was a mistake, sure to infuriate allies. She placed a hasty phone call to Secretary of State Colin Powell, who said he would come right over. Buy some time, he urged.

Cheney's letter for Bush skated off to one side of staff secretariat procedures, which ordinarily gave cabinet officers and top-ranking White House aides an opportunity to weigh in on presidential documents. Some saw this one, some did not. The text had grown more soothing, but its transactional language—the words that turned the wheels of government—followed exactly in the path mapped out by Cheney's staff the previous week. "I support a comprehensive and balanced national energy policy that takes into account the importance of improving air quality," the letter said. "I do not believe, however, that the government should impose on power plants mandatory emissions reductions for carbon dioxide, which is not a 'pollutant' under the Clean Air Act." Such a step—the very step Bush proposed as a candidate—could not be justified "given the incomplete state of scientific knowledge of the causes of, and solutions to, global climate change." The president planned to launch, instead, a wide-ranging examination of "innovative options."

Whitman's meeting did not last long. Cheney had already been and gone, Bush's signature in hand. The president apologized for moving without her, but said he had made up his mind: with an energy crisis brewing, this was no time to impose new burdens on utilities and their customers. Some government experts doubted a crisis, in fact, existed. A briefing memo prepared for the energy task force the same month said that "on the whole, U.S. energy markets are working well, allocating resources and preventing shortages." But Cheney made crisis a running theme, and his final report would open with the statement that "America in 2001 faces the most serious energy shortage since the oil embargoes of the 1970s."

As a dispirited Whitman left the Oval Office, Cheney walked briskly past in an overcoat, heading for the weekly Senate Republican lunch. "Do you have it?" the vice president asked an aide, who passed him an envelope. The vice president was taking no chances: he would deliver Bush's letter by hand. By afternoon, the president of the United States had aligned himself with fringe-group claims that the causes and significance of global warming remained unproved.

Cheney's motorcade departed before Colin Powell passed through the White House security gate. Too late, Rice told the secretary of state. "They all got together . . . and said to hell with everybody else and they just signed it with no reference to our allies, no reference to 'Let's work with them and find a way forward on carbon emissions,'" Powell later said.

On other questions, too, the energy task force became a creature of Cheney's worldview, eliding differences of emphasis with the president. Bush had asked Cheney for a plan to "encourage conservation on the one hand, and bring more energy into the marketplace." Cheney set off a brouhaha, three months later, with a speech describing conservation as "a sign of personal virtue," not a basis for policy. He ridiculed the idea "that government should step in to force Americans to consume less energy." Bush had not said otherwise, exactly, but Cheney reframed the marching orders as he followed them. Some of Bush's advisers, including White House counselor Karen Hughes, saw a draft of that speech and urged Cheney to "green it up." A lot of voters cared about the environment. Perhaps the vice president could find a less provocative form of words? Cheney saw no point in skirting controversy. The test of a speech, as one aide recalled his reply, was "whether it serves a purpose . . . in solidifying a goal that the vice president believes in."

Conservation, for Cheney, was ultimately a matter of supply and demand. Bush spoke of helping the working stiff, the driver who couldn't afford to fill his tank. The vice president, according to White House speechwriter Michael Gerson, held the antipodal view: "Markets would take care of" reducing consumption, Cheney argued, "as gas prices rise."

Bush loved to hear about new technology. He was smitten, especially, with hydrogen's potential as a boundless source of clean and renewable power. Cheney "was in a different place," one close observer said—the insistent pragmatist, guardian against soft sentiment. What the country needed, Cheney said, was a near-term boost in domestic energy production. In the real world, that meant coal and oil and nuclear power. Decades of overregulation, in Cheney's view, had stifled their growth. Somebody had to break down legal barriers—against drilling for oil in the Arctic, against building new coal-fired power plants, against a long-debated plan to store radioactive waste under Nevada's Yucca Mountain. No Yucca, no nuclear construction. Karen Knutson, one of Cheney's energy advisers, said he questioned her in intricate detail about the alternative fuels that captured Bush's fancy, the better to understand their limits. Many of them had been touted by the environmental movement for years— electric cars, biofuels distilled from corn, and the ne plus ultra of hydrogen fuel cells. "The vice president was keen on developing a realistic approach," she said. "Right now, you use more energy to create the hydrogen than the hydrogen would replace."

Cheney prepared his energy plan at the greatest possible distance from public view. Before starting work, he directed David Addington, his general counsel, to devise a structure that would leave the task force beyond the reach of the Federal Advisory Committee Act. That was the open-government law that gave so much grief to Hillary Clinton in 1993, exposing the records of her health care task force to political attack. "He was very critical at many points at the way in which he felt presidents would yield in giving up information," said Michael Malbin, a long-standing ally of Cheney on executive secrecy. Cheney decided to "put down a marker," and his task force was "deliberately set up to be different" from Clinton's.

The key point of legal contrast, based on Addington's advice, was the limitation of task force "membership" to employees of the executive branch. Cheney could meet with all the lobbyists he liked, but they must have no official status on the panel.

Thus did Cheney and his staff receive advice—and policy drafts—from visitors, or guests. One of the first, on a list that went undisclosed for more than six years, was James J. Rouse. Then vice president of ExxonMobil, Rouse had been a major donor to the Bush-Cheney inauguration fund. A week later, February 21, came Kenneth Lay, the soon-to-be-indicted chairman of Enron Corporation and another big donor. March 5 brought more Enron and Exxon-Mobil executives, along with Duke Energy, Florida Power & Light, El Paso Energy, and other utilities. In the weeks to come a procession of oil companies, including Conoco, Shell Oil, and BP America, met with Cheney or his aides. Environmental groups—more than a dozen of them—were crammed together into a single meeting on April 4, expending half their allotted time on introductions. Cheney did not attend. Lundquist, the task force chief of staff, later said there was no point in talking to environmentalists again. Had he followed their advice, he said, "the president and vice president would have fired me."

All those meetings were secret. Cheney made clear to those who attended, according to participants, that public mention of their visits would be unwelcome. More than four years later, oil company representatives—including the chief executives of ExxonMobil and the since-merged ConocoPhillips—still flatly denied their companies had taken part. (Shell's chief executive, more cautious in his testimony before the Senate Energy and Commerce committees, said his company had played no role "to my knowledge.") The *Washington Post* obtained an attendance list, based on Secret Service records, that placed Rouse at one of the task force meetings. Interviewed by telephone, the retired Exxon vice president gamely stood by his denial. "That must be inaccurate, and I don't have any comment beyond that," he said. Angry Senate Democrats spoke of pursuing criminal charges if any witness had made a "materially false, fictitious or fraudulent" statement. Those threats came to nothing.

In the spring of 2001, Cheney's task force faced formal demands for information from two House committees, the General Accounting Office, and outside litigants.

Cheney and Addington welcomed the fight. Lundquist, who ran the energy meetings, believed his own integrity was in question: critics were saying the secrecy smelled of cover-up. He recommended that Cheney open the books. "Don't ever suggest that to me again," Cheney told him.

The vice president believed in what his old friend David Gribbin called "the demonstrative use of power." An early stand for presidential authority, aides said, sent a strong signal of intent. Victory would discourage other challenges and prepare the ground for further offensives. Cheney persuaded Bush, against the advice of his political staff, to pursue a long and costly struggle to the nation's highest court. "We were hiding something we shouldn't be worried about," Dan Bartlett recalled, describing his advice to Bush. "We were looking too secretive when it didn't matter."

Looks meant little to Cheney. Secrecy meant a great deal, though not for the reasons commonly supposed at first. Critics alleged that the former chairman of Halliburton, an oil services firm, was intent on lining the pockets of his cronies—or even, perhaps, his own. They had a decent circumstantial case. The Bush-Cheney campaign, a ticket of two oil men, had hauled in record contributions from the industry. And it was hard to deny that expanded drilling, or looser pollution controls, would please those donors. But such considerations, by just about every inside account, were no more than incidental to Cheney. In interviews with nearly two dozen close observers of the energy task force, many of whom were not in the vice president's camp, none ascribed political motives of any kind to Cheney. The way he went about his work, one senior official said without pleasure, "actually showed he didn't give a rat's ass about the politics." Cheney was a true believer: national security and economic health required a boost in energy production, and that in turn required a rollback of stifling rules. On issues of this magnitude, Cheney would show again and again that he brooked little compromise.

Nor did Cheney stand to gain financially from Halliburton's good fortunes, despite loose accusations then and since. The University of Pennsylvania's Annenberg Public Policy Center, which eventually obtained and analyzed the relevant records, concluded that the vice president was correct to assert "no financial interest in Halliburton of any kind." He had received $1.6 million in deferred salary, weeks before becoming vice president, and another $398,548 after taking office. But that money was earned before Cheney left the company, and by contract the size and dates of payment were fixed. Though hardly anyone knew it, Cheney had sacrificed valuable assets to ensure he had no conflict of interest as vice president. Two days before the inauguration, Dick and Lynne Cheney quietly gave away an estimated $8 million in stock options from Halliburton and six other companies. Typically opaque, even when transparency would serve him, Cheney made public no details. Years later, the Annenberg Center reviewed a copy of the irrevocable "Gift Administration Agreement." The agreement established a charitable trust, funded the trust with all proceeds of the Cheney stock options, and named three beneficiaries: the University of Wyoming, the medical faculty at George Washington University, and a charity that pays private and religious school tuitions. Even then, there remained a theoretical conflict of interest. What if Halliburton folded before paying out the last of Cheney's deferred salary? To eliminate that motive to protect the company's financial health, Cheney bought a $15,000 insurance policy. The policy would replace Cheney's remaining Halliburton income if the company somehow went bust.

Accusations of venality, after all those precautions, were among the very few things that could pierce Cheney's detachment. Rob Portman, who played John Edwards in preparation for the 2004 vice-presidential debate, pushed every button he could "to make him bite."

"I really got under his skin," Portman said, with "the Halliburton thing."

The same year, on June 22, the vice president had a chance encounter with Senator Patrick Leahy. The Vermont Democrat had accused Cheney of collusion in awarding sole-source contracts to Halliburton in Iraq. The Democratic National Committee declared a "Halliburton Week" to flog the story. Leahy approached Cheney on the Senate floor, put out his hand. No hard feelings.

"Fuck yourself," Cheney said.

Aides were divided afterward, but most of them agreed with Portman's assessment: it was another demonstration shot.

"He doesn't lose control," Portman said. "He sometimes says, 'You've gone over the line here.'"

Cheney, at bottom, did not promote secrecy for fear of embarrassment. Neither his advisers nor their advice embarrassed him. Cheney favored stealth, in part, because it gave him practical advantages. As he demonstrated neatly with the global warming letter, it was easier to win a battle when opponents did not show up. For the vice president, however, there was a much larger question of principle at stake.

In Cheney's estimation, a president's authority was close to absolute within his rightful sphere. Congress and courts had their own spheres, separate and unshared. With its very first word, Article II of the Constitution vested "the" executive power in the president. Like other advocates of a "unitary executive," Cheney believed the president's inherent functions—command of the Army and Navy, direction of the cabinet, execution of the law—were indivisible. Exercise of those powers was beyond the reach, in principle, of legislative or judicial review.

Secrecy was only one outgrowth of that belief, though an important one. Neither the public nor other branches of government had a right to look behind the curtain in the White House, Cheney believed. A president, he said often, could not expect free and candid advice except in secret.

"He firmly believes—believes to the point where, when he talks about it, his eyes get a little bluer—that for the presidency to operate properly, it needs to be able to have confidential communications," said Scooter Libby, Cheney's chief of staff. (Libby drew an analogy then that he might not have chosen two years later, comparing Cheney's prerogative to a reporter's protection of confidential sources.) Political debate about the energy task force, and about nearly any other executive function, should properly be confined to what the president said and did in public.

This was a profoundly revisionist view of the American plan of government, a departure from two centuries of legal scholarship. Mainstream historians had long agreed that the Constitution's checks and balances relied not on a literal "separation of powers" but more nearly on a system of overlapping control. The framers made plain that their animating purpose was to thwart the emergence of a new tyrant dressed in constitutional garb. None of the most potent powers of government—taxing and spending, making law, punishing criminals, waging war—was assigned to a single branch. The legislature defined crimes; the executive prosecuted; courts decided guilt and imposed sentence. The president commanded troops in combat, but Congress declared war, raised armies, and defined "rules for the government and regulation of the land and naval forces." The president could veto legislation, but with sufficient support the Congress could override him. The president proposed treaties and nominees for high office, but the Senate could withhold consent.

Cheney and Addington did not invent their revisionist view, which came into vogue in the Reagan administration. But the vice president and his lawyer became, by far, its most influential adherents.

Like other "presidentialists," Cheney and Addington drew authority from *Federalist* No. 70, one of Alexander Hamilton's tracts on behalf of the as-yet unratified Constitution. "Energy in the Executive is a leading character in the definition of good government," Hamilton wrote. "It is essential to the protection of the community against foreign attacks; it is not less essential to the steady administration of the laws." The first quality of an energetic executive, Hamilton wrote, was "unity."

In a rare exposition at length of his constitutional views, published almost exactly two hundred years later, Cheney described Congress as "a collective, deliberative body" that tended to "slow down decisions" and "subject them to compromise." The presidency, by contrast, "was designed as a one-person office to ensure that it would be ready for action. Its major characteristics, in the language of *Fed-*

eralist No. 70, were to be 'decision, activity, secrecy and dispatch.'" By reasons of size and diffuse responsibility, Cheney argued, Congress was prone to reckless leaks and feckless changes of heart. In a dangerous world, therefore, a president sometimes had to defy congressional demands for information and legislative attempts to restrict his use of power. "On the scale of risks, I am more concerned about depriving the president of his ability to act than I am about Congress's alleged inability to respond," Cheney wrote.

Cheney's admiration for Hamilton, displayed in several citations to *Federalist* No. 70 over the years, did not extend to the Founding Father's prior writings. There is no public record that Cheney mentioned *Federalist* No. 69, published four days before No. 70 in the same New York newspaper. And yet the earlier piece is the one in which Hamilton addressed Cheney's subject most directly. In No. 69, Hamilton weighed executive powers explicitly against those of Congress, in order to demonstrate the limits of the former—even in war. In comparison to that of a monarch, or even that of the existing governor of New York, "the power of the President would be inferior," Hamilton wrote. The president would command "the militia of the nation" only after Congress declared war or called up troops to suppress insurrection or repel invasion. The president's authority as commander in chief "would be nominally the same with that of the king of Great Britain, but in substance much inferior to it." That balance evolved over the decades, especially after World War II, but this was the originalist view of Hamilton and his fellow framers.

In *Federalist* No. 70, by contrast, Hamilton was not talking about Congress at all. The passages quoted by Cheney arose from Hamilton's dispute with opponents who believed the executive power should be vested in a committee, not a single president. Hamilton, in other words, was not comparing the relative merits of the president and Congress in the energetic conduct of the people's business.

He was describing the advantages of a unified *presidency* over a divided one.

One Cheney sympathizer, a former federal prosecutor of terror crimes, maintained that the vice president's critics were no less guilty of cherry-picking the *Federalist* papers. Accusing Cheney of disregard for No. 69, according to Andrew McCarthy, "ignores the selfsame Hamilton's admonition, in *Federalist* 73, against 'the propensity of the legislative department to intrude upon the rights, and to absorb the powers, of the other departments.'" That is not a persuasive rejoinder. Hamilton acknowledged the risk of congressional overreach precisely in the course of explaining its constitutional cure. His exclusive purpose in No. 73 was to justify two provisions for the president's self-defense: the power to veto laws, and a guaranteed salary. Absent fixed compensation, Hamilton argued, a regnant legislature could "reduce him by famine, or tempt him by largesses." Absent the veto power, a president "might gradually be stripped of his authorities by successive resolutions, or annihilated by a single vote." Nothing in this was relevant to Cheney's claim that the commander in chief may refuse to disclose his acts in office or disregard a law once it has passed. Hamilton's case for restraining Congress, in fact, began with the premise that its lawmaking and spending powers would be binding.

On his first full day at work, White House counsel Alberto Gonzales gathered his legal staff and delivered their prime directive from the president. Bush had told him, Gonzales said, "I want to leave the presidency better off than I found it." That imperative—to protect and expand executive authority—originated with neither Bush nor his lawyer, according to six members of the White House staff.

Bush had just left a governor's post that, by constitutional structure, was among the weakest in the nation. In Texas, most top officials were elected on their own, not beholden to the governor for their jobs. Independent commissions ran state agencies. Bush's lieutenant governor, Robert Bullock, was a Democrat—and the powers of his position were arguably superior. Bush was obliged to forge bipartisan coalitions. He did it well, and made that style of governance a selling point in the 2000 campaign. When Bush arrived in Washington, aides said, he looked forward to the elbow room of his new job, but he brought no particular grievance against Congress.

The vice president did. He had left the Ford White House in 1977 with an abiding belief that post-Nixon reforms unduly hobbled the commander in chief. "You had the nadir of the modern presidency in terms of authority and legitimacy," Cheney later said.

In his efforts to cover up the Watergate scandal, Nixon discredited the pillars of presidential authority. He claimed falsely that an FBI investigation of the campaign burglary would expose national security secrets. He fired a prosecutor who tried to subpoena Oval Office recordings, and he asserted executive privilege over audiotapes that demonstrated his complicity in a crime. Nixon's further deceptions about the Vietnam War, and exposure of intelligence abuses in congressional probes led by Frank Church and Otis Pike, touched off an avalanche of new laws. Congress laid on one after another: the War Powers Act (no troops in combat after ninety days without congressional approval) . . . the Budget Control Impoundment Act (president can't refuse to spend money appropriated by Congress) . . . an expanded Freedom of Information Act (public access to government records) . . . the Intelligence Oversight Act (advance notice to Congress of covert action) . . . the Clark and Boland amendments (no intervention in Angola and Nicaragua) . . . the Foreign Intelligence Surveillance Act (no domestic spying without special warrant) . . . the Presidential Records Act (White House papers preserved as public property) . . . the Independent Counsel Act (special prosecutor can't be fired).

"All these things were marginalizing presidential power," said Bruce Fein, who played a role in the Reagan administration's successful campaign to recapture the president's lost autonomy. In his 1980 meeting with Jim Baker, the very first substantive point Cheney made, according to Baker's notes, was this: "Pres. seriously weakened in recent yrs. Restore power & auth to Exec Branch—Need strong ldr'ship. Get rid of War Powers Act—restore independent rights." In the margin of his legal pad, Baker drew six stars and noted that Cheney called this the "central theme we ought to push."

Many scholars, not only conservatives, agreed that Congress had swung the pendulum too far after Nixon. Bill Clinton, who had his own reasons, happily allowed the Independent Counsel Act to expire, and he followed Reagan's lead in avoiding invocation of the War Powers Act.

David Gergen, who worked with Cheney during the Ford years, said the vice president's "zealous reassertion of the power of the presidency" arose from the experience of a White House under siege. "He felt that what had become known as the imperial presidency during Nixon had become the imperiled presidency," Gergen said. "Where a number of us part company with him is that a number of us believe that through Reagan, those powers had been substantially restored. When George W. Bush became president, I didn't think that should or would be a major priority."

But Cheney had a way of framing the issue that got a rise out of Bush. In an interview with reporters that, according to aides, echoed words he had spoken years earlier to Bush, Cheney said the president "should not have to reveal . . . to a member of Congress who he talked to that morning."

White House officials said Cheney's long-held constitutional views fit well with Bush's determination to show a strength his father was accused of lacking. This would not be a "prudent," compromising White House, and Bush would not disparage, as his father had, "the vision thing." A bold presidency called for bold use of power. Here again, Bartlett said, the vice president pushed on an open door with Bush. And so it was Cheney's message of executive supremacy that the president conveyed to Alberto Gonzales in January.

Just after Cheney left the Ford White House, his wife wrote a roman à clef of the Cheney philosophy. Lynne Cheney's *Executive Privilege,* published in 1979, stars a heroic president from out west (Montana, not Wyoming), brisk and businesslike and principled. A leaked logbook of his Oval Office meetings brings politically damaging speculation that he is under psychiatric care. (His scheming Number Two, in an entertaining subplot, spots an opportunity to make "the vice presidency more important.") President Zern Jenner lies to the public without apology in order to protect a foreign policy objective— regime change. More important, he says (pacing the West Wing "with a determined stride"), he is protecting the prerogatives of "the office itself."

Jenner—say it fast and it sounds a little familiar—is a barely camouflaged stand-in for Dick Cheney. He is a man of modest tastes and simple habits, embarrassed by the red-jacketed servants who bring him coffee. Jenner's wife is a close lifelong partner, but "she and he had never been given to examining each other's feelings and motives the way she knew some of their married friends did." He has a famous "tenacity and self-control," which even so are "nothing compared to hers." Jenner's dedicated aides, like the man they serve, bring overstuffed briefcases home every night, compelled by urgent business to snatch another few minutes of work. An ally who shares the president's views even praises "martial law tribunals" for terrorists, twenty-two years before the September 11 attacks. In this, as in her other novels, Lynne Cheney writes in sex-positive prose, but she modestly sets those scenes ("Take off your clothes, you gorgeous man") far from the First Bedroom. She dedicates the book to "Dick, who has shaped my life—and even one or two of my opinions."

The pedagogical center of *Executive Privilege* comes in soliloquies describing the fictional president's guiding principles.

"I have a right to confidentiality from the press just as much as from Congress and the Courts," the president says. "The national interest would not be served by my telling them about those meetings. How can I expect the discussions in this office to be open and free if everyone has to sit around and worry about how his words will look on the front page of the *Post*?

"As I think back on the other men who've worked in this room," he continues, "it seems to me that the history of the presidency in the twentieth century is the history of a gradually weakening institution."

This goes on for a few hundred words.

"Well, I for one am not going to help in the process of making this office more vulnerable," Jenner concludes.

The good guys in the novel are contemptuous of "kiss-and-tell books" by former aides. One of them says the president "deserved at least one person around him whose silence he could depend upon." The bad guys are mostly reporters. Riding high after Watergate, the journalists are disrespectful and inclined to "unkempt dress and slouching demeanor." They lie, sleep with sources, and steal documents off unguarded desks.

One character embodies two Cheney family villains in one. Nicholas Frye is a former staffer at the Senate Watergate committee who moves on to the *Washington Post*. The narrator implies he got the job as "payment for services rendered" after leaking committee secrets to the (unnamed) Bob Woodward and Carl Bernstein. The dust jacket says Frye "would betray anyone, do anything, for a story," and so he does. The *Post* blithely publishes secrets of CIA operations and "a new and deadly weapons system." Another disclosure, in *Newstime* magazine, leads the president to tell an editor that he is no more than a spy.

Environmentalists and Native American advocates take a few shots as well, for wasting fossil fuel reserves. Whitefeather Indians, a fictional tribe that Lynne Cheney seems to have named after a 1955 film, are claiming land rights over coal-rich tracts in Wyoming and Montana. The president intervenes because, he says, "this country needs that coal."

Enter the energy task force. On April 19, 2001, the ranking Democrats on two House committees—John Dingell and Henry Waxman—sent a letter asking for the names of all task force members, the dates of its meetings, and "copies of all documents and records produced or received." The same day, they enlisted the help of the General Accounting Office, the investigative arm of Congress, which oversees the use of public money. In an increasingly testy exchange of correspondence, David Addington warned that the GAO, as a legislative body, could not "intrude into the heart of Executive deliberations." The GAO, in fact, had sought and received just this sort of information from Republican and Democratic White Houses before. When Addington would not budge, Comptroller General David Walker issued a rare "demand letter" directly to Cheney. The vice president replied not to Walker but to the full House and Senate, saying the comptroller general's demand "would unconstitutionally interfere with the functioning of the Executive Branch."

Walker scaled back his demands, but he also began to talk of a lawsuit, the GAO's first in eighty-one years. White House political aides became alarmed. The Bush administration had taken a beating in public opinion, with even conservatives asking what Cheney had to hide. Stonewalling Congress, Hughes and Bartlett and others argued, was not an obvious way to build support for a legislative agenda.

For Cheney, this *was* the agenda. A president possessed of his rightful powers, untrammeled by Congress, could work great change by regulation and executive order alone. Enhancing that power, he argued, mattered more than public relations or the fleeting good graces of Congress. The decision came to Bush. Karen Hughes, Dan Bartlett, Andy Card, Al Gonzales, Karl Rove, and David Addington joined the president and vice president in the Oval Office.

"We decided to stiff the Comptroller General," recalled associate White House counsel Brad Berenson, who had reviewed the documents and found nothing especially sensitive. "The easiest thing politically would have been to turn them over. What surprised me is that the president was willing to burn political capital to protect the records."

The sides were drawn. *Walker v. Cheney* reached federal court on February 22, 2002. The vice president's legal arguments included a stunner. Because each branch of government had unique spheres of authority, and the executive powers vested solely in the president, Congress had no enforceable right to demand *any* information from the executive branch that was not already available to the public. Courts, Cheney said, had no part in the dispute. If unsatisfied with the vice president's voluntary disclosures, Congress had no option save the "appropriately cumbersome" tools of "political self-help": the whole House could attempt to cut off funding to his office, order his arrest for contempt by the sergeant at arms, or vote articles of impeachment. Once Congress appropriated funds, Cheney argued, it had no lawful power to scrutinize their use in policymaking "within the unitary structure of the Executive." Walker's reply brief noted, without exaggeration, that Cheney "seeks to work a revolution in separation of powers principles, one that would drastically interfere with Congress's essential power to oversee the activities of the executive branch." If accepted, the vice president's argument would "create a new and unbounded immunity from oversight based on constitutional provisions that have never before been invoked in an interbranch dispute over documents. Indeed, under defendant's conception of 'our government of separated powers,' . . . no such disputes could ever again reach the courts."

The court ducked, declining to rule on the substance of the case. Walker's cause was taken up from the unlikeliest of directions. Judicial Watch, a conservative foundation that had tormented the Clinton administration in court, filed a similar demand for information before a second federal judge.

That suit, too, failed in the end, but not before it unearthed some intriguing snapshots. It was Judicial Watch that obtained and made public the memo from Haley Barbour on "eco-extremism" and carbon regulation. The same organization, by way of a legal side trip to the Commerce Department, found that Cheney's energy task force had been studying a map of Iraqi oil fields, pipelines, refineries, and terminals, along with charts detailing "Foreign Suitors for Iraqi Oilfield Contracts." The context for these documents, dated March 2001, was never explained.

In order to learn what the fight was about, U.S. District Judge Emmet Sullivan ordered the vice president to make a private showing, in chambers, of the disputed documents. Cheney refused to comply. He filed an "interlocutory appeal," interrupting the lower court case before it was resolved. The judicial branch had no more right than the legislative, the vice president argued, to compel him to disclose anything about his work. One federal judge, a frequent ally of the Bush administration who was not involved in the energy case, said in an interview that it was extraordinary for the vice president to open a second front against the judiciary. "The classic debates on executive power are between the executive and Congress," the judge said. The U.S. Court of Appeals for the D.C. Circuit ruled against Cheney. And so Cheney, with Bush's blessing, took the unusual step of asking the Supreme Court to issue a writ of mandamus—a direct command to the lower court to halt its work.

The high court declined to issue the writ, but it found errors in the appeals court ruling and sent the case back down. After another procedural victory for Cheney, the lawsuit died. The court did not accept the vice president's sweeping constitutional claims, but his take-no-prisoners litigation strategy achieved a practical result that Walker described as "literally devastating to the General Accounting Office's ability to obtain any information from the executive branch under any circumstances." By the time the case ended, in 2005, the struggle over executive authority would spill across a much wider federal landscape.

"You should not underestimate the impact of that experience on Cheney and his office," said Dan Bartlett. What Cheney took away "was 'You see, it didn't matter what all these blowhards were saying'" in Congress and the press. Yet the risk of pure principle, Bartlett said, was that "you win the battle but lose the war."

Of the energy task force proposals that required new laws, most died in Congress. Arctic oil drilling, the Yucca depository, construction of new nuclear power plants—none of those things happened. The House and Senate did not pass an energy bill at all until Bush's second term. Even so, Cheney and his allies would find—as he had predicted— that they could work a world of change with executive tools alone.

Chapter Five

Very Hard and Very Quick

On a closed patch of desert in early summer, the U.S. government built a house for Osama bin Laden.

The al Qaeda leader would have recognized the four-room villa. He lived in one just like it outside Kandahar, Afghanistan, whenever he spent a night among the recruits at his Tarnak Qila training camp. The stone-for-stone replica, in Nevada, was a prop in the rehearsal of his death.

On and off for nearly a year, "Operation Afghan Eyes" had been searching for bin Laden with a remote-controlled aircraft called the Predator. Until this moment, despite its fierce name, the mosquito-shaped drone had had no sting. CIA ground controllers caught a glimpse of bin Laden now and then, but all they could do was take his picture. That changed in the first week of June 2001. A modified Predator, on a test flight over the Nevada desert floor, fired a prototype missile from four miles out. The shot carried true. Forensic analysis of the mock bin Laden villa measured blast and shrapnel effects that would probably have left no one inside alive.

This was not a Bush administration initiative. The project had begun under orders from President Clinton and continued on inertia in those last six months. By whatever provenance, the U.S. government now had in its hands what one participant called "the holy grail" of a three-year quest—a weapon that could find and kill bin Laden in real time.

This might have been important news for Cheney, because Bush had given him the lead White House roles on both terrorism and intelligence. The vice president also took the hardest rhetorical line, harder than the president himself. When suicide bombers attacked the USS *Cole* shortly before the 2000 election, killing seventeen sailors and nearly sinking the Navy destroyer, candidate Dick Cheney said, "Any would-be terrorist out there needs to know that if you're going to attack, you'll be hit very hard and very quick. It's not time for diplomacy and debate. It's time for action." This was an essential point of comparison in the 2000 campaign: the strength and resolve of the Bush-Cheney team in contrast to the ditherings of Clinton and Gore.

At the time, the *Cole* bombing looked like al Qaeda's doing, but U.S. intelligence lacked proof. Bush and Cheney, on the campaign trail, vowed to retaliate once the perpetrators became clear. Soon after they took office, the facts were in.

Cheney told his authorized biographer, "I don't recall it cropping up." That is surprising. At 4 p.m. on February 9, 2001, less than three weeks after arriving in the White House, Cheney received a briefing that featured this slide: "Al Qaeda responsible for: Nairobi, Dar [es Salaam], Tirana, Kampala, Yemen, WTC, NYC tunnels, Jordan millennium, Boston, LA, Washington state bomb materials, USS *Cole*." (The list, expounded orally by the briefers, included U.S. embassy attacks in Africa, the 1993 truck bombing of the World Trade Center, and other plots, some of them disrupted, in the United States and overseas.) Six days later, in a memo sent directly to Cheney, a senior director on the National Security Council staff suggested that the CIA should be ready to "definitively conclude that *al-Q'ida* was responsible" for the *Cole*. Richard Clarke and others in his counter-terrorism directorate peppered Cheney, Condi Rice, and Steve Hadley with additional evidence—and recommendations for a military response—at least five more times in writing during the spring.

The vice president, like his colleagues, had other priorities.

Three months before September 11, 2001, when the armed Predator became available, Osama bin Laden had not yet reached the pinnacle of villainy in the American public mind. But he was well known inside the U.S. government. In an annual review of global threats, Director of Central Intelligence George Tenet said for three years running—in 1999, 2000, and 2001—that al Qaeda topped the list of most dangerous and immediate adversaries. By the summer of 2001, Tenet and Clarke "had their hair on fire" with warnings that a large-scale al Qaeda terrorist attack appeared to be imminent. On August 6, Bush and Cheney received the now-famous Presidential Daily Brief titled "Bin Ladin Determined to Strike in US," the thirty-sixth time in less than eight months that the CIA drew their attention to bin Laden or al Qaeda. John McLaughlin, Tenet's deputy, expressed frustration that "some policymakers, who had not lived through such threat surges before, questioned the validity of the intelligence or wondered if it was disinformation." An authoritative source said he was referring primarily to Cheney and Deputy Defense Secretary Paul Wolfowitz. The CIA responded with a briefing titled "Bin Ladin Threats Are Real." Though far from specific about the time, place, or manner of an attack, the briefings did allude to terrorist discussions of hijacking aircraft and to surveillance of targets in New York City. Cheney later downplayed the summer warnings, describing them as "noise in the system" and saying he was not especially alarmed.

The CIA and the Air Force practiced the Predator strike against bin Laden and prepared military plans against al Qaeda bases in Afghanistan. According to Donald L. Kerrick, a retired three-star Army general who served on the White House national security staff until early that summer, they could not get the attention of Bush or his top advisers. A working group held over from the Clinton administration met weekly to develop options, but "candidly speaking I didn't detect any" interest from the vice president or cabinet-rank officials, Kerrick said. "We told them we are going to be hit again, we have no idea where or when, and they just had to be prepared." The Predator was grounded, its missile unfired, in part because the Air Force and CIA could not agree who would pay for a $3 million replacement if the drone was lost. "We question whether it is advisable to make such an investment before the decision is taken on flying an armed Predator," John McLaughlin, the deputy director of central intelligence, wrote to Steve Hadley. The national security "principals," Cheney and the cabinet-rank advisers, declined to decide.

By early spring, at least three congressional committees had announced hearings on U.S. preparedness against terrorist threats. Fearing embarrassment, the White House cut a deal: cancel the hearings and let the president take decisive steps himself, without looking pushed. On May 8, Bush announced the new Office of National Preparedness for terrorism at the Federal Emergency Management Agency. Bush also said Cheney would direct planning for "consequence management" of a domestic attack, adding, "I will periodically chair a meeting of the National Security Council to review these efforts." He did not. Cheney's planning did not progress beyond a staff review of past advisory commission reports. Former Virginia governor Jim Gilmore and retired lieutenant general James Clapper briefed Cheney on one such report, saying "an attack was likely . . .

and there wasn't a plan in place to respond," said one participant. "Nobody gave a crap about this. It was theoretical."

The president mentioned the word "terrorism" only one other time in his first eight months, leaping rhetorically from terrorists to the need to "get rid of the ABM Treaty." That was spin. Terrorists did not possess ballistic missiles or much prospect of acquiring them. Cheney and Defense Secretary Don Rumsfeld cared about missile defense against other potential enemies—Iran, Iraq, North Korea, China, some future Russia gone bad. When the Senate Armed Services Committee proposed to strip $600 million from the missile defense budget, and spend it instead on counterterrorism priorities identified by military commanders, Rumsfeld said he would recommend a veto. The veto threat came on September 9.

Second- and third-level Bush administration officials asked career staffers, meanwhile, to prepare ever more ambitious drafts of a strategy against terror, National Security Presidential Directive 9. No new resources were assigned to the fight with bin Laden, but the declared objective grew ever grander. The goal evolved from "rolling back" to "permanently eroding" and, in the last draft, to "eliminating" al Qaeda. On September 4, the NSC staff's long-frustrated counterterrorism chief urged the cabinet principals to make an actual commitment of American military, political, and economic power.

"Are we serious about dealing with the al Qida threat?" Richard Clarke wrote in his agenda memo for their first meeting on terrorism since taking office. "Is al Qida a big deal? . . . *Decision makers should imagine themselves on a future day when the [government] has not succeeded in stopping al Qida attacks and hundreds of Americans lay dead in several countries, including the US. What would those decision makers wish that they had done earlier?* That future day could happen at any time." Seven days before September 11, the principals approved the outlines of a multiyear strategy, but again deferred decisions on what to spend, which steps to implement, and when.

"I can tell you the strategy we had, the sequencing we had in mind," Steve Hadley said in an interview four months later. "I guess I can't prove to you that we would have done it."

"Turn on the TV."

It was Brian McCormack, Cheney's personal aide, on the phone. A few minutes earlier, at 8:46 a.m., American Airlines Flight 11 had slammed into the North Tower of the World Trade Center. Smoke poured from the wounded structure.

"It's already on," replied Debbie Heiden, the vice president's executive assistant.

The remote control rested by Cheney's right hand, untouched.

"How in hell could a plane hit the World Trade Center?" he asked.

At just about that moment, 9:03 a.m., it happened again. The vice president watched live as United Airlines Flight 175 banked into the South Tower at 590 miles per hour, vanishing inside a fiery gash in the glass exterior.

Terrorism. No more doubt about it. Cheney picked up a direct line to the mobile communication team in Florida, where Bush was visiting Sarasota's Emma E. Booker Elementary School.

"I need to talk to the president," Cheney said, and hung up.

Aides streamed in. McCormack joined Scooter Libby, Condi Rice, Mary Matalin, Josh Bolten, and speechwriter John McConnell around the vice president's desk.

"The cabinet is going to need direction," Cheney said, and he set about providing it while awaiting word from Bush.

Four or five Secret Service agents arrived, submachine guns in hand. Like the firefighters in Manhattan, who leaped from their trucks with axes and spades to face a million tons of burning wreckage, the agents reached for their usual tools but found no place to employ them. The threat they now faced, according to an emergency call from the control tower at Reagan National Airport, was a third jetliner—"coming at you and not talking with us." American Airlines Flight 77, unidentified as yet, was flying fast and low toward the White House.

Jimmy Scott, one of the Secret Service guys, pushed through the staff gaggle around the vice president at 9:36 a.m.

"Sir, we need to move you—now," he said.

Cheney nodded, his body language saying just a minute. He turned to say a word to someone else.

The agent brought down the flat of his hand—loud—on Cheney's desk.

"Now!" he commanded.

Scott grasped Cheney's shoulder and the back of his belt and frog-marched the vice president of the United States out of his office. Joined by a second agent at the door, Scott wrangled Cheney through the marble Rotunda and into an unmarked staircase in the East Wing.

The three men were racing a jet aircraft on foot. Official accounts do not mention it, but if the White House had been the target, Cheney would have lost the race. The vice president did not reach the entrance to an underground bunker until 9:37 a.m., exactly as American 77 struck the Pentagon. The al Qaeda pilot had banked through a broad turn and doubled back; absent that change in course, the plane could have arrived minutes sooner at 1600 Pennsylvania Avenue. In previous jobs, the vice president had studied "decapitation attacks," intended to wipe out a nation's senior leadership. Now it was his own head on the line. For the briefest of moments, as the Secret Service propelled him to shelter, Cheney's implacable mask gave way. His expression, said a witness who knew him well, displayed "the intensity of the situation. . . . This was the real deal."

Once through the first vaulted door of the Presidential Emergency Operations Center, Cheney entered a tunnel equipped with bunk beds built for apocalypse. The shelter had been dug in secret for Franklin Roosevelt in World War II, then hardened during the cold war. Cheney spotted a bench with a telephone and stopped, still in the tunnel. He was in a hurry to speak to the president. Eight minutes passed before Cheney found Bush aboard Air Force One, at 9:45 a.m. With an attack in progress and Washington under fire, the constitutional line of succession was at risk. "I urged him not to return until we could find out what the hell was going on," Cheney later explained. Lynne Cheney, arriving separately, joined him in the tunnel during the ten-minute call.

A minute or two later, the Cheneys passed through a small communications studio, then turned left into a larger conference room. The vice president sat at the center of a long wooden table, coffee and snacks and Diet Coke within reach. A white telephone for encrypted conversations was mounted in a sliding drawer to his left. Side-by-side flat screens on the wall showed an interagency crisis team on one monitor, cable television news on the other.

At 9:59 a.m., the vice president had his eyes locked on CNN, chin resting on interlaced fingers, when the South Tower of the World Trade Center collapsed.

"There was a groan in the room—that I won't forget, ever," said one person present. "It seemed like one groan from everyone"— among them Condi Rice, Steve Hadley, Lynne Cheney, Scooter Libby, Josh Bolten, economic adviser Lawrence Lindsey, and Transportation Secretary Norman Mineta. A White House photograph of the moment caught a stifled scream from counselor Mary Matalin, eyes wide and hands pressed hard against her mouth.

Cheney said nothing. He made no sound. He did not move in his seat.

"I tried not to gawk, but I knew the vice president's reaction was going to be an important one" for history, said the witness, who filled a notebook with observations that day and read it aloud as he described the scene. "I was looking into his eyes. I remember turning my head and looking at the vice president, and his expression never changed. His chin was still in his hands, and you could tell that whatever change there was in his demeanor was inside."

Lynne Cheney, her face slack with horror, reached for her husband's arm. Still, he did not react.

Finally, Cheney closed his eyes. After one long, slow blink, he turned away.

Rumors and false reports competed for Cheney's attention, along with scraps of fact. The bunker's aging technology did not help. Secure telephone lines were dropping calls. The audio system played sound from only one video monitor at a time. Lynne Cheney kept muting the videoconference of the government's crisis response team so she could listen to CNN. In the Situation Room, maybe a hundred yards away, government officials needed guidance from Cheney and the leaders gathered around him. Richard Clarke and his staff made repeated calls to the only number they knew. That turned out to be the telephone next to Cheney. The vice president waited impatiently for links to Bush, Rumsfeld, Mayor Rudy Giuliani in New York. Every time the phone rang, he grabbed it briskly. "He thought the president was calling," one aide recalled.

"*Y'ello,*" Cheney said.

It sounded like "yellow," emphasis on the second syllable. Or "yeah-hello" bitten down.

Clarke asked for Mike Fenzel, his liaison in the bunker.

Cheney handed the Army major his receiver.

"Always happy to answer the phone for you, Mike," Cheney said, smiling tightly.

Clarke wanted an open line to the bunker. He called again. Then again.

Cheney kept answering, still expecting Bush. He stopped saying anything when he heard Clarke's voice, just put the receiver down.

"Who's the asshole who keeps answering the phone down there?" Clarke demanded, after finally getting his man back on the line.

"That would be the vice president," Fenzel replied.

Cheney, by many accounts, was the coolest head in the room, working calmly to gather data, digest it, and direct the cabinet. In another administration, that would have been the national security adviser's job, or the chief of staff's. Andy Card was with Bush aboard Air Force One, but his deputy, Josh Bolten, was in the bunker. Condi Rice worked a few seats down from Cheney. Participants in that morning's events described surprisingly little contact between them. The vice president took briefings, conferred with Scooter Libby in a voice too low for anyone else to hear, then got on the phone with heads of agencies.

"He was holding the fort," said one White House staff member who watched him all day in the bunker. "He was the man in charge. We were trying to bring information to him. The vice president saw himself as the man responsible for teeing decisions up for the president. Dr. Rice saw herself as organizing and coordinating the rest of the NSC."

Anything airborne might yet be a weapon. The bunker staff brought Cheney a stream of fresh—and erroneous—threat reports.

One staff member's notebook, made available to the author, displayed the chaos. Briefers misreported the flight number of the first suicide plane. They mistook the third one, which hit the Pentagon, for a helicopter. Three inbound jets from overseas—United Flight 947, Air Canada Flight 65, and Continental Flight 57—formed a suspected terrorist phalanx because they "failed to respond" to air traffic control. (They had been diverted elsewhere or canceled.) The transcript of an "air threat conference call," which Cheney periodically joined, included spurious reports of a hijacked Delta flight and of another unknown plane out of New York's John F. Kennedy Airport.

Two jetliners were reported down, one in Pennsylvania (true) and the other on the Kentucky/Ohio border (not). Both reports referred, without knowing it, to United Flight 93.

At around 10:03 a.m., barely five minutes after Cheney walked into the conference room, United 93 took on a third identity in the situation reports. This time it was an unknown jetliner racing toward Washington at five hundred miles an hour. By then the plane had already crashed, passengers having tried to overpower the hijack crew. But the Federal Aviation Administration, apparently relying on a projection after losing live radar data, issued rapid updates on the phantom bogey. The plane was eighty miles out, then sixty, then ten.

Sometime between 10:10 and 10:15 a.m., a military aide asked the vice president a question never faced by the U.S. government in its own airspace. The jetliner was presumed hostile, but packed with innocents. Should the Air Force shoot it down? Cheney paused for "about the time it takes a batter to swing, maybe starting from the windup," Scooter Libby said later. Then he answered: Yes.

Explaining the decision afterward, Cheney used the vocabulary of personal choice. He called it "painful, but nonetheless clear-cut.

And I didn't agonize over it. . . . You're asking American pilots to fire on a commercial airliner full of civilians. On the other hand, you had directly in front of me what had happened to the World Trade Center, and a clear understanding that once the plane was hijacked, it was a weapon."

A few minutes later, according to Libby's time-logged notes, Cheney repeated the order: "10:15–10:18: Aircraft 60 miles out, confirmed as hijack—engage? VP: Yes." And then a third time: "Take it out."

On what authority? Twelve years earlier, when a far less momentous decision loomed and another President Bush was out of town, Cheney told Dan Quayle correctly that the vice president had no lawful place in the chain of command. After September 11, Cheney and Bush insisted that the president issued the "weapons free" command and Cheney did no more than pass it along. Republican and Democratic members of the 9/11 Commission said in interviews that they had strong doubts. The measured language of their final report said "there is no documentary evidence for this call, but the relevant sources are incomplete." Commissioner Slade Gorton, a former GOP senator who was one of Bush's appointees, recalled, "They said one thing. There were no records to indicate that it took place. You can determine whether or not you thought they were lying." Suppose he were on a jury and had to decide? "Now that is a very interesting question," said the onetime Air Force officer and state attorney general. "I am not going to answer. If I were not a 9/11 commissioner I would probably answer your question, but I was."

Categorical proof of a negative is seldom possible. But there are three strong reasons to conclude that the alleged conversation did not take place.

The commission explored only one of them. If Bush gave Cheney shootdown authority, the two men must have spoken sometime after Cheney's arrival in the bunker's conference room (that is, after 9:56) and before his first order to destroy the incoming aircraft (that is, no later than 10:15). The parties to that call, if it happened, were among the most thoroughly monitored people on earth. A single document should have answered the question, because communications to and from Air Force One are routed and logged by the White House secure switchboard. As it happened, there were seven additional sets of official records tracking the calls made by Bush and Cheney that day: the Secret Service Log, the Situation Room Log, the PEOC Watch Log, the PEOC Shelter Log, a recording of the "air threat conference call," the routine Communications Log kept by the White House Military Office, and the special "9/11 Log" created that morning. The 9/11 Commission reviewed handwritten notes, in addition to these, from Scooter Libby and Lynne Cheney, who stayed at the vice president's side, and from Ari Fleischer aboard Air Force One. (The author obtained access to the handwritten notes of a fourth person in close proximity to Cheney, who did not show them to the commission.) Altogether, there were a dozen sets of contemporary records.

None of them logged a Bush-Cheney call between 9:56 and 10:15. Though the commission did not say so directly, there was no other alleged gap in the president's telephone records. Significantly, the very same logs—covering the same two parties, in the same two places—did show a call between Cheney and Bush at 10:18 a.m. That two-minute conversation began shortly *after* the vice president cleared Air Force fighters to open fire. According to John Farmer, a senior member of the commission's professional staff, the Bush administration did not allow investigators to ask the military switchboard operators about the discrepancy. "It was quite clear that the staff that looked at the records did not believe the vice president when he said he talked to the president" before the shootdown order, commissioner Jamie Gorelick said.

A second set of circumstantial clues is scattered around the commission report but unassembled in the narrative. The 9/11 commissioners asked and answered a narrow question: Was there evidence that Bush spoke to *Cheney* in advance about the change in Air Force rules of engagement? (The commissioners found none.) They did not examine explicitly whether Bush spoke to *anyone* about the issue, or otherwise displayed awareness, before Cheney gave the shootdown order. Did the president know that fighters were racing to intercept a jetliner bound for Washington? If so, he did not mention it to Andy Card, Karl Rove, or Navy Captain Deborah Lower, the director of the Situation Room, all of whom accompanied Bush on Air Force One. Nor did any of them hear the president allude on the phone to the most urgent decision of the day. Press Secretary Ari Fleischer, mindful of history, had planted himself in front of Bush with a pen and pad. Ten words, halfway through a footnote in the fine print of the commission's report, summarized the evidence from all sources: "Fleischer's 10:20 note is the first mention of shootdown authority" by anyone aboard Air Force One. It was 10:20 when Bush hung up from a two-minute call with Cheney and told Fleischer he had just approved the use of force against any hijacked airplane still aloft. By the commission's calculations, Cheney had given the order five to ten minutes earlier.

There is a third reason to doubt the official narrative, which as far as the author knows has not been noticed before. Cheney made a crucial change in his story, just at the moment when it became susceptible to disproof.

In a long interview with *Newsweek* toward the end of 2001, Cheney specified that Bush gave him shootdown authority as Cheney stood in the tunnel outside the main White House bunker. The time of that call was well documented: it took place from 9:45 to 9:55. According to the vice president, Rumsfeld had ordered fighters to guard the skies over Washington. Cheney told Bush, he said, that the pilots would need rules of engagement. "I recommended that we authorize them to shoot," Cheney told *Newsweek*. "We talked about it briefly. And he said, 'OK, I'll sign up to that.' He made the decision."

There was no record of what was said in that telephone call. Cheney had no reason to believe his account could be disputed. But the vice president alluded to external events, and the times of those events could be established with precision. As more records emerged, it became evident that the tunnel conversation could not have happened as Cheney described it. When the conversation began, Rumsfeld was still unreachable and the North American Aerospace Defense Command, or NORAD, had yet to call its aircraft to battle stations. Steve Hadley, the deputy national security adviser, did not even request a "combat air patrol" over Washington until 9:59 a.m.

If Bush was the one to authorize lethal force, the conversation must have been later than Cheney recalled. By itself this was hardly damning; anyone can miss by a few minutes. The problem for Cheney, and for Bush, was that the next documented call between them came too late. By then, Cheney had already issued the shootdown order. The president and vice president now had only two choices: retreat from the core assertion, that Bush made the shootdown decision, or describe a third telephone call for which no evidence existed.

It is worth taking note of when the story changed. According to White House records, Cheney sat for his *Newsweek* interview on November 19, 2001. By December, Democrats were pressing for an investigation of the events of September 11. An independent examination of records would demonstrate that the vice president's initial story was not true. When the *Washington Post* reconstructed the shootdown order, two months after *Newsweek,* Cheney and Bush had a new version. (The contradiction has apparently not been noticed before.) Now, for the first time, the two men described a conversation that took place shortly past 10:00, a few minutes after Cheney arrived in the conference room. Otherwise it followed roughly the script that had been provided to *Newsweek.* When Cheney recommended the shootdown order, Bush told the *Post,* "I said, 'You bet.' We had a little discussion, but not much."

There was another change in the account that Bush and Cheney gave to the *Post,* an important one. In this version, Bush approved Cheney's idea but then conveyed it to Rumsfeld, who "passed the order down the chain of command." That is the lawful procedure for transmitting military instructions: from the president through the defense secretary to the general or admiral in charge of the combatant command.

By this account, the whole sequence went exactly by the book. That assertion was demonstrably incorrect, and the White House eventually retreated. When Bush spoke to Rumsfeld at a few minutes after 10:00, the 9/11 Commission discovered, "the subject of shoot-down authority was not discussed." At 10:33, by which time the White House staff believed U.S. fighters had destroyed at least one aircraft, Steve Hadley was still telling military commanders that it was "the vice president's guidance" that "we need to take them out." Most telephone records that morning disclosed only the times and parties of each call. There was, however, a transcript of the conversation in which Rumsfeld learned that his pilots were licensed to kill. At 10:39 a.m., nearly half an hour after issuing the order, Cheney had this exchange with the defense secretary: "Pursuant to the president's instructions I gave authorization for [hijacked aircraft] to be taken out," Cheney said.

A pause.

"Hello?"

"Yes, I understand. Who did you give that direction to?" Rumsfeld asked.

To the pilots, Cheney said, by way of the White House operations center and NORAD.

"It's my understanding they've already taken a couple of aircraft out," Cheney added.

What are we to make of this? Suppose the mystery had more pedestrian stakes and players with names that were not Cheney and Bush. With evidence like this, nearly anyone would conclude that Leader B made a tough choice and Leader A gave his blessing after the fact. The president and vice president of the United States, using all the moral authority of their offices, staved off that verdict by daring a bipartisan commission to call them liars.

Does it matter? Recall the scenario. A suicide pilot is inbound. Time is short, communication slow. In military parlance, the enemy has fought its way "inside the decision curve" of the government, offense outpacing reaction from the defense. Does anyone really want the vice president to stand on legal niceties and permit another devastating attack? True, by 10 a.m. on September 11, decapitation was no longer a risk—for the executive branch, at least. Bush was airborne; Cheney underground. But the busy Capitol Building might have been destroyed, and with it a quorum of Congress. Likewise the Supreme Court, where Chief Justice William Rehnquist happened to be hosting a conference of federal judges from around the country. The Treasury Department. The Federal Reserve. Each of those structures was big and distinctive enough to pick out from the air on a clear, sunny day. The nation would have found a way to cope, but another plane might have struck a terrible blow. Exigencies do not get a whole lot more exigent. If the vice president set the law aside at such a moment, he had very strong grounds.

Yet Bush and Cheney did not say that. They did not mount a necessity defense, as Abraham Lincoln did after "suspending" the right of habeas corpus. They simply denied that any departure took place. Perhaps an untested president could not abide his absence at the moment of greatest peril, knowing how much the nation would count on his leadership. Perhaps Cheney saw the risks in a narrative of usurped command.

It is possible, in theory, that the Cheney-Bush account of the shootdown order is untrue and yet sincerely believed by one or both of them. One scenario, which fits the known facts, is that Cheney did not tell Bush, when they spoke at 10:18, that he had already issued the order. In that case, a logical possibility for which there is no proof at all, Bush would naturally suppose his approval came in advance.

In another scenario, for which there actually is some evidence, the president's recall of events is merely garbled. Bush mangled the facts in other stories he told about that morning, with no apparent motive to mislead. Twice he gave a folksy account of passing by a television at the Florida elementary school just as a jetliner slammed into "the first building." At a town hall meeting less than two months afterward, he said: "I was sitting outside the classroom waiting to go in, and I saw an airplane hit the tower—the TV was obviously on. And I used to fly myself, and I said, 'Well, there's one terrible pilot.'" He told that story again in January 2002. Nothing very much like it could have happened. There was no live coverage of the first plane strike, and no such footage was even discovered until the next day. Bush arrived at the school, in any case, after American Flight 11 struck the North Tower. Nor could Bush have seen the live collision of the second plane, because that one hit while he was reading "The Pet Goat" to second graders. It is possible that the president watched a *replay* of the *second* strike in a holding room *after* leaving class. (The story would not make much sense that way, because there was no more talk of pilot error once the second tower was hit.) If so, he confused both the sequence and content of what he saw, a transposition not unlike the one alleged about the shootdown order.

If Bush and Cheney simply lied, as substantially all the evidence but their own suggests, then a template for "this crusade, this war on terrorism" was established from the moment it began. Again and again the two men would display a shared sense of danger, an instinct for the precedent-busting response, and a willingness to blur the line between discretion and subterfuge.

On September 11 and afterward, Cheney staked out decisions of great national moment without explicit authority from Bush. In that he resembled a much younger man, the Army general that Cheney most admired. David Petraeus, who went on to become the four-star chief of U.S. Central Command, was known in the service as a leading practitioner of the art of UNODIR. That is military shorthand for "unless otherwise directed," a valuable if risky tool for the commander who values autonomy. The way it works is, you take initiative in the heat of the moment. Then you send a well-timed UNODIR message ("unless otherwise directed, I will continue to . . ."). Hearing no objection, you have a patina of authority for decisions that higher headquarters have neither approved nor forbidden. In less skillful hands, this can easily end a career. As a division commander in 2003, Petraeus would make UNODIR oil deals and spend UNODIR military funds to advance the mission as he understood it in northern Iraq. Unorthodox but effective, he would seldom be overruled. One way to understand Dick Cheney is as the UNODIR vice president writ large. He did not defy the commander in chief, but he certainly did not always wait for orders.

As morning passed in the White House bunker, Cheney consumed information as fast as the staff could produce it. There were casualty reports, not all of them accurate:

FLIGHT	PAX	ATTENDANTS	CREW
United 175	56	7	2
United 93	38	5	2
American 11	8	9	2
American 77	58	4	2
TOTAL: 266			

Some people in the bunker did back-of-the-envelope math. Figure one hundred floors, one hundred victims to a floor—good God, there could be ten thousand dead in each tower. Cheney did not want speculation. He asked for hard facts: How many minutes between collision and collapse? What was the available evacuation time? He paced his briefers with little nods, moving his head wordlessly when he was ready for the next point. "There was only so much information we could provide him," another staff member said. "He wasn't taking part in any small talk at all."

One fragmentary set of briefing notes referred to the presumption that al Qaeda was behind the attack. Analysts expected bin Laden to empty known facilities, such as a camp called Derunta, in order to thwart a retaliatory strike. Using the U.S. government's transliteration of bin Laden's initials, the notes said:

> *Responsibility → UBL*
> *Checking for evacuation from training camps in Afghanistan*
> *Tend to tie al Qaeda with mujahedin . . . Derunta?*
> *UBL Task Force is going through all traffic (NSA)*

Three people present, not all of them admirers, said they saw no sign then or later of the profound psychological transformation that has often been imputed to Cheney on September 11. What they saw was self-containment on a heroic scale—and a rapid shift of focus to the machinery of power.

Less than an hour after reaching the bunker, Cheney did something remarkable. He called for David Addington, his counsel. Who had time for lawyering now? The attack was not even over, so far as he knew. He had the lead on "consequence management," and first responders—police and firefighters and medical workers—were overwhelmed. The president demanded to return to Washington; the Secret Service urged Cheney to dissuade him. A jam-packed agenda awaited the National Security Council. Intelligence update. New security measures at borders, embassies, key domestic assets. Outreach—what to say to the public, to Congress, to foreign leaders? Resume commercial air traffic—when? Reopen financial markets—how?

These were today's decisions, tomorrow's. Cheney was looking much further ahead. The conflict he envisioned that morning would call upon lawyers as often as soldiers and spies.

Like everyone else in the Eisenhower Executive Office Building, Addington had been given no choice. Evacuate. *Run,* the Secret Service agents commanded. Addington, colleagues said, tried to return to the West Wing but was barred at the gate. He headed for the Pentagon on foot, hoping he could link up with the general counsel there, his friend William J. Haynes II; if not, he would work from home. Around the time he reached the Memorial Bridge, which spans the Potomac River between Washington and Virginia, the White House switchboard managed to get through.

Turn around. The vice president needs you.

Down in the bunker, official photographs of the day show Addington in diffident poses, arms behind him or leaning against a wall. In one of them he stands next to the presidential seal, in earshot as Cheney confers with Bush by phone. In others he defers, in his body language, to Condi Rice and Karen Hughes and members of the cabinet.

The vice president had something in mind for Addington that could not wait. From time to time as the day progressed, the two men conferred in soft tones. The question they asked would launch a legal revolution.

What extraordinary powers would the president need in the coming war?

Chapter Six

ENEMIES, FOREIGN AND DOMESTIC

I f a mandarinate ruled America, the recruiting committee on
September 11 would have had to find someone like Cheney. "I
don't want to get too poetic about this, but it's almost as if his
whole life had been but a preparation for this moment in history,"
said Jack Kemp, who used to be a future vice president himself.
Scooter Libby quoted that line, too, giving due credit to Winston
Churchill. Cheney professed no knowledge of fate. He had some
acquaintance, though, with force and counterforce. Al Qaeda having struck on his watch, Cheney made clear by word and deed
that he would take a leading role in the nation's reply. So, too, did
Libby and David Addington. The three of them simply knew what
had to be done, a considerable advantage in the debate that would
soon follow.

Churchill was prime minister when he mused on his destiny. In-
voking him on Cheney's behalf had a certain lèse-majesté, but the
breach of protocol was no great surprise. The unseasoned president
would lean heavily, for a time, on his Number Two.

The question that Cheney asked Addington in the bunker—what

new authority will the president need?—was nothing new to either man. Both had given long attention to the aftermath of catastrophe. In the 1980s, as a member of Congress, Cheney made no-notice deployments to secret military facilities, playing White House chief of staff after a simulated nuclear strike on Washington. Since then he had been absorbed in nightmare scenarios involving biological weapons. Cheney and Addington had a long to-do list.

The vice president shifted America's course, more than any terrorist could have done. Al Qaeda took a terrible toll, in lives and property. But if "everything changed," as the shock persuaded so many people to believe, it was not so much because the event was nonpareil. For September 11, the National Center for Health Statistics recorded a 44 percent spike over the expected daily death rate, followed by a return to normal on September 12. The year-end tally showed 2,922 lives lost to "terrorism involving the destruction of aircraft (homicide)," a figure that was comparable to the 3,209 pedestrians killed by cars, pickup trucks, or vans. (Non-terrorist homicides exceeded 17,000.) The economic damage was extensive, but no match for the losses of Hurricane Katrina or the subprime mortgage meltdown in Bush's second term.

These measurements obviously did not capture the full meaning of September 11. A familiar terrorist threat announced itself that day with frightening new proximity and ambition. But decisions made in the White House, in response, had incomparably greater impact on American interests and society.

Cheney freed Bush to fight the "war on terror" as he saw fit, driven by a shared belief that the government had to shake off old habits of self-restraint. With Bush's consent, Cheney unleashed foreign intelligence agencies to spy at home. He gave them legal cover to conduct what he called "robust interrogation" of captured enemies, using calculated cruelty to break their will. At Cheney's initiative, the

United States stripped terror suspects of long-established rights under domestic and international law, building a new legal edifice under exclusive White House ownership. Everything from capture and confinement to questioning, trial, and punishment would proceed by rules invented on the fly.

To accomplish those goals, the vice president and his lawyer had to set the government's legal direction. In the favored Cheney metaphor, they put an oar in the water. Cheney preferred to steer the boat unobtrusively, not to propel it in plain view. He and Addington sat astern, dipping their blades quietly to alter the vessel's course.

By the afternoon of September 11, Addington had made contact with Timothy Flanigan, the deputy White House counsel. Flanigan's boss, Alberto Gonzales, was stranded in Norfolk, having departed Dulles International Airport that morning an hour before the ill-fated American Flight 77. No matter. His deputy was the one Addington wanted.

Flanigan, forty-eight, was another of the Cheney allies in place just below the top ranks of government. Like many of them, he was overqualified. Some of Flanigan's résumé was par for the course: law clerk to the late Warren Burger, the "strict constructionist" chief justice of the United States; alumnus of the first Bush administration; promoter of executive power at the Federalist Society. Flanigan's best credential, though, made the deputy White House counsel job look like a demotion. A decade earlier, he had served as chief of the Justice Department's Office of Legal Counsel.

That little-known office is crucial to understanding what happened in the Bush-Cheney years. Run by a Senate-confirmed appointee, the Office of Legal Counsel is akin to the Supreme Court of the executive branch. Two of its alumni—William Rehnquist and Antonin Scalia—went on, in fact, to join the high court. When government agencies disagree about what the law means, they ask the OLC.

When the attorney general wants to know, *he* asks the OLC. The resulting opinion is binding on every cabinet department.

Nobody with authority like that went unnoticed by the vice president. Cheney believed in central White House control. If anyone could tell the whole unitary executive branch what it could and could not do, there had better be a sharp eye keeping watch.

The logical overseer would be the White House counsel. George Bush's choice was not going to be that guy. Bush named a loyal Texan to the post, not a legal powerhouse. At forty-six, Alberto Gonzales had never held an out-of-state job. Bush called him "Fredo," which gave rise to unflattering conjecture. (In the *Godfather* movies, Fredo was Vito Corleone's middle son, the dumb one.) That was unfair. The new consigliere to the president, the second of eight children born to migrant cotton workers, was nobody's fool. Raised in Humble, Texas, by an alcoholic father and a mother with a sixth-grade education, Gonzales managed to work his way through college and Harvard Law School. Gonzales met Bush as a young corporate lawyer in Houston, and Bush loved his up-by-the-bootstraps tale. As governor, Bush hired Gonzales to be his legal adviser. Gonzales was discreet and self-effacing. He knew how to boil things down for Bush, explain complex legal matters in layman's terms. But he had neither the federal experience nor the force of intellect, many colleagues said, to play in the big league of the Washington legal game.

Tim Flanigan had both. The deputy's job promised him unusual influence. Flanigan would backstop his boss and serve as mentor to the Justice Department office he once ran.

Flanigan was in the Situation Room on September 11. When Addington reached him from the bunker, Flanigan patched in the Justice Department Command Center across town. There he found a young attorney named John C. Yoo. The thirty-four-year-old son of anticommunist émigrés from South Korea, Yoo had taken leave from university life to join the Office of Legal Counsel as a deputy.

Calm and soft-spoken, Yoo made his name at Berkeley's Boalt Hall Law School with provocative writings on presidential power. His analysis held that the president has "plenary powers" as commander in chief, meaning that they belong exclusively to him, and that the president is the "sole organ of the nation in its foreign relations." The president also enjoys "plenary authority" to interpret international law, and his interpretation should be granted "almost absolute deference" from courts. Alternatively, he may "violate international law and treaties, if he so chooses." With important qualifications, those claims would have attracted support from many legal historians. In government, Yoo pushed them well beyond the bounds of accepted scholarship, even among those who shared his presidentialist bent. Yoo declared in the most expansive terms that the commander in chief need take no account of restrictions set by the coequal legislative and judicial branches. Responding to a request from Flanigan, Yoo wrote two weeks after the al Qaeda attacks that no law "can place any limits on the President's determinations as to any terrorist threat, the amount of military force to be used in response, or the method, timing, and nature of the response. These decisions, under our Constitution, are for the President alone to make." Yoo later acknowledged that his understanding of the Constitution "differs, at times sharply, from the conventional academic wisdom." Beginning on September 11, he was empowered to turn beyond-the-edge arguments into the law of the executive branch.

Yoo's impact might have been more modest had it not been for the vice president's canny lawyer. Yoo had a predilection for big, brawny answers, but there had to be questions first. Addington, working almost invariably through proxies, requested OLC opinions on subjects calculated to elicit broad replies. Addington insisted on strict secrecy, preventing the circulation of drafts to agencies that might challenge Yoo's analysis. With the rulings in hand, the vice president's counsel wrote the regulations, directives, and executive orders that changed events.

Gonzales, Bush's lawyer, played his own important role. He "was not a law of war expert—he didn't purport to be," Yoo said, and Gonzales had no "developed views" on the separation of powers. His job naturally inclined him, though, to a favorable view of his client's authority. Gonzales became the interpreter and salesman of new legal theories to Bush, without whose signature nothing big could happen.

Thus formed the core legal team that Cheney oversaw, directly and indirectly, in the years after September 11. "Addington, Flanigan, and Gonzales were really a triumvirate," recalled Bradford A. Berenson, then an associate White House counsel. "Gonzales had the relationship with the president. Addington had the relationship with the vice president. And Flanigan, as a former OLC head, had the legal expertise. It was a flying wedge of staffers backed up by the president and the vice president, and it doesn't get much better than that."

There was not a lawyer in government, of more than three dozen interviewed, who doubted Addington's status as first among equals. He had a size on him, everything writ large—the physical presence, the booming anger, the cutting intellect, the certainty of belief, the presumption of purview over whatever caught his eye. Addington attended pretty much every meeting of significance in Gonzales's wood-paneled office, the two of them facing the visitor's sofa in matching chairs. Often he did most of the talking. Though he usually deferred to Gonzales in manner, Addington made clear that neither he nor his office was subordinate. Just as the vice president was an independent constitutional officer, Cheney's staff reported to no other authority. Nor did Addington hesitate to contradict Gonzales. When the Office of Legal Counsel was assigned to draft an executive order on presidential records, according to a lawyer who watched the process, Addington laid out a framework for keeping more secrets and keeping them longer. Later, the drafting attorney made changes at the White House counsel's direction. Addington telephoned, furious, and ordered that his original instructions be obeyed. They were. At the Pentagon, a senior lawyer told a similar story, declining to specify the subject.

Yoo, Berenson said, "was a supporting player" for the triumvirate, but his importance would be hard to overstate. A back channel to the Office of Legal Counsel, sometimes kept secret from Yoo's own superiors, became the key to Cheney's dominance of the "war on terror." With the OLC's writ, any federal agency could do as the vice president asked.

Yoo never rose beyond deputy assistant attorney general, but he was the fulcrum of the lever that Cheney pulled to move the world. In a prolific run of opinions that fall and winter, Yoo claimed without limitation that the president could disregard laws and treaties prohibiting torture, war crimes, warrantless eavesdropping, and confinement without a hearing. The breadth of his language was stunning.

Cheney and Addington found Yoo's analysis congenial. In a public debate in 1983—at a time when his own paycheck came from the House—Cheney said Congress gave the president "prior approval" to make war as he saw fit, simply by hiring soldiers and buying their gear. "We have appropriated the funds and raised the army and purchased the equipment and built the missiles and the bombers," he said. By virtue of his exclusive constitutional role, "the president has the authority to make decisions about how to use those things." (Cheney made clear he intended the definite article.) Gerald Ford, the former president he served, did not agree. "Questions of war and peace, which are the responsibility of the president in the White House and of the Congress, are too serious not to be of dual responsibility," Ford said at the same conference. Here again, a nuanced argument along Cheney's lines, especially when it came to command of troops on the battlefield, would not have been controversial. But Cheney took his position to the extreme. His arrival at the Pentagon in 1989, with Addington at his side, brought striking new claims that the commander in chief could disregard even peacetime regulation of the armed services by Congress.

There were those who wondered, though no one is known to have dared ask directly, whether Addington spoke entirely for the vice president. People who saw them up close had little doubt.

"I would say he was a perfect agent, and not one eyelash different than Cheney," said Jack Goldsmith, who would come to clash titanically with both of them. "In a way, Cheney is not subtle, and he has never hidden the ball. The amazing thing is that he does what he says. Relentlessness is a quality I saw in him and Addington that I never saw before in my life. They cared more than anybody else. I admired Addington even though I disagreed with him. It was impressive, even if it was bizarro. It was a will to power."

An added feature of Cheney's model, especially after September 11, was near-hermetic secrecy. Not only the conduct of policy but even the law itself, as Yoo and Addington and Flanigan rewrote it, was classified. The new legal framework was meant to be invisible, unreviewable—its very existence unknown by legislative or judicial actors who might push back.

By every appearance these were Cheney's committed views, advanced regardless of which party held the White House. They were far from the mainstream, nonetheless, even among conservative Republicans. One high-ranking lawyer, a Bush appointee still in office as the administration neared its end, described Cheney's constitutional philosophy as "monarchical." "The President is Article Two, and there are three articles of the Constitution," the lawyer said.

Cheney and his staff did not bother much with the legislative agenda after September 11. This was war, and war belonged to the executive branch. No other branch could move with the speed and unity required to protect the country. Power, initiative, decision—they flowed naturally to the executive in a crisis, and the vice president placed himself at the center.

Addington mostly sat out the Patriot Act debate and, before that, the Authorization for Use of Military Force, which the president signed on September 18. Flanigan drafted the force resolution, with help from Yoo. They wrote it as broadly as possible, Yoo said, because "this war was so different, you can't predict what might come up."

Cheney could predict. What came up for him first was intelligence. To kill your enemies, you had to find them. To defend against attack, you had to hear it coming.

As always, the vice president moved fast.

"I don't think you can ignore the idea of time on task in policymaking," said John Ashcroft, who was then attorney general. His meetings with Cheney, he said, "were among the most economical in terms of time consumption I've ever had."

While the wreckage in lower Manhattan still smoked, Cheney invited George Tenet to his West Wing office. As director of central intelligence, Tenet oversaw not only the CIA but a federation of fourteen other agencies and offices.

What can you do against al Qaeda, Cheney asked, that you're not already doing?

It was a sensible question in the aftermath of a costly failure. Were there unused capabilities that might avert the next attack? Cheney was inviting Tenet to redeem himself and the $30 billion enterprise he led.

The vice president brought a point of view. He had lived through the intelligence scandals of the 1970s, exposed by journalists such as Seymour Hersh and committees led by Representative Otis Pike and Senator Frank Church. Cheney fought losing battles in Congress against reforms he believed unwise. As he described the new legal landscape, case officers had to follow Marquis of Queensbury rules that were alien to their missions and their natures. On pain of criminal penalties, they could no longer consort too closely with bad actors, the criminals and tyrants overseas who knew what the U.S. government wanted to know. They could not wink at rough interrogations. They could not spy on foreign agents in the United States without permission from a court. Intelligence officers were second-guessed by congressional committees, inspectors general, and the FBI. Predictably, the CIA and its sister agencies had become more afraid of legal risk than of failure.

Cheney's first conversation with Tenet focused on the National Security Agency, which had the biggest budget and largest workforce. The NSA sifted signals intelligence through the most powerful computer hub on the planet. Outsiders spoke of wiretapping, but agency employees had a saying: Outsiders "don't know SIGINT from Shinola." Telephone calls were one thin slice of the electromagnetic spectrum. If information flew on a photon, the agency tried to catch it—microwave or radio wave, visible light or infrared light or laser. (The agency hunted electrons, too, but old-fashioned copper wire carried less and less of the traffic.) The NSA's physicists and linguists and computer scientists could extract meaning from just about any man-made source of radiation. Some of their work involved signals between machines, executing a transaction or reporting the position of a device. Some involved communications between people, speaking by phone or computer or fax. Traffic analysis looked for patterns in the volume and timing of communications. Link analysis looked for patterns in who talked to whom. Headquartered on a five-thousand-acre campus at Fort Meade, Maryland, the NSA could aim its globe-spanning apparatus anywhere, in or out of U.S. territory.

It could, but it did not.

Abuses exposed by the Church Committee in 1975 traumatized the agency. Richard Nixon used the NSA, on a relatively modest scale, for political espionage. Senator Frank Church, speaking after the release of his committee's final report, warned that total tyranny would result if the agency "were to turn its awesome technology against domestic communications." Congress passed a web of new laws to prevent that, including the Foreign Intelligence Surveillance Act. The NSA grew a culture of respect for the Fourth Amendment, displayed in large-type posters all over Fort Meade: "The right of the people to be secure in their persons, houses, papers, and effects, against unreasonable searches and seizures, shall not be violated, and no Warrants shall issue, but upon probable cause." Americans, while in the United States, were no longer targeted without a warrant. If their communications were scooped up inadvertently, so-called minimization procedures (usually) expunged their names.

Cheney asked George Tenet to find out what the NSA might do differently if unleashed. Michael Hayden, its director, came back with an answer in the last week of September. He brought a Venn diagram, three ovals with overlapping edges. One oval represented the spymaster's ideal—everything desirable that SIGINT might provide. A second showed what could be done with present technology. The third oval included only what was legal. The agency, Hayden told the vice president, worked inside the space "where all three of those ovals intersected."

Years later, explaining what happened next, George Bush said: "After September the 11th, I spoke to a variety of folks on the front line of protecting us, and I said, 'Is there anything more we could be doing, given the current laws?' And General Mike Hayden of the NSA said there is."

Bush got it wrong on two counts. It was Cheney who asked the question, or asked it first, and it had little to do with "current laws."

The vice president looked at Hayden's three ovals—desirable, possible, legal.

Set aside the third one, Cheney said. For purposes of discussion, forget about the law. What could you accomplish if you stopped closing your eyes and ears to communications inside the United States?

Another sensible question, hypothetically. Maybe the law needed changing. The most dangerous kind of terrorist would be the one in our midst. After September 11, the working assumption in the U.S. government was that al Qaeda "sleeper cells" were already in place, preparing to strike again. "The database is being built, and the FBI is running down leads every day and reporting on them every day," National Security Adviser Condoleezza Rice said then. Finding the bad guys would be harder if the NSA looked only overseas.

There was a lawful procedure for spying on foreign agents and terrorists inside the United States. The government could apply for a secret warrant in the Foreign Intelligence Surveillance Court, a closed federal tribunal that met on the Justice Department's sixth floor—or anywhere handy, from a judge's chambers to the back of a car, in the urgent months after September 11. Before the attacks, the court was granting 750 to 1,000 warrants a year and had yet to reject an application. The number doubled quickly after that. But FISA warrants, as they were called, required probable cause and a known suspect. They were issued one at a time. What Cheney and Hayden wanted was a way to find unknown terrorists and unsuspected plots. To do that, the NSA had to fish with a big net, not a hook.

In discussions over the next few days, in a small group that included George Tenet, Scooter Libby, and David Addington, Cheney and Hayden devised the outlines of a new surveillance program. They would not tell the FISA court. They would not seek legislation. They would rely on the president's asserted authority as commander in chief to defy explicit prohibitions of law.

Cheney brought the proposal to Bush, along with a draft directive prepared by Addington. On October 4, 2001, Bush signed the first Presidential Authorization. The program went operational on October 6.

John Bellinger began to bump into something mysterious that winter. He was the senior national security lawyer in the White House, counsel to Condoleezza Rice. People who worked in the program sometimes assumed that he must be "read in." He was not.

Cheney and Addington drew a very tight circle, keeping the program secret from anyone whose loyalty was in doubt. Bellinger, forty-one, was an experienced intelligence hand. He had been special assistant to CIA director William Webster, counsel to the Senate Intelligence Committee, and a senior national security attorney in the Justice Department. Addington did not see him as a true believer. Something about the guy, on an almost pheromonal level, aroused Addington's "open contempt," as one among many colleagues put it. Maybe it was the prep school pedigree, St. Albans and Princeton and Harvard Law. Maybe the years of service under Clinton, even as a nonpolitical appointee. Maybe the instinct for compromise, promoting the kind of "interagency treaties" that the vice president's lawyer despised. More than once Addington accused Bellinger to his face of selling out presidential authority for convenience, or public relations.

"David is extremely principled and dedicated to doing what he feels is right and can be a very tough customer when he perceives others as obstacles to achieving those goals," said Brad Berenson, who worked with them both as a White House lawyer. "But it's not personal in the sense that 'I don't like you.' It's all about the underlying principle."

One day an NSA official passed Bellinger in a hallway.

"See you at the meeting this afternoon," he said.

"What meeting?" Bellinger asked.

"Oh, you're right," the official said, haltingly. "Never mind. Must be the vice president's special program."

Bellinger heard it from someone else. And then again.

Three times, same cryptic phrase. The vice president's special program.

Bellinger had had his fill of it. This was his job. He could only imagine what they were telling his boss if Rice was not allowed to consult her legal adviser. Bellinger walked down two flights of stairs in the Eisenhower Executive Office Building and confronted Addington in his second-floor office.

"David, I know you're up to something," he said. "One, you need to know people are talking about it, and, two, I hope you're doing this the right way. You don't have me, the NSC's lawyer, involved."

Addington glowered.

"I'm not going to tell you whether there is or isn't such a program," he said. "But if there were such a program, you'd better go tell your little friends at the FBI and the CIA to keep their mouths shut."

In the damage-control effort four years later, after the *New York Times* disclosed the operation, the White House rebranded it for public consumption. The president called it the "Terrorist Surveillance Program," and he summed it up like this: "It seems like to me that if somebody is talking to Al Qaeda, we want to know why." That description had little to do with the program. The surveillance was attempting to *detect* terrorist plotters—to establish *whether* a person was dangerous—not to monitor people on existing suspect lists. By definition, that meant nearly all of the targets would prove innocent.

The U.S. government was sweeping in e-mails, faxes, and telephone calls made by its own citizens, in their own country. Transactional data, such as telephone logs and e-mail headers, were collected by the billions. Content was reviewed from a much smaller number of targeted suspects—five hundred to six hundred at a time, thousands in the course of a year. Analysts seldom found information even remotely pertinent to a terrorist threat. No one expected otherwise, unless al Qaeda had somehow infiltrated thousands of sleeper agents into America. An intelligence officer did not look at things that way. A valuable clue was no less so if it came in one of a million intercepts. From a legal point of view, on the other hand, the washout rate mattered.

The program branched out from the NSA. Other government agencies, including the CIA, the FBI, and elements of the Defense Department, used information gleaned from the NSA to do additional surveillance. Vehicles could be tagged. Cell phones could be located, even when switched off. Cash machines, credit cards, bank transfers, changes of address, air and hotel and rental car reservations—all of these could help the government track not only the activities but the physical locations of its targets. In an interview about a related intelligence tool, the "national security letter" that enables the FBI to review a person's telephone and banking records, a senior FBI official gave an explanation that others used privately to justify the NSA program. If agents could not comb through a person's digital life without specific grounds for suspicion, they would already know what they were trying to find out, said Joseph Billy Jr., then the FBI's deputy assistant director for counterterrorism. "It's all chicken and egg," he said. "We're trying to determine if someone warrants scrutiny or doesn't." Billy said he understands that "merely being in a government or FBI database . . . gives everybody, you know, neck hair standing up." Innocent Americans, he said, "should take comfort at least knowing that it is done under a great deal of investigative care, oversight, within the parameters of the law." He added: "That's not going to satisfy a majority of people, but . . . I've had people say, you know, 'Hey, I don't care, I've done nothing to be concerned about. You can have me in your files and that's that.' Some people take that approach."

Much of the program's operation remains unknown even now. But enough evidence emerged to say the government collected information on a scale that potentially touched every American. After his second secret briefing on the program, Senator Jay Rockefeller wrote a letter to the vice president. When he heard "the direction the administration is moving with regard to security, technology and surveillance," he said, "what sprung to mind" was the Pentagon's Total Information Awareness project. Alarmed at the civil liberties threat, Congress had suspended the TIA five months earlier. In it, the Defense Department was trying to compile and mine information from every available computer data bank. Confirmation that Rockefeller was on the right track came from none other than John Yoo. In a memoir of his government service, Yoo did not refer to the program directly, but he described the scope of "data mining" required to locate al Qaeda terrorists. He emphasized that it must include domestic communications:

> *Rather than being able to focus on foreign agents who are already known, counterterrorism agencies must search for clues among millions of potentially innocent connections, communications, and links. . . . Members of the al Qaeda network can be detected by examining phone and e-mail communications, as well as evidence of joint travel, shared assets, common histories or families, meetings, and so on. . . . It is more important to chase them down quickly inside the United States than outside. NSA critics want to place bureaucratic impediments precisely where the danger to America is greatest and flexibility is most important.*

Hayden, the National Security Agency director, gave the most authoritative confirmation that the program worked like a "drift net" across the national communications grid. He did so, ironically, in the course of explaining why he did not lie when he denied it.

In January 2006, after Bush confirmed a portion of the program, Hayden gave a bravura performance at the National Press Club. He had earned a reputation as one of the most persuasive briefers in Washington, lucid and reassuring. Here he was telling reporters and a live television audience that there was no cause for alarm:

> *The intelligence community has neither the time, the resources nor the legal authority to read communications that aren't likely to protect us, and NSA has no interest in doing so. These are communications that we have reason to believe are al Qaeda*

communications. . . . This program is not . . . a drift net over
Dearborn or Lackawanna or Fremont grabbing conversations that
we then sort out by these alleged keyword searches or data-mining
tools or other devices that so-called experts keep talking about.

Five months later, Hayden faced a Senate hearing as nominee for a new job as director of the CIA. With a confirmation vote as leverage, the Senate Select Committee on Intelligence had finally obtained its first secret briefing on the program.

"General, having evaluated your words, I now have a difficult time with your credibility," Senator Ron Wyden, an Oregon Democrat, told Hayden. "After you admitted you were wiretapping Americans, you said on six separate occasions the program was limited to domestic-to-international calls. Now the press is reporting that the NSA has amassed this huge database that we've been discussing today, of domestic calls."

Wyden was following the rules, citing the press instead of the classified briefing he had just received.

"So, with all due respect, General, I can't tell now if you've simply said one thing and done another, or whether you have just parsed your words like a lawyer to intentionally mislead the public."

"I chose my words very carefully," Hayden replied, "because I knew that some day I would be having this conversation." In his own mind, he said, his National Press Club remarks involved only the activity that Bush acknowledged, not anything else the NSA might be doing.

"At key points, key points in my remarks, I pointedly and consciously downshifted the language I was using," Hayden said.

"When I was talking about a drift net over Lackawanna or Fremont or other cities, I switched from the word 'communications' to the much more specific and unarguably accurate 'conversations.'"

In other words, there *was* a drift net over America. It was not Hayden's fault if we understood him to assure us of the reverse. He was talking only about "conversations"—the words we typed or spoke on the telephone. There was no drift net for content. But Hayden made no such denial about "communications." He did not spell it out for Senator Wyden, because the rest of the answer was still classified. The drift net collected the so-called metadata of domestic communications—the Web links we clicked, the numeric addresses of our computers, the "to" and "from" and "subject" lines of our e-mails, the telephone numbers we dialed, the parties and times and durations of our calls. FISA or no FISA, all those had become fair game for collection without a warrant.

This was the program that Cheney built, and it fell to him, as it did on other matters, to make the most extravagant claims of success. Asked about the surveillance in December 2005, he replied: "The fact of the matter is, it's a good, solid—and it's saved thousands of lives."

Even at the risk of contradicting the vice president, Mike Hayden would not go along with that, telling senators he "cannot personally estimate" a figure. In private meetings, he said flatly that there was no evidence to support it. "This may not be important now, but it's going to be important later," Hayden said at one such gathering.

FBI director Robert Mueller also declined a senator's invitation to vouch publicly for the vice president. A close associate said later that Mueller "doesn't agree with Cheney that TSP saved thousands of lives. He says it is useful."

There were places Hayden refused to go with the program. He took issue with Cheney's suggestion that no one in Congress had a need to know. Hayden feared the day when he might be hauled up as a witness. He knew the history. The Church Committee had skewered his onetime predecessor Lieutenant General Lew Allen Jr. Hayden wanted buy-in, at least, from the chairmen and vice chairmen of the intelligence committees.

"One of the contributions that I gave to the conversation was congressional notification," Hayden later testified, without mentioning opposition from Cheney. "When we were discussing this, I literally said in our small group, 'Look, I've got a workforce out there that remembers the mid-1970s.' And forgive me for a poor sports metaphor here, but the line I used is, 'Since about 1975, this agency's had a permanent one-ball, two-strike count against it, and we don't take many close pitches.'"

Hayden went along with warrantless surveillance of metadata, the transactional stuff. He deflected suggestions from Cheney and Addington that his agency could equally read the content of domestic e-mails or listen to domestic telephone calls. *But there's no legal difference!* Addington told him. As a technical matter, Hayden's lawyers agreed. If the president could ignore one part of the FISA law, he could ignore another. "Legal but stupid, there is that category," said one participant in the government's internal debate. "It was a bright line for everybody" except the vice president that it would be "unwise and institutionally disastrous" to collect purely domestic communications.

"OVP wanted to go further, and I drew the line," Hayden told one visitor, referring to the office of the vice president. As long as one party to a conversation was overseas, Hayden could tell himself and anyone else that the NSA held fast to its foreign intelligence mission.

That was why Hayden hated it when reporters and commentators talked about "domestic surveillance."

"I've taken literally hundreds of domestic flights," he said. "I have never boarded a domestic flight in the United States of America and landed in Waziristan."

It sounded good. But the surveillance statutes said a warrant was required if *either* end of the conversation was on U.S. territory. The American side of the program—the domestic surveillance—was its distinguishing feature. That was the part that took Hayden and Cheney and the rest of them outside the law.

At the Justice Department, a senior career lawyer named James A. Baker stumbled across the program, much as John Bellinger had done at the NSC. He was chief of the Office of Intelligence Policy and Review, the U.S. government's liaison to the special surveillance court. Some of the classified files he saw had unexplained gaps, information that should have been sourced but seemed to come from nowhere. According to colleagues, he became convinced that there was a signals intelligence operation he did not know about.

Because FISA warrants are issued in single-party proceedings, with only the government talking to the judge, Baker had an especially strong legal and ethical obligation to disclose every pertinent fact. Colleagues and judges called him a stickler for the rules. He was not prepared to tolerate the use of extralegal spying to produce information for legitimate warrant applications. Baker requested briefings for himself and for the chief judge of the FISA court, Royce C. Lamberth, on any warrantless electronic surveillance in the United States.

Word came back from the White House. If there was such a program, it would be none of his business, or the court's. Baker threatened to notify Lamberth that he could no longer vouch for the integrity of his evidence.

"He forced it," Lamberth said in an interview.

Addington passed word through Gonzales that Attorney General John Ashcroft could read in Baker and the chief judge, but no other judge on the court. Lamberth, a Vietnam veteran who talked like a gunslinger and wore cowboy boots under his robes, sat down with Ashcroft and Mike Hayden around Christmas 2001. The judge was astonished to learn that even Deputy Attorney General Larry Thompson, who often signed FISA certifications in Ashcroft's absence, was not cleared for the program. "He specifically told me I could not discuss it with Thompson," Lamberth said.

Unsatisfied with Ashcroft's legal explanation, Lamberth got a second briefing, this time from John Yoo. The young lawyer told him that FISA, which described itself unambiguously as the "exclusive" authority for domestic intelligence gathering, did not even apply. "Unless Congress made a clear statement in the Foreign Intelligence Surveillance Act that it sought to restrict presidential authority to conduct warrantless searches in the national security area—which it has not—then the statute must be construed to avoid [such] a reading," Yoo wrote at that time.

Even if Congress forbade the surveillance, Yoo told Lamberth, the president could do it on his own authority as commander in chief.

Later, the Justice Department would make a new argument, claiming that Congress not only did not forbid but actually invited warrantless domestic surveillance when it passed the Authorization for Use of Military Force. The theory was that surveillance is inherent in war, and this war was fought just as much at home as overseas. That made little sense to Lamberth. When laws appear to conflict, the general gives way to the specific. Yoo was claiming implicit authority for something that was expressly forbidden in two other statutes. The program was also gathering intelligence on a broader range of targets than the ones identified by Congress in the use-of-force resolution, which was limited to the "nations, organizations, or persons" responsible for September 11.

"They had gotten it enacted, and they thought it gave them authority to do all kinds of things that I didn't think it did," Lamberth said.

When Lamberth first heard of the program, however, Ashcroft said "the president was going to do it for forty-five days, and it might be renewed but might not," Lamberth said. "So what I thought we were talking about was a very short-term emergency thing, perhaps until we got a legislative fix, and certainly not something that would end up going on for years."

A legislative fix was not on the agenda. Hayden persuaded Cheney to brief four members of Congress, but the vice president wasn't asking them for permission.

On October 25, 2001, the chairmen and ranking minority members of the intelligence committees were summoned to the White House. The program was one of the government's most closely compartmented secrets. Under Presidents George H. W. Bush and Bill Clinton, a conversation of that gravity would involve the commander in chief. When the four lawmakers arrived in the West Wing lobby, an aide led them through the door on the right, away from the Oval Office.

"We met in the vice president's office," recalled former senator Bob Graham. Bush had told Graham already, when the senator became committee chairman, that "the vice president should be your point of contact in the White House." Cheney, the president said, "has the portfolio for intelligence activities."

Conceiving the surveillance, supervising the plan, pitching it to Bush, controlling the information supplied to judges and Congress—

none of this meant there was such a thing as "the vice president's special program." Not according to Andy Card, the White House chief of staff.

"You're trying to say, 'Who was standing at the top of the pyramid?'" Card said in an interview. "And the president was standing at the top of the pyramid. Did he seek counsel from lots of different people? Yes. Were some voices louder than others? Yes. Were some voices more knowledgeable than others? Absolutely."

David Addington carried the U.S. Constitution in his suit jacket. It was a well-thumbed pocket edition—white paperback cover, maybe three by six inches, a few dozen pages of very small type. A lot of people noticed that, because he had a habit of brandishing the text when he wanted to make a point about presidential authority.

Not many people knew what Addington taped to index cards tucked inside.

"One of the possible functions of the vice president is to succeed the president if he has to," said William J. Haynes II, an old friend of Addington's who served as general counsel at the Pentagon. "Please don't read too much into this. He has all the executive orders and statutes on succession. He shrinks down the text."

Understudy was actually the vice president's only executive function. There was a puzzle, even so, about the thoroughness of Addington's pocket library—excerpts from the Presidential Succession Act of 1947, Executive Order 12656, Presidential Decision Directive 67. There were complex contingencies on who would succeed to the nation's highest office if the vice president was *not* in the picture. Cheney had a guaranteed spot at the head of the line.

As usual for the vice president's lawyer, it was a question of principle.

Addington believed the statutory line of succession was an unconstitutional infringement on the unitary executive branch.

The Constitution does not specify the order of succession, leaving it to Congress to say "what officer shall then act as President" if the vice president is dead or disabled. Congress made its last major rewrite in 1947. After the vice president, the succession moves to the Speaker of the House and the president pro tempore of the Senate, followed by cabinet secretaries in the order in which their departments were established, beginning with State, Treasury, and Defense. Addington, colleagues said, did not think a member of the House or Senate could qualify as a constitutional "officer."

Two government lawyers said in interviews that Addington approached them, separately, with that question. One replied that he would have to give the matter some thought. The other said there might be a pretty good case against the succession law.

"He *loved* that answer," said a witness to the second conversation.

There was a practical aspect to the discussion, one colleague said, "when Strom was alive." He meant Senator Strom Thurmond, the Senate's president pro tempore, whose faculties were diminished long before he died at age one hundred. "We had discussions of whether we really considered Strom Thurmond to be in the succession, and David made the point that members of the legislative branch shouldn't even be in the succession."

None of this was academic to Addington. He was consumed with the risk of a decapitating attack on Washington.

Bush alluded to such an attack in explaining the warrantless surveillance program. The initiative arose, he said, from "threats to the continuity of our government." Continuity of government is a term of art. Loss of continuity would mean the death of the president and his successors. It is a threat to the constitutional order itself.

Back when Cheney played White House chief of staff in the 1980s exercises, Addington was one of his advisers. Rand Beers, then at the State Department, worked on a parallel team under mock chief of staff Donald Rumsfeld, who was then in the private sector. Each of three teams, deploying simultaneously from Andrews Air Force Base, included a cabinet member to play the president. The Speaker and president pro tem were never brought along, Beers said. "They were always dead" in the exercise scenarios. "There was always the question" of whether the legitimate line of succession "means that the Speaker becomes the president. I don't remember if we ever answered that specifically. From my perspective it was an interesting intellectual issue, but it wasn't an issue I had to worry about."

On September 11, the U.S. government activated contingency plans to disperse its leaders to hardened locations outside Washington, a step it had not taken even in the moments of greatest crisis in the cold war. The Bush administration evacuated Speaker Dennis Hastert and President Pro Tem Robert Byrd, but both insisted on returning to the capital before the all clear. At the urging of NSC staffer Richard Clarke, another alumnus of the 1980s exercises, Cheney pressed to keep the shadow government active indefinitely. "The whole premise was that Washington, without prior notice, could be rendered uninhabitable," said another participant in the planning. "Think about that. We have never, ever believed that possible before."

The administration requested secret funding to replace the Roosevelt-era White House bunker, the Presidential Emergency Operations Center, where Cheney spent September 11. Plans called for a new facility with upgraded technology—accessible from the White House but dug deeper and located more securely. The House and Senate established alternative locations to convene in Washington, and top legislative leaders were equipped with special communications gear to be carried at all times by their Capitol Police escorts.

Cheney was not alone in his exile to undisclosed locations. Joseph Hagin, the deputy White House chief of staff for operations, kept a rotating cadre of 70 to 150 senior managers from across the executive branch on twenty-four-hour bunker duty in a hollowed-out mountain away from Washington. "In the case of the use of a weapon of mass destruction, the federal government would be able to do its job and continue to provide key services and respond," Hagin said.

There was always one eligible successor to the president in the bunker. Not once was that "standby president" the Speaker or president pro tem. "They never included a member of Congress in the COG shadow government after September 11," said Norman Ornstein, who studied the deployments as senior counselor to the Continuity of Government Commission.

Wayne Downing, the president's senior terrorism adviser after September 11, said the fault belonged to the legislators themselves, who refused to take the operation seriously. "One of the biggest problems you got is to get the people who are supposed to get to the alternate locations to get their worthless asses out," he said. "We could lose two-thirds or three-quarters of the Congress, and don't tempt me to say it, that could damn well be an improvement."

More than a year after September 11, a visitor in Scooter Libby's office, EEOB 276, asked him whether the Bush administration was working on a change in the line of succession.

"I think it would be a reasonable issue for people to look at, if we were," Libby said, in the cryptic way he had of speaking about classified subjects.

Six months later, Cheney hosted the Continuity of Government Commission in his ceremonial office. Norm Ornstein returned for a private meeting with the vice president, urging him to propose a legislative repair to the succession statute. Cheney passed Ornstein to his deputy chief of staff, Dean McGrath, who was not encouraging.

"He told me, 'Pursue this all you want, but I don't think there's any chance we'll be doing anything legislatively on this,'" Ornstein said.

One commission insider, a Cheney admirer who did not want to be named, said the vice president and his staff "had their plans" for presidential succession, "and their plans were going to be by fiat."

Chapter Seven

DARK SIDE

Before, the vice president's motorcade stopped at red lights. Now it sped through blocked-off streets. Life changed fast for Cheney, personally as well as officially. He was spending a lot of time at the presidential retreat at Camp David, a moment's scramble from "Site R," the underground military command center burrowed into Raven Rock Mountain nearby. There were other undisclosed locations for Cheney while the president was in Washington, some no more secure than a fishing lodge. Stealth, more than fortresses, protected him. Unable to attend meetings in person, Cheney beamed in by secure video link, his disembodied head ducking off the screen when he bent to take notes. Cheney's car, already armored, was fitted with equipment to seal its air supply in case of need. A large hump in the backseat, a friend re-ported, contained a chemical-protective suit. The Secret Service gave special lapel pins to visitors, ejecting anyone without a pin from the vice president's vicinity.

The sense of danger was urgent, palpable. Wayne Downing, a retired four-star general, arrived at the White House that fall to help launch the war with al Qaeda. When he reviewed the intelligence, he said, "one of the things that was sobering to me was all the work they had done on looking at chemical weapons, radiological dispersion devices, and their fascination with nuclear weapons."

"Mr. Vice President, are we going to be okay?" Nina Rees, one of Cheney's domestic advisers, asked him nervously in a staff meeting after September 11.

"We're working as hard as we can to protect you, but we are a target," Cheney replied. "Understand that. You don't need to stay, but I'm staying."

Cheney explained what he meant by "as hard as we can" a few days later. The United States had a fine military, he said, and would use it where appropriate.

> We also have to work, though, sort of the dark side, if you will. We've got to spend time in the shadows in the intelligence world. A lot of what needs to be done here will have to be done quietly, without any discussion, using sources and methods that are available to our intelligence agencies, if we're going to be successful. That's the world these folks operate in, and so it's going to be vital for us to use any means at our disposal, basically, to achieve our objectives.

"Dark Side" came to define him in the public mind, and inside the White House, too. Bush, the nicknamer in chief, called Cheney nothing more disrespectful than the Veep. There were other names in use behind the vice president's back. One of them was Big Time, a reference to a profane exchange with Bush delivered accidentally into a live microphone. Another was Management, an homage from Karl Rove, with usages such as "Better check with Management first." (Three colleagues reported Rove's paternity; he denied it.) Much later, after a hunting accident, it was Deadly Dick.

But the most prevalent nickname for Cheney in the first term was Dark Side.

Cheney was easy to cartoon, and critics found imaginary subtexts in some of his words. But the thing about the "dark side" interview was that Cheney made himself so clear. He was not referring only to the absence of light. There would be secrets, yes. But another kind of darkness as well.

Dark Side meant something in popular culture. Twenty-four years after its debut, the *Star Wars* movie franchise had brought an enduring vocabulary to American politics. The Dark Side was the nether region of the Force. Fueled by anger and hatred, it conferred great power at some expense to humanity. Jokes about the Dark Side and its high priest, Darth Vader, were staples of the 2000 campaign and the Florida recount.

If Cheney was somehow unaware of the image he summoned, he embraced it afterward. CNN's John King, interviewing the vice president at his residence, asked why even old friends thought he had "become this dark, nefarious force." Cheney replied, "We need to be able to go after and capture or kill those people who are trying to kill Americans. That's not a pleasant business. It's a very serious business. And I suppose people sometimes look at my demeanor and say, well, he's the Darth Vader of the administration." By 2007, Cheney was dressing his dog as Lord of the Sith for Halloween and alluding to Vader as a warm-up joke in speeches.

Any means at our disposal, basically.

Here the vice president brought the language of darkness to the terrain of human nature, human behavior. He believed in the "hard power" of compulsion far more than the "soft power" of persuasion, said Aaron Friedberg, the director of planning on his foreign policy staff. Whenever a subject arose "where there was no room for idealism or sentimentality, you'd find the vice president there," said

Brad Berenson, the White House lawyer. The speechwriter Michael Gerson called him "the most dour and pessimistic person in the room." Cheney might have put it differently, others said, if he were less averse to self-reflection: he was not so much disillusioned as without illusion. Tom Foley, a Democrat and former Speaker of the House who calls Cheney a friend, said the vice president "feels very, very strongly that the country is at risk and *everything has to be done* to protect it." Anthony Fauci, whom Cheney consulted on biological weapons threats, found him "determined to do *whatever is necessary* to protect the American public." Juleanna Glover, a Cheney adviser, said he viewed himself as "a pragmatist, realistic about human nature," asking, "What motivates basic human behavior? Is it the carrot or the stick?" His answer? "If you have a very big stick, use what's at hand."

Just past the Oval Office, in the private dining room overlooking the South Lawn, Cheney joined Bush for lunch on November 13, 2001. The two of them shared the round parquet table once a week, most often on Thursdays. It was a chance to talk alone, no staff and no fixed agenda.

Cheney brought a four-page text. David Addington, his lawyer, had drafted it in strict secrecy.

The United States was at war in Afghanistan, Osama bin Laden's base of operations. It was the first substantial response to September 11. Now U.S. troops faced a question: What should they do with a captured fighter from al Qaeda or the Taliban?

Questions like that nearly always get scrubbed in an "interagency review." Secretary of State Colin Powell appointed Pierre Prosper, ambassador-at-large for war crimes, to lead a working group. You couldn't just shoot prisoners. Couldn't let them go. Should they get federal trials? Courts-martial? Something else? Prosper convened representatives from Justice, Defense, and the Joint Chiefs of Staff. Condi Rice and Alberto Gonzales sent lawyers. They met in a conference room down the hall from Powell's seventh-floor suite. Weeks passed. "Once you start diving into it, and history has proven us right, these are complicated questions," Prosper said.

Cheney's staff did not show up. Addington knew what his client wanted, and "the interagency was just constipated," said Jim Haynes, his ally at the Pentagon.

Addington typed out an order that stripped foreign terrorist suspects of access to any court—civilian or military, domestic or foreign. They could be confined indefinitely without charge. They would be tried, if at all, in closed "military commissions," modeled on the ones Franklin Roosevelt set up for Nazi saboteurs in World War II. Addington was not the first to think of that idea, Tim Flanigan said later, but he was the "best scholar of the FDR-era order" among their small group of trusted allies. "He gained a preeminent role by virtue of his sheer ability to turn out a draft of something in quick time."

By relying on Roosevelt's model, and on the 1942 Supreme Court case upholding it, Addington discarded six decades of intervening laws and treaties. Since then the United States had led the world in creating international institutions and international law, some of it enacted into U.S. statutes. The United Nations, headquartered in New York, passed the Universal Declaration of Human Rights in 1948. More than 190 countries signed the Geneva Conventions, negotiated under U.S. sponsorship beginning in 1949. The armed services built a whole new legal system, the Uniform Code of Military Justice. Congress enacted a torture statute and the War Crimes Act.

Cheney's lawyer needed backup from the Justice Department. He turned once again to the Office of Legal Counsel. John Yoo and his colleague Patrick Philbin paved the way for military commissions in a pair of memos, dated November 6, 2001, and January 9, 2002. The president, they wrote, did not need approval from Congress or federal courts. International treaties did not apply. Yoo said in an interview that he saw no need to show drafts to the State Department, which hosts the archives of the Geneva Conventions and the government's leading experts on the law of war. "The issue we dealt with was: Can the president do it constitutionally?" Yoo said. "State—they wouldn't have views on that."

Attorney General John Ashcroft got wind of the proposal. It gave exclusive authority to the Pentagon to decide which alleged terrorists to try in military commissions. Over Veterans Day weekend, on November 10, Ashcroft took his objections to the White House.

The attorney general found Cheney and Addington, not the president, at the broad conference table in the Roosevelt Room. Ashcroft minced no words.

He was the president's senior law enforcement officer. He supervised the FBI. He oversaw terrorism investigations and prosecutions nationwide. There was no way he was going to hand over suspects to tribunals over which he had no say.

"We've already spoken to your OLC," Cheney replied. "They recommend otherwise."

Who? Ashcroft demanded.

John Yoo.

The attorney general turned red. Raising his voice, Ashcroft talked right over Addington—no mean feat—and brushed aside interjections from Cheney. "The thing I remember about it is how rude, there's no other word for it, the attorney general was to the vice president," said one of those in the room. Asked later about the confrontation, Ashcroft replied curtly: "I'm just not prepared to comment on that."

According to Yoo and three other officials, Ashcroft made no headway. He was not going to have any role in the choice of venue for terrorist trials. Cheney tweaked his draft to say the president would make that decision, but in practice Bush would delegate it to Don Rumsfeld at the Pentagon.

It was difficult to tell what the president knew, if anything, about the military order now heading toward his lunch table. Certainly he approved the idea that this was going to be a new kind of war, without a lot of lawyerly coddling for terrorists. When details became important, someone was supposed to tell him. Was he aware of Ashcroft's objections? Had anyone offered a heads-up on the legal risks, or the likely reaction of allies? Did Bush intend to keep his national security adviser and secretary of state out of the loop?

Cheney liked to remind the White House staff that "the president's most precious commodity is his time," said Ron Christie, one of the vice president's advisers. It must not be wasted. Jack Marsh, an old friend and colleague, said that Cheney, like Don Rumsfeld, believed "you get off the president's plate everything that you can." When Cheney cared about an issue, he did what he did with barbecue when Lynne wasn't looking: he piled his own plate high.

Every administration struggled with this question. The president should not be asked to make choices below his pay grade, but he had to know enough to decide when he wanted to intervene. In other White Houses, the time-is-precious maxim meant that "only things that involved disputes among high-level people should go to the president," said Ron Klain, chief of staff to Vice President Gore. If the vice president made the call, as Cheney did in swatting down

Ashcroft, "who is going to bring that to the president? Who has that brief?"

Ashcroft could have walked a few yards down the hall. He was not close to Bush, but the attorney general got an appointment when he asked. How many times did a cabinet officer want to dip into that well? Ashcroft turned left at the door from the Roosevelt Room, away from the Oval Office, and back out toward the street.

Three days later, Cheney brought the order to lunch with the president. No one told Colin Powell or Condi Rice. No one told their lawyers, William H. Taft IV and John Bellinger. No one told Pierre Prosper, who was waiting for a reply to the option paper he sent the White House. Jim Haynes, the Pentagon lawyer, said the order "was very closely held because it was coming right from the top."

Cheney emerged from lunch with a thumbs-up from the president. Flanigan could not believe how fast it all happened.

"I was astonished," Flanigan said. "David and I were huddled in my office, realizing that the bureaucracy was not going to be a bit pleased to see the president act this way, on his own without their blessing—and without the interminable process that goes along with getting such a blessing." That was a good thing, he judged. "Every once in a while it is healthy for the president to do this. It shakes the bureaucracy up. It shows them the need to move quickly to meet his policy objectives."

The vice president chanced no last-minute protest. He sent the order on a swift path to execution, leaving no trace of his touch.

In less than an hour, the document traversed a West Wing circuit that gave its words the power of command. It changed hands four times, with emphatic instructions to bypass staff review. Cheney's days of "orderly paper flow," of shunning "oh, by the way decisions," were long behind him.

From Addington, then Flanigan, the text passed to Brad Berenson, an associate White House counsel. The vice president's link to the document broke there: no one told Berenson its provenance.

Staff secretary Harriet Miers was away. Berenson walked the order to her deputy, Stuart W. Bowen Jr. His instructions were to prepare it for signature at once. Bush was about to depart for his ranch in Crawford.

"This has to be staffed," Bowen said.

"No, it's been taken care of," Berenson responded.

Bowen wasn't buying.

"What we do here with documents like this," he said, "is we staff them."

Exacting rules in the secretariat required a "chop," or sign-off, from every assistant to the president with a stake. In this case that would include at least Andy Card, Condi Rice, Steve Hadley, deputy chief of staff Josh Bolten, the White House counsel's office, Nick Calio at Legislative Affairs, and the communications counselor Karen Hughes.

Not only that. There should have been a routing slip that showed the Office of Management and Budget had circulated the order to the cabinet. There was supposed to be a certification, too, that Justice checked the order's "form and legality." Bowen was looking at four pages of type on plain white paper. Thousands of presidential documents passed through the office. None like this.

Berenson played his trump card.

"The president has already approved it."

"If that's the case, you should just walk it yourself down to him," Bowen said. "Why are you bringing it to me?"

No, it had to be a formal directive. It was urgent. Matter of national security. The president was waiting. Outside on the White House lawn, low-throated turbines were spinning on the president's helicopter, Marine One.

Bowen relented. In retrospect, he wished he had not.

"It's by no means a picky procedural matter. It is fundamental to advising the president," Bowen said. "The staffing process exists to ensure the president receives complete and accurate advice that has been vetted by his most senior advisers, and therefore helps the president avoid mistakes."

Berenson, looking back on the incident, said he knew only that "someone had briefed" the president, securing approval. "I don't know who that was," he said.

Bush was standing, ready to depart, when Bowen arrived in the Oval Office. Addington's words were now bound in a blue portfolio, embossed with the presidential seal. Bush reached for the folder and turned to the last page. Bowen held it open. Bush pulled out a Sharpie from his breast pocket and signed, slashing upward in the diagonal line that marks his first decisive stroke.

Bush was airborne for Crawford when CNN broke into its broadcast with the news. Condi Rice, furious, sent John Bellinger to complain.

Colin Powell had the television going in his office. He picked up the phone to Pierre Prosper.

"What the hell just happened?" he asked.

The next day, November 14, 2001, Cheney took another bold step. He told the U.S. Chamber of Commerce that a terrorist does not "deserve to be treated as a prisoner of war."

The president had not yet made that decision. Ten weeks passed, and his advisers fought a fierce internal brawl, before Bush ratified the policy that Cheney declared: the Geneva Conventions would not apply to al Qaeda or Taliban fighters captured on the battlefield.

Since 1949, Geneva had accorded protections to civilians and combatants in a war zone. Those protections varied with status. Scholars had identified gaps in the language that theoretically left some parties, in some circumstances, uncovered. But the negotiating history, and decades of practice under U.S. leadership, interpreted Geneva to confer a minimum set of rights on everyone. Under Ronald Reagan in 1987, the United States had refused to ratify an additional protocol, arguing that it would have given prisoner-of-war status to terrorists. But that was far from claiming that accused terrorists had no Geneva rights at all. The American government had never been in the business of looking for that kind of loophole.

Rumsfeld, elaborating on the position Cheney staked out, cast the old rubric aside. All captured fighters in Afghanistan, he said at a Pentagon news briefing, are "unlawful combatants" who "do not have any rights" under Geneva.

At the White House, Bellinger sent Rice a blunt warning. The Cheney-Rumsfeld position would place the president, personally, in breach of international law. ("Protect your client," Navy general counsel Alberto Mora urged Rumsfeld's lawyer at a comparable moment the following year.) As a practical matter, Bellinger wrote, even the closest allies could be expected to stop handing over suspects to U.S. custody. Faxes had been pouring in from overseas since Bush signed the order for military commissions. The first one had come from the British lord chancellor, noting pointedly that London's cooperation was based on accepted legal norms.

Powell asked for a meeting with Bush. The same day, January 25, 2002, Cheney's office struck a preemptive blow. It appeared to come from Gonzales, the president's lawyer. Hours after Powell made his request, Gonzales signed his name to a memo that cut the legs out from under the secretary of state. The subtly mocking tone did not sound much like Gonzales. Addington, in fact, had written the text, basing it in part on John Yoo's memorandum of January 9. Flanigan passed it to Gonzales, and Gonzales sent it as "my judgment" to Bush.

If Bush consulted Cheney after that, as he did on most things, the vice president became a sounding board for advice he originated himself.

Addington, under Gonzales's name, appealed to the president by quoting Bush's own declaration that "the war against terrorism is a new kind of war." Addington described the Geneva Conventions as "quaint," casting Powell as a defender of "obsolete" rules devised for another time. If Bush followed Powell's lead, Addington suggested, U.S. forces would be obliged to provide athletic gear and commissary privileges to captured terrorists.

That was a parody of what Powell proposed. According to David Bowker, a State Department lawyer, Powell did not argue that al Qaeda and Taliban forces deserved the privileges of prisoners of war. Powell said they were entitled to a review of their status. He predicted that few, if any, would qualify as POWs, because they did not wear uniforms on the battlefield or obey a lawful chain of command. "We said, 'If you give legal process and you follow the rules, you're going to reach substantially the same result and the courts will defer to you,'" Bowker said.

The vice president's lawyer made no attempt to keep his January 25 memorandum under wraps, distributing it around the White House and cabinet departments. Late that afternoon, as it began to circulate, Addington turned to Flanigan.

"It'll leak in ten minutes," he predicted.

The next morning's *Washington Times* carried a front-page article in which administration sources accused Powell of "bowing to pressure from the political left" and advocating that terrorists be given "all sorts of amenities, including exercise rooms and canteens."

It was a nearly perfect hit. Addington found a way to top it. He blamed the State Department itself for leaking a story to the right-wing newspaper most likely to portray the secretary of state as a patsy. The breach of secrecy, Addington said, proved that Will Taft, Powell's legal adviser, could not be trusted. Taft—the great-grandson of a Republican president and deputy defense secretary under the first president Bush—joined John Bellinger on a growing blacklist.

"I was off the team," Taft said.

The vice president's lawyer had marked him an enemy. Taft did not know he was at war.

"Which, of course, is why you're ripe for the taking, isn't it?" Taft added.

He laughed at the memory, briefly.

The arguments over Geneva and military commissions were stage setters, means to an end. Cheney had several goals, but the most important was to extract intelligence from captured enemies.

For that purpose, the vice president and his allies had to construct what Will Taft called the "legal equivalent of outer space"—a place where detainees had no status, where no rules and no jurisdiction applied. As a territorial matter, that place became Guantánamo Bay, a U.S. naval base built on a broad natural harbor at the southeast tip of Cuba. Fidel Castro's government did not recognize the perpetual lease obtained by Theodore Roosevelt, free of charge, in 1903. That was convenient for the Bush administration. It enabled David Addington and friends at OLC to argue that there was no sovereign authority at all. Neither Cuban nor American nor international law applied.

Congress was not invited. Jane Harman, a hawkish Democrat on the House Intelligence Committee, went to see Addington one day at the White House. She had been thinking a lot about terrorists and how to question them. She gave a speech at Georgetown University, "Intelligence Gathering in the Fog of Law." She wanted to work with the White House on new rules. "I said, 'We need to do this. I have proposals for what these rules could look like,'" Harman recalled. She came armed with the Constitution. Addington, she figured, would like that. Article I, Section 8, gave Congress the power to "make rules concerning captures on land and water."

"That doesn't apply," Addington said. "That's about piracy."

When the so-called captures clause was written, Addington said, the context was the role of privateers—mercenaries with quasi-legal authority—in the struggle to control commercial and military sealanes. The rules in question, he said, were about property, not people. Anyway, terrorists were not pirates. Congress had no say. "I just found that astounding," Harman said. Legal historians, in fact, are divided on the question, but the most extensive recent scholarship said Harman was right: the original intent of the framers, and admiralty law at the time of the constitutional convention, "covered enemy persons as well as property." The military commissions order, an extraordinary departure from the status quo, was the first step toward years of trouble and frustration for Bush. "That is where the disaster began," said a conservative lawyer, loyal to Bush, who saw the order at birth. "The lack of due process, the artifice of treating Gitmo as outside the jurisdiction of U.S. law, the failure to bring charges, and the un-American, if you will, evidentiary rules—I think it led directly to torture," he said.

A close ally of Cheney's said the vice president's role on legal policy was vital precisely because of people who worried about "due process" for terrorists. "On detainees, you need to understand the landscape," he said. The Office of Legal Counsel at Justice—Yoo and company—was "usually pretty muscular." Same went for the Defense Department. The National Security Council staff played the middle. Then there was the State Department, "which is basically an al Qaeda cell." Someone had to make sure the right voices were heard. "Since the vice president understands military and intelligence matters, and as a former White House manager, he's in a unique position to guide the process."

The second or third time Cheney guided the process around Rice and Powell, blindsiding them with another ruling from the OLC, the two of them decided to send a message. They synchronized an appearance to lodge a complaint—with Al Gonzales.

Powell at her side, Rice blazed with anger.

"There will be no more secret opinions on international and national security law!" she commanded.

If it happened again, she would go straight to the president.

Powell remarked admiringly as they emerged that Rice dressed down Gonzales "in full Nurse Ratched mode." He had just compared the national security adviser to the head nurse in the 1975 film *One Flew Over the Cuckoo's Nest*. Which happened to be set, a colleague pointed out, in a mental hospital.

No one believed poor Fredo was in charge of the decision to exclude Rice and Powell. But neither of them raised a ruckus with the vice president, or even Addington. When it came to Cheney in those days, Rice's voice, like Nurse Ratched's late in the movie, was choked to a whisper.

The first accused terrorists reached the U.S. naval prison at Guantá-namo Bay on January 11, 2002. Shortly after that, a delegation from CIA headquarters arrived in the Situation Room. The agency presented a delicate problem to Al Gonzales, who had next to no experience on the subject. The vice president's lawyer, who had plenty, sat alongside.

The meeting marked "the first time that the issue of interrogations comes up" in the White House, according to John Yoo, who was there. "The CIA guys said, 'We're going to have some real difficulties getting actionable intelligence from detainees'" if interrogators worked within the polite confines of Geneva.

From that moment, if not sooner, the vice president turned his attention to the practical business of forcing an unwilling captive to talk. His office played a central role in shattering limits on coercion, commissioning and defending legal opinions that the Bush administration would later have to abandon.

Cheney had been thinking about the power of cruelty since at least 1984. In March of that year, the CIA's chief of station in Beirut, William Buckley, fell into the hands of Hezbollah. "He was kidnapped and tortured," recalled Tom Smeeton, a former CIA officer who served then as minority staff director of the House Intelligence Committee. Cheney, a committee member, followed the Buckley case closely, reviewing a secretly obtained videotape of the station chief's decline. Cheney "was quite concerned about the implications of his torture and what that could mean in terms of revelations of various intelligence operations going on in the Middle East," Smeeton said. The presumption they shared, with foreboding, was that torture worked.

After September 11, Cheney and his allies pioneered a distinction that the U.S. government had not claimed before. "Torture," narrowly defined, would remain out of bounds. But violent, cruel, or degrading methods, the terms of art in Geneva, were perfectly lawful. The vice president's office did not originate every idea to rewrite or reinterpret the law, but Cheney and Addington promoted those ideas and translated them into the operational language of government.

Addington set the agenda in the January 25 memorandum signed by Gonzales, the one about the quaintness of Geneva. He had a far more serious purpose than embarrassing Colin Powell. The impetus was the recent CIA visit. Geneva's "strict limits on questioning of enemy prisoners," Addington wrote, hobbled efforts "to quickly obtain information from captured terrorists."

No longer was the vice president focused on procedural rights, such as access to lawyers and courts. The subject now was elemental: How much suffering could U.S. personnel inflict on an enemy to make him talk—"quickly"?

For the first of many times to come, Cheney's lawyer alluded to the dangerous line the government was about to cross. Future prosecutors, with motives "difficult to predict," might bring criminal charges against interrogators, he wrote. Or against the people who told them what to do. That was exactly Mike Hayden's fear about warrantless surveillance. Jim Haynes, at the Pentagon, had the same concern. "You have also asked," John Yoo wrote in a memorandum to Haynes, "whether U.S. interrogation of al Qaeda and Taliban detainees could lead to liability and potential prosecution before the International Criminal Court."

Geneva rules forbade not only torture but also, in equally categorical terms, the use of "violence," "cruel treatment," or "humiliating and degrading treatment" against a detainee "at any time and in any place whatsoever." The War Crimes Act of 1996 made any grave breach of those restrictions a U.S. felony. The best defense against such a charge, Addington wrote, would combine a broad presidential directive for humane treatment, in general, with an assertion of unrestricted authority to make exceptions.

The vice president's counsel proposed that President Bush issue a carefully ambiguous directive. Detainees would be treated "humanely and, to the extent appropriate and consistent with military necessity, in a manner consistent with the principles of" the Geneva Conventions. There were people who read that line with relief. It looked pro-Geneva. They were not reading very closely.

To the extent appropriate . . . military necessity . . . consistent with . . . the principles of . . .

Addington's proposal had almost boundless room for maneuver. It committed the U.S. government to nothing. When Bush issued his public decision two weeks later, on February 7, 2002, he adopted that formula verbatim. Again, the vice president's counsel had written the words that Bush turned into law.

In a radio interview later, Cheney said, "We don't torture." What he did not acknowledge, according to Alberto Mora, the Bush-appointed Navy general counsel, was that the Geneva decision had the primary purpose of making room for cruelty. Addington and Yoo had built a new legal structure with a back door to places unseen.

How far would they go? Yoo was summoned again to the White House in the early spring of 2002. This time the question was urgent. The CIA had taken custody of Abu Zubaida, then believed to be a top al Qaeda operative, on March 28. He was not at Guantánamo Bay. Even the legal equivalent of outer space was not remote enough. He was completely off the map, in a secret prison maintained by the CIA overseas.

Now, Yoo said, the CIA officers wanted to know "what the legal limits of interrogation are."

The CIA could not have been blunter about its motives. Six years later, Ralph S. DiMaio of the agency's National Clandestine Service filed a sworn statement in federal court. "The requests for advice," he wrote, "were solicited in order to prepare the CIA to defend against future criminal, civil, and administrative proceedings that the CIA considered to be virtually inevitable."

It took four months for Yoo to produce a formal opinion. Meanwhile—in secret consultations with Gonzales, Flanigan, Addington, and CIA lawyers—Yoo gave interim authority for most of what the agency wanted to do. According to an authoritative source, Yoo rejected one proposed technique: the CIA could not bury a subject alive, even if it planned to dig him back up in time. Convincing a person of his imminent death was torture, open and shut. Other proposed methods, Yoo said, were fine.

Because the advice came from the OLC, it was authoritative for the executive branch. Officials who relied on it had something close to an "*ex ante* pardon," advance immunity if their actions were later deemed a crime. Dick Cheney knew all about *ex ante* pardons. Gerald Ford had given one to Richard Nixon.

According to two U.S. government sources, George Tenet wanted more. Associates said Tenet was convinced that he and his people would one day be hung out to dry. He insisted on political as well as legal backing.

Tenet told Dick Cheney and Condi Rice, in separate meetings, that he needed approval from the top for the new "enhanced interrogation" techniques. If he went down, the rest of them were going with him.

And so it passed. Beginning in the second quarter of 2002—and periodically until at least early 2005, longer than previously reported—Cheney and Rice and the war cabinet sat with George Tenet and his successor in the Situation Room. The vice president led meetings with Don Rumsfeld, Colin Powell, and John Ashcroft, among others, to decide which torments exactly would be inflicted on each of the "high-value detainees." According to one source, Tenet and his briefers gave details of each method employed, sometimes showing photographs. Tenet was determined not to accept what an adviser called "a wink and a nod." One participant in the meetings said, "I don't blame him for trying to get individual cover, but you don't necessarily let everybody bring everything they want into the White House. It was insane, I think, to be discussing techniques to use against individual detainees." Bush's advisers, the participant said, "didn't want the president talking about these techniques," but they briefed him in detail. "He was fully knowledgeable." When ABC News revealed the cabinet-level meetings, years later, Bush confirmed that he knew exactly what the principals were doing, and he approved.

Cheney considered the gloves-off questioning, as Tenet did, an absolute necessity. There were any number of euphemisms, but the bald fact was that if an important detainee would not talk, the U.S. government did what it took to break his will.

Any means at our disposal, basically.

Psychologists who treat torture victims tend to focus more on duration and cumulative effect than on any one "technique" of questioning. A twenty-hour interrogation is exhausting and disorienting. Many of them on consecutive days induce sleep deprivation so acute that State Department human rights reports before September 11 routinely defined it as torture.

For a century at least, the government said that some forms of treatment were torture all on their own. One of them was "waterboarding," an ordeal with roots in the Spanish Inquisition. The U.S. government held war crimes trials for those who practiced it, Americans and foreigners, beginning in 1902. Cheney and the cabinet principals approved waterboarding for at least three men: Abu Zubaida, Abd al-Rahim al-Nashiri, and Khalid Sheikh Mohammed.

There are more and less delicate ways to describe what that means. A Pentagon memo, approved and later withdrawn by Don Rumsfeld, said the technique is meant to "induce the misperception of suffocation," which makes it sound like a misunderstanding on the subject's part. In that form of waterboarding, interrogators strap a man down, incline his feet above his head, blindfold him, and stretch a wet towel over his face, dripping enough water over his nose to cut off nearly all air. It is more like smothering than drowning. Interrogators keep it up until the victim's pulse and blood pressure reach dangerous thresholds. According to an intelligence officer who has been through it himself, there is not much you can do to a person that instills greater panic. After a pause, it begins again.

In another variant, interrogators force water into the subject's nose and mouth. When he can no longer hold his breath, he sucks in liquid, choking and coughing explosively. It is not a simulation, exactly. He is drowning, and then he is rescued. Interrogators give him time to recover, and repeat.

The reliability of information thus obtained became a matter of much debate, but those arguments settled very little. The government did not say nearly enough—about what interrogators learned, and when, and how—to allow outsiders to judge. A braver question, which not as many people wanted to address, was whether Americans were prepared to be a nation that did this sort of thing, torture or not-quite torture, if it worked. Did we feel that frightened? That ruthless?

"At the time, you really did have to understand what the cabinet principals were faced with, which was an intensely high threat situation," said an associate of Condi Rice's, who said she gradually came to believe that waterboarding should be renounced. "We really thought we were going to be attacked—possibly chemical, biological, even nuclear, the potential that they could blow up entire American cities. And it appeared that al Qaeda wanted to do all that. And then they captured a couple of these people. And then CIA came and said, 'You know, this is the only way to question these people. Our experts say this is the only program that will work.' And Justice said that the [Geneva Conventions] didn't apply . . . and that the agency program did comply with the torture statute. When we asked the CIA, 'Were there alternatives?' they said there were no other alternatives. It essentially left the principals with no real other options there."

Rice declined to discuss those meetings or the techniques she voted to support. But by 2008, when she paid a call on Google headquarters (corporate motto: "Don't be evil"), she did allude to changes in her thinking. Law and values played a role, but she began and ended her answer with The Threat. The deciding factor, she made plain, was fear.

"We were in an environment in which saving America from the next attack was a paramount concern," she told Google employees in a freewheeling question-and-answer session. Since then, Rice said, "there has been a long evolution now of American policy about detainees and about interrogation techniques. We now have in place a set of laws that were not there in 2002 and 2003. . . . And these issues have evolved. They've evolved in the context of a democracy. They've evolved in the context of a constant debate about our values and what

President Ford, Chief of Staff Dick Cheney *(far right),* and others in the Oval Office in May 1976. *Left to right, behind desk:* Press Secretary Ronald Nessen, Deputy Press Secretary John Carlson, unknown, counselor Robert Hartmann, legislative assistant Max Friedersdorf.

President George H. W. Bush at a Department of Defense briefing during the first Persian Gulf War, with *(left to right)* Vice President Dan Quayle, General Colin Powell, and Secretary of Defense Dick Cheney, in Washington, D.C., January 1991.

On the campaign trail in August 1999, Republican presidential nominee George W. Bush arrives onstage alongside Oklahoma governor Frank Keating, who will come to regret his bid to become Bush's running mate.

When President Bush met with Alan Greenspan, Cheney always sat in. Behind the scenes, the vice president took steps to neutralize the Fed chairman's advice against the tax cuts of 2003.

The president and vice president often reached a meeting of minds for entirely different reasons, arriving at the same position by separate paths.

Cheney confers with Bush by phone from the White House bunker on September 11, 2001, as *(left to right)* counselor Karen Hughes, vice presidential counsel David Addington *(standing)*, National Security Adviser Condoleezza Rice *(sitting)*, and counselor Mary Matalin listen in. Addington and Cheney began work that morning to reshape U.S. law for the "war on terror."

President Bush meets with his war cabinet on September 15, 2001, at Camp David. *Left to right:* Attorney General John Ashcroft, Cheney, Bush, Secretary of State Colin Powell, Secretary of Defense Donald Rumsfeld, Deputy Secretary of Defense Paul Wolfowitz.

An estimated seventy-seven thousand salmon, some of them the endangered coho species, washed up dead on the banks of the Klamath River in California *(pictured)* and Oregon after Cheney pushed through a diversion of water. Later, the government declared a "commercial fishery failure" on the West Coast.

President Bush receives a military and intelligence update in the Oval Office on March 20, 2003, the first day of war with Iraq. *Left to right:* Cheney *(back to camera),* Director of Central Intelligence George Tenet, the president, Chief of Staff Andrew Card.

With Cheney looking on behind them *(left to right),* Condoleezza Rice, Colin Powell, and Donald Rumsfeld listen as President Bush and Afghan president Hamid Karzai hold a joint press conference in the White House Rose Garden on June 15, 2004.

Jack L. Goldsmith, who led the Office of Legal Counsel in 2003 and 2004, clashed titanically with Cheney's lawyer, David Addington.

Cheney waits with Chief of Staff Scooter Libby for Bush to make a statement on the retirement of Supreme Court justice Sandra Day O'Connor, on July 1, 2005. Cheney would play the leading role in choosing her replacement.

Deputy Attorney General James B. Comey *(center)* during an April 12, 2005, news conference announcing the indictments of three British nationals on terrorism charges. His standoff with the vice president over warrantless domestic surveillance, one year earlier, came close to bringing about a mass resignation that would have done great damage to Bush. Behind Comey are prosecutor George Z. Toscas *(left)* and Assistant Attorney General Christopher Wray.

Left to right: FBI director Robert Mueller, Attorney General Alberto Gonzales, and Cheney look on as Bush speaks after a meeting with his counterterrorism team at the J. Edgar Hoover FBI Building on August 3, 2007.

Cheney, code-named "Angler" by the Secret Service, has approached the levers of power obliquely, skirting the orderly lines of authority he once enforced as White House chief of staff.

our values call us to do. . . . It is a different environment now than it was then, thank God."

By then the CIA had a new director. Mike Hayden, the former chief of the National Security Agency, had worked on the frontiers of surveillance, not interrogation. Waterboarding did not happen on his watch. But the scars of political battle, on both subjects, had led him to reconsider the Venn diagram he once showed Cheney.

The sketch Hayden made for the vice president had three ovals, overlapping at the bottom and fanning out like a hand of cards. Their labels were "useful," "lawful," and "tech poss." When he sat down with a reporter for the *Washington Post* in the spring of 2008, he grabbed a slice of stationery ("The Director, Central Intelligence Agency") and drew it again, just the same way. "I used to always describe, 'OK, that's our work space, right in there,'" he said, shading the region where all three ovals overlapped. But three no longer seemed to be enough. Hayden made a fourth oval and labeled it "pol. sustain." Politically sustainable. Now the sketch looked like a lumpy propeller. The "work space" for interrogations had shrunk. Hayden drew heavy crosshatched lines, marking the new boundaries of the forbidden. Therein a thing might be legal, if you asked the right lawyer, but voters were apt to be repulsed.

And there it was, in the innermost sanctum on Langley's seventh floor: a map of the Dark Side itself. "We exist in a political context," Hayden said. "We cannot have, for example, an approach to terrorism . . . that has an on/off switch every other November. It has to have stability." Intelligence agencies had to do their work within the limits of political tolerance. This was a decidedly un-Cheney-like way of thinking, but in Hayden's mind it was no more than provisional. "You can always go here for the short term," he said, pointing toward the Dark Side region of his sketch—the thing you can get away with legally but cannot expect the public to stand behind. "But what you really want is where you've got all four. . . . Otherwise, you are starting and stopping. And I think that, by the way, allows me to say what I said: 'No, we're not doing waterboarding anymore.' 'But waterboarding's unlawful, isn't it?' Well, I never said that. I said we're not doing it."

Public opinion shifts. Circumstances change. What happened once might happen again. Hayden was inclined to look back without judgment on the people who sat in the Situation Room in 2002, 2003, and 2004. "I'm glad I didn't have to make those decisions. I respect the people who did. And I am not in a position to question them."

Hayden was tired, in fact, of all the questioning. He had long been the spook of choice for opinion leaders, the house intellectual in an operational world. But now he invoked a different crowd, the blue-collar football fans of his native Pittsburgh. "I would say that elite commentary, and you know what I mean by that—I'm not talking about getting an Iron City [beer] before going into Heinz Field," Hayden said. "Elite commentary seems to focus less on the threat and more on the tactics the nation has chosen to have dealt with the threat."

Al Qaeda still aspired to another devastating attack.

"We remain worried, and frankly, I wonder why some other people aren't worried, too," he said.

John Yoo delivered his written opinion on "standards of conduct for interrogation" on August 1, 2002. (Jay Bybee, who ran the Office of Legal Counsel, was the author of record, but Yoo and others said Bybee did little of the substantive work.) Another one, substantially similar but addressed to the Defense Department, came on March 14, 2003.

Having concluded that the Geneva Conventions did not apply, Yoo delved instead into the Torture Act, the American law that gave force to an international treaty in 1987. According to the Convention Against Torture, the term meant "any act by which severe pain or suffering, whether physical or mental, is intentionally inflicted on a person," without exception.

Yoo's analysis said the U.S. adoption of that standard left room for many forms of "cruel, inhuman, or degrading treatment." He noted, correctly, that the "mere infliction of pain or suffering" did not count as torture. Torture, according to the statute, meant "severe pain." Yoo maintained that in order to count as illegal torture, "severe pain" would have to reach "the level that would ordinarily be associated with . . . death, organ failure, or serious impairment of body functions."

If an interrogator were one day charged with a torture crime, Yoo wrote, the prosecutor would have to show that torment of this utmost intensity was "the defendant's precise objective." If the interrogator had a good-faith belief that the pain he inflicted was more bearable, he would not be guilty. (Reading medical and other professional literature, Yoo suggested, would help show good faith.) Even if an interrogator had "certain" knowledge that his actions would cause extreme pain, he would not commit torture unless the pain itself, not another goal, were his "express purpose."

Should all those distinctions fail, the opinion said, an interrogator could mount either of two legal defenses: "necessity" (to prevent catastrophic harm) or "self-defense" (to save the country and the interrogator himself).

Yoo's final fallback position was that the president, as commander in chief, had unlimited authority to decide the methods of interrogation. Anything he ordered, even flat-out, undeniable torture, would be lawful.

As a matter of policy, Yoo said he warned Addington and Jim Haynes, the Pentagon lawyer, against the risks of letting military interrogators use the harshest forms of treatment. A second official, with authoritative knowledge, confirmed Yoo's account. The armed services, Yoo told Haynes and Addington, had too many people and too little training in special interrogation methods. They might easily overuse the tools or overstep the limits. "I always thought that only the CIA should do this, but people at the White House and at DOD felt differently," Yoo said.

The following month, on September 25, 2002, a small passenger plane touched down at the airstrip serving Guantánamo Bay. Into the tropical Cuban heat stepped a delegation of lawyers in business suits: Addington, Haynes, and acting general counsel John Rizzo of the CIA, among others.

"It was definitely the jacket-and-tie brigade," said Lieutenant Colonel Diane Beaver, a midlevel Army lawyer who advised the task force running interrogations. "When you're at the bottom of the pile" and you receive a visit from "the vice president's attorney, the CIA— I mean, this is an august group. You don't need to be told, 'This is important.'"

The visitors toured Camp Delta, most of its construction still improvised. When they asked to observe an interrogation, their hosts walked them to a double-wide trailer. A narrow corridor inside led to a room with a mirrored, one-way window, the kind you see on every TV cop show. The lawyers donned headphones and watched a "Tiger Team" throw questions at a young man wearing an orange jumpsuit and chained to a bolt on the floor. Each team had an FBI agent, an Army or Navy criminal investigator, and a military intelligence officer. They played by FBI rules, no rough stuff.

"Mr. Addington appeared to be the leader of the group, if you will," Beaver said. "Mr. Haynes by nature is quiet. . . . Addington was more vocal."

The visitors asked a lot of questions about Detainee 063, Mohammed Qahtani. Recent evidence suggested that Qahtani had tried to meet the lead plotter, Mohammed Atta, in Orlando a month before September 11. It was possible they had found the twentieth hijacker, somebody who might know what was coming next. The U.S. government believed another attack, maybe bigger, was on its way.

Addington and company, Beaver said, "were asking, 'What do we know about this guy? How much do we know? Have we got anything out of him?'"

Recalling the visit later, after being transferred to a Pentagon job that reported to Jim Haynes, Beaver took pains to cast no blame for anything untoward that may have happened next.

No one suggested she throw out the rule book, she said. There were no winks, no nods. Nothing more than a statement of plain fact: Qahtani might know something vital.

"They know you have important detainees like Qahtani, so yeah: 'Whatever you need to do to get the job done.' But not anything illegal," Beaver said. "Just that it's important. You should be working hard to get results, or these people wouldn't even be there."

"I didn't see it as pressure," she said. "Maybe other people did."

One of Addington's questions, Beaver said, gave her mission a new intensity.

"Are the medical doctors checking for vaccination marks on these detainees?" Addington asked. "Smallpox vaccinations?"

This was the consuming fear in the vice president's office, the nightmare scenario of a terrorist with a weapon of mass destruction. Smallpox, history's most lethal pathogen, had been eradicated in the human population. Dick Cheney, Scooter Libby, and David Addington focused great attention on the danger that al Qaeda might somehow get a live culture and set it loose in the United States.

"I thought that was insightful, but frightening all the same," Beaver recalled. "I remember thinking, 'Oh my gosh, they're actually talking about this at the White House,' where, you know, people who have vaccinations might be the ones testing smallpox virus." She added, "To me, it just brought home that I could be in a place where if al Qaeda could bring smallpox in, that's what al Qaeda would do."

As the visitors waited to board a ferry to their plane across the bay, Addington and one or two others stood off to the side. They were talking to Major General Michael Dunlavey, commander of Joint Task Force 170. Beaver did not hear what was said.

Dunlavey later told Philippe Sands, a British lawyer specializing in international tribunals, that Qahtani was resistant to questioning. "They wanted to know what we were doing to get to this guy, and Addington was interested in how we were managing it," Dunlavey said, according to Sands. "They brought ideas with them which had been given from sources in D.C."

General James T. Hill, the four-star chief of U.S. Southern Command, was the highest-ranking officer in the chain of command over Guantánamo that day. He did not learn until years afterward that Addington and his group had been there.

"It should never have happened that way," Hill said. "It should *never* have happened that way.

"Something of that magnitude should have been known by the guy in charge of the whole area, which was me," he said. "Because those are policy decisions. It was a high-ranking-enough party, with enough policy implications, that the guy in charge of the policy in that area—*me*—should have known about it, and should have been asked about it. Would I have said, 'Yes, let them come?' The answer's probably yes. Would I have sent my lawyer down there to be with them? Answer's yes."

By October 11, two weeks after the visitors departed, Major General Dunlavey had completed a twelve-page request for permission to begin more aggressive forms of questioning. He listed eighteen techniques, from hooding and yelling to isolation, stress positions, twenty-hour interrogations, and the use of "individual phobias (such as fear of dogs) to induce stress." He also asked permission for waterboarding. Diane Beaver, his lawyer, had four days to analyze the proposal. She wrote that members of the armed services who did some of those things would be committing crimes under the Uniform Code of Military Justice. There should be training and health safeguards in place. The legal problem might be solved, she wrote, with "permission or immunity in advance from the convening authority, for military members utilizing these methods."

There it was: the *ex ante* pardon. If the president gives authority, it's legal. According to disputed minutes of a meeting Beaver attended, a CIA lawyer conveyed John Yoo's analysis and added that the meaning of torture is "subject to perception."

In logs recording the subsequent handling of Detainee 063, Qahtani was stripped naked, shaved of his beard, menaced with dogs, bound in painful positions, subjected to extremes of heat and cold, and forcibly injected with intravenous tubes when he refused to eat or drink. Three teams of interrogators took turns with him, twenty out of twenty-four hours.

These were the rudiments of Soviet-style interrogation, denounced by Ronald Reagan and other pillars of the cold war in the annual Helsinki meetings on human rights. There were reports that Guantánamo methods were reverse engineered from the training

U.S. pilots received on how to withstand the abuses of the Soviet foreign intelligence service. "The basic KGB technique, they adopted—sleep deprivation, stress positions, cold," said Tom Malinowski, the senior Washington official for Human Rights Watch.

Over forty-nine days, the logs on Detainee 063 described the subject's reactions: "urinated on himself . . . began to cry . . . asked God for forgiveness . . . broke down and cried . . . bit the IV tube completely in two . . . moaning . . . began crying hard."

On the fiftieth day, Navy general counsel Alberto Mora threatened to file an official written protest, saying the methods employed against Qahtani "constituted, at a minimum, cruel and unusual treatment and, at worst, torture." Rumsfeld rescinded authority for the new methods the same day.

Another year passed, and the U.S. military replaced Saddam Hussein as landlord of Baghdad's Abu Ghraib prison. On January 13, 2004, a military police sergeant, disgusted by what he saw there, slipped a compact disc of photographs under a door at the Army's Criminal Investigation Command. The photos, hundreds of them, showed stomach-turning scenes—chained and naked Iraqi prisoners, cowering in terror before snarling dogs or piled in sexually humiliating poses. One iconic image featured a prisoner draped in a black shroud and clamped to electrodes. American soldiers in the photos gloated sadistically. CBS News obtained the photos and broadcast them.

"This is going to kill us," Alberto Gonzales murmured as the images played across his television screen, the volume turned down, in the last week of April.

As allies recoiled and public sentiment in Arab and Muslim countries turned savage, John Bellinger composed a memo for George

Bush. Bellinger told Condi Rice, his immediate superior, that the president had to demonstrate his outrage at a moment of national disgrace. He wrote a formal transmission memo, with a cover note to Rice and a draft directive from Bush to Rumsfeld. The president would tell the defense secretary that he was deeply troubled by this taint upon the nation, directing him to report back in thirty days with an explanation and a plan of action.

And then Bellinger found out something that, in three years as a top adviser to Rice, he had never known. Every time he wrote a memo to his boss, a blind copy was routed to the vice president's office. Libby, according to one official, made the arrangement with Steve Hadley, Rice's deputy. It was not advertised, and neither was it reciprocated: what happened in Cheney's office stayed in Cheney's office.

Someone there sent Bellinger's memo, intended as blunt, private advice, to Rumsfeld. His deputy, Paul Wolfowitz, phoned Hadley. This was an important channel in the Rumsfeld-Cheney alliance, and it worked in both directions. "Sometimes it was OSD to OVP to Hadley," one colleague said, using the initials for office of the secretary of defense and office of the vice president. "Sometimes it was OVP to OSD to Hadley." Five of Hadley's staffers said, in separate interviews, that the deputy national security adviser became nervous when either side was angry. Richard Armitage, the deputy secretary of state, said privately that Hadley was "Cheney's mole."

The president must absolutely not send that memo, Wolfowitz told Hadley. What are you doing over there? It would look like a slap at the defense secretary—as if the president believed the Abu Ghraib abuse had been policy.

Hadley phoned Bellinger.

"What are you doing?" Hadley asked. OSD, he said, is pretty steamed.

Bellinger's memo went through draft after draft. Rice and Hadley thought a more diplomatic version would be a good idea. After much toning down, Rice brought the draft directive to Bush. The president, the vice president, and the national security adviser consulted.

"The vice president talked him out of it," said one close observer of the episode.

John Yoo's torture memos, and the aggressive turn that interrogations took at Guantánamo, became public early that summer in a pair of stories by the *Wall Street Journal* and the *Washington Post*.

Cheney and Addington, with Gonzales going along, pressed Bush to ride out the storm—explain nothing, release nothing, reverse nothing. John Ashcroft dutifully took the heat in a Senate hearing, saying the government "rejects torture" but adding, "I am refusing to disclose these memos because I believe it is essential to the operation of the executive branch that the president have the opportunity to get information from his attorney general that is confidential." Other Bush advisers—including Dan Bartlett, Colin Powell, and Condi Rice—were horrified. They said the president had to jettison the torture opinions, and fast.

Before the White House could reach consensus, the Justice Department's Office of Legal Counsel pulled the plug. Yoo had departed, and so had Jay Bybee, his nominal boss. The new team said it would announce a retraction of the torture opinions on June 22.

Gonzales and Haynes scheduled a competing news conference that day. Yoo's memoranda, Gonzales told reporters, were exercises in "abstract . . . legal theory" that had nothing to do with the White House. "They're interesting for lawyers to debate," he said, but "in reality, they do not reflect the policies that the administration ulti-mately adopted."

That claim was breathtaking in its dishonesty. The most brutal interrogations ever sanctioned as government policy were under way as Yoo prepared his 2002 opinion. More than that: the opinion was commissioned specifically to give formal blessing to methods the vice president and war cabinet had authorized in the White House Situation Room. The CIA itself had never asked for a broad theory of torture and its limits. The agency only wanted a clear yes or no on a list of proposed techniques. Yoo delivered that in a separate and still-classified opinion. His fifty-page disquisition on torture, which gave legal guidance to the vice president and cabinet principals, was titled "Memorandum for Alberto R. Gonzales."

In an interview after leaving government, Yoo said Addington and Flanigan assisted in the preparation of that memo, with Gonza-les attending the meetings. Yoo did the writing, but the triumvirate reviewed the major lines of argument and portions of the draft.

Addington advocated the memo's most jarring claim: that the president may authorize any interrogation method, even if it indis-putably constitutes torture. U.S. and treaty laws forbidding "any" person to commit torture, that passage stated, "do not apply" to the commander in chief, because Congress "may no more regulate the President's ability to detain and interrogate enemy combatants than it may regulate his ability to direct troop movements on the battlefield."

At their June 22 news briefing, Gonzales and Haynes did not talk about those things. For nearly the whole two hours, they deflected attention toward a new trove of documents they chose to release that day. The Guantánamo interrogations, by their account, had been an up-from-the-bottom initiative.

Look over here: a memo from Major General Dunlavey, requesting tough new techniques. The legal work was all done down at the base. Some lieutenant colonel, it seemed, name of Diane Beaver. Haynes gave out her memo, left her name on it. Hundreds of news stories in coming weeks put the onus for abuse at Guantánamo on Beaver and her boss.

Another year passed, and Diane Beaver moved on to a new legal job at the Pentagon. She had been battered by her experience. She had also reconsidered: "If I had it to do all over again, I might have been more thoughtful about—" She stopped, collecting her thoughts. "Even if something's legal, you want to consider the policy implications," she said.

Jim Haynes was still the top lawyer at the Pentagon, a job that rated a power office on the E Ring. For a while, he had to move out for renovations. Visitors to his temporary suite, Room 3B710, traversed a narrow hallway past Beaver's desk.

Around Thanksgiving 2005, David Addington turned up. Beaver was in civilian clothes. He had not seen her for more than three years.

Addington remembered her, remembered her name. He remembered her opinion, too, the one that said permission from the top could immunize interrogators from charges of abuse. The president's delegated authority made any method lawful.

The White House and the Justice Department had abandoned that line of reasoning, at least in public. Beaver had walked away from it herself.

"I still think you were right," Addington said.

He smiled.

"Great minds think alike," he said.

He walked on down the hall to visit with Haynes.

The Bush administration stopped saying openly that there were no legal limits on the president's interrogation authority. But behind the standard talking points, the silhouettes of Cheney and Addington could still be made out. Critics lamented that the White House turned "torture" into an empty label. Spokesmen denied that the United States engaged in any such thing, but refused to discuss particulars. The critics missed something important. The formula was not empty. It was a syllogism, informed by the same old claim of unlimited power. "Torture" was *defined* as what "we do not condone," as Bush put it. Whatever Bush did permit, Al Gonzales said, "does not constitute torture."

Quod erat demonstrandum.

Chapter Eight

Matching the Science

Very early one morning, a voice-mail indicator began to blink in Room 6140 of the Interior Department. Sue Ellen Wooldridge played the message when she arrived.

"This is Dick Cheney. I understand you are the person handling this Klamath situation, and I have some questions. Please call me at—"

Long pause.

"I guess I don't know my own number. I'm over at the White House."

Yeah, right.

Who would fall for that? Wooldridge, forty, was the nineteenth-ranking official in a department that did not exactly bask in White House attention.

"I thought to myself, 'Someone is fucking with me,'" Wooldridge said.

She pressed *D on the keypad. Delete.

Late that afternoon, Wooldridge returned from a meeting.

Another message. Guy named Ron Christie from the White House. Cheney's deputy domestic policy adviser.

Any special reason, he asked, why you're not returning the vice president's call?

Oh, God.

Not a prank.

Really sorry.

There are three miles of corridors in the Interior headquarters, an austere limestone structure at Eighteenth and C streets Northwest. It has six wings, seven floors, and twenty-two hundred rooms.

Dick Cheney found his way through that labyrinth, to just the right woman in just the right place, because the thing on his mind at that moment was about to land on her desk. How he knew that, Cheney did not say. He liked to "reach down"—that was his term—through layers of management. He wanted his information direct, unfiltered. If a decision was coming, Cheney made sure to find out when and where and how it would be made.

"The vice president of the United States was and remains the consummate staffer," Christie said. "He understands how the bureaucracy works and, when the bureaucracy is not working, how to cut through it. He'd pick up the phone all the time and call people around the building and the government."

This time the vice president had spotted a political threat in Oregon, a battleground state that the Bush-Cheney ticket lost by less than half of 1 percent in 2000. Not to say the matter was only political. It looked like one of those big-government follies that got right under Cheney's skin.

Thousands of farmers and ranchers were struggling to keep their croplands and pastures from turning to dust. Drought had struck hard in the Klamath River basin, just north of the California border. Growers were counting on a century-old complex of dams and canals to irrigate four hundred square miles of potato and alfalfa and grazing range.

All of a sudden the Bureau of Reclamation was getting ready to close the gates. Federal biologists announced that the Endangered Species Act left the government no choice: survival was at stake for three imperiled species of fish. Divert the water, they said, and the fish might die.

This was just the kind of thing that drove so many Westerners around the bend. Bad enough that the federal government owned half the land in thirteen states, a fact that East Coast visitors had a hard time even believing. Now some bureaucrat in Washington was going to tell a whole farming region, a quarter million acres, to shut down for a season and kiss its crops good-bye?

For what? Shortnose suckers. Lost River suckers. Coho salmon.

"They swim upstream and up to the ocean, where they are caught by fishermen and served up on plates in San Francisco," said Roger Marzulla, a lawyer representing the irrigators. "What kind of endangered species is this? If you really want more salmon, open a hatchery!"

The thing did not make any more sense to Cheney. He picked up his telephone.

There would be plenty of interventions to come, most of them invisible. Other at-risk species, from right whales and polar bears to cutthroat trout, would give way to the vice president's priorities on commerce, recreation, and energy. Car, truck, and coal plant emissions would be viewed through the lens of supply and demand. Snowmobiles and those who loved them would attract an unexpected bounty of attention.

Yellowstone Park, the nation's oldest, would be nominated for removal from the list of protected World Heritage Sites after Paul Hoffman, a former Cheney aide, rewrote the park staff's professional assessment. "We sent the report back and forth a couple of times," said John Varley, then director of the park resource center. "Paul made it very clear that the administration wanted to get Yellowstone off that list." That move, it emerged, would permit construction of a coal-fired power plant in the Bull Mountains nearby, which Interior Department scientists identified as a threat to the park. Still later, a smart reporter noticed that applications had quintupled around the country for permits to build coal-powered plants near national parks. "We can have our power and clean air too," Hoffman told the *Washington Post*.

No one filed an environmental impact statement on the vice president. Cheney worked through proxies, and proxies of proxies. Well into the second term, Cheney's influence—on air and water quality, wildlife protection, and preservation of parklands—remained largely unknown to public interest groups and congressional committees. It was scarcely better understood in the White House. Press secretary Scott McClellan, whose memoir called Cheney "the magic man," described the vice president's range of influence in the usual limited terms: energy, national security, and executive power.

There is a fascinating artifact of Cheney's stealth in the *Federal Register,* whose three columns of small gray type do not often inspire that adjective. Cheney arrived in office to find a gold mine of authority over environmental and other rules. None other than Bill Clinton conferred it on him, aiming, at the time, for Al Gore. In Executive Order 12866, Clinton established that "the Vice President is the principal advisor to the President on, and shall coordinate the development and presentation of recommendations concerning, regulatory policy, planning, and review." Nearly any power seeker in Washington would seize upon that kind of mandate.

Cheney accepted the power, but not the public profile. Bush amended Clinton's order twice, in 2002 and 2007. The president concentrated greater authority in the White House, requiring central approval for "policy guidance" by federal agencies, not only for regulations. Bush changed one other thing, at Cheney's request. He deleted every reference to the vice president, all twenty-five of them, from Clinton's order. Cheney would wield all the regulatory power that Gore did, and more, but the government's official record showed no sign of him. Rather than directing the process openly, Cheney interceded through allies at the Office of Management and Budget, including at various times two former top aides, the man who played John Edwards in his campaign debate rehearsals and his son-in-law, Philip J. Perry. As in the Klamath case, Cheney also worked through eager-to-please staffs at Interior, Commerce, Energy, and their subagencies.

"We gave him [proposed] changes to endangered animals, when they were listed or delisted," and tracked rule-making issues in other departments, said Karen Knutson, a member of the vice president's domestic staff. One time it was something about an endangered minnow playing hell with the water supply in Albuquerque. Another time, a new glitch in the Yucca Mountain nuclear storage plan. Cheney worked to undo an order banning timber cutting and road building in national forests, arranging broad exceptions that were justified in terms of fire prevention.

"Make sure the process is run on this, so there will be a full policy analysis," Cheney told Knutson.

The White House review process, he meant, preventing the agency from acting without approval. The vice president might want to put an oar in.

"I saw him weighing in on almost all of the panoply of issues," said Jay Lefkowitz, who was then deputy general counsel at the Office of Management and Budget. "Lots of environmental issues early on. The administration inherited a whole bunch of regulatory issues from the Clinton administration." Roadless rule, arsenic rule, snow-mobile rule. "There were a lot of those rules, and he had a staff that kept him fully advised."

The Klamath basin episode was the granddaddy of all interventions. Like most of the others, it involved a policy objective that ran up against law and science. Cheney took them both on, one at a time.

Bob Smith was a worried man. A former Oregon congressman who served with Dick Cheney on the House Interior Committee, he represented increasingly desperate farmers. When Cheney phoned during the transition for advice on appointees, Smith took the opportunity to bend his ear about Klamath. The vice president, Smith said, shared his views on property rights and the ill effects of government meddling.

"He saw, as every other person did, what a ridiculous disaster shutting off the water was," Smith said. "He understands how cherished water is. Water is our existence, our future."

Whose existence, though? Property did not have much to do with the question. It was big-government action that Smith and his clients wanted. The public owned the water, the dams, and the land on which the river flowed. The issue was who would get how much of a scarce government resource.

"There's a saying: 'Whiskey's for drinking because water's for fighting over,'" said Paul Hoffman, the former congressional aide to Cheney who went on to land two senior posts at Interior.

Upstream, at the river's source, Native American tribes wanted to keep the waters high in Upper Klamath Lake, where they fished for subsistence and income. Their interests aligned with the two endangered species of suckers, because federal scientists said low lake levels would harm the fish. Farmers and ranchers wanted the lake water to flow downstream, but depended on diverting it from the river to their land. Commercial fishermen and native tribes farther downstream, whose interests aligned with the threatened salmon, opposed the diversion for farmers.

The law gave strongest protection to the fish and the native tribes. The Endangered Species Act was categorical: the government could not take a step that would harm protected wildlife. When economic claims came into play, the tribes had water rights that preceded those of the farmers. Federal courts had given them a "priority date" of "time immemorial."

The political economies of Oregon and Washington pointed elsewhere.

Long before others at the White House, Cheney perceived a threat to the Republican Party. The Jim Jeffords defection, brought about in no small measure by Cheney himself, had left the Senate effectively in Democratic hands. White House hopes for taking back control depended on winning tight races in the 2002 midterm election. Oregon's GOP senator, Gordon Smith, faced a well-funded challenger. The Bush administration could not afford to anger thousands of solidly Republican farmers and ranchers.

The vice president was the first to see something that "at first blush didn't seem like a big deal," but actually had "a lot of political ramifications," said Dylan Glenn, a special assistant to Bush who got involved later. The case became a test as well for national conservatives who looked to the White House to draw new lines between environmental and economic interests. Karl Rove and the White

House Office of Political Affairs took up the Klamath issue, too, months after Cheney did.

"This wasn't about fish. It was about politics," said California representative Mike Thompson, a Democrat, who emphasized the next presidential campaign. "They thought they could influence voters in '04 by siding with the agricultural interests. The president wanted to win six electoral votes in Oregon."

Sometime after Bob Smith spoke to Cheney, the telephone rang on Ron Christie's desk. White House telephones show caller ID by name. Christie glanced at the display. It said "The VP."

"Hello, it's Dick," the vice president said. "I want you to look into something. The Klamath basin."

"What is that?"

"It's out on the border of California and Oregon."

Big fight about water, Cheney said. Track it down.

Christie came back with a briefing. The Endangered Species Act did not leave a lot of room for maneuver.

"What does the statute say?" Cheney asked.

In detail, he meant. Christie explained.

"Isn't there some way around it?" Cheney asked.

Right about then, the vice president decided it was time to check on Interior. His staff scouted ahead, trying to find out who had the big picture on Klamath. There were too many offices involved—the Fish and Wildlife Service, Bureau of Reclamation, National Marine Fisheries Service, Environmental Protection Agency. The list went on.

Sue Ellen Wooldridge was deputy chief of staff to interior secretary Gale Norton. She got tagged with the assignment.

Cheney never told Wooldridge what to do or how to do it. That was not the way he worked, not usually. Cheney set a goal, an outcome.

What the vice president said, according to Wooldridge, was: "If we're going to put a bunch of farmers out of business, we've got a problem. We've got a massive problem." The department was aware of the problem, she said, but Cheney's call "heightened our attention to it and our need to make sure we were paying attention."

Cheney made sure attention did not wander. According to Bob Smith, the vice president called the interior secretary to emphasize his interest. Cheney's staff called Wooldridge every week.

"I never got any directives," Wooldridge said, only questions: "What is the status? What is happening? What decisions do you need to make? What discretion do you have?"

Every week Cheney's schedule included a briefing from his domestic policy staff. The evening before each briefing, Ron Christie and his boss, Cesar Conda, delivered a memo for the vice president to take home. He liked to read at night. The memo offered background on the issue of the week: the budget, Bush's education plan, Social Security.

Nearly every week, month after month, Cheney finished each briefing with a question.

"So, Ron, what about a Klamath update?"

By spring, protests against the federal water cutoff were edging toward violence. Farmers and their families organized a symbolic bucket brigade of eighteen thousand men and women on May 7, 2001, then staged raids in June and July, using blowtorches and a chain saw to open irrigation gates that the Bureau of Reclamation welded shut. Some of them clashed with U.S. marshals, who were called out when local law enforcement officers refused to intervene. One group of protesters formed a mounted cavalry, organizing a "Klamath T Party" of civil disobedience. Antigovernment forces from out of state, including militia activists from Montana, Michigan, Idaho, and Nevada, gathered in August for a "Freedom Day" demonstration at Klamath Falls.

Even after September 11, amid all the intensity of war, Cheney returned with discipline to the river and the farmers and the fish.

"It became a sort of running joke with me and Cesar," Christie recalled. "The thing that was not on the agenda but that always was on the agenda."

Usually, "I'd say, 'Things aren't going well.' It was so emotionally charged—you had farmers sitting in front of the locks. It was a very explosive situation. He did not accept that we couldn't find a way to make sure that the farmers could farm and the fishermen could fish and the environment could be adequately taken care of. He was adamant: there had to be a solution."

At around the same time, in August, Cheney lost patience on another issue. He had made clear since February, when the energy task force got going, that he placed a high priority on easing pollution controls on coal-fired power plants and oil refineries. Months had passed with no result.

Christine Todd Whitman, the former New Jersey governor, had known the vice president since they both worked for Don Rumsfeld in the Nixon administration. Cheney got her the job as administrator of the Environmental Protection Agency. She was not working out.

Whitman's cell phone rang in Steamboat Springs, Colorado, where she was enjoying the alpine meadows with her husband, John, and their two kids.

Cheney's tone was brusque.

Why was EPA dragging its feet on emission rules? Cheney had

promised change. The president had signed his task force report three months before.

"You haven't moved it fast enough," Cheney said.

Whitman disagreed. She was responsible for enforcement of the Clean Air Act. It was one of the touchstone achievements of the environmental movement in the 1960s and 1970s, along with parallel laws on water quality, wildlife, and preservation of parklands "unimpaired for the enjoyment of future generations." Protecting air quality saved a lot of lives, and it happened to be popular with voters. Cheney's sympathies leaned more toward the conservative backlash that began in the Reagan administration. Environmentalists were a special interest that had tilted the law too far against industry and recreation.

One of Whitman's jobs under the Clean Air Act was known as "new source review." A lot of old smog and soot-producing plants were grandfathered against rules requiring modern pollution controls. If they upgraded their facilities, they became a "new source" of pollution and had to install scrubbing technology. The only exception was for routine repair and maintenance. For years, the industry game had been to see how much a plant could upgrade or expand and call it maintenance. During the Clinton administration, electrical utilities and oil refiners complained bitterly that they were hit with undeserved federal lawsuits and penalties.

Dick Cheney was one of the complainers. As chairman of Halliburton, he helped prepare an industry study in mid-2000 that denounced "recent EPA enforcement actions," saying they "could significantly hinder the industry's ability to continue its historical capacity expansion rate." Not so coincidentally, Cheney's energy task force took the same view one year later. The final report directed Whitman "to encourage the development" of new heat and power plants by reducing the time required for permits and "ensuring consistent implementation" of the rules. In plain English: back off the Clinton enforcement standards, and get rid of the pending lawsuits.

During task force meetings, Whitman had been stunned by unquestioned claims that the EPA was responsible for stifling new construction. "I was upset, mad, offended that there seemed to be so much head nodding around the table," she said.

Back then, Cheney tried to take "new source" enforcement away from Whitman altogether, floating a proposal to shift the job to the Energy Department. Whitman fought "tooth and nail," appealing to White House chief of staff Andrew Card. She agreed that the agency ought to clarify the meaning of "routine repair and maintenance," but not in a way that undercut the ongoing Clinton lawsuits. A lot of them had merit, she said.

Whitman proposed a political trade with industry. New source rules would be eliminated. Instead, polluters would buy emission rights. Let the market work its magic. Whitman did not find any takers. Cheney was offering to drop enforcement for free.

On the telephone now from Steamboat Springs, Whitman warned the vice president that the Bush administration had to move cautiously. She could not redefine "routine repair and maintenance" so broadly that everything qualified.

"Document this according to the books," Whitman told Cheney, "so we don't look like we are ramrodding something through. Because it's going to court."

"I felt if we took it to the point where the cases went away," it would look completely illegitimate, she said. Cheney just "wanted it done fast . . . in a way that didn't hamper industry."

Though still feeling the sting of her last attempt, when Cheney rolled her so easily on global warming, Whitman asked for a meeting with the president. She brought an armful of news clippings and laid them in two stacks on the Oval Office coffee table.

This stack, she told Bush, pointing to the short one, two and a half inches high, was the press reaction to the arsenic decision. Cheney had backed that one, too: the White House reversed a Clinton administration rule to cut arsenic in drinking water from a maximum fifty parts per billion to ten. The World Health Organization, the European Union, and American public health research had set the new arsenic standard. The White House review team said it needed more study.

Whitman pointed to the second stack of articles, four or five times taller.

"If you think arsenic was bad," she told Bush, "look at what has already been written" about the proposal to back off air pollution controls. She was appealing to her shared history with Bush as a pragmatic, environmentally moderate governor.

It was exactly the wrong thing to say, if Cheney had any influence on the president. You didn't govern by opinion polls, and you didn't trim sound policy in hope of persuading the news media to make nice.

Cheney sat impassive, saying nothing while Whitman was in the room. She walked out with a feeling that "the decision had already been made."

Cheney made no effort to impede her access to Bush, Whitman said. But there was nothing she could do about the fact that "you leave and the vice president's still there. So together, they would then shape policy."

Long story short, the White House review process gutted the rules. Instead of measuring actual emissions, the EPA would compare the pollution levels of an expanded plant against the "potential" emissions before the upgrade. "Potential" was defined as the theoretical output of pollutants if the original plant had operated twenty-four hours a day, seven days a week. Which, in fact, it had not. The rules also redefined "routine repair and maintenance" to permit an upgrade of up to 20 percent of a facility each year. Over five years, the nation's dirtiest plants could rebuild themselves from the ground up without installing new technology to cut emissions.

Whitman announced her resignation, with the usual Washington dodge about spending more time with her family.

"I just couldn't sign it," she said. "The president has a right to have an administrator who could defend it, and I just couldn't."

Whitman warned Cheney there would be a legal fight, and there was. A federal appeals court rejected the 20 percent rule, saying the White House had redefined the Clean Air Act in a way that could be valid "only in a Humpty-Dumpty world."

By then, the former New Jersey governor was long gone. So was Eric Schaeffer, the chief of EPA's Office of Regulatory Enforcement.

In his resignation letter, Schaeffer said the nine companies he sued "emit an incredible 5 million tons of sulfur dioxide every year (a quarter of the emissions in the entire country) as well as 2 million tons of nitrogen oxide." The agency's uncontested scientific data showed that 10,800 people died prematurely each year because of that pollution. The White House, he said, had snatched "defeat from the jaws of victory" because most of the plant owners had been ready to settle. Two of them withdrew from consent decrees.

As the second Bush-Cheney term neared an end, final rules had yet to be written or enforced.

"Every day you can postpone saves them a lot of money," Schaeffer said in an interview, speaking of plant owners. "It's a *lot* of money.

In the long run, finally, finally, most of these power plants will have scrubbers, but they've dragged it out for thirty years."

Early in the Klamath debate, the Interior Department passed word to Cheney that there was a procedure for exemptions in the Endangered Species Act. He did not have to find a way around the law. The vice president could ask Interior to convene the "God Squad."

A panel of seven cabinet officials, known formally as the Endangered Species Committee, could grant the farmers their water if it found that their hardship was grave enough to warrant extinction of protected wildlife. It was a high bar to clear, but every member of the panel would be a Bush appointee.

Cheney rejected that course, according to Bob Smith. Convening the panel would have been a public act, and very controversial. The Bush administration would openly have to "play God and decide that because of the hardships . . . we're essentially going to let the species go," Wooldridge said.

Cheney had another idea. The law did not seem to be helping. Maybe they ought to go after the science.

By that time, Wooldridge said, "everybody had their own scientists. The irrigators had their own scientists saying the science used by Fish and Wildlife Service was wrong. The Indians had scientists. It was a science war."

The vice president understood immediately, aides said, that he did not have to win that war. All he really needed was a draw. If scientists had no consensus against a diversion of water, then the law would cease to be an obstacle. Science here was a little bit like Alan Greenspan in the tax cut of 2001. Endorsement would be nice, but ambiguity served fine.

"We have to match the science," Cheney said, according to Smith.

Two federal agencies had already issued formal Biological Opinions. Cheney told Smith he would bring in the National Academy of Sciences, a society of distinguished academics who volunteered their advice under government charter.

That sounded like a roll of the dice to Smith. Academy panels were politically independent. Their members received no payment and had to reach conclusions that could withstand peer review. "It worried me that these are individuals who are unreachable," Smith said.

Cheney expressed no such concern.

"The National Academy of Sciences is a very busy institution," Smith said. "To create a priority in a small place in a small corner of the country is difficult, and that's what he helped us do. He called them and said, 'Please look at this—it's important. Please go out and take a look at that.'"

Cheney left no trail. William Kearney, a staff member there, said he had canvassed his colleagues, and "as far as I know the vice president never contacted the National Academy of Sciences regarding Klamath."

It was interior secretary Gale Norton who announced in October 2001 that the academy would be asked to take on the case. Cheney did not need to twist her arm. Norton made her name at the Mountain States Legal Foundation, fighting federal regulators in court. Her boss there was James Watt, the Reagan administration interior secretary who once proposed to sell off national parklands.

But even cabinet secretaries could not make the academy jump. There was a lengthy application process, and studies were usually scheduled long in advance. Rounding up panel members, from all around the country, normally took still more time. At least one request for a Klamath study had already been languishing for months.

Once Cheney got involved, Smith said, "everyone just went flying at it."

Smith said that "everyone chipped in, including the vice president," to prepare the formal request: "Petitioned them. Pointing out the issues. The problems. And making them recognize that this is really a national issue."

As the vice president had demonstrated before, the right question made all the difference. Cheney did not ask the academy how much water the fish needed, or how much danger they faced. He made a much smarter inquiry, for his purpose: Just how sure was the evidence that fish would die if water levels fell?

Environmental science depends on models, not controlled experiment. Certainty is elusive.

Cheney was not looking for answers. He was shopping for doubts.

"We had four documents to review," said Suzanne Van Drunick, the study director. "And the charge was very, very narrow. Just to review those four documents."

For the initial report, the only one that mattered for the current growing season, the academy did its business in a single sitting.

"We had one meeting on November 9, after the committee was assembled, and decided what the findings were," Van Drunick said. A thirty-seven-page report was drafted and circulated for external review. By January 2002, the panel had released its interim findings. "That's a whirlwind schedule," she said.

William M. Lewis, who chaired the panel, said his report "was produced very quickly because the Bureau of Reclamation was under a lot of pressure over how to manage water in the upcoming year. Because they were taking a lot of heat from the [affected] farms."

What the panel found, he said, was that "there wasn't enough evidence to justify severe water management practices as a reliable way of preventing damage to the species of concern."

That formula troubled other academy scientists, and the Klamath report provoked an unusual degree of academic controversy. The academy was not supposed to consider the "severity" of water management or the consequences of withholding water from farmers.

"The protocol is you do the science first without this sort of big shadow," said Stuart Pimm, a biologist who is a member of the academy and of the committee that appoints its panels. "Many people raised their eyebrows," he said, at "the fact that economic interests seemed to be coming to the table."

The Lewis committee "went beyond the science," Pimm said. "They went in and adjudicated water rights."

Bob Smith, the farmers' lobbyist, was ecstatic.

"Now we had science on our side," he said.

George Bush and Karl Rove flew to Oregon with the good news in February 2002, assuring farmers and ranchers of their support.

Interior's Bureau of Reclamation took the academy's report as a green light to give the farmers their maximum allocation of water. J. B. Ruhl, a co-author of the academy's report, said the bureau's move was not "supported by our recommendations." The panel had said it did not know how much water the fish needed, "not that more water wouldn't be better," according to Van Drunick, the study director.

Gale Norton flew out to Klamath on March 29, 2002, with plenty of television coverage, to open the headgate as farmers chanted, "Let the water flow!" And seizing on the report's draft findings, the Bureau of Reclamation wrote a new ten-year plan that gave the farmers the same generous share every year. The needs of native tribes and

California fishermen would be addressed by new water sources, as yet unidentified.

A senior Interior biologist said the ten-year plan was scientifically baseless. Politically appointed superiors deleted those objections from his report. The biologist, Michael Kelly, resigned and said in a whistle-blower claim that "someone at a higher level" had plainly given the orders. Later, a federal appellate court would rule that the ten-year Klamath plan did not even pretend to support the endangered species until year nine. By then, "all the water in the world" would not save the fish, "for there will be none to protect."

In late September 2002, the first of an estimated seventy-seven thousand dead salmon began washing up on the banks of the Klamath River where it passed through Yurok tribal lands. The threatened cohos were dying—but so, in even larger numbers, were chinook salmon, the staple of commercial fishing in northern California. State and federal biologists found other contributing factors, but the studies agreed that the kill would not have happened without the diversion of water to farms. As California's Department of Fish and Game noted in a lengthy analysis, the only risk factor "that can be controlled to any degree" is the amount of water diverted to irrigation.

Cheney achieved his objective. The 2002 planting season was saved. The farmers farmed. The native tribes, the fishermen, and the fish themselves bore the brunt.

Had the national academy not given him support, according to his aide Ron Christie, Cheney would have considered other options.

"The situation resolved itself before we had to pull out all the tricks in our bag," Christie said.

Chapter Nine

DEMONSTRATION EFFECT

The vice president leaned over a coffee table, unrolling secret documents across the top. He had an audience of one. It was late September 2002, the same week David Addington flew to Gitmo. A different theater of war held Cheney's attention today. Dick Armey, the House majority leader, had strayed off message. Way off. Armey saw no need for a scrap with Saddam Hussein, and he did not mind saying so in public. Saddam was a tyrant and a clown, okay. But a menace to the United States of America? Come on. The White House pulled out all the stops to change Armey's mind. Bush invited him for a parlay in the Cabinet Room, flew him to Camp David, arranged a special briefing from George Tenet. Armey did not budge. He was Cheney's project now.

And so here sat the majority leader on a couch in room H-208, the vice president's borrowed Capitol hideaway. Cheney took a facing chair, coffee table between them, looking his old friend in the eye. They had been allies going on eighteen years, Armey following Cheney up the GOP ladder in the House. Cheney could still give a briefing with the best of them. He had that knack for reading upside down, turning a document so the other guy could see. Cheney laid out big maps and photographs, some of them more than three feet long. The vice president was ready to open the bag, let Armey in on secrets he had never heard before.

"I want to share with you some things, and I know when I'm done you will agree with me that this is the right course of action," Cheney said. It was a curious opening. "He didn't say 'agree with the president,'" Armey recalled. "He said 'agree with me.' I don't know why that stuck in my craw." Armey and Cheney were already cast as point and counterpoint. The vice president had been beating war drums since August 7. If someone did not stop Saddam, "it's the judgment of many of us that in the not-too-distant future he will acquire nuclear weapons," Cheney said. Armey chose the very next day to say Bush should let the Iraqi leader "rant and rave all he wants." Armey told reporters, "I don't believe that America will justifiably make an unprovoked attack on another nation."

This guy was no Mod Squad Republican. A tax-hating Texas good ol' boy, Armey favored armadillo boots and had earned a lifetime rating of 97 percent from the American Conservative Union. He was co-architect of the Republican Revolution of 1994, a promilitary Republican with a Republican commander in chief. He should have been an easy vote on Iraq. Instead, Armey had made himself one of Cheney's pivot points. Congress would decide on war authority, yes or no, in another two weeks. A lot of members were unsure, but no one liked to look weak in an election year. "You remember, at the time Congress was in a panic about this," Armey recalled. "Everybody was scared to be seen as the guy that didn't want to go cut somebody's throat." If Armey could oppose the war, he gave cover to every doubter in waiting. Look at it that way, and Armey became the center of gravity of the political opposition. Cheney had to neutralize him, end of story. "I was in a position, they feared, to stop the legislation," Armey said.

Cheney prepared carefully, a habit of decades. For a full hour he walked the majority leader through a blood-chilling narrative, the graphics produced on cue by a military aide. The vice president by then had dialed up his public rhetoric, warning not only that Saddam had an arsenal but that "the United States may well become the target." What he told Armey was worse. "The upshot of the briefing is, it's a gathering threat that's really *more* imminent than we want to portray to the public at large," Armey recalled.

In the privacy of his office, for this one crucial vote, Cheney leveled claims he had not made before and did not make again. Two of them crossed so far beyond the known universe of fact that they were simply without foundation.

The vice president brought the disquieting news that Iraq's "ability to miniaturize weapons of mass destruction, particularly nuclear," had been "substantially refined since the first Gulf War," Armey recalled. Cheney mentioned biological weapons, too, but the nuclear part made the biggest impression. "They were developing weapons, they were miniaturizing weapons, developing packages that could be moved even by ground personnel," Armey said. It was the suitcase-nuke scenario, the ultimate nightmare. Why had Armey not heard about this from Tenet? Well, because the CIA had not even entertained the hypothesis. U.S. intelligence got a lot of things wrong, but not *that* wrong. Several agencies assessed (incorrectly, it turned out) that Saddam's government was shopping for equipment to enrich uranium. None of them claimed to have evidence that Iraq was making progress on warhead design. Iraq produced partial schematics for two types of weapons in the 1980s, but "they didn't know how to build a bomb, period," said a government scientist with a central role in assessing the evidence before the war. Neither of the Iraqi designs would have fit a missile, let alone a suitcase, and neither of them would have worked as they were drawn. Four months before Cheney sat down with Armey, the Defense Intelligence Agency acknowledged that there was "no firm evidence of a current nuclear weapon design effort." (It cited no infirm evidence, either.) The other intelligence agencies concurred.

According to Armey, Cheney also reported that al Qaeda was "working with Saddam Hussein and members of his family." What that meant, Cheney said, was that "we now know they have the ability to develop these weapons in a very portable fashion, and they have a delivery system in their relationship with organizations such as al Qaeda." Inside the government, Cheney and Scooter Libby were in a distinct minority of officials—backed by none of the fourteen U.S. intelligence offices—who maintained that Iraq and al Qaeda had operational links. But even the vice president did not claim to have evidence for what he told Armey: that Saddam had personal ties to Osama bin Laden's terrorist network.

Some of Cheney's talking points had more support, at least at the time. Cheney unrolled a full-scale photograph of an aluminum tube, three feet long and three inches in diameter. Intelligence officers had intercepted thousands on their way to Iraq. Cheney told Armey they were centrifuge rotors made of highly specialized aluminum—an alloy called 7075 T6, the strongest known. With that many centrifuges, Saddam could enrich enough uranium for a bomb in under a year. *I got an aluminum tube looks just like that,* Armey thought. *Keep my fly rod in it. Seen irrigation pipe out west, looks like that, too.* Armey did not say so. "I was trying to be respectful, without being openly cynical," he said. "I had to sort of take the vice president's word on what are these things I'm looking at. Because what do I know? I assumed that what he's telling me is verifiable intel."

What Cheney told Armey was not a fact, but the CIA did promote it as a theory. A midlevel analyst named Joe Turner had come up with the idea that the tubes were centrifuge parts. He was an engineer working in export controls, not a scientist. A full year before Cheney briefed Armey, the Energy Department asked eminent nuclear physicists to evaluate the tubes. Houston G. Wood III, founder of the centrifuge department at Oak Ridge National Laboratory, said he and his colleagues reported they could not imagine a way to use the tubes for uranium enrichment. Science discourages talk of the impossible, he said, but "I would like to see, if they're going to make that claim, that they have some explanation of how you do that. Because I don't see how you do it."

An alternative explanation for the tubes had been in hand since 1996, when UN inspectors discovered thousands of them on a rocket assembly line at the Nasr Company, a few miles north of Baghdad. Even so, six years later, Cheney had CIA support. The agency backed Turner to the hilt, commending him for outstanding service. The idea that Saddam wanted the tubes for artillery rockets, Turner said, was a transparent cover story. Nobody would use a specialized alloy for something so basic.

Cheney unrolled more big sheets, satellite photos of Tuwaitha, Ash Shaykhili, and other nuclear sites that UN inspectors destroyed between 1991 and 1995, after Iraq's defeat in the first Persian Gulf War. There were new roofs, new construction. Iraq was reconstituting its nuclear establishment. *What does a roof tell you?* Armey thought. *Who knows what's under there?*

Armey could not put his finger on it, but something felt wrong. "I remember leaving the meeting with a very deep sadness about my relationship with Dick Cheney," he said. "It's an intuition thing. I felt like, 'I think I just got a good BS'ing.' If you'll pardon the Texas vernacular, I felt like I deserved better from Cheney than to be bullshitted by him. I reckon that's about as plainspoken as I can put it."

Cheney barely mentioned to Armey the central point of his briefing three weeks earlier for the Gang of Four—the Senate majority and minority leaders, the Speaker of the House, and the House minority leader. Cheney had asked to see them on September 3, immediately after the Labor Day recess, with utmost urgency. There was alarming new intelligence about Iraq's unmanned aerial vehicles, or UAVs. In the 1980s Iraq had tried to fit the drones with sprayers for biological agents. Now Iraq had another UAV program. (The Air Force Intelligence Agency, the U.S. government's main source of expertise on UAVs, assessed the purpose as reconnaissance, not biowar. Cheney did not mention that.) The really ominous part, the vice president said, was a recent discovery that Iraq had clandestinely acquired electronic maps of the eastern United States. Connect the dots: Saddam could put drone aircraft on a freighter, steam them across the Atlantic, and use the route-planning software to dispatch lethal microbes anywhere from Miami to Boston.

Cheney's briefings on the tubes, the roofs, and the drones were already controversial in September, subjects of dispute inside the intelligence world. Soon afterward, the U.S. government acquired powerful new evidence that the threats the vice president described did not exist. Cheney did not choose to correct the record. Armey and the Gang of Four did not learn until years later that important pillars of Cheney's argument had turned to sand.

The CIA theory of the aluminum tubes fell apart when UN inspectors returned to Iraq in November 2002. At least one American, a Los Alamos employee named Frank Pabian, was on the team that reached the Nasr plant on November 18, the first of several visits to check the Iraqi rocket story. Sure enough, the inspectors found production lines and files recording the manufacture of thirteen thousand artillery rockets. Conventional weapons, nothing illegal. There were plenty of aluminum tubes on hand, but open-air storage corroded them. Thousands of half-built rockets, with motors and fins, sat crated at the assembly lines, awaiting new tubes. Inspectors also solved the mystery of the special aluminum alloy. Iraqi scientists had copied an Italian rocket called the Medusa, which used identical tubes—same special alloy, same dimensions. Pabian brought back samples in December. Joe Turner stuck to his story, but it turned into that old barstool joke: Who you gonna believe, me or your own lying eyes? Same went for the new roofs on old buildings. UN inspectors, again with Americans among them, visited Tuwaitha and the other suspected nuclear sites on December 6, 7, 9, 10, and 11, 2002. They were under the roofs, walking around inside. No forbidden program. Around the same time, the report about Iraq's purchase of electronic U.S. maps was debunked at the source. The Australian Secret Intelligence Service notified the CIA that its initial information was wrong. It turned out that an Australian vendor, pitching the sale of unrelated equipment, offered to throw in commercial mapping software. Iraq declined.

By the end of 2002, nearly three months before the United States' invasion of Iraq, the Bush administration knew those things. Leaders in Congress did not. Faced with so much certainty, Armey lost faith in his doubts. The vice president had found his pivot point, nudged an obstacle, and tipped the result, just as he did on taxes and torture and global warming. Armey shut up about the war. Later, when he discovered the truth, Armey found it hard to swallow. "If I tell you something and it turns out I later find out, 'Gee, I wasn't right about that,' I think I have a responsibility to come back and tell you otherwise," he said. "Did Dick Cheney, a fellow who had been my trusted friend—did he purposely tell me things he knew to be untrue? I will go so far as to say I seriously feel that may be the case. I can't know that, but I am seriously concerned that might have been the case." He added, "Had I known or believed then what I believe I know now, I would have publicly opposed this resolution right to the bitter end, and I believe I might have stopped it from happening, and I believe I'd have done a better service to my country had I done so."

A great big spiderweb of a chart, traced across poster-size sheets of artist's stock, mapped the terrain of Cheney's fears after September 11. David Wurmser, forty, the Swiss-born neoconservative who drew it, was connecting dots he believed the CIA had missed. He worked "in splendid isolation, just thinking, researching" his long-held theories about terrorists and the states that sponsored them. In his previous studies, at the American Enterprise Institute, Wurmser relied on open source material. For a time he had access to classified information as a Navy reservist, assigned one weekend a month as a desk officer at the Defense Intelligence Agency. But Wurmser's job in the Alert Center, watching incoming threat reports, offered little opportunity to probe subjects of interest. In October 2001, a Cheney ally in the Defense Department gave Wurmser access to the raw intelligence files he craved. Douglas Feith, the undersecretary for policy, set Wurmser up in an office on the D Ring of the Pentagon's second floor. The cramped work space, inside a communications center called OSD Cables, came equipped with a terminal for the Joint Worldwide Intelligence Communications System, or JWICS. With security clearances approved by Feith, Wurmser now had direct access to a wide array of sensitive source materials. His research blossomed. The spiderweb, depicting links among states and terrorist groups, grew more intricate.

"It covered half the wall," Wurmser said. "Sadly, it looked like that scene in *A Beautiful Mind*." The movie, he meant. The one where

Russell Crowe played a delusional genius who covered a shed with charts of imagined conspiracy. Wurmser knew about the jokes some people made, but he also knew what he believed. For months he drew lines through data points—names, phone numbers, places, dates—and deduced relationships where the lines converged. "Link analysis," which Wurmser described as his method, is a burgeoning field in applied mathematics, and intelligence services hope it will one day bring order to their vast electronic files. The field is not yet ripe. One challenge is filtering noise in the system—the false, imprecise, and outdated reports that coexist with valuable leads. The mathematical problem is more basic: Even if all your data are perfect, how do you distinguish meaningful links from trivial coincidence? Wurmser concerned himself with none of that, relying on intuition and inference.

In his early twenties, Wurmser worked on *Hydra of Carnage,* a study published in 1985 that found signs of Soviet sponsorship in apparently unrelated acts of terrorism. Feith contributed a chapter. Wurmser wanted to update *Hydra,* but his ambition did not stop there. "I imagined something very much like George Kennan's 'Long Telegram,' maybe even NSC-68," he said. Those were seminal works of twentieth-century foreign policy, the intellectual foundations of the cold war. Kennan, the severe and brilliant diplomat, dictated his 1946 telegram from his sickbed, flat on his back, describing a strategy of containment that would frame U.S.-Soviet relations for decades. In National Security Council Report 68, Paul Nitze gave Kennan's strategy a more aggressive cast, calling for a military buildup to confront an enemy driven by "a new fanatic faith, antithetical to our own."

The spider chart was meant "to create a strategic picture, and that strategic picture is the foundation of policy change," Wurmser said. "It helped you visualize, because if you saw, say, twenty relationships between X and Y, and twenty between Y and Z, then there's at least a suspicion that Z and X are interacting through Y." A map like that could bring insight, but there were perils in surmising too much. Suppose X and Y were Dick Cheney and Colin Powell. Twice they served in senior posts under presidents named Bush. In the early 1990s, they worked at the same address and were spotted together on international flights. They communicated frequently, encrypting their secrets. Back then, Cheney hired Powell for a very big job, elevating him over people far more senior. Ten years later, with Cheney in charge of recruiting, Powell got an even bigger job. From all this a person might figure that Powell was an agent of influence for Cheney. Lawrence Wilkerson, a colonel in Cheney's Pentagon who became Powell's State Department chief of staff, might be Agent Z on Wurmser's chart, taking Cheney's instructions through a cutout. As it happened, though, Powell was Cheney's bitter antagonist in the second Bush administration, and Wilkerson called Cheney every angry name from "ruthless," "dangerous," and "arrogant" to the "leader of a cabal." This business of links and relationships could get tricky.

Wurmser's spider diagram became a presentation of 110 slides. Included were nuggets of information—"Yes, raw intel," Wurmser said—with reliability labeled "undetermined" in the classified databases. "I let the reader judge," he said, referring to charges from professional analysts that he used dubious sources that fit his beliefs. "What I was focused on was ignored information. They say it was cherry-picking. To me, I was more laboring against obsolete assumptions rather than cherry-picking." The "Saddam–al Qaeda connection," Wurmser said, took up no more than 5 percent of his presentation until public statements from Bush and Cheney turned his attention to Iraq. "I saw this as a much broader war than Saddam," he said. "I thought it was an epic struggle between a whole category of nations and us, literally the seven state sponsors of terror and us." When Wurmser transitioned to the office of John Bolton, who owed his job as undersecretary of state to Cheney, he began focusing more intensively on the potential transfer of nuclear, biological, and chemical weapons to terrorists.

These were Wurmser's projects, not Cheney's. It would be risky to presume a full coincidence of views, though not perhaps as risky as presumptions Wurmser made. Indisputably, the vice president valued Wurmser's work and promoted it. Cheney deployed William Luti, a member of his own staff, to oversee and expand the operation Wurmser founded. It became known as the Policy Counterterrorism Evaluation Group inside Luti's Office of Special Plans. Air Force Lieutenant Colonel Karen Kwiatkowski, a military intelligence officer who worked for him, said Luti interrupted an early staff meeting to berate an aide for failing to respond quickly enough to a request for information from the vice president's chief of staff. "Scooter wants it and you have to get it over there right away," Luti barked. Kwiatkowski said, "The connectivity continued throughout. These guys are our first customers." Wurmser gave updates on his work to other members of Cheney's foreign-policy team, John Hannah and Samantha Ravich, and the three of them shared close ties to Ahmed Chalabi, the Iraqi exile who supplied them with some of their source materials about Saddam. Wurmser's path through the Bush administration brought him to Cheney's office full-time on September 4, 2003. He assumed positions of increasing responsibility over the next four years. "As time went on I had more and more direct contact with Scooter and more and more direct contact with the vice president himself," Wurmser said. Cheney did not take all of Wurmser's advice, and on many subjects his own views were opaque. But the core of Wurmser's work—the search for points of convergence among terrorists, hostile states, and weapons of mass destruction—was fundamental to Cheney's view of the world.

Speechwriters recall little if any input from Cheney on the "axis of evil" passage in Bush's second State of the Union address. But the strategic concept belonged to the vice president. Cheney might not have chosen the axis phrase himself, because it sounded too much like an old-fashioned national alliance. The vice president's name for his nightmare was "nexus." He and Don Rumsfeld "both used that term a lot, the nexus," said Feith, the Pentagon's chief of policy. "Cheney and Rumsfeld hammered on this idea that the main strategic problem after 9/11 for the United States was the nexus of terrorist groups, WMD, and state supporters of terrorism." Before September 11, Feith said, the prevailing wisdom was that "terrorists want a lot of people watching, not a lot of people dead." Now terrorism was no longer political theater. "Cheney made a very big deal out of this idea that the enemy in the war on terror is a network of terrorist organizations and their state sponsors," Feith said. "The problem was a network; it wasn't just a terrorist group." By September 2002, Bush had adopted Cheney's worldview more precisely. "Our greatest fear is that terrorists will find a shortcut to their mad ambitions when an outlaw regime supplies them with the technologies to kill on a massive scale," he said.

Aaron Friedberg, a Princeton professor of international relations, arrived in Cheney's office a few weeks before Wurmser, in the last days of summer 2003. His instructions were sparse, and he searched for clues to his employer's state of mind. "I came to the conclusion after a while that much of what I needed to understand about what he cared about, and wanted to have people pay attention to, could be explained by making the assumption that after September 11 he took very, very seriously this possibility of a terrorist attack with WMD," he said. "In a sense that's not saying anything surprising, but my sense is that many people find it very difficult to hold that idea in their head, really, and conjure with it, and see what it implies."

To bring around someone like Dick Armey, Cheney was prepared to bend the truth, maybe break it. Politicians, editorial writers, the public—they were looking for a certainty that intelligence could not provide. A leader in this kind of war could not wait for categorical proof. Cheney believed in his bones that the risks were mortal and real. One of the first things Friedberg heard on the job was the story of the vice president's reaction on September 11. "It would have been so much worse if they had had weapons of mass destruction," Cheney said that day. Why would Cheney go there? Al Qaeda had wreaked catastrophe with box cutters and muscle, lessons at a flying school that anyone could attend. It was about as low-tech as terror could get, requiring no shadowy link to a rogue regime. Why leap from an event like that to a state-sponsored mushroom cloud? Cheney took the leap because al Qaeda did. Osama bin Laden wanted that kind of power, talked openly about acquiring it, and nobody could guarantee he would not succeed. The vice president sought out worst-case scenarios. Warding them off was a leader's highest calling. "This problem of an event that's presumably of low probability but has very, very high impact—what do you do about it?" Friedberg asked. "Also, how do you know when you've done enough? A lot of people just said, 'We're doing what we can.' I think this is something that he thought about every day, and maybe he spent a lot of his time thinking about on many days."

Terrorists were hard to find, maybe impossible to deter. States were neither. To break potential links between them, it made sense to concentrate on the latter. Governments had known addresses, interests that could be held at risk. The question was where to begin. As Wurmser noted, the State Department designated seven "state sponsors" of terrorism: Iran, Iraq, Libya, Syria, Sudan, North Korea, and Cuba. Among those, the two most dangerous, and the subjects of the most important new intelligence, were North Korea and Iran. The Pyongyang government was hostile, unstable, economically desperate, armed with one or two nuclear weapons, and capable of quickly building half a dozen more. Its Dear Leader, Kim Jong Il, was apparently willing to sell nearly anything, from drugs and counterfeit $100 bills to missile technology. The government in Tehran, also hostile, appeared to be more rational. That was not all good news. Iran had an exceptionally competent intelligence service, which left few fingerprints on its work. American officials blamed it for orchestrating the Khobar Towers bombing of U.S. forces in Saudi Arabia in 1996, and for abetting an attack in Riyadh in May 2003. Iranian embassies around the world equipped Hezbollah and other terrorist groups with money and weapons and top-of-the-line fake passports.

There was fresh evidence of clandestine nuclear programs in Iran and North Korea, both of which started from a position far ahead of Iraq's. In the first half of 2002, the Bush administration discovered that Iran had already built a secret nuclear enrichment facility in Natanz. The same summer, British and American intelligence services learned that the Pyongyang government was among the customers of Abdul Qadeer Khan, the father of Pakistan's atomic bomb and the world's first private black market supplier. Khan seemed to have sold tens of thousands of centrifuges to North Korea. "That intel was very, very sensitive," said Stephen Yates, Cheney's senior Asia policy adviser. Until then, North Korea was believed to be a nuclear power with "one or possibly two" weapons and no immediate prospect of more, according to declassified CIA reports. Its existing arsenal had been built with plutonium from spent reactor fuel, the balance of which was held under United Nations seal. A centrifuge plant would give Pyongyang an alternate route to the bomb, using uranium instead of plutonium. By September, the CIA reached the dismaying conclusion (later in doubt) that a "production-scale" centrifuge facility was nearly complete. On October 5, 2002, North Korean diplomats gave truculent confirmation to Assistant Secretary of State James A. Kelly.

"This North Korea stuff was popping up at an inopportune time," Yates said, because by then Bush and Cheney were committed to war with Saddam Hussein. The White House dispatched Kelly to brief allied ambassadors. When a French official proposed to take the matter to the UN, Kelly replied, "The Security Council is for Iraq." The White House withheld the North Korea news from Congress and tried to keep information about Iran's secret enrichment project under wraps. When an exile group held a press conference in August to disclose the Iranian program, the Bush administration deflected attention back to Saddam. That month Cheney made three alarming public statements about an Iraqi nuclear threat.

By his own declared measurements of danger, Iraq should not have been the center of the spiderweb for Cheney. The nexus, if it was anywhere, was in Pakistan—a nuclear state whose national hero sold parts to the highest bidder, whose intelligence service backed the Taliban, and whose North-West Frontier Province became a refuge for al Qaeda. Saudi Arabia, too, had a lot more links to bin Laden than Iraq did. As Cheney saw it, there was nothing decisive to be done about those countries. Washington needed whatever help the Saudis and Pakistanis were willing to provide, and if either government fell, the successor was almost sure to be worse. Equally powerful circumstances handcuffed the United States in North Korea and Iran, terror-supporting states that had nuclear programs more advanced than Iraq's.

On the Korean Peninsula, military geography left the vice president with little taste for risk. Nothing fundamental had changed since his Pentagon days, when the DIA told Cheney that North Korea had more than ten thousand artillery pieces in range of Seoul, the South Korean capital. One-quarter of the South's population was literally under North Korean guns. The classified "Net Assessment on Military Balance in Korea" said there was a small chance that North Korea could actually win a conventional war. If Pyongyang threw half its forces against Seoul and sent the other half down the east coast, it might "checkmate" U.S. reinforcements at their points of entry in Pusan and Kimhae. The reaction of China, the giant to the north, was also hard to predict. As vice president, Cheney was "mindful of just how hard it is to come up with military plans" for North Korea, Yates said. Cheney sometimes said "targeted military strikes might be something we'd have to consider, but I never heard him as an advocate. We never satisfied him with an adequate set of options where we could reasonably put a lot of pressure on the North Koreans and the Chinese without having an unacceptable level of risk."

Much the same applied to Iran. It had a larger, better-equipped, and more proficient army than Iraq. The twenty thousand U.S. troops across its Afghan border were too few to pose an invasion threat but offered Iran a lot of inviting targets. Iran's navy and missile forces were potent threats to unarmed tankers in the Persian Gulf, and Tehran controlled the world's fourth-largest oil reserves. Iran's Quds Force, intelligence ministry, and Hezbollah clients were regarded by U.S. analysts as the "A-team" of international terrorism, more capable than al Qaeda and far from fully engaged against the United States. "Anytime the question would come up, 'Can we do X or do Y against Iran,' the immediate response was, 'What can they do back to us?'" Friedberg said.

The world's last remaining superpower, Cheney believed, must not stand helpless against the dangers of a state-terror nexus. A defensive crouch was not an option. The United States could not destroy every potential foe, unseat every hostile government, but tackling one would send a powerful message to the rest. Bernard Lewis, a British-born historian who was among Cheney's frequent advisers on Islam and the Middle East, said Cheney believed that "the image which we should avoid is that we are a harmless enemy and an unreliable friend." Yates, Cheney's Asia adviser, heard him say the same thing. "The vice president seemed to be quite concerned about the perception of American strength," Yates said. "That is easily spent, and very slowly rebuilt." Friedberg said part of Cheney's calculation was to show "we were able and willing to strike at someone. That sends a very powerful message."

"Demonstration effect"—that was Friedberg's term for it. "The demonstration effect is not just to be a tough guy but to reestablish deterrence," he said. "We had been hit very hard, and we needed to make clear the costs to those who might have been supporting or harboring those who were contemplating those acts." People close to Cheney had observed this thinking before. In his Pentagon days, according to David Gribbin, an old friend who then served as chief of legislative affairs, Cheney established authority with two demonstrative blows to the military brass. On the eve of the 1991 Persian Gulf War, Cheney concluded that the Navy was lying about the progress of its troubled A-12 bomber. He did something defense secretaries almost never do. He canceled the program outright. Not long before that, General Michael J. Dugan, the Air Force chief of staff, made epically indiscreet remarks to reporters about the coming war in the gulf. Cheney had warned the Air Force about freelance policy. He checked with the president, then fired Dugan. (Behind the scenes, he let Dugan know it was nothing personal. Cheney urged the Senate

Armed Services Committee, against its inclinations, to let Dugan retire with a four-star general's pension. That sent a message, too.) "It was educational," Gribbin recalled. "That's the use of power. I think he thought he was using his authority to serve the American people, and he's obviously not afraid to be a rough opponent. When he fired Dugan, no one had ever done that since Truman. . . . The message was, 'Civilians are in control here, for heaven's sake. Let's not be confused about that.'"

Cheney, in the end, did not press for war with Iraq because Saddam really topped the list of "grave and gathering threats," as he led the Bush administration in asserting. The United States would take him down because it could. The war would not preempt immediate danger, a more traditional ground for war, but prevent a danger that might emerge later—from Baghdad or anywhere else in the viewing audience. Part of the point, as Voltaire explained about a public execution in *Candide,* was "to encourage the others." Michael Gerson, a White House counselor and speechwriter, said Bush shared that outlook on prevention to a point. "I think the president has always felt like this is also part of the war on terror, and he's glad to have the vice president on top of the issue," he said. He added, "It's fair to say that the vice president's foreign-policy emphasis is the realistic confrontation of threats to the American people, while the president, unusually for a conservative, is a root-cause thinker. When he looks at the Middle East, the question he asks is, 'What's the root cause, and what's the long-term solution?' And in this case, it's not a military solution, it's the development of hopeful societies that don't produce ideologies and individuals that murder our citizens." Two Cheney advisers said he sympathized with aspirations to freedom, but he was realistic enough to understand that free elections might bring bin Laden and like-minded figures to power in much of the Islamic world.

Iraq brought Bush and Cheney to their most fateful intersection.

They arrived by largely divergent routes. Gerson saw a perfect confluence, joining vice-presidential Realpolitik with presidential ideals. "It would not have turned out any differently," he said, whichever man decided. Maybe so, if the story ended on invasion day. Bush saw Iraq as a demonstration model, just as Cheney did. But what message did the war demonstrate? Love us, or fear us? Walk with us, or keep out of our way? Was America Don Quixote, riding to the rescue in a world of hope, or had we become Jack in *Lord of the Flies,* the toughest hunter on a very dangerous island? Bush and Cheney reached the gates of Babylon with an undivided will to destroy Saddam Hussein. But the ambiguity of purpose at the heart of the war would do much to explain its undoing.

Just before Christmas 2003, the U.S. government sounded urgent internal alarms. Yates and Friedberg remembered warning notices, but neither was privy to the closely held details. For public consumption, the Department of Homeland Security declared an Orange Alert on December 21. In the president's top circle of advisers, anxieties blew right across the red line. There was a big spike in the daily Threat Matrix, the compilation of terrorist "indications and warnings." Most of them were probably spurious, and nearly all were vague. But the increase in volume alone had to mean something. Leads poured in from detainee interrogations, from allied governments, and from signals intelligence. A lot of the chatter pointed to something big. Intelligence analysts likened their work to assembling a mosaic. That made it sound like a jigsaw puzzle, but in truth the job was harder. The analysts had to put together a picture using fragments from a mountain of broken tiles. Most of the tiles they needed might be missing. Some of the tiles they had might not belong.

Nobody claimed to know for sure, but the intelligence suggested plans for a spectacular attack around New Year's Eve. New York, Los Angeles, and Las Vegas, the biggest venues, got most of the public attention, with conspicuous new security precautions. With just a day or two left in 2003, something scarier came across the transom. Scary enough for George Tenet to seek an emergency meeting of the principals. The president's top advisers had scattered for the holiday, but they and some of their deputies convened by secure video. Cheney beamed in from Wyoming. Marine General Peter Pace, vice chairman of the Joint Chiefs of Staff, held the fort at the Pentagon's National Military Command Center. Defense Secretary Don Rumsfeld teleconferenced from New Mexico. Condi Rice and Colin Powell appeared on the SVTS screen, too. Each participant filled a small window on the side, appearing in the big center panel when he or she spoke.

Tenet went first. Newly gathered intelligence, combined with what the agency had in hand, showed a credible risk of an imminent attack on Washington. The sources were ambiguous. But it looked real enough and big enough that Tenet was ready to take a chance of crying wolf. From the vibe of the intelligence, he told the principals, the bad guys hoped for damage on a scale that sounded an awful lot like a nuclear weapon. Those last two words stopped the conversation for a beat. Pace, the four-star general near ground zero, mentioned a point of procedure. Ordinarily the Joint Staff would beef up its command center on a big alert, but "we won't cancel leaves and bring back key personnel, because if this report is true it just means we'll all be dead," he said, keeping his voice nice and even. Rumsfeld, 1,600 miles away, offered that "somebody ought to be writing all this down, in case it doesn't turn out well." A few minutes later, a stenographer appeared. In the Pentagon. Nobody questioned the logic.

Cheney hunched over his notes as Tenet briefed the details. If terrorists had somehow got hold of a transportable nuke, the likeliest scenario involved a warhead stolen from the former Soviet arsenal. What kind of operation could buy, handle, smuggle, deliver, and detonate such a device? It seemed to Cheney there had to be state sponsorship of some kind. Nuclear terrorism would require sophisticated tradecraft, a big pile of cash, fake travel papers or ship manifests. It wouldn't be Russia, even if the theft happened there. It couldn't be Saddam Hussein; U.S. Special Forces had pulled him out of a hole near Tikrit a couple of weeks before.

"We need to get a nonpaper to Iran immediately," Cheney decided. That was jargon for an official-but-unofficial message. Rumsfeld quickly agreed. There would be no government letterhead, no formal démarche. But the text would be crystal clear. "If this happens," Cheney said, summarizing, "the consequences for Iran will be unimaginably grave." In diplomacy, "grave consequences" was the accepted euphemism for military force. Euphemism offered ambiguity, providing room for maneuver and leaving the other fellow guessing. The vice president was not looking for ambiguity. "Unimaginably grave" would come with a mushroom cloud.

Why Iran? Tenet had little or no indication that the plot, if plot there was, had support from the Islamic republic. But if the CIA could draw inferences, so could Cheney. Iran had capabilities and a history of using them. Tehran had become a temporary home for some al Qaeda figures who had fled Afghanistan, though not nearly as many or as senior as those in Pakistan. The CIA said they appeared to be under some kind of house arrest; the vice president had his doubts. "Policymakers are allowed to argue with the intel," said Mark Lowenthal, assistant director of central intelligence for analysis, who declined to confirm or discuss the New Year's alert. "He thinks very, very quickly. He processes quickly. He's one of the fastest people in the room, and some of the people in the room are none too shabby."

Iran *might* be involved, might know something. With stakes this high, there was no time to wait for proof. This was a dark-side moment: motivate your enemy with a stick. Iran needed every incentive to find and stop the coming attack, just in case it could. Rice and Powell did not think like that, did not have enough information to choose a course. They took no immediate position. The meeting ended with Cheney and Rumsfeld in sync. "These are ruthless men, and they were completely credible in the role of making ruthless threats, and that was exactly what they believed the situation required," said one participant. "It's not every day you make a threat to obliterate a country when you have no evidence at all. They had no idea whether Iran in fact had any role."

December turned to January, and nothing blew up. No one was arrested. The chatter grew quiet. Over at Homeland Security, Tom Ridge ended the Orange Alert on January 10, 2004. What happened in the interim remains unknown. Authoritative sources said no U.S. warning was passed to Iran through the official Swiss diplomatic channel or through British intelligence, which served as an occasional substitute. A high-ranking Iranian official said he should have heard of a warning like that, regardless of how it was conveyed. He had not. Did Bush reject the message Cheney proposed? Did the vice president learn something that changed his mind? Did the CIA stand down from its alert? Did the warning in fact find its way to Iran, teaching the mullahs they faced mortal retribution whether guilty or not, and maybe better beef up their own deterrent? Even Iran watchers in the U.S. government could not say. What struck close observers of the New Year's alert was Cheney's decisiveness, his autonomy. Some wondered how the president could have failed to join such a gathering, even assuming he was briefed on the result. "You know who's in charge in a room. You know who's in charge in a meeting. Cheney was in charge," said a witness.

Cheney was on the lookout for Iranians he could talk to, hosting exiles to discuss the prospect of unseating the clerical regime. One of Cheney's unannounced visitors was Reza Pahlavi, eldest son of the Iranian ruler who lost his throne to the Islamic revolution of 1979. Sometimes called the "baby shah," Pahlavi was nineteen years old when the ayatollahs took power. He had come to the United States for Air Force training and a degree at the University of Southern California, and he pretty much never left. He saw himself as Iran's rightful monarch, delivering "Messages to the Nation" on a Web site and by audio and video broadcasts. One Bush administration official said Cheney first met the aspiring shah, by now a man of middle age, in Colorado, then invited him to the White House.

"Reza Pahlavi came to see Cheney four or five times," said Hillary Mann, the National Security Council director for Iran. Like all Cheney's meetings, these were unadvertised. When Mann heard through the grapevine, "I was not allowed to be in the room." Wurmser, who described himself as "pretty much the point man on Iran" for Cheney, downplayed those meetings, which have not been disclosed before. "The attitude was we need to listen and work with whoever palatable was out there, but I never heard a value put on his currency in Iran or his utility for an opposition movement," Wurmser said. "He was a decent guy, the baby shah, but we never really got in any discussions I can remember over the quality of his leadership of the opposition movement." Mann said she understood otherwise. The vice president was "sizing him up, whether he could be a Chalabi type, form a government in exile or rile up the students" who staged angry demonstrations in 1999.

Wurmser and John Hannah, a senior staff member who later became Cheney's national security adviser, met other opposition figures as well. One of them was Shahriar Ahy, an adviser to Reza Pahlavi who once served as the shah's informal liaison to the White House. Another, unexpectedly, was the grandson of Grand Ayatollah Ruholla Khomeini, the late leader of the Iranian Revolution and scourge of the Great Satan in Washington. The son of his son, Sayyid Hussein Khomeini, had become a political apostate. He followed his family's religious path, earning the rank of ayatollah, but he denounced his government's "dictatorship of the clerics." In the summer of 2003, after American-led troops toppled Saddam Hussein, Khomeini crossed the border and installed himself in Baghdad. Iranians just as much as Iraqis "need freedom now, and if they can only achieve it with American interference I think they would welcome it," he told a correspondent for the *New York Observer*. "As an Iranian, I would welcome it." Wurmser and Hannah, with an assist from Michael Ledeen, a longtime advocate of regime change in Iran, lost no time in bringing the ayatollah's grandson to Washington. Khomeini's CIA dossier, according to someone who read it, described "a long history of heroin abuse," but Hannah and Wurmser sat down with him on the periphery of a public event at the American Enterprise Institute. Khomeini told the audience that his countrymen would welcome U.S. assistance to any leader "who is willing to step into the field, who has the will-power and the dynamism to lead Iranians into freedom." He left unspoken whether he ascribed those virtues to himself.

"It would be great if we could use him," Hannah told Hillary Mann after the speech. Wurmser, recalling the event, said, "Did I sit and coordinate" a political plan with the ayatollah? "No. But I was listening to what a lot of people were saying."

Cheney's concept of regime change was widely misunderstood, in and out of government. It was not all about bombs and boots on the ground. The vice president knew how to use a hammer, but his strategy for international conflict had much more nuance. Usually it looked to the long term, expecting no immediate result. Cheney adapted to circumstances and probed for tools to shift them. His threshold question, Wurmser said, was, "Can you modify regime behavior without regime change?" If not, were there instruments available to bring such change about? How long might it take, and what were the risks? Why should anyone think the successor government would be an improvement? Which policies would best serve U.S. objectives in the interim? A top-ranking adviser, who would not speak on the record because he remained in Cheney's employ, said, "It would be a very bad mischaracterization to say this guy has a theology about regime change, he has a formula about regime change, he has some sort of red line that we cannot engage diplomatically with enemies." The vice president's policies were "situation-driven," the adviser said.

Cheney did not share the zeal of his neoconservative advisers for democracy through revolution. What he did share was a judgment that some governments, by nature, were irreconcilable at their roots with U.S. interests. Cheney was less likely than his staff to describe such regimes as "evil," though aides said he did not disagree. "Regime change starts with a diagnosis, but it doesn't necessarily lead him to the prescription that the way to deal with it is by the use of force," Friedberg said. "What do you do if your judgment is that no agreement they make will be kept? The real concern may be that because of the fundamental nature of these regimes, you can't reach tolerable agreements with them."

For Cheney, Friedberg said, "the collapse of the Soviet Union was really a profound experience. For one thing, the standard experts will tell you things are going to be tomorrow the way they are today. He was reading CIA assessments of the resilience and stability of the Soviet regime right up to December of '91," when it fell apart. "The conventional idea—that the way to improve relations with the Soviet Union was by convergence and negotiations, and that will be the way the cold war will end—was wrong. You had to have a fundamental change of regime, and that change was possible." Cheney came to the view, as well, that "you don't want to get in the way by doing things that delay the collapse of the regime by propping them up."

Similar scenarios were weighed and refined for North Korea, but Cheney remained cautious. The United States had limited leverage, said Steve Yates, his Asia adviser, but "he was supportive of trying to grow those instruments." Cheney did not take for granted that it would be a good idea to use them. "What evidence do we have that we know who would come in after him?" Cheney asked. "What evidence do we have that implementing a strangulation or induce-ment strategy would increase or decrease the risk of proliferation? If you take away all sources of income but weapons of mass destruction, does that lead him to sell the weapons of mass destruction?" Accord-ing to Yates, Cheney's fundamental focus was on consequences— "balance of power and all those other things that come from the Kissingerian world. His priorities were hierarchical. Is someone for regime change? It's different from saying we have a policy or strategy to bring it about. But who wouldn't wish for the Korean people to live better?"

Friedberg said the Bush administration found no coherent policy. That would have been possible only "if you hadn't had Powell or you hadn't had Cheney and Rumsfeld. As it was, you got a resultant vec-tor that didn't satisfy either." If Cheney had had his way, Friedberg said, "we wouldn't have had the six-party talks" that put U.S. and North Korean diplomats in a room with representatives of Russia, China, Japan, and South Korea. "What you would have had instead is pressure, with others, to either squeeze them or contain them. What you ended up with was negotiations and partial pressure. It has clearly not stopped them from testing nuclear weapons, and it has locked us into a process we can't get out of even after they tested."

John Hannah, who eventually replaced Scooter Libby as Cheney's national security adviser, began his career in Soviet studies and shifted focus to the Middle East. He was a speechwriter and policy planner in the State Department under Bush's father, then moved to the Washington Institute for Near East Policy, a spin-off of the American Israel Public Affairs Committee. According to Hillary Mann, who remained a friend of Hannah's despite policy disagreements, he was known waggishly "as Jihad John," a sobriquet arising from "his very muscular rhetoric" about the region. "A *lot* of people call him that," she said. Hannah "would talk about the Iranian regime and Syrian regime as dictatorships, just like the evil empire, and by sitting with evil regimes you confer legitimacy on them."

"Our model was something Martin Malia wrote about the Soviet Union," Wurmser said, referring to the conservative scholar's prescient forecast in 1990 that the Communist government was at imminent risk of collapse. Malia maintained that external pressure had forced Soviet rulers into a corner from which they could not escape. If they maintained their repressive system at home, their economy and military strength would fail. If they relaxed internal controls, pressure from below would bring about the regime's demise.

Wurmser and Cheney, along with Steve Hadley, met periodically with Uri Lubrani, an Israeli government figure who had long proposed a similar strategy for Iran, asserting that the Iranian people were "ripe for a change." Lubrani did not advocate invasion, but he believed it essential to isolate the regime as completely as possible. Negotiations would be tantamount to recognition of the regime, discouraging internal opponents and opening the door to further concessions from Europe. Lubrani brought proposals to give quiet assistance to dissident organizers. "If for instance there will be a strike in the oil industry of three to four weeks, the regime is done, finished," he told his White House contacts. "If you have the transport workers, the electrical workers, and the teachers strike, the regime is finished. The question is, 'Are the people ready?' Yes, I think they're ready." Cheney and his daughter Liz, running the Iran-Syria Operations Group at State, led an effort to channel clandestine funds to fomenters of trouble in and out of Iran.

Marine General Anthony Zinni, the chief of U.S. Central Command in the late 1990s, knew Cheney from his visits to the region as chairman of Halliburton. "He seemed to be so well grounded, so commonsensical," Zinni said. Later, during and after his brief assignment as Bush's special envoy to the Middle East, Zinni "started hearing the term 'constructive destabilization'" from people in and around the vice president's office. "They believed you could light this spark, cause a dramatic shift. Anybody who knows this part of the world knows you've got to be careful which spark you light."

"How dare he? This is illegal!" Eric Edelman said, looking up from a stack of stapled intelligence traffic from the National Security Agency. "He has no instructions to do that. What are we going to do about it?"

Edelman was Cheney's principal deputy national security adviser. It was the second week of January 2003. What Edelman was reading, according to a colleague, was the NSA transcript of an American diplomat's conversation in the Persian Gulf. Richard Haass, the State Department's director of policy planning, was in Abu Dhabi, a T-shaped island that formed one of the city-states of the United Arab Emirates. Haass had been battling the Pentagon and the vice president's office in a tug-of-war over "engagement" with Iran. A close White House adviser to the senior President Bush, Haass favored efforts to find points of common interest with the leading power in a globally important region. Cheney and Rumsfeld backed strict isolation in order to undermine the regime.

Like other senior officials, Edelman received daily transcripts from the NSA that touched on subjects of his responsibility, delivered in a manila envelope with his name typed on a white cover page. Ordinarily when eavesdropping on "U.S. persons" abroad—the legal term for American citizens, residents, and corporate entities—the agency removed their names from the transcript. But policymakers could obtain a name by special request if they affirmed that the speaker's identity was required to understand the intelligence. John R. Bolton, a Cheney ally who was undersecretary of state, made a practice of asking the NSA to provide that information. From time to time, on a scale unknown, the vice president's office took advantage of the prerogative, too.

Edelman, according to a witness, believed he saw evidence of face-to-face talks between Haass and a diplomat from Iran. "Look what he's saying," Edelman exclaimed. Cheney's office had been working hard to stop such contacts, which flourished briefly in 2002 when the interests of the two nations were joined against Afghanistan's ruling Taliban. In a previous job at the United Nations, Hillary Mann was authorized to speak to her Iranian counterpart, Kourosh Ahmadi, about those Afghan issues. One day a friend at the State Department warned that her meetings, too, were monitored. "Be careful," the friend warned, alluding vaguely to high-ranking figures in the White House. "Your name is coming up in intercepts. Protect yourself."

Haass, years later, said he had met Iranian diplomats during the Afghan talks of 2002, but he did not recall speaking to an Iranian in Abu Dhabi. "I had conversations with UAE officials in which Iran came up," Haass said, but he denied exceeding instructions. "I wrote so many memos saying that regime change was an unrealistic foreign-policy goal for the United States. The disagreements were over the regime's stability and the tools we had for affecting that." Nonetheless, he said, "when I was overseas I was working for this administration, whether I agreed with the policies or not. Nothing ever got back to me that anybody was unhappy about what I said on that trip." He declined to say what he thought about the use of communications intelligence to monitor his meetings, but he had a question. "If that was intel, I'd want to know that whatever was done was in line with law and regulations," he said.

Information was power. Cheney sought it widely and creatively, and used it to shape what the president learned and when. Unlike any vice president before him, Cheney reviewed the president's CIA briefing before Bush did. Cheney typically woke at 5:45 a.m. at his residence on the grounds of the Naval Observatory. He browsed four newspapers during his workout on an elliptical trainer, preferring the originals to clippings from the White House staff. By 7:00 a.m. Scooter Libby arrived from his home in suburban Virginia. A senior CIA analyst walked them through the President's Daily Brief, which was akin to a highly classified newsletter, with short articles on current intelligence and longer ones on trends. Cheney's briefing was a dress rehearsal for the one Bush received an hour later in the Oval Office. The vice president, who despised redundancy, almost never failed to sit in. "If the vice president is in town he'll always be there," said Josh Bolten, who was deputy chief of staff and chief of staff for Bush. "If he's out of town, he'll almost always be on the SVTS. . . . Doesn't matter if it is five a.m. Cheney time, the vice president is going to want to be in, and that happens not infrequently because [Bush will] be here and the VP will be out on the West Coast."

Cheney delved into subjects of interest, and in his prebriefing he often suggested that the agency expand on an item and draw it to the president's attention. "He'll come into the briefing with the president often already knowing the information that the briefer is giving the president and sometimes more because he will have dug into what the intel reports are saying," Bolten said. Steve Hadley, the national security adviser, said Cheney "will periodically in that morning meeting come out and he will say, 'Mr. President, I went out to the agency yesterday, and I spent an hour and a half taking a deep dive on subject X. And they're doing some really good work out there, and you need to see it, Mr. President.'"

One example involved Iran and North Korea. The latter was a nuclear power, the former a suspected aspirant. Cheney and Rumsfeld were advancing the theory that Iran had a secret uranium enrichment program, a plausible suspicion for which the CIA had found no evidence. The Natanz facility, made public in the summer of 2002, was under UN monitoring. If Iran was enriching uranium for a weapon, it had to be doing that somewhere else, with centrifuges yet undiscovered. One day Cheney's CIA briefer alluded to missile sales from North Korea to Iran. "He's a very good reader of intelligence," Hadley said. "The vice president sees all these intelligence reports and contacts between the two of them, and he says, 'Don't the same entities involved in missile technology have some ties to nuclear technology?' So, had we looked for ties between North Korea and Iran in their nuclear program? Very interesting question." Hadley called the question "classic Cheney," which was true in more than one way. In fact, the CIA had considered Cheney's question closely, and had not changed its answer—U.S. analysts saw no trace of a secret Iranian centrifuge program. By asking again, Cheney "cues the President to come in with a series of questions and task a little analysis," Hadley said. More analysis meant more time, and that suited the vice president fine. He and Rumsfeld were locked in a multiyear struggle against advocates of an agreement with the Iranian government. Deadlock amounted to victory for Cheney. Did the new study bring new evidence? "Not so far that we've found," Hadley said.

There were other ways to guide information and policy. Condi Rice assigned Ben Miller, a CIA analyst on detail to the National Security Council staff, to be White House liaison to the Iraqi opposition before the invasion. Like the agency he represented, Miller was profoundly skeptical of Chalabi, telling colleagues that Chalabi was a liar and possibly a double agent for Iran. During one heated argument, according to Hillary Mann, "Ben said something Chalabi didn't like and he said to Ben, 'We know where you go to church.'" Miller refused to deal with him again. Eric Edelman, John Hannah, and Doug Feith at the Pentagon complained to Hadley. Then Cheney's chief of staff stepped in. "Scooter Libby had him fired," Mann recalled, sending him back to Langley.

Aaron Friedberg was an innocent amid the bureaucratic cloak-and-dagger, but he saw how hard the vice president and his staff worked to keep tabs on what other agencies said and did. When trying to manage policy toward rogue regimes, he said, "it's one thing to try to make something good happen. It's another, and sometimes equally important, to make sure nothing bad happens." The logic of negotiations, he said, put the government "under a lot of pressure to cut deals we shouldn't cut."

The final days of 2003 found Ahmed Chalabi in a Baghdad homecoming turned bittersweet. The president had decided not to install his government-in-exile, the Iraqi National Congress, as Saddam's replacement. He protested bitterly when Zalmay Khalilzad, a senior White House official, broke the news. According to one witness,

Chalabi invoked the vice president's support. "Next time I'll check with management," Khalilzad replied drily. There was some consolation in Chalabi's return to Mansour, the wealthy Baghdad neighborhood of his youth. He and his men had somehow claimed the Hunting Club, the pleasure den of Saddam's older and more dissolute son Uday, as well as a selection of nearby stately homes. Chalabi sat in the well-appointed upstairs library of one of those homes, which rightfully belonged, he said, to a relative. There were fine marble floors and fine carpets, and technicians had set him up with satellite voice and data links. After a chef-prepared meal as Chalabi's guest, the author wished to ask about weapons of mass destruction. Chalabi had worked tirelessly since the 1990s to persuade Americans that Iraqi nuclear, biological, and chemical weapons posed a mortal threat. His intelligence chief, Entifadah Qanbar, who dropped in on our library chat, had run the congressionally funded Information Collection Program, which "cultivated and analyzed" reports from defectors and other "raw intelligence" about illegal weapons, according to a memo Qanbar wrote nine months before the war. The principal consumers of his intelligence, identified by name and direct-dial telephone number, were William Luti, the former Cheney aide at the Pentagon, and John Hannah, then the vice president's special assistant for national security. Not much of Qanbar's intelligence turned out to be true. Now, eight months after the fall of Saddam, the weapons hunters of the Iraq Survey Group were in their last throes. David Kay, who led the group, would soon return to Washington empty-handed. Chalabi did not want to discuss the subject, he said, "because of the hassle we got out of it."

Once persuaded, Chalabi pointed with satisfaction to a shelf of books he had recently acquired. They belonged to Jaffar al-Jaffar himself, dean of the Iraqi atomic establishment. Look for yourself, Chalabi said: a knowledge base for Saddam's nuclear resurgence.

Upon inspection they were reference works on particle physics and quantum mechanics, forty-year-old textbooks from Jaffar's graduate schooling in Birmingham, England. Did Chalabi, who held a mathematics Ph.D. from the University of Chicago, really see something sinister on that shelf? "My men have only just found these," he said with an air of important disclosure. "I said, 'Where did you get them?' 'We went to his house.' 'What else did you find?' 'Crates and crates of papers. The Americans have not read them.'" Chalabi shook his head, appalled at the incompetence of the invaders. "Astounding," he said. "It's just unbelievable. Jaffar wanted to build a bomb since the 1960s. They had an active program for weapons of mass destruction."

Only that week, Chalabi confided, he had dined with Nissar Hindawi, a scientist on Saddam's biological weapons team. For some years the Iraqi National Congress had shopped Hindawi's story to its friends in government and the press. Back in April, Judith Miller of the *New York Times* wrote that she had interviewed him "in the protective custody of the Iraqi opposition leader Ahmad Chalabi." Hindawi's claims checked out when he spoke of Iraq's historic weapons programs, but not so on matters more recent. "'I know how to weaponize anthrax,' he told me," Chalabi confided. He laughed. "He's a little man, who looks like he can be a haberdasher in Harrods." Saddam's men were everywhere. "They can hide things very well, but he had the weapons themselves, that's my scenario." Even Vx, the lethal nerve agent? "Oh yes, he had stabilized Vx," Chalabi said.

And what if no evidence turned up for any of that? Chalabi waved off the question.

"Turn off the tape," he said finally.

The author complied. An aide inspected the recorder, making sure.

"It doesn't matter," Chalabi said. "I am not concerned. We have liberated Iraq, and it does not matter why. It is a good thing."

Less than three months later, Dick Cheney invited MSNBC's Lester Holt to his ceremonial office in the Eisenhower Building, where he sat behind a desk first used by Theodore Roosevelt. "The search is going to go on," Cheney said. "That work will probably continue for another year or two, and it's not complete yet." Maybe Saddam did not have stockpiles, but "he had biological weapons programs that could have produced, on relatively short notice, because he had the basic laboratories, he had the technology and the people who had done it before." Could have. Had done. Like Chalabi, the vice president did not see that as the main point, anyway. "I think on balance, overall, there's no question we did the right thing in Iraq," Cheney said.

Back when he briefed Dick Armey, long before the weapons hunt died and an insurgency came to life—even then Cheney entertained doubts about the project. A leader should not show ambivalence, but the vice president let it surface in private on the day he won the Battle of Congress. Armey had cast his reluctant vote for war, weeping in the well of the House, on Thursday afternoon, October 10, 2002. The Senate debate lasted longer, pushing the vote past midnight. Early Friday morning, the White House victory was complete. That evening at One Observatory Circle, Cheney's turreted official residence, he held a small dinner party for an author he admired. Sideboard candles and a chandelier reflected warmly off celadon walls, but the mood in the formal dining room was dark. Cheney had been reading *An Autumn of War,* a collection of essays by the military historian Victor Davis Hanson. He liked it so much that he bought copies for his staff, telling them the man had captured his own views exactly. A scholar of the ancient Greeks, Hanson cited Hellenic philosophy. War was "innate to civilization," a terrible thing, but not necessarily unjust. Citizens often faltered, putting leaders to the test. That was one of the things on Cheney's mind. He usually asked his guests to prepare a talk, starting the conversation in an after-dinner salon. The vice president asked Hanson to make a twenty-minute presentation on the roles of leaders in unpopular wars.

Hanson thought that remarkable. He was not the kind of classicist who thought only of Sparta and Troy. Based at the Hoover Institution at Stanford, he was a regular in policy combat at *National Review Online*. He knew a lot of people in Washington, and he heard too much easy euphoria about the prospect of war with Iraq. Cheney was far from euphoric. Hanson found him "reflective, quiet, sober." This was a just war, Hanson told him. Cheney sat at the end of the table, playing devil's advocate. "He was very depressed about both the options of going to war and not going to war," Hanson said. "He didn't think either were good options."

The vice president asked Hanson to stay behind when the other guests left, ushering him to a white armchair in the library. Gilbert Stuart's austere *John Adams* stared down from the mantel. Lynne Cheney said this was one of her husband's favorite rooms, with a buffalo in bronze and other western sculptures that reminded him of home. For a while, Hanson said, "we didn't talk about Iraq. We talked about human nature." Cheney projected melancholy, resignation.

"You have only bad and worse choices," the vice president said.

Hanson knew George Bush, had met with him more than once. The president had "a lot more propensity to be idealistic and see that democracy is the innate right of mankind," he said. Bush meant it when he said America "should be the one to offer the world our values." Cheney's view "is much more tragic," Hanson said. "The vice president would say, 'This is a messy transition, and I don't know whether or not it's going to work, and I don't know whether people in the Middle East are capable of democracy.'"

In private Cheney had regrets about the way his last war had ended. In 1991 he supported the first President Bush in choosing to halt U.S. tanks well short of Baghdad. Three years later, in remarks that would be replayed millions of times on YouTube, Cheney explained why Bush had made the right decision.

He was strikingly younger looking then, thinner faced and darker haired than the man who sat with Hanson at the fireplace. Cheney's reasoning was Kissingerian—cost and benefit, balance of power, the marshaling of resources for national gain:

> *If we'd gone to Baghdad, we would have been all alone. There wouldn't have been anybody else with us. There would have been a U.S. occupation of Iraq. . . . It's a quagmire if you go that far and try to take over Iraq. The other thing was casualties. Everyone was impressed with the fact we were able to do our job with as few casualties as we had. But for the 146 Americans killed in action, and for their families, it wasn't a cheap war. And the question for the president, in terms of whether or not we went on to Baghdad, took additional casualties in an effort to get Saddam Hussein, was how many additional dead Americans is Saddam worth? Our judgment was, not very many, and I think we got it right.*

Cheney was not a man who aired second thoughts in public, but to a few confidants he lamented the slaughter of Iraqi Kurds and Shiites who rose up after the war. He had done his part to lead them on, believing that Saddam would fall. When the Iraqi president saw that Washington would not intervene, he crushed the rebellions and exacted awful revenge.

Cheney still thought first and foremost about the national interest, but according to Hanson and some of his staff, the vice president was beginning to see it in new ways. He did not "necessarily think that every person deserves freedom on a platter from the United States," Hanson said, but after September 11 Cheney was open to the view that a liberation strategy "might be a way to check the jihadists." Hanson saw Cheney that evening as "an old-school realist who has changed because of his experience. He's gone back and reexamined everything he did, and he's come to a new realism." The essence of realism was to live without illusion, to accept the world as it is. That night, as Hanson saw it, Cheney was redefining what that meant.

"He's not dealing with a world the way it always has to be," Hanson said. "He's dealing with a world that can be changed."

Some of Cheney's advisers thought so, too. When Saddam Hussein fell, not quite six months after the Hanson dinner, people like Yates and Hannah and Wurmser prepared to press on. The dreadnought USS *George W. Bush* had steamed right over a tyrant, and they wanted to follow the bow wave. "The United States was ten feet tall," Yates said. "The Chinese were paying a lot more attention to what we might potentially do. That might have been an opportune time for a bold initiative on North Korea, with a bit of a swagger."

The demonstration effect. Thing was, it cut both ways. If the war went badly, what would it demonstrate then? Not love us. Not fear us. It would project just the image Cheney wanted to avoid: America as harmless enemy, unreliable friend. Cheney refused to contemplate defeat, but that did not mean he expected the war to be easy. Yates found he "had no audience" for his big plans. "I was having a hard time getting access to the vice president, or even Scooter or Eric Edelman," he said. Samantha Ravich, another Asia specialist on Cheney's staff, told a colleague that the vice president "put North Korea on the back burner." Iraq consumed more and more of Cheney's time. "In terms of his appetite for paper, we began exercising judicious editorial control on how much you could send the vice president that was not about Iraq," Yates said.

Aaron Friedberg joined the vice president's office at the turning point in the summer of 2003. He could feel it, and he hesitated when Scooter Libby invited him to interrupt his academic career. What persuaded him was the possibility that he might yet witness world-changing events. "The way I thought to myself about it was, this is either going to be like 1947 or it's going to be like 1967," he recalled. "I mean, it's either going to be *Present at the Creation,* a whole bunch of things going on, building institutions and reshaping of the world, or—" Friedberg broke off the sentence, looking for the right way to put it. *Present at the Creation* was Dean Acheson's memoir of halcyon days just after World War II: the Marshall Plan, resuscitation of Europe, reformation of Germany and Japan. Had Friedberg named a book in counterpoint, which he did not, he might have chosen Neil Sheehan's *A Bright Shining Lie.* Sheehan's book about Vietnam described a history of self-delusion, the drowning of pretty hopes in jungle mud. Friedberg's question that summer was whether Iraq would become the quagmire Cheney foresaw in 1994. He was thinking of the Vietnam before the Tet Offensive of 1968, when the war took its irreversible turn. "I guess for me, '67 is when things have escalated," he said. "It's not clear how it's going to turn out, but it's obvious that it's kind of an inflection point. In one case things broaden out," and the United States can follow victory with success elsewhere. "In the other, they narrow down." The vice president, as Friedberg saw it, must be an optimist. Why else hire a long-range planner? "I think the reason he wanted someone to do what he asked me to do was the hope, the assumption, of broadening out," he said.

Chapter Ten

SUPPLY SIDE

Air Force Two touched down just after sunset at Greenbrier Valley Airport in West Virginia, delivering Cheney to a GOP congressional retreat. This was the one chance each year for House and Senate Republicans to step away from the daily roll call, think about big ideas. They called their annual event the "Congress of Tomorrow," and the faint echo of Disney suited the venue. The Greenbrier was a charming resort with a scary old museum underneath. The historic hotel had been equipped for holocaust in the 1950s, not long after Stalin got the Bomb. Its cavernous underground bunker, intended to shield a postnuclear Congress beneath twenty-ton blast doors, became a tourist attraction after the cold war. Since then the place had been refurbished in style. The Greenbrier was set in the Allegheny highlands. It looked like what you'd get if you moved Jefferson's Monticello estate to the mountains and built a much bigger house. Weather smiled on the governing majority. Temperatures climbed to the fifties that week. A lot of legislators found time for a massage, a round of golf, or a soak in the famous white sulfur springs.

The vice president was all business. He had spent the morning, February 6, 2003, at a memorial service for seven astronauts who died aboard the space shuttle *Columbia*. War was coming soon in Iraq. The economy was stalled. Corporate scandals—Enron, Adelphia, WorldCom–made the stock market look like a bad neighborhood. The Dow Jones had shed a fifth of its value since summer. An hour or so before Cheney arrived, the market closed at 7,929, well below the trough after September 11.

Cheney came to sell his party on the president's plan for recovery. But it was not Bush's plan he sold, not exactly. Months of preparation and debate had shaped another big tax cut, $674 billion. This plan was even more Cheney's baby than the last. He had consulted widely, delved deeply. He outworked and outmaneuvered rivals who cautioned against paralyzing budget deficits. Cheney had largely won over the president. His proposal had three main pieces, and Bush liked only one of them at first. He came around on the second one. But Bush said no to the third: a deep cut in the tax on capital gains.

If you bought stock low and sold it high, the government took a slice of your profit, or capital gain. Cheney felt strongly that this discouraged investment and made it more expensive to move money around a dynamic economy. Glenn Hubbard, then chairman of the Council of Economic Advisers, said "many of the people the president trusted felt differently." "There were legitimate concerns about the budget," and there was also the question of appearances. A capital-gains cut would skew in favor of the rich. "Certainly the vice president was on the right economic side of this," Hubbard said. "High earners are where the entrepreneurs are."

The politics, and Bush's populist instincts, pointed elsewhere. There were breaks for the wealthy in his tax plan already. The previous tax cut, in 2001, had been criticized as a gift to the highest-paid 4 percent of taxpayers. "The president's attention and energy was always engaged by personal stories," said chief speechwriter Michael Gerson. "For the whole first campaign it was the waitress who faced this unfair high marginal tax rate." Bush talked about his "compassion agenda," Gerson said, as much in White House meetings as he did on the stump. "The president often personalized policy issues, related them to the lives of ordinary people. It's fair to say that the vice president's economic concern was much more macro."

The president made his decision at the end of 2002: Cheney's capital-gains proposal was out. "There was a question of priorities and how to fit things in," said Karl Rove, Bush's chief political adviser. "And ultimately the president made the call."

For the moment.

Back in 1974, in the second week of October, Dick Cheney got his first "supply-side" economic briefing. In contrast to "demand-side" economists, who focused on consumer spending as the engine of economic growth, supply-siders looked to boost production. Anything that helped create new businesses and new jobs, or made old ones more productive, was good for the economy. Most of the time the supply-side advocates were talking about lower taxes.

Cheney's first encounter with those ideas came in a sketch on a cocktail napkin. The story became well known in conservative circles after author Jude Wanniski told it four years later. Cheney was deputy to Don Rumsfeld, President Gerald Ford's chief of staff. Inflation was raging. Ford had just given a speech proposing to "Whip Inflation Now" with a temporary tax surcharge. There were campaign-style buttons, red and white with big block letters, saying WIN. Arthur Laffer, a former Nixon administration economist, invited Cheney to join him at dinner with Rumsfeld at the Washington Hotel, across the street from Treasury. Laffer told them Ford's tax surcharge was a dumb idea. He picked up a pen and a napkin and drew the soon-to-be-famous Laffer Curve, which looked like the launch and descent of a rocket. At first, increasing tax rates (the left-right axis) brought more revenue (the up-down axis), and so the rocket arced upward in a nice parabolic curve. Sooner or later, the trajectory reached its peak. When tax rates got high enough, people started losing their motivation to work harder and take more risk. The rocket ran out of fuel and started plunging back down. From that point, increasing tax rates would actually bring lower revenue. Laffer did not invent the idea, but he made it popular. "They got it," Laffer said. "They got it clearly."

Maybe so, but Cheney was no supply-sider yet. He did not buy the argument that tax cuts were the most important tool of economic policy. Cheney believed in old-fashioned federal budget discipline. The government should spend no more than it takes in. Like his mentor, Alan Greenspan, Cheney leaned toward monetarist economic theories, which focused on interest rates and the money supply. That emphasis placed the most consequential decisions in the hands of technocrats who ran the Federal Reserve, the government's central bank. Cheney distrusted politicians to manage an economy. The best thing a president and Congress could do, he maintained, was to leave the Fed alone and keep the budget in balance.

If budget deficits were bad, then tax cuts had to be viewed with caution. In 1983, when supply-side conservatives launched an attack on Federal Reserve chairman Paul Volcker, Cheney broke party ranks to defend him. The subtext here was politics. Republicans wanted Volcker to juice the economy for President Ronald Reagan's reelection in 1984. Representative Mickey Edwards, an Oklahoma Republican, said Reagan had saved the economy "by reducing tax rates," and Volcker was dragging it backward. Cheney, then Wyoming's sole congressman ("it was a small delegation, but it was quality," he often joked), disagreed. On the same broadcast, he said the Fed ought to be independent, free of politics. Cheney praised Reagan less for his tax cuts than "for not having berated the Fed, not having tried to undermine or undercut what Volcker was doing." The Fed chief "does deserve a lot of the credit on the inflation front because Congress, frankly, has failed on the deficit. Mickey, you would agree that the $200 billion certainly is outrageous."

At the American Enterprise Institute, a conservative think tank, Cheney ran into economist Lawrence Kudlow not long after Reagan left office in 1989. "I'm not convinced that the Reagan tax cuts worked," Cheney said. Sometime in the early 1990s, according to supply-side enthusiast Jack Kemp, Cheney came around. No longer was he "caught up in a very conventional Republican 'balance the budget *über alles*' as the solution to every problem."

"He was a late convert," said Cesar Conda, Cheney's domestic policy adviser in the White House.

The federal budget, nearing $2 trillion a year when Bush and Cheney took office, is a president's way of putting money where his mouth is. But overseeing the budget was exactly the kind of serious, vital, boring work that glazed George Bush's eyes. He had people for that. The vice president thrived in the vacuum.

In Bush's first year, the White House created a panel called the Budget Review Board. Cheney took the chair. The board set priorities and gave guidance to the agencies on their spending requests. Even so, no agency got everything it asked for. Thousands of times each year, the Office of Management and Budget turned down a request. In a tiny percentage of those cases, the relevant cabinet secretary would refuse to take no for an answer.

In previous administrations, that kind of fight came to the Oval

Office. Not under Bush. Now the conflicts came to the Budget Review Board. Theoretically, a cabinet chief could still go over Cheney's head. Mitch Daniels, the Bush administration's first budget director, said it never happened. "In the three budgets that I prepared for the president, the total number of appeals taken to the president was zero," said Daniels, now governor of Indiana. "When I spoke to old budget hands"—including Leon Panetta, Bill Clinton's budget director and then chief of staff—"they thought that was stunning. I attributed that in the main to the respect people had for the vice president. The sense people had was if that particular group didn't agree with them, then the president wasn't likely to either."

The board, in fact, was "rigged," as one member put it, to keep budget disputes "off the president's plate." That Cheney Diet again. Watch Bush's plate. Protect the commander in chief from indigestion. If a fight came to the Budget Review Board, it meant that one of the president's top appointees regarded the stakes as high. The board saw its share of parochial nonsense, but most of the time there were hard questions and real trade-offs to resolve. These were the questions that Cheney kept off Bush's plate, and the president preferred it that way.

Most often the review board sent the cabinet chief home empty-handed. The OMB decision stood. Sometimes Cheney put his finger on the other side of the scale. "One that comes to mind is one involving some Homeland Security funding that he thought was mandatory," said Josh Bolten, who succeeded Daniels. "And he gave some support to Governor [Tom] Ridge as secretary, and urged me as budget director to rethink the shuffling of the money."

Wise cabinet secretaries, and budget directors, too, vetted their proposals with Cheney in advance. Bush's third chief of the Office of Management and Budget, Rob Portman, said he used Cheney as a "sounding board" on spending matters that might become contentious. "He never, ever has said to me, 'Do this.' Never. Which is interesting, because that might be the perception of how he operates," Portman said. "But it is, 'What do you think of this?' Well, he's the vice president of the United States—and obviously I'm interested in his point of view."

In the second half of 2002, the vice president began meeting more frequently with outside advisers. The government had plenty of smart economists. The Treasury Department, just next door, could fill an arena with them. Cheney wanted to hone his thinking in private.

Recession was at hand. New York, the financial capital, had not finished recovering from September 11. The technology bubble—that irrational exuberance for tech stocks, every Silicon Valley start-up the Next Big Thing—had finally popped. Companies that fetched $30, $40 a share were penny stocks. Nobody wanted to invest in traditional securities, either. Corporation after corporation got nailed for making up profit claims, and even the financial cops could not be trusted. Arthur Andersen LLP, the stodgy old accounting firm, went out of business that summer after shredding evidence of Enron's cooked books.

"The economy had suffered a series of body blows," said Rob Nichols, then an assistant secretary of the treasury. "There was an acknowledgment that something needed to be done. But the vice president was *the* driving force."

Cheney became implacable once he made up his mind, but first he liked to hear a lot of competing views. He took government seriously, thought hard about what would work and what would not. Larry Kudlow, to whom Cheney once confessed his doubts on

Reaganomics, now became a valuable partner. Kudlow had advised Ronald Reagan, and he rose to chief economist at Bear Stearns before alcohol and drug abuse cost him the job. He came roaring back as a television host on CNBC's *Kudlow & Cramer* (later *Kudlow & Company*), which became a favorite Cheney vehicle for promoting economic plans. Cheney's brainstorming sessions brought together "a mixed group—not just supply-siders like me," Kudlow said. The vice president "loves to hear a good debate in front of him," and "he absorbs it all. He asks a lot of questions. The notion that he likes to surround himself with people who all think like he does is totally wrong."

Cheney seemed to have an endless appetite for detail: truck tonnage, freight-car loadings, seasonal variations. Michael J. Boskin, a Stanford professor who was top economic adviser to the first president Bush, found himself closely questioned about the best way to measure inflation. The consumer price index? The personal consumption expenditures deflator? The new "chained" consumer price index, which tracked spending shifts from one type of good to another? "Each of these have their pros and cons. It's pretty subtle," Boskin said. "It's a level of intelligence and intellectual curiosity and hard work and good staffing. To have a sitting vice president, who has to be dealing with an immense range of issues—to be that savvy is very impressive."

Arthur Laffer, the man with the curve, was another of Cheney's regulars. "He understands detail as far down as you want to go," Laffer said. "Most politicians are, 'If it's not on one page, don't give it to me.' You know who I mean." Cheney read the reports, and then he read the appendices. On and off airplanes, and in the car, he carried a brown leather briefcase, one of those triple-wide models that lawyers used to bring to trial before rolling bags came along. Toted it himself, taking no airs. Aaron Friedberg, a senior staff member, said the typical contents were "a thick stack of briefing books, on top of which was a copy of *Field & Stream* magazine." Brian V. McCormack, his former personal aide, said, "The ride up to the Capitol Building for the policy lunches on Tuesday—it's an eight-minute ride and he's using it."

Cheney would ask for a presentation in depth. He made jottings on breast pocket note cards embossed with the vice-presidential seal. Cheney's script was compressed and forward-leaning, letters longer than they were tall, as if his hand raced to keep up with his thoughts. He would ask a visitor to speak for ten full minutes, uninterrupted, before he began to probe. Briefings for Bush were, well, briefer. "It's 'Marty, what do you think of where we stand today?'" said Martin Feldstein, a Harvard professor who once served as chief economic adviser to Ronald Reagan. "If I were to make a ten-minute presentation to the president . . ." Feldstein trailed off. Wouldn't be invited back? He laughed.

Cheney was far from indifferent to politics, but he looked to other kinds of advisers for that. People who had never campaigned for dogcatcher should stick to what they knew. "A couple of times I made the mistake of giving my political views on some policy, and he'd shoot me down," said Conda, the vice president's domestic adviser.

"I hired you to give me policy advice," Cheney said.

The vice president had an outdoorsman's vocabulary. Sometimes he left a meeting and handed a note card to the staff. "Take soundings on this," he said. If information proved elusive, he said, "Run it to ground." Alone with his staff or with his visiting brain trust, Cheney kept that poker face, signaling nothing. "He was a total listener," said John Makin, an economist and visiting scholar at the American Enterprise Institute. "I never came away with the feeling that 'Oh, I know what the vice president is thinking.'"

By summer, Cheney knew. The question was not whether to cut taxes. The question was how to structure the cut.

The vice president usually sent a staff member to the Wednesday lunch of antitax activists hosted by Grover Norquist of Americans for Tax Reform. Norquist said Cheney was never going to be part of the "don't cut taxes, there's a deficit" crowd, which included Treasury Secretary Paul O'Neill. That is why Cheney designed a tax proposal himself. "The munchkins at Treasury would ruin it," Norquist said.

Traditional conservatives, like O'Neill and budget director Mitch Daniels, still focused on the gap between spending and revenues. George Bush had inherited a surplus, but it was long gone. Cheney no longer worried much about budget deficits. He had become convinced that lower tax rates created new jobs, and the new jobs in turn produced more income to be taxed. The Laffer Curve was back. It was the best of all worlds: the tax cuts paid for themselves. This was a point of faith for supply-siders. They had abolished the "no free lunch" maxim of Milton Friedman, the Nobel-winning libertarian who once was Cheney's economic guru. O'Neill and Alan Greenspan, another strong influence on the old Cheney, told him the supply-side claim was less than half true: lower rates did spur economic growth, but not nearly enough to make up for all the lost tax revenue. Cheney had other rejoinders. If the government had less money, it could always spend less. Better to leave cash in the hands of entrepreneurs and investors who created wealth in the first place. Wasn't the main idea to set the economy on its feet? Putting the health of the federal budget first was backward.

At an economic summit at Baylor University on August 13, 2002, business executives invited by Cheney pitched Bush on the idea of reducing the dividend tax. The president liked their argument. The way the system worked now, they said, corporate income was taxed twice. First the company itself paid tax. When it distributed income to shareholders as dividends, the shareholders paid tax on it again. Bush saw no reason to allow double taxation at all. Why cut the tax, he asked, when we can abolish it? That would be a game changer, a declaration of principle.

Cheney had two more items on his agenda. One was to speed the reduction of top income tax rates, allowing the highest earners to pay less. The other was to cut the tax on capital gains. "He got this idea from Art Laffer on capital-gains tax reductions and he was just hot on that," said Conda, the vice president's domestic adviser. Anyone who bought a stock and held it for three years could sell it after that and pay no tax at all on the profit.

Cheney hardly ever circulated his own proposals, preferring to leave the job to allies. For the capital-gains idea he made an exception. "We were not responsible for originating memos," Conda said. "It wasn't our job. Except this one time . . . He kept asking me about it."

"Where are we on this?" Cheney asked. "Let's put it in the White House policymaking process."

On September 4, 2002, O'Neill took his stand: the economy did not need another tax cut, and the country couldn't afford it. Bush had expensive plans for homeland security, a war to finish in Afghanistan, and another one looming in Iraq. According to author Ron Suskind, who based his account on O'Neill's notes, the treasury secretary told Bush the revenue loss would mean "you won't have any money to do anything you want to do . . . for the rest of your term. Now's the time to keep your powder dry. Any other path is not responsible."

Meanwhile, the director of Bush's National Economic Council, Lawrence Lindsey, made the mistake of speaking much too candidly in a newspaper interview. War with Iraq, he said, would cost 1 to 2 percent of the gross domestic product. That translated to a price tag of up to $200 billion. Lindsey's remark ignited a firestorm, inside the administration and out. Talking about the cost of war was no part of the White House plan. Don Rumsfeld at the Pentagon denounced the estimate as "baloney." Bush told his press secretary that Lindsey's statement was unacceptable. Cheney made no public statement, but this was not the kind of breach he forgave. Lindsey had committed a classic Washington "gaffe," as the writer Michael Kinsley defined the term: an inadvertent blurting of the truth. Or a piece of the truth. As Bush and Cheney prepared to leave office, the war's financial toll quadrupled Lindsey's worst-case estimate.

O'Neill kept at his message of "fiscal crisis" in November. "Reagan proved deficits don't matter," Cheney replied, according to the treasury secretary's account. "The vice president really got a sense of where O'Neill was coming from and surmised it was a problem," Conda said.

Cheney's old friend had become an obstacle. He was not, however, immovable.

Alan Greenspan, another old friend, posed a different challenge. He had been uneasy about the 2001 tax cut but had stepped out of the way. Now he was alarmed by the burgeoning deficit and its inflationary risks. He assumed that Cheney was, too. Cheney knew better than to ask Greenspan what he planned to do about it. Interest rates and money supply were the province of the Federal Reserve alone. But the vice president cared about the answer, and he collected intelligence as best he could.

Periodically Cheney invited Wayne Angell to come in for a talk. A former member of the Fed's board of governors, Angell had left the central bank to start his own firm. He had worked closely with Greenspan, and played tennis with him on weekends. He no longer had inside knowledge, but he was well positioned to forecast the Fed's next steps. Cheney's Greenspan watch took on urgency as an election year approached. Economic torpor augured badly for 2004. If the White House wanted healthy expansion by then, it would have to act soon. "The vice president was certainly aware of the importance of economic success in regard to the reelection program for 2004," Angell said.

What Cheney wanted to know was this: would Greenspan use his central banker's tools to "swing decidedly toward restraint before the 2004 election?" If so, the Fed could spoil Cheney's plans. "It would not have made a lot of sense, for example, for the vice president and the president to rely upon the expansionary impact of lower tax rates if that expansion would have been shut down by monetary policy," Angell said. "He wanted to know what I thought the Federal Reserve might do." This was a subtler version of the game that Mickey Edwards and other Republicans had played two decades earlier, looking to the Fed for help with Reagan's reelection. Cheney did not pressure Greenspan, but he devoted a lot of energy to divining Greenspan's intentions. Angell predicted, correctly, that Cheney and Bush would make it to election day "with a very, very accommodating Federal Reserve."

Greenspan and Cheney spoke often. The Fed chairman counted on the vice president as his conduit to Bush. Greenspan brought Cheney a new study, modeling the impact of burgeoning federal budget deficits. The bigger the deficit, the greater the increase in long-term interest rates. The government already borrowed so much money that it raised the cost of loans for everyone. Greenspan said the model showed that higher interest rates would choke economic growth. A new tax cut might bring short-term stimulus—a horizon that happened to include 2004—but the higher interest rates would wipe out those benefits quickly. Within a year or two the economy would be worse off.

A principled leader, the Fed chief believed, would not make that kind of trade. As far as Greenspan could tell, according to an authoritative account of his views at the time, Cheney agreed with him. The vice president had never been one to wear his thoughts on his sleeve, but over the years Greenspan had learned to read doubts in Cheney's questions. On this matter the two men seemed to have a meeting of minds. Greenspan felt confident that Cheney would pass his warning to the president.

Not until years later did Greenspan learn what Cheney did next. Cesar Conda, the vice president's adviser, said Cheney asked him to critique the Fed chief's study. Conda had experience as a tax lobbyist and congressional staffer, but he was no economist. His academic training stopped at an undergraduate degree. The paper Conda reviewed was a twenty-page technical analysis by Thomas Laubach, a Princeton Ph.D. who was senior economist in the Fed's macroeconomic and quantitative studies department. It was dense with regression analysis and mathematical derivatives. Conda said he reviewed the paper and wrote a short, punchy memo explaining that the Federal Reserve "turned out to be completely wrong" about its own data. Conda attached his rebuttal to Laubach's study and passed it around to supply-side allies in the White House.

Conda could not say what, if anything, Cheney gave to Bush. "It wasn't my job to know," he said.

The president gathered his economic team in the Roosevelt Room on November 26, 2002. Every chair was filled around the long walnut table, and lower-ranking officials lined the walls on both sides. Cheney was in some undisclosed location. The White House Communications Agency brought a portable video link, setting down the high-tech equipment alongside Chippendale furniture and cream-colored walls.

Cheney's head filled an oversize screen, like the great and powerful Oz without the flames. In truth, the screen diminished him. The Secure Video Teleconferencing System had given rise to a new government verb, to SVTS, pronounced *sih-vits*. "He can SVTS into something," said one participant, "but it's not the same when you're on the SVTS as when you are in the room." Subtle signals and private eye contact are lost; interjections cannot be timed with precision. In Cheney's case, the participant said, the video link took away a major advantage: only somebody in the room could "stay behind when everyone else leaves."

Bush still liked the dividends tax cut, and he decided to abolish the tax completely. He was skeptical about cutting the tax rate on regular income for earners in the highest bracket, a central plank in the vice president's platform. Hubbard and Lindsey, the two senior White House economic advisers, backed Cheney. Josh Bolten, Paul O'Neill, and Mitch Daniels worried that, as Bolten put it, "this burns a big hole in the budget." Daniels eventually backed down from his challenge to Cheney. "I was late to that party," he said.

The president had questions. Was it necessary to reduce income taxes again for the richest Americans? Didn't we already give them a break by getting rid of double taxation on dividends? "What are we doing on compassion?" Bush asked. The meeting meandered, as large ones do. According to Hubbard, Daniels, Conda, and others, Cheney pushed hard for the top rate cut—and for a cut in the capital-gains tax as well.

When Bush unveiled his tax package on January 7, 2003, Cheney carried the day on one but not the other. Bush did not include the capital-gains proposal in his bill. "It goes to show you," said Cesar Conda, the vice president's chief domestic policy adviser at the time. "He wins and he loses, and he lost on that one."

Losses were not always permanent for the vice president. Nor were they obvious, because Cheney cloaked them in loyal public support.

He stepped aside when Bush felt strongly, swallowing disagreements over the No Child Left Behind Act, the expansion of Medicare drug benefits, and Bush's middle-of-the-road position on affirmative action. (Cheney had joined Ted Olson, the solicitor general, in urging opposition in principle to any race-based preference.) The vice president considered it absurd that the government should pay the unemployed a bonus for finding work, a notion Bush endorsed. He advised against a bailout for Argentina's defaulting central bank, but Bush backed a plan proposed by European allies.

When the president made tactical decisions, though, or when Cheney thought his own preferences better served Bush's principles, he sometimes circled back. In trade negotiations, Karl Rove proposed a deal with Congress: Bush would support a tariff on steel imports if Congress gave him special authority to negotiate new trade agreements. Free-trade purists like Glenn Hubbard hated the steel tariff, but when Bush accepted Rove's advice, even Hubbard did not know Cheney was on his side.

Instead of grousing about the tariff, Cheney asked his staff to research options to roll it back. Once Bush got what he wanted from Congress, Cheney arranged a repeal for the steel tariff, fifteen months before it was due to expire.

"Yes, sir?" Paul O'Neill said.

Vice president on the line.

"Hey, Paul."

It was December 5, 2002, nine days after Bush's meeting in the Roosevelt Room. There would be a lot of work ahead to guide the tax plan through the House and Senate. Got to do it right. O'Neill had made it clear he was not with the program.

"What can I do for you?"

"Paul, the President has decided to make some changes in the economic team."

Pause.

"And you're part of that change."

Cheney suggested that O'Neill make the usual excuse about wanting more time with his family. The treasury secretary declined. He was too proud to pretend he had not been fired. He cleaned out his desk the next day.

Larry Lindsey, the man with the $200 billion crystal ball, departed the same day as O'Neill. For Cheney, the field was clear.

"I was a big advocate of his, without question," Cheney said later, talking about the treasury secretary. "And it's turned out to be a big disappointment. . . . It was time to make a change, so we made the change."

When George Bush came to the Greenbrier for the Congress of Tomorrow, he addressed the GOP caucus at a casual Sunday lunch. It was a few minutes after eleven on February 9, 2003, and the president took full command of the friendly crowd. He razzed Tom DeLay and Rick Santorum, big men on campus in the House and Senate. He teased the room with an old joke comparing Congress to a herd of cats. Then he turned serious.

"There's a lot of people paying attention to what's happening overseas," the president said. Today he wanted to talk about his plan "to grow our economy."

He spelled it out. He would address unemployment by cutting income taxes for top earners. That would "put more money into the pockets of the entrepreneurs of America, which is good for those who are looking for work." Abolition of the dividend tax would serve to "help our seniors and to make the Tax Code more fair." Bush cited the "10 million seniors who receive dividend income." The president did not mention capital gains. He had deep-sixed that proposal two months before.

By the time Bush spoke, the vice president had been and gone. Cheney's visit, three days earlier, was not about a speech to the whole caucus. The vice president worked the side rooms. Bush almost certainly did not know it, but his tax plan was on life support and Dr. Cheney had come to do some surgery.

"We were deciding how to proceed," recalled Representative Adam H. Putnam, who later became the third-ranking Republican in the House. "Are we going to put all our eggs in the dividends basket, or are we going to move on capital gains? As I recall, he was a very strong advocate on both counts, but particularly capital gains in terms of its potential to unleash the economy." Cheney made an impression. "The vice president is sort of the Moses of the economic message," Putnam said, "in that when he speaks, being a House guy, having been in the House and having been the CEO of a major company, he just oozes credibility."

The key to any deal would be Cheney's friend Bill Thomas, chairman of the Ways and Means Committee. Same guy who lent

Cheney an office in the Capitol. Thomas did not think abolition of the dividends tax would make it through Congress, certainly not the Senate. He liked Cheney's idea better: reduce the dividends tax instead of wiping it out. Use the extra money to cut the tax on capital gains. A little from each. Looked less radical that way.

"The president advocated a particular policy," Thomas said, but "zero dividends would not become law." Cheney helped shape a realistic alternative, Thomas said. "His usefulness is not so much packaging it—we did that," Thomas said. "It's to get people to 'yes' that's sometimes more difficult." One person in particular. The fellow in that big white mansion up Pennsylvania Avenue.

As committee chairman, Thomas proposed the amendment to Bush's tax bill. Cheney kept his name and his advice out of view. "We can use each other, in the best sense of using each other," Thomas said. They had been doing it for close to thirty years. Sometimes one of them made a proposal and the other backed his play. Sometimes "we switch roles," Thomas said. The Ways and Means chairman guided his amendment through committee, and then the full House. Along the way, a key section of Bush's tax bill changed its name. The president submitted a "Dividend Exclusion to Eliminate Double Taxation of Corporate Earnings." Now the section was called "Reduction in Taxes on Dividends and Capital Gains."

The Senate was a tougher sell, less enthusiastic about tax cuts in general and capital-gains tax cuts in particular. John McCain was among the leading skeptics. Finance Committee chairman Chuck Grassley was unsure. Cheney tapped outside allies, including Larry Kudlow, to lobby the Senate. Bill Kristol, watching from afar as the editor of the *Weekly Standard,* noticed that the vice president was bringing proxies into the debate. Nothing unusual for officials who thought they were losing, but Kristol found that telling. "He can't just snap his fingers and make things happen," Kristol said. "It struck me then that he wouldn't need to do it if he were as powerful as people think."

Kristol misjudged. Cheney needed proxies because it would be bound to get out if he lobbied for the capital-gains cut directly. He was backing a substitute for the president's proposal. Hardly anyone, in or out of the White House, knew that. "The Senate had our version," said Candi Wolff, the senior White House lobbyist, referring to the president's proposal. "The House had a different one."

A decision point came when Bush invited Bill Thomas and Chuck Grassley, the two committee chairmen, to the White House residence. Which version of the bill would come out of the conference committee, which reconciles differences between the two houses of Congress? Cheney sat in. He and Thomas had worked it out: Thomas would make his best argument on the capital-gains tax cut "and then Cheney could support me because he didn't want to pitch the policy," Thomas said.

The vice president held his silence until after the legislators were gone. "I wasn't in the room after the meeting," Thomas said. "My assumption is that the vice president, as is usually the case, was persuasive. Probably explaining that making law at that level is better than making a statement at some other unachievable level." He added, "That's why the administration changed its position." Glenn Hubbard, who chaired the Council of Economic Advisers, said Bush had always "accepted the economic arguments" about capital gains, but "I would say he was concerned about the appearance. The non sequitur was that he felt that way, but then made the decision he did."

The tax bill came to the Senate floor May 23, 2003, two months after war began in Iraq. The capital-gains amendment was attached.

Every senator showed up, and they deadlocked, fifty-fifty. Cheney sat in the chair reserved for the president of the Senate. When the tally came in, the vice president gave one of his enigmatic smiles. Then he used his only stated constitutional power. He cast the tie-breaking vote.

Chapter Eleven

OFF THE TRACKS

A burst of ferocity stunned the room into silence. No other word for it: the vice president's attorney was shouting.

The president doesn't want this!

You are not going to see the opinions.

You are out . . . of . . . your . . . lane!

Five government lawyers had gathered around a small conference table in the Justice Department Command Center. Four were expected. David Addington got wind of the meeting and invited himself. If Addington smelled revolt, he was not far wrong. No rebels lay in wait that day, but unwelcome questions had begun to find their voice. The vice president's grip on the law of war was softening. As George Bush closed his first term and began the second, federal courts and Congress sought to check the unbridled powers claimed in his name. Behind the scenes, Cheney and Addington struggled with insurgency-minded lawyers in the executive branch itself.

Months would pass before Bush became aware of the turmoil within his government. By then, the vice president and his lawyer had stoked dissent into flat-out rebellion. The president would face a dilemma, and the presidency itself a historic test. Cheney would come close to leading them off a cliff, man and office both.

On this second Monday in December 2003, Addington's targets were a pair of would-be auditors from the National Security Agency. He had displeasure to spare for their Justice Department hosts. The new man at the Office of Legal Counsel, whose credentials Addington had vetted personally, was beginning to look like a mistake. Perfect example, right here. A couple of NSA bureaucrats breeze in and ask for the most sensitive documents in the building. And Justice wants to tell them, *Help yourselves?* This was going to be a very short meeting.

Joel Brenner and Vito Potenza, the two men wilting under Addington's wrath, had driven twenty-six miles from Fort Meade, the NSA's eavesdropping headquarters in Maryland. Their subject was codeword-classified, so closely held that its name could not be uttered in public. The group convened in a windowless room, shielded against every manner of snoopery. In spy parlance it was a SCIF, a Sensitive Compartmented Information Facility, the real-world counterpart to the "Cone of Silence" used by television secret agent Maxwell Smart.

Brenner and Potenza were conducting a review of their agency's two-year-old special surveillance program. They already knew the really secret stuff: the NSA and other intelligence agencies had been unleashed to turn their machinery inward, collecting "signals intelligence" inside the United States. The program, a hybrid of new espionage activities on U.S. territory, had spread its tentacles to the FBI, the CIA, the Defense Intelligence Agency, and others, each of which used the data to conduct additional surveillance. Brenner and Potenza did not know why exactly the Bush administration believed all this was legal.

It was an awkward question. Potenza, the acting general counsel, and Brenner, the inspector general, were supposed to be the ones who kept their agency on the straight and narrow. That's what Cheney and their boss, Lieutenant General Michael Hayden, told doubters among the very few people who knew what was going on. It was one thing to say the president's politically appointed lawyers green-lighted domestic surveillance. It was another to claim a go-ahead from career civil servants, unbeholden to the White House. Cheney, who chaired briefings for select members of Congress, said repeatedly that the NSA's top law and ethics officers had approved what their agency was doing. Hayden, a reassuring uniformed presence who did most of the talking in Cheney's briefings, likewise said the new operations were "thoroughly reviewed by the NSA's general counsel and inspector general." Later, in public, Bush repeated their formula, and even made reference to Brenner. "I was concerned about the legality of the program, and so I asked lawyers—which you got plenty of them in Washington [laughter]—to determine whether or not I could do this legally. And they came back and said yes," he said. One of them, he added, was "an IG that is very active at the NSA."

None of that was true, not without one of those silent asterisks that secretly flip a sentence on its tail. Brenner and Potenza had told Hayden that the *agency* was entitled to rely on a military order from the president. America was at war with al Qaeda, intelligence gathering is inherent in war, and the Constitution appoints the president commander in chief. For a military organization, as a rule, that sufficed. They were well aware, according to other lawyers conversant with their advice, that the legal issues for the government were more complex. Potenza and Brenner were not constitutional lawyers. They had not even been asked to offer written opinions. They relied on assurances that the Justice Department's Office of Legal Counsel had made a careful review of the law. That was not true either, at the time. When the program began, on October 4, 2001, Addington's indispensable ally John Yoo had not yet been read in. Several weeks later, with colleague Robert Delahunty, Yoo wrote a broad but generic memorandum claiming "ample authority" for domestic intelligence collection. Only later did Yoo provide explicit authority for the warrantless surveillance. Now Yoo had left the department and returned to Berkeley. The NSA was hearing that Justice had new doubts. Brenner and Potenza figured it was time to read the opinions for themselves.

"This is none of your business!" Addington exploded.

He was massive in his swivel chair, taut and still, potential energy amping up the menace. Addington's pugnacity was not an act. Nothing mattered more, as the vice president and his lawyer saw the world, than these new surveillance tools. Without the program, they said in White House meetings, the nation would stand helpless before future plots. We hadn't seen the last attack coming. The next could be catastrophically worse. Maybe—maybe—the program would help head it off. Bush had made a decision. Debate could only blow the secret, slow down vital work, or call the president's constitutional prerogatives into question. Somehow it always fell to Addington to make these points. *Did no one else care?*

If Brenner and Potenza had replied with the auditor-equivalent of "you're not the boss of me," they would have been right. The two men could have pressed their document request and told the big, loud man from the White House to get out of their way. But that kind of thing did not happen often to an emissary of the vice president, Addington least of all. The NSA lawyers returned to their car empty-handed and drove back up the Baltimore-Washington Parkway. Hayden, who spoke so often of his reliance on their advice, did not intercede on their behalf. That was not the way things worked in the dance between the NSA director and Cheney. "Hayden is a very accomplished military officer, but you don't end up where he's at without being a savvy bureaucrat," said a contemporary chief of another U.S. intelligence organization. "You think Hayden hasn't figured out that crossing Addington would be bad for him personally?"

Addington had good reason to keep the legal papers under wraps, according to a government official who later took part in the dispute. Yoo's legal memos had not relied entirely on the "commander in chief override," the assertion that a president may disregard a statute or a court ruling he deems unconstitutional. In order to justify the program, Yoo had to describe it and place it in the context of existing law. The technical, operational, and legal issues were elaborate. Brenner and Potenza understood the NSA machinery and its intricate body of rules—the Foreign Intelligence Surveillance Act, the Electronic Communications Privacy Act, the Telecommunications Act, Executive Order 12333, attorney general guidelines for foreign intelligence collection, U.S. Signals Intelligence Directive 18. No novice could master all that quickly, and experts who read his work later said Yoo made a mess of it. "If NSA lawyers had seen the NSA opinions, they would have cried foul, because the opinions were incompetent in areas the NSA lawyers knew everything about," an official said. That, it turned out, was the point: Brenner and Potenza were just the kind of cautious bureaucrats, to Addington's way of thinking, who crippled a workforce of tens of thousands of spies with a risk-nothing, gain-nothing "culture of compliance." If that were not enough, Potenza was a registered Democrat. Addington did not mention it, but colleagues said he made a practice of knowing things like that.

The NSA's lawyer and inspector general made sure the agency carried out its orders to the letter. What they could not do was judge for themselves that the orders were legal.

The command center of "the President's Program," as Addington usually called it, was not in the White House. Its controlling documents, which gave strategic direction to the eavesdropping apparatus at Fort Meade, lived in a vault across an alley from the West Wing—in the Eisenhower Executive Office Building, on the east side of the second floor, where the vice president headquartered his staff.

The vault was in EEOB 268, Addington's office. Cheney's lawyer held the documents, physical and electronic, because he was the one who wrote them. Each authorization package included a fresh assessment, prepared by the CIA director, of the ongoing threat from terrorists and the value of intelligence gleaned from the special surveillance. There was also a signature from Attorney General John Ashcroft attesting to each order's proper "form and legality." But the source documents of the program—in which new forms of domestic spying were created and developed over time—were Presidential Authorizations that Addington typed on a Tempest-shielded computer across from his desk.

It is unlikely that the history of U.S. intelligence includes another operation conceived and supervised by the office of the vice president. Back in 2001, it had been Cheney who brought Bush a radically new concept of electronic surveillance at home. Through his lawyer, the vice president now guided the program's expansion and development. Words, once signed by the commander in chief, became orders for the nation's espionage machinery. And it was Addington who wrote those words, defining the reach of warrantless intrusion into the lives of Americans. On national security matters, the president's own lawyer, White House counsel Alberto Gonzales, did little more than review documents that Addington prepared. None of this meant that Cheney had usurped the president. Bush gave his blessing. The vice president and his lawyer translated broad concepts into the language of action, and thereby acquired power.

White House chief of staff Andrew Card had "no idea," he said, that the presidential orders were held in a vice-presidential safe. An authoritative source said the staff secretariat, which kept a comprehensive inventory of presidential papers, classified and unclassified, possessed no record of these. In an interview, Card said the Executive Office of the President, a formal term that encompassed Bush's staff but not Cheney's, followed strict procedures for handling and securing presidential papers. "If there were exceptions to that, I'm not aware of them," he said. "If these documents weren't stored the right way or put in the right places or maintained by the right people, I'm not aware of it." Asked why Addington would write presidential directives, Card said, "David Addington is a very competent lawyer." After a moment he added, "I would consider him *a* drafter, not *the* drafter. I'm sure there were a lot of smart people who were involved in helping to look at the language and the law."

For the first eighteen months, the helper's job belonged to John Yoo. Gonzales and Addington assigned Yoo to prepare the program's supporting legal opinions, and they instructed him to tell no one else, including his direct superior. By the time the NSA auditors came calling, a new man, Jack Goldsmith, was chief of the Office of Legal Counsel. Soon after Goldsmith arrived on October 6, 2003, the vice president's lawyer invited him to EEOB 268. Nobody from the NSA or White House staff was in the room. Addington pulled out a folder with classification markings that Goldsmith had never seen.

"David Addington was doing all the legal work. All the important documents were kept in his safe," Goldsmith recalled. "He was the one who first briefed me."

That turned out to be the norm. Initiates to the program often received their first briefings from Addington or Cheney himself. Addington had de facto control of read-ins, according to three officials with personal knowledge. Among those kept out of the circle were Jay Bybee, ostensibly John Yoo's boss and the Bush administration's chief interpreter of laws, and two successive deputy attorneys general, whose jobs might require them to certify the program in Ashcroft's absence, Larry Thompson and James B. Comey. Then there was John Bellinger, the legal counsel to National Security Adviser Condoleezza Rice. "Bellinger didn't know," said Bryan Cunningham, then Rice's deputy counsel. "That was a mistake." Addington's effort to regulate access to the program was unrealistic, in one sense, because signals intelligence is mass-produced by tens of thousands of workers on an eight-square-mile campus. Hayden had to brief close to a hundred employees on the program's first day, and those were supervisors. But the vice president's office could and did make sure that, in policy and political circles, only essential allies found out.

Goldsmith's new assignment gave him final word in the executive branch on what was legal and what was not. He had not been anyone's first choice. Cheney and Addington had suggested John Yoo to run the Office of Legal Counsel after helping Yoo's boss move out to a federal judgeship. Attorney General John Ashcroft balked, accusing Yoo (accurately) of working back channels to the White House. Ashcroft's own candidate was deemed insufficiently reliable.

Goldsmith, the compromise appointee, landed the position without exactly applying. A forty-one-year-old Chicago law professor, he had worked for Addington's friend William J. Haynes II, the Defense Department's general counsel. He was already scheduled to return to academic life. Goldsmith had a rock-ribbed conservative reputation, making his name as a legal scholar with critiques of "the creeping influence of international law" on American courts. Before coming to Justice he wrote a memo to Don Rumsfeld, warning that "various nations, NGOs, academics, international organizations, and others in the 'international community' have been busily weaving a web of international laws and judicial institutions that today threatens USG interests." He urged the government to fight the claim that treaties and customary international law—for example, human rights conventions—establish obligations that may be enforced in U.S. courts. He had thrived among academic elites, earning first-class honors at Oxford University, emerging from Yale Law School as a conservative "after an allergic reaction to Yale's left-wing jurisprudence," and clerking for Supreme Court justice Anthony Kennedy.

Addington was "the biggest presence in the room" during a job interview ostensibly conducted by Alberto Gonzales. The vice president's lawyer made clear he had read and approved Goldsmith's scholarly writings, some of them fairly obscure. If there were an all-time highlight reel for job interviews, Goldsmith might have made the cut with his answer to a stock question on potential embarrassments: "The only thing I could think of, I said, was that my stepfather was Jimmy Hoffa's right-hand man and a longtime suspect in Hoffa's disappearance." That jaw-dropper did not evince much interest from Addington, who walked Goldsmith through a checklist of the administration's new frontiers in national security law. The two lawyers agreed on everything—military commissions to try terrorists, the denial of POW status to al Qaeda and Taliban fighters, the legality of the invasion of Iraq. But they did not discuss the subjects that brought them to loggerheads in coming months: the NSA's special surveillance and the gloves-off interrogation of "high-value" terror suspects. Goldsmith did not yet know those programs existed.

How much could it matter? Goldsmith did not have the looks of a guy who posed a threat to the government's alpha lawyer. He was easy to underestimate, rumpled and self-conscious on first impression. At University College, Oxford, in the 1980s, Goldsmith mostly kept to himself in the small walk-up lounge where graduate students drank instant coffee and read the British tabloids. Round-faced and bookish, he gave off a misleading aura of softness. He had lettered in football, baseball, and soccer at Pine Crest High School in Fort Lauderdale. The son of a Miss Teenage Arkansas and a father who "blew through his trust fund" and disappeared, Goldsmith spent his teenage years with the mob-connected Teamster who married his mother. He was not a bare-knuckled brawler in Addington's mold, but Goldsmith arrived at Justice with no less intellectual self-confidence and strength of will.

Goldsmith does not recall saying a word during Addington's eruption at the NSA visitors on December 9. But the vice president's lawyer had already learned to keep an eye on the newbie at the OLC. In his first week on the job, Goldsmith delivered an unwelcome ruling that Iraqi combatants held by U.S. forces there, unlike al Qaeda and Taliban troops in Afghanistan, were entitled to rights under the Geneva Conventions.

Then Goldsmith stepped in to protect a staff member in a dispute with Addington. According to two former lawyers in the office, the vice president's counsel somehow found time to read OLC "bill comments" on every piece of legislation before Congress. These were routine internal memos for the record, committing the government to nothing. It made no sense to anyone that the vice president's man would care. "There was nothing at stake," one lawyer there said. Yet Addington interceded repeatedly as an editor. One day during Goldsmith's first month, Addington sent a scathing e-mail to an OLC line attorney, complaining that the attorney failed to consider the question of congressional jurisdiction. He cited a 1995 case and demanded a rewrite. Goldsmith read the case, disagreed with Addington, and told the attorney to leave his memo as it was. If the legal issue was inconsequential, Goldsmith's independence was not.

Meanwhile, Goldsmith had been studying the special surveillance program with growing unease. Addington's behavior with the NSA auditors was "a wake-up call for me," Goldsmith said, warning him that he had better look even more closely. Cheney and Addington, Goldsmith came to believe, manipulated the legal advice they sought. "They were geniuses at this," Goldsmith said. "They could divide up all these problems in the bureaucracy, ask different people to decide things in their lanes, control the facts they gave them, and then put the answers together to get the result they want."

December 9, 2003, was the beginning of the end of that strategy. The days of easy victory, of fundamental policy made in secret without opponents showing up, were winding down for Cheney and his staff.

The program still required Ashcroft's signature every forty-five days. For several months—from John Yoo's departure in May 2003 to Goldsmith's arrival in October—a lawyer named Patrick Philbin had been handling the classified paperwork. Addington hand-picked Philbin for the job, regarding him as a loyal soldier. With Yoo, he had written muscular memos after September 11 on the president's wartime authority, approving for example the detention of foreign suspects at Guantánamo Bay with no access to American courts. Philbin had walked the stations of the conservative legal establishment—Federalist Society, a clerkship with Judge Laurence Silberman, another with Supreme Court justice Clarence Thomas. (Those were John Yoo's credentials exactly.) At the Pentagon, Rumsfeld presented

Philbin with the "Exceptional Civilian Service Award for Support to the Secretary of Defense in the War on Terror."

The easy thing for Philbin would have been to cut and paste from previous legal memos. The program had been certified a dozen times. But this was not a routine matter, and the facts kept changing. There were updates in the threat reports, in the nature of the surveillance itself, and in the intelligence gleaned. All those things could affect the program's legality.

The more questions Philbin asked, the less he liked the answers. Parts of the program fell easily within the constitutional powers of the commander in chief. Others looked dicier. Philbin had to study the intersection of three complex systems: telecommunications, spy technology, and the statutory regimes that governed surveillance. Some of the things the program did seemed to need permission from Congress or the courts.

On its face, the program violated two felony statutes forbidding electronic surveillance without a warrant. The specified exceptions in those statutes did not apply. It was possible to argue that Congress had created an implicit exception in its use-of-force resolution after September 11. That was a controversial claim, but if it was true, the exception covered only surveillance of "nations, organizations or persons" responsible for the New York and Washington attacks. Other laws required the president to notify Congress about the program. The meaning of "timely" notice had some wiggle room, but not enough to cover a two-year delay. Lawyers could debate which of two possible notification requirements applied, but the White House was conforming to neither. There was a case to be made that telephone and Internet customers waived their privacy rights in the fine print of their service contracts. Some government lawyers said the companies could therefore hand over any communications they liked. Maybe that argument could protect the companies from civil lawsuits. Maybe not. But it did not do much to help the government address the Fourth Amendment problems or the statutory limits on its own intrusions into privacy. Then there was the question of what the government did with the intelligence. If it led to information that produced a warrant application, or a criminal indictment, the program could be tainting evidence presented in court. Another issue was e-mail, which turned out to be legally trickier than expected. Unless the program rejected surveillance laws altogether, it should have been making sharp distinctions between its handling of e-mail and of telephone calls. Voice travels by wire or radio waves, which are covered by one set of rules. E-mails move across the same electronic highways, but each one is chopped into "packets" that travel separately, often by different routes, and are reassembled only upon arrival. If the NSA "acquired" e-mail at its source or destination, rather than during transit, it would be subject to stricter legal standards. Another problem for e-mail surveillance was the difficulty of knowing whether the parties were in the United States or overseas, a legal distinction the program tried to maintain. You can send a message to someone while he is in Paris, but he may not receive it until he logs in from New York. Advocates of the program found it absurd that the legality of surveillance should "depend on the mode of communication selected by the target," as one official put it. But that anomaly and others faced anyone engaged in a serious study of the law.

Jack Goldsmith took over the account in December. After a few weeks, he decided the program "was the biggest legal mess I'd seen in my life." He approached Ashcroft in December.

"Do what you have to do to fix it," Ashcroft said. "We have to make sure this is being done lawfully."

At the time, the attorney general had no reason to believe the White House would resist. Cheney clearly had the lead on this. That could be a big plus. The vice president had "a history of being one of the best-prepared people" when it came to troubleshooting, Ashcroft said in an interview, without referring to NSA surveillance. "He reserved his comments for a time when you were pretty sure this was not just air moving in the room," Ashcroft said. "He was the E. F. Hutton in the room. When he talked, everybody would listen." If Cheney saw things as Justice did, there was no more important ally.

Goldsmith wanted another pair of eyes on the problem at Justice. He asked for permission to read in Ashcroft's new deputy, Jim Comey, "one of the quickest and shrewdest lawyers I have ever met." Ashcroft liked the idea, but he did not have that power. Goldsmith had to bring the request to the White House. As always, he found Addington waiting with Gonzales in the White House counsel's corner office, one floor up from the chief of staff. They sat in parallel wing chairs, much as Bush and Cheney did in the Oval Office.

"The attorney general and I think the deputy attorney general should be read in," Goldsmith said.

Addington replied first. "Forget it," he said.

"The president insists on strict limitations on access to the program," Gonzales agreed.

Weeks passed. Goldsmith kept asking. Addington kept saying no. "He always invoked the president, not the vice president," Goldsmith said. In January 2004, Goldsmith began threatening that Ashcroft might withhold his certification if he could not obtain advice as he saw fit. Comey was not exactly Mr. Popular at 1600 Pennsylvania Avenue. He had arrived at Justice as a six-foot-eight golden boy, smooth and polished, with top chops as a terrorism prosecutor in Virginia and New York. Then came December 30. A political spat with a Cheney critic had led to the leak of his wife's identity as a clandestine officer of the CIA. The investigation was beginning to point to the White House. Ashcroft recused himself. Then Comey did something unforgivable: he appointed an independent counsel.

People around the president began calling him "Cuomey," morphing him with the liberal Democrat from New York. It was not a compliment. Bush said it too, and probably said it first, but it may have been one of his innocent garbles. At a campaign rally in Iowa that summer, Republican activist Maurene Failor, a $2,000 contributor to Bush-Cheney 2004, introduced herself to the president as Comey's mother-in-law.

"Jim Cuomey's a great American," Bush said.

"It's *Comey,* Mr. President," she replied.

"Hey, Rudy!" Bush called out to former New York mayor Rudy Giuliani, correcting himself, "this is Jim Comey's mother-in-law!" There were warm greetings all around.

In late January, Goldsmith and Addington cut a deal. Comey would get his read-in. Goldsmith would get off the fence about the program. "They'd get a definitive answer from me by the next deadline," he said.

"You're the head of the Office of Legal Counsel, and if you say we cannot do this thing legally, we'll shut it off," Addington told him.

Feel free to tell the president that his most important intelligence operation has to stop.

Your call, Jack.

Goldsmith wanted to fix the thing, not stop it. He and Philbin traveled again and again to Fort Meade, each time delving deeper into what the program did and how it worked. They were in and out of Gonzales's office, looking for changes in the parts they could not justify. Addington bent on nothing, swatting back every idea. Gonzales listened placidly, sipping Diet Cokes from his little refrigerator, encouraging the antagonists to keep things civil.

There would be no easy out, no middle ground. Addington made clear that he did not believe for a moment that Justice would pull the plug. The stakes were way too high. Goldsmith could not disagree on that point. By saying no to the commander in chief, he told a Senate panel four years later, he "worried very, very much that people were going to end up being killed by it. And if that had happened, I would be here on this green felt table and people would be saying . . . 'You legalistic, pin-headed lawyer, you. Look, you told the president he couldn't do something and a lot of people got killed.'"

Mike Hayden and Vito Potenza drove down from Fort Meade after lunch on February 19, 2004, to give Jim Comey his first briefing on the program. In the Justice Department's sixth-floor SCIF, Hayden got Comey's attention fast.

"I'm so glad you're getting read in, because now I won't be alone at the table when John Kerry is elected president," he said. The witness table, Hayden meant. Congressional hearing, investigation of some kind. Nothing good. Kerry had the Democratic nomination just about locked up and was leading Bush in national polls. Hardly anyone in the intelligence field believed the next administration would climb as far out on a legal limb as this one had. That was one reason Hayden pushed for some kind of congressional notification.

Back in his office after the meeting, Comey met with his chief of staff and Philbin.

"Holy shit, what is the head of the NSA about to tell the deputy attorney general, that he begins with that introduction?" Comey told them, recounting his reaction. The briefing was a mindblower, but the spell was dissipating already. "Hayden was all dog and pony, and this is probably what happened to those poor folks in Congress, too," Comey told them. "You think for a second, 'Wow, that's great,' and then if you try actually to explain it back to yourself you don't get it. You scratch your head afterward and you think, 'What the hell did that guy just tell me?'"

By the end of the month, Goldsmith and Philbin reached their conclusion: parts of the surveillance operation had no support in law. They walked Comey through the program, in far greater depth than Hayden had. Comey was so disturbed that he drove to Langley one evening to compare notes with Scott Muller, the general counsel at the CIA. Muller "got it immediately," agreeing with the Goldsmith-Philbin analysis.

"At the end of the day I concluded something I didn't ever think I would conclude, and that is that Pat Philbin and Jack Goldsmith understood this activity much better than Michael Hayden did," Comey said. "They drilled down, understood things in a way that more senior people didn't."

On Thursday, March 4, Comey brought the findings to Ashcroft, conferring for an hour one-on-one. The two men "agreed on a course of action," Comey later testified. Three senior Justice Department officials said in interviews that Ashcroft gave his full backing to the Office of Legal Counsel. He was not going to sign the next presidential order—due in one week, March 11—unless the White House agreed to a list of required changes.

Ashcroft was reviewing notes for a news conference in Alexandria, a few hours later, when his color changed and he sat down heavily. An aide, Mark Corallo, ducked out and returned to find the attorney general laid out on his back. By nightfall, Ashcroft had been rushed to George Washington University Medical Center in severe pain, suffering acute gallstone pancreatitis. The complications would come close to killing him. On Friday, Comey became acting attorney general.

The next day—Saturday, March 6, five days before the March 11 deadline—Goldsmith brought the Justice Department verdict to the White House. He told Gonzales and Addington for the first time that Justice would not certify the program.

"If you rule that way, the blood of the hundred thousand people who die in the next attack will be on your hands," Addington roared.

"The president is free to overrule me if he wants," Goldsmith said. Most constitutional scholars agreed. Article II, Section 3, said the president "shall take Care that the Laws be faithfully executed," and that made him their chief interpreter in the executive branch. But in the legal and political culture of the postwar United States, that was not an attractive option. Nor was the alternative that Goldsmith offered that morning. "The president can also ignore the law, and act extralegally," he said.

A long silence fell. It lasted three full days.

Gonzales phoned Goldsmith at home before sunrise on Tuesday, March 9, with two days left before the program expired. There was bad chemistry, he realized, with Addington. Why not come in and talk, just the two of us? Goldsmith arrived at the White House in morning twilight. Alone in his office, Gonzales begged the OLC chief to reconsider. Gonzales tried to dispute Goldsmith's analysis, but he was in over his head. At least let us have more time, he said. Goldsmith said he could not do that, either.

The time had come for the vice president to step in. Proxies were not getting the job done. Cheney was going to have to get hold of this thing himself.

Cheney did not enlist the president. Bush was across the river in Arlington, commending the winners of the Malcolm Baldrige awards for quality improvement. Campaign season had come already, and the president was doing a lot of that kind of thing. That week he had a fund-raiser in Dallas, a "Bush-Cheney 2004 event" in Santa Clara, and a meet and greet at the rodeo in Houston.

Soon after hearing what had happened between Goldsmith and Gonzales, the vice president asked Andy Card to set up a meeting at noon with Mike Hayden, FBI director Robert Mueller, and John McLaughlin (subbing for George Tenet) from the CIA. Cheney spoke to them in Card's office, the door closed.

Four hours later, at 4:00 p.m., the same cast reconvened. This time the Justice contingent was invited. Comey, Goldsmith, and Philbin found the titans of the intelligence establishment lined up, a bunch of grave-faced analysts behind them for added mass. The spy chiefs brought no lawyers. The law was not the point. This meeting was about telling Justice to set its qualms aside.

The staging had been arranged for maximum impact. Cheney sat at the head of Card's rectangular table, pivoting left to face the acting attorney general. The two men were close enough to touch. Card sat grimly at Cheney's right, directly across from Comey. There was plenty of eye contact all around.

This program, Cheney said, was vital. Turning it off would leave us blind. It would be a profound mistake. Hayden, the NSA chief, pitched in: even if the program had yet to produce blockbuster results, it was the only real hope of discovering sleeper agents before they could act.

"How can you possibly be reversing course on something of this importance after all this time?" Cheney asked.

Comey held his ground. The program had to operate within the law. The Justice Department knew a lot more now than it had before, and Ashcroft and Comey had reached this decision together. "I will accept for purposes of discussion that it is as valuable as you say it is," Comey said. He and his colleagues had their doubts, actually, but they did not need to have that argument, too. "That only makes this more painful. It doesn't change the analysis. If I can't find a lawful basis for something, your telling me you really, really need to do it doesn't help me."

"Others see it differently," Cheney said. There was only one of those, really. John Yoo had been out of the picture for nearly a year. It was all Addington.

"The analysis is flawed, in fact facially flawed," Comey said. "No lawyer reading that could reasonably rely on it." Gonzales said nothing. Addington stood by the window, over Cheney's shoulder. He had heard a bellyful. "Well, I'm a lawyer and I did," Addington said, glaring at Comey.

"No *good* lawyer," Comey said.

In for a dime, in for a dollar.

Addington started disputing the particulars. Now he was on Jack Goldsmith's turf. From across the room the head of the Office of Legal Counsel jumped in. And right there in front of the big guys, the two of them bickered in the snarly tones of a couple who knew all each other's lines.

As the sun went down on Tuesday, the president of the United States had yet to learn that his Justice Department was off the rails. A train wreck was coming, but Cheney wanted to handle it. Neither Card nor Gonzales was in the habit of telling him no.

"I don't think it would be appropriate for the president to be engaged in the to-and-fro until it is, you know, penultimate," Card said in an interview. "I guess the definition of 'penultimate' could vary from four steps to three steps to two steps to one step. That's why you have White House counsel and people who do the legal work."

Participants in the Tuesday-afternoon meeting, including some of Cheney's recruits, left the room shaken. Mueller worked for the attorney general, and the FBI's central mission was to "uphold and enforce the criminal laws of the United States." Hayden's neck, and his agency, were on the line. The NSA director believed in the program, believed he was doing the right thing. But keep on going when the Justice Department said no?

Early the next morning—Wednesday, March 10, with twenty-four hours to deadline—Hayden was back in the White House. One colleague saw him conferring in worried whispers with Homeland Security Adviser John Gordon, a mentor and fellow Air Force general, much the senior of the two. They huddled in the West Wing lobby, Hayden on the love seat and Gordon in a chair. The conversation must have been somewhat cramped: even the homeland security adviser, according to the vice president's office, had no "need to know" about homeland surveillance. But the two officers had been around the block a few times, and they knew how to talk without quite talking.

Jim Comey was in the White House that morning, too, arriving early for the president's regular eight-thirty terrorism brief. He had heard nothing since the discouraging meeting the day before. Comey found Fran Townsend, an old friend, waiting just outside the Oval Office, standing by the appointment secretary's desk. She was Bush's deputy national security adviser for combating terrorism, but Comey had known her since their days as New York mob prosecutors in the 1980s. Since then, Townsend had run the Justice Department's intelligence office. She lived and breathed surveillance law.

Comey took a chance. He pulled her back out to the hallway between the Roosevelt Room and the Cabinet Room.

"If I say a word, would you tell me whether you recognize it?" he asked quietly.

He did. She didn't. The program's classified code name, Stellar Wind, left her blank. Comey tried to talk around the subject, haltingly. He looked worried.

"I think this is something I am not a part of," Townsend said. "I can't have this conversation." Like Steve Hadley and John Gordon and Secretary of Homeland Security Tom Ridge, she was out of the loop.

Oh God, Comey remembers thinking. *They've held this so tight. Even Fran Townsend. The president's counterterrorism adviser is not read in?*

Comey towered over his diminutive friend. He chose his words carefully.

"I need to know," he said, "whether your boss recognizes that word, and whether she's read in on a particular program. Because we had a meeting here yesterday on that topic that I would have expected her to be at." He was hoping for an ally, or maybe rescue. "I don't know what I was looking for, to be honest," Comey recalled. "I felt very alone, with some justification. The attorney general is in intensive care. There's a train coming down the tracks that's about to run me and my career and the Department of Justice over. I was exploring every way to get off the tracks I could."

Chapter Twelve

U-TURN ON
CONSTITUTION AVENUE

F ran Townsend had a pretty good guess about the problem on Jim Comey's mind. Anyone in a senior national security post, by then, had an inkling of the warrantless-surveillance program, if only from sourceless intelligence reports, unexplained silences in meetings.

"I'm not the right person to talk to," Townsend told Comey in the hallway outside the Oval Office. "You should talk to Condi. I'm going to tell her you've got concerns."

Comey's concerns no longer interested Cheney. The battleground had shifted. Tuesday had been for backing Comey down, or Jack Goldsmith. Either one would have to fold without the other. Wednesday was for taking the fight somewhere else. "They probably thought there was a palace coup in the Justice Department," Goldsmith said, looking back on it in 2008. "They'd known for months I had problems with the program and that Ashcroft was on board with my position. But I can imagine how they were thinking. Is it really a coincidence that twenty-four hours after Ashcroft goes to the hospital we come in and say we can't approve this? These are 'unitary executive' people. 'Are you telling me the fifth-ranking person in the Justice Department is going to tell the president what he can't do?' They were just offended by that idea."

On Wednesday, March 10, Comey learned that Cheney had called a meeting of congressional leaders to update them on the program. The acting attorney general smelled a rat. He asked an aide to let the White House know he was coming. The answer came back promptly. "You're not invited," the aide said.

Cheney convened his meeting in the Situation Room. Bush, even now, was nowhere in the picture. He was stumping the battleground state of Ohio, talking up the economy in Cleveland. Around the vice president were Hayden, Gonzales, and the Gang of Eight—the four ranking members of the House and Senate, and the chairmen and vice chairmen of the intelligence committees. This was for their ears only. No staff, no notes. Some of them, Cheney said, were about to learn for the first time about an exceptionally sensitive matter. Hayden walked through the program's vital mission, his personal commitment as an officer to collect what the law allowed and not one photon or one electron more. Gonzales said the top lawyers at NSA and Justice had green-lighted the program from the beginning. Now Ashcroft had fallen ill, and the new man, Comey, took the view that the president lacked authority.

More than three years later, Gonzales would testify that "we were there asking for help, to ask for emergency legislation." Gonzales presented to the lawmakers, he testified, "in the most forceful way that I could the disagreement that existed." Under questioning, he acknowledged that he spoke only of Comey, but he said it would be "logical for them to assume . . . that perhaps the Office of Legal Counsel might also have that same position." As Gonzales told the story, there was "consensus in the room" from the legislators, "who said, 'Despite the recommendation of the deputy attorney general, go forward with these very important intelligence activities.'" By this account, four Democrats and four Republicans, duly informed that the Justice Department had ruled something unlawful, said the White House should do it anyway.

Tom Daschle, then Senate minority leader, said the Gonzales story "does not conform at all to my recollection. It is completely untrue." Jane Harman, then the ranking minority member of the House Intelligence Committee, said, "We were briefed on the operational details, period. We were not briefed on the legal underpinnings. . . . I was never told, I figured this out after these briefings basically stopped, that they had substantially failed to follow FISA over the years."

According to participants, Cheney appeared to be skeptical of a legislative solution anyway. (In White House discussions he had opposed the idea in principle because asking for permission means the president thinks he needs it.) Cheney showed the lawmakers no proposed bill that day, said nothing particular about what a law might say. The question he framed came close to answering itself. Could Congress hold hearings and write a new law, giving new authority under the Foreign Intelligence Surveillance Act, or FISA, for the program, without tipping off anyone that something was afoot? Gonzales described the reply: "It would be very, very difficult to obtain legislation without compromising this program."

Later, Jane Harman would ask for a private appointment with Cheney. She sat down with him one-on-one in room H-208, just off the House floor, shortly before an address to a joint session of Congress. "I felt so strongly that the full committee should be briefed," she said. That would enable her to consult the committee's staff attorney. "I could do the legal research, do a deeper dive into the legal underpinnings," she said. Harman came as an ally. The program was vitally important, she believed, but it had to be done by the book. "I said, 'I'm the one who's coming to you. I'm someone who believes these programs are important, provided they comply with the law. I believe you have an obligation to brief the full committee.' And he looked at me and he said, 'No.'"

"Enough people have been briefed," Cheney said.

Royce Lamberth, the chief FISA judge in the program's first year, said the Bush administration had no interest in changing the law. "We could have gone to Congress, hat in hand, the judicial branch and the executive together, and gotten any statutory change we wanted in those days, I felt like," he said. "And I felt like there was a way the statute could have been tweaked in a way that they could have lived with. But they wanted to demonstrate that the president's power was supreme, and the judiciary was just a tagalong when necessary, but not appreciated."

Late that Wednesday afternoon, Bush returned from Cleveland. Soon afterward, the phone started ringing in the makeshift command center next to John Ashcroft's hospital room. Janet Ashcroft had been at her husband's side for six days. He was in intensive care, sedated, recovering from emergency surgery to remove his gallbladder. Mrs. Ashcroft's orders were unequivocal: no calls, from anyone, for any reason. According to two people who saw the FBI's handwritten logs, the White House operator—on behalf of Gonzales or Card, it was unclear which—asked to be connected to the attorney general. The hospital switchboard, following orders, declined.

That evening, the FBI logged a call from the president of the United States. No one had the nerve to refuse him. The phone rang at Ashcroft's bedside. Bush told his ailing cabinet chief that Alberto Gonzales and Andy Card were on their way.

The next hour or two of the story, or some of it, is now well known. After that, there is a lot that has never been told. Janet Ashcroft called her husband's chief of staff, David Ayres. Ayres called Comey, who was on his way home. Comey told his driver to make a U-turn on Constitution Avenue. The driver switched on the siren, slapped a flashing light onto the roof of the car, and stepped on the gas. At 7:20 p.m., en route, Comey got through to Mueller at a restaurant with his wife and daughter. "I'll meet you at the hospital right now," the FBI director said. Goldsmith got a similar call. He stood up abruptly from dinner at home and raced to Twenty-first and Pennsylvania Avenue, phoning Philbin from his car. It was a stock scene from Hollywood's Washington: men in their forties and fifties, stamping on the brakes, abandoning double-parked vehicles, and running up a hospital stairwell as fast as their legs could pump.

Comey, Goldsmith, and Philbin converged on the room before Gonzales and Card arrived. As soon as he saw the layout, Comey placed another call. He spoke a few words to Mueller and handed the phone to an agent on Ashcroft's FBI guard detail. Mueller instructed the agent "not to allow me to be removed from the room under any circumstances," Comey said later. The attorney general was semiconscious. Comey sat at his bedside, quietly telling Ashcroft what was happening. Goldsmith and Philbin stood behind him.

In came the White House chief of staff and White House counsel, proferring an envelope.

"How are you, General?" Gonzales asked.

"Not well," Ashcroft said.

Gonzales tried to tell Ashcroft the afternoon's manufactured news: the Gang of Eight had spoken, and they wanted the program to carry on. The White House counsel used a peculiar formula.

"We've achieved a legislative remediation that will address Justice's concerns," he said.

"I remember thinking, what the *hell* does that mean?" Comey said. Ashcroft had relinquished his legal authority. He looked half dead. What if Gonzales actually tried to put a pen in his hand? The White House counsel testified later that "there are no rules" that prevent a disabled official from deciding, "I'm feeling well enough" to return to duty.

The showdown with the vice president, the day before, had been excruciating, the pressure "so great it could crush you like a grape," Comey said. This was worse. Was Comey going to sit there and watch a barely conscious man make his mark on a piece of paper? "I didn't know what I was going to do," Comey said. Right about then, Ashcroft raised himself up stiffly. He glared at his visitors and said they had no business coming. He gave a lucid account of the reasons that Justice had decided to withhold support. And then he went beyond that. Ashcroft said he never should have certified the program.

"You drew the circle so tight I couldn't get the advice that I needed," Ashcroft said, according to Comey. He knew things today, he said, that he should have known before they first asked for his signature. If it were up to him now, he would refuse to approve. But it was not up to him. Gesturing at his deputy, Ashcroft said, "*There* is the attorney general." Spent and pale, Ashcroft sank back down. As Gonzales and Card retreated, Janet Ashcroft "shook her head and stuck her tongue out," Goldsmith recalled. "It wasn't funny at all. It was completely serious. He was really, really sick. He'd just expended himself. I was worried he was going to die."

Mueller, who arrived soon afterward, spent a private moment with Ashcroft. He leaned over the bed.

"Bob, I'm struggling," Ashcroft said.

"In every man's life there comes a time when the good Lord tests him," Mueller replied. "You have passed your test tonight."

Later, Card said privately that the hospital visit was among his greatest regrets. That night, he directed his fury at Comey. As soon as he reached his office, Card telephoned the acting attorney general. Harsh words were spoken. Card demanded that Comey march over to the White House—right away.

Not alone, Comey said. Not after the conduct he had just seen.

"What conduct? We were just there to wish him well," Card said.

"After what I just witnessed, I will not meet with you without a witness, and I intend that witness to be the solicitor general of the United States," Comey repeated.

By now, Goldsmith was out the door. He telephoned Ed Whelan, his deputy, who was at home bathing his kids. "You've got to get into the office now," Goldsmith said. "I'll tell you when I get there." He couldn't tell much. Whelan was not cleared. Goldsmith said he had just come from an astonishing scene of courage in the face of official misbehavior. "Please draft a resignation letter for me," he told Whelan. "I can't tell you why."

All hell was breaking loose at Justice. Phone calls and BlackBerry messages pinged around the senior staff. Lawyers streamed back to the building from the suburbs, converging on the fourth-floor conference room. Comey spoke privately with Solicitor General Ted Olson, then chaired a meeting that lasted over an hour. Associate Attorney General Robert McCallum, the third-ranking official at Justice, joined in. So did David Ayres and David Israelite, Ashcroft's chief and deputy chief of staff. Daniel Levin, Ashcroft's counselor, and Chuck Rosenberg, Comey's chief of staff, were there, too. Some of them had to leave when Comey talked about the substance of the dispute. Apart from Goldsmith and Philbin, only Levin and Rosenberg (from previous jobs) knew about the program.

Everyone in the room could see the White House had crossed some kind of line that Comey could not abide. A decision was beginning to coalesce: if Comey quit, none of them were staying.

At the FBI, they called Mueller "Bobby Three Sticks," playfully tweaking the Roman numerals in his fancy Philadelphia name, Robert Swann Mueller III. But the joke was all about the three-fingered Boy Scout salute. Mueller was fifty-nine years old, a lawyer and a G-man and a marine, but he had Boy Scout written all over him. Late that evening, word began to spread. It wasn't only Comey. Bobby Three Sticks was getting ready to turn in his badge.

Like every federal agency, Justice had filled its top ranks with political loyalists. They admired George Bush, wished him well, hoped to see him reelected later that year. In and around the building that night, questions began to be asked. Whatever just happened, was it really Bush who did it? As far as the senior staff could tell, some kind of decision seemed to be imminent. Had anyone explained to the president what was at stake?

Ed Whelan, Goldsmith's deputy, pulled out his BlackBerry. He fired off a message to White House staff secretary Brett Kavanaugh, a friend whose position gave him direct access to Bush. "I knew zilch about what the matter was, but I did know that lots of senior DOJ folks were on the verge of resigning," Whelan said, declining to discuss the subject further. "I thought it important to make sure that the president was aware of that situation so that he could factor it in as he saw fit."

Kavanaugh had no more idea than Whelan. As the man who directed paperwork in and out of the Oval Office, he had heard policy tantrums and murmurs of resignation before. Whelan's message did not sound like the usual fit of pique. Kavanaugh passed word right away to Andy Card.

The timing was opportune. Just about then, around 11:00 p.m.,

Jim Comey finally responded to his summons from the chief of staff. Whatever Card had planned to say earlier, he had calmed down fast. There was something new on his mind. Card was "concerned," Comey said later, "that he had heard reports that there were to be a large number of resignations at the Department of Justice." Comey gave him no comfort. "I don't think people should try to get their way by *threatening* resignations," Comey told Card. "If they find themselves in a position where they're not comfortable continuing, then they should resign."

"He obviously got the gist of what I was saying," Comey recalled.

It was close to midnight when Comey got home, long past the president's bedtime. Bush's sleep went undisturbed by news that his government was coming apart.

Trouble was still spreading. The FBI general counsel, Valerie Caproni, told colleagues she would leave if the president reauthorized the program over Justice Department objections. At the CIA, general counsel Scott Muller said the same. Muller predicted that his boss, George Tenet, would also leave. (Asked that question in 2008, Tenet denied any such intention. He declined to explain his reasons.) Assistant Attorney General Christopher Wray, who ran the Justice Department's criminal division, stopped Comey in a hallway. "Look, I don't know what's going on, but before you guys all pull the rip cords please give me a heads-up so I can jump with you," he said.

James A. Baker, the counselor for intelligence, thought hard about jumping, too. He had been battling the White House for nearly two years about the program, on an entirely separate front. He supervised applications for domestic surveillance, known as FISA warrants, in the closed tribunal established by Congress for that purpose.

He had helped broker a deal between the White House and the court. The Bush administration would keep the chief judge fully informed on the program, and no evidence gleaned by warrantless surveillance would be allowed to taint a warrant application. Twice since 2002, when Colleen Kollar-Kotelly took over as chief judge, colleagues said Baker had felt obliged to alert her that he was unsure those promises had been kept. Royce Lamberth, who preceded Kollar-Kotelly as chief judge, said that "she concluded they weren't being forthcoming, but I don't know all the circumstances that led to her concluding that."

"I was determined to stay there and fight for what I thought was right," Baker said in an interview, declining to say what the fight was about, on or off the record. He had obligations, he said, to the lawyers who worked for him in the Office of Intelligence Policy Review. "If it had come to this, if people were willing to go to the mat and tolerate the attorney general and deputy attorney general resigning, that's pretty serious. God knows what else they would have come up with. I was going to protect my troops. . . . I had substantial institutional knowledge and could better serve the country by staying than leaving."

Baker seldom had direct dealings with the White House, but he accompanied Jack Goldsmith and other Justice officials to see Gonzales and Addington not long before the Comey crisis peaked. They discussed arrangements for resolving Kollar-Kotelly's doubts.

"Jim, we have a lot riding on your relationship with the FISA court," Addington said. "I hope you come through for us." Addington hated the court's involvement, believing the president was empowered to make surveillance decisions alone. Moments later, he vented his frustration. "We're one bomb away from getting rid of that obnoxious court," he said.

At the White House on Thursday morning, the president moved in a bubble so tight that hardly any air was getting in. It was March 11, decision day. If Bush reauthorized the program, he would have no signature from the attorney general. But by now that was nowhere near the president's biggest problem.

Many of the people Bush trusted most were out of the picture. The political and policy staffs could not run traps at Justice, check around to see how bad things really were. Communications and Legislative Affairs could not forecast the likely fallout on public opinion and Capitol Hill. Karl Rove was not cleared for the program. Neither was Dan Bartlett or Karen Hughes, who had returned to Texas but still spoke to Bush as many days as not. Condi Rice had the clearance, but Cheney did not invite her to the meetings that mattered.

Bush gave a speech to evangelical Christians that morning and left the White House for an after-lunch speech and fund-raiser in New York. In whatever time he took to weigh his options, Cheney, Addington, Card, and Gonzales were all he had. Two of them knew exactly where they stood, unswerving in their commitment to keep the program just as it was. The other two, colleagues said, were loath to take a strong position. According to accounts they gave afterward, Card and Gonzales were beginning to turn that Thursday morning. Gonzales told two confidants that he had broken with Addington—a first on any issue of consequence. As a matter of prudence, Gonzales counseled the president against reauthorizing the program without Justice on board. Card, too, told colleagues he had tried to bring Bush around.

"My job was to communicate with the president about the peripheral vision, not just the tunnel vision of the moment," Card said, deflecting questions on how and when he may have suggested a change of course.

Did peripheral vision mean a broader view of the consequences?

"Yes," Card replied. "It was like—I don't want to limit it to this particular matter, but that's part of a chief of staff's job. A lot of people who work in the White House have tunnel vision, and not an awful lot of people have peripheral vision. And I think the chief of staff is one of the people who should have peripheral vision."

Card did not really need the corner of his eye to see a disaster at hand. Even so, Bush did not know what his subordinates knew that morning. Cheney and Addington, Card and Gonzales, had plenty of data. Card had heard the news directly from Comey the night before. On Thursday, the chief of staff summoned Bob Mueller to the White House at noon. The FBI director's daily log, released later in censored form, recorded a full page of blacked-out single-spaced notes on that forty-minute meeting—an eternity at the staccato pace of the West Wing. Mueller made a point of seeing Gonzales on his way out, so both of them knew where he stood. The president liked and admired the FBI director. By the next day it became clear that Bush had no idea that Mueller was ready to bail.

If Gonzales and Card made unequivocal stands, then Bush took Cheney's side on the biggest legal decision of his presidency, against the unified advice of his Justice Department, White House counsel, and chief of staff. If they told him that mass resignations were coming, then Bush chanced an exodus of top appointees without pausing to ask one of them why. One White House adviser, a close student of the way Bush made decisions, said, "His behavior makes no sense to me if he knew." Card and Gonzales, the adviser said, had reasons to soft-pedal the scale of the uprising. Whatever else he did, Card had miscalculated the "penultimate" moment. By Thursday, "to go in and say 'By the way, we've been arguing about this for months' would be to say they hadn't told him about a big problem that's been going on for a long time."

For Cheney, it did not matter much whether one official or ten or twenty took a walk. Maybe they were bluffing, maybe not. The principle was the same. The vice president could be deft in deflecting conflict, pragmatic in resolving it on many issues. But on fundamentals—national security, presidential authority—you didn't bow to terrorists, you didn't bow to Jim Jeffords, and you didn't allow a threat to divert you from what needed to be done. "The president of the United States is the chief law enforcement officer—that was the Cheney view," said Dan Bartlett, who was later briefed into the program and the events of the day. "You can't let resignations deter you if you're doing what's right." Cheney and Addington "were ready to go to the mat," he said, and the vice president's position boiled down to this: "'That's why we're leaders, that's why we're here. Take the political hit. You've got to do it.'"

Addington returned to the Eisenhower Executive Office Building and opened the codeword-classified file on his computer. He had a presidential directive to rewrite.

It has been widely reported that Bush executed the March 11 order with a blank space over the attorney general's signature line. That is not correct. For reasons both symbolic and practical, the vice president's lawyer could not tolerate an empty spot where a mutinous subordinate should have signed. Addington deleted the Justice Department from the document. He typed in "Alberto R. Gonzales," the White House counsel, on a substitute signature line.

What Addington wrote for Bush that day was more transcendent than that. There was a point of principle to be made, and there was a practical problem to solve. An unsigned certification of lawfulness would be a pretty obvious warning flag, but the White House counsel was nowhere in the chain of authority that defines the criminal law. Legal jeopardy might one day face a person who followed an order with no better backing than that.

The specter of future prosecutions hung over the program that week, now that Justice had taken its stand. "Pardon was in the air, but no one ever mentioned pardon," said one of the lawyers involved. Cheney and Addington often said fear of the law had neutered intelligence agencies since the 1970s. If the Justice Department ruled the program illegal, did those who carried it out commit crimes? Hayden's nervous joke about John Kerry was even less funny now. It was possible to construct a case, one Bush administration lawyer said, in which the high-ranking officials who planned and authorized the program were engaged in a criminal conspiracy. That would be tendentious, this lawyer believed, but with a change of government it could not be ruled out. Warrantless wiretapping had been one count in the articles of impeachment voted against Richard Nixon in 1974.

"I'm sure when we leave office we're all going to be hauled up before congressional committees and grand juries," Addington told one colleague in disgust. "I'm not going to get a lawyer." The message was that Addington had followed his conscience. If it came to that, he would stand up proudly.

Meanwhile, he did not stop at adding a legally meaningless signature line for Gonzales. Addington drew up new language in which Bush relied on his own authority to certify the program as lawful. Addington's words remain classified, but Bush expressly overrode the Justice Department and any act of Congress or judicial decision that purported to constrain his power as commander in chief. The rewritten directive declared in sweeping terms that Bush had the final word. Addington's formula may have been the nearest thing to a claim of unlimited power ever made by an American president, all the more radical for having been issued in secret. Not only would the will of Congress be flouted, but if the White House had its way Congress would never know it.

George W. Bush signed the directive before leaving for New York around lunchtime on Thursday, March 11, 2004. Gonzales, despite his advice to the president, duly countersigned. The program would carry on, Justice or no Justice. Andy Card did what he always did, cleaning up the mess. He spoke to at least one member of the Gang of Eight, delivering the good news that the trouble had passed. "As you know, the attorney general is in intensive care and the acting attorney general—the deputy attorney general, Jim Comey—is not comfortable signing in his place," Card said, according to a record of the call. "And so the president has reauthorized with the White House counsel signing."

Just a little more comfortable that way.

Jim Comey got word of Bush's decision in the middle of the afternoon. He called another staff meeting, and meanwhile typed a letter.

> Dear Mr. President:
>
> At my confirmation hearing, I was asked what I would do if I concluded that a course of action was fundamentally wrong and I could not convince my superiors of that fact. I replied:
>
>> You are asking me to imagine an apocalyptic situation that I don't expect to encounter. I would not take

this job if I thought I was going to be working with people who didn't share my love of the law and love of the institution. So I don't think I'll ever find myself in that position. I can commit to you though that—because I talk so much about integrity and about this great group behind me—that's what I really care about. I don't care about politics. I don't care about expediency. I don't care about friendship. I care about doing the right thing. And I would never be part of something that I believe to be fundamentally wrong. I mean obviously we all make policy judgments where people disagree, but I will do the right thing.

Over the last two weeks I have encountered just such an apocalyptic situation, where I and the Department of Justice have been asked to be part of something that is fundamentally wrong. As we have struggled over these last days to do the right thing, I have never been prouder of the Department of Justice or of the Attorney General. Sadly, although I believe this has been one of the institution's finest hours, we have been unable to right that wrong. . . .

Therefore, with a heavy heart and undiminished love of my country and my Department, I resign as Deputy Attorney General of the United States, effective immediately.

Sincerely yours,

James B. Comey

There was no pretense in it, not a hint of praise for the president. Confronting Bush, not serving him, had been the department's finest hour. In Comey's fourth-floor conference room, the senior leaders of the Justice Department reconvened to prepare a collective document for the White House. Many of them, like Comey, had already written their resignation letters. David Ayres, Ashcroft's chief of staff, pleaded with Comey to wait a few days. He was certain that Ashcroft would want to quit alongside him.

Well past eleven o'clock that night, Patrick Philbin steered his BMW through darkened suburban streets, Jack Goldsmith in the passenger seat. They turned onto Laurel Hill Road in Vienna, Virginia. With them was a classified pouch from the Justice Department. There was no more maybe about it. Tomorrow, Friday, was the last day of work for something like two dozen Bush appointees.

Alberto Gonzales came to his door in pajamas, bathrobe, and slippers. The three men had not seen one another since the hospital, but there was no anger. They were drained, physically and emotionally. Gonzales invited them in.

Goldsmith and Philbin had brought the document composed at Justice a few hours before. For the record, for whatever review might one day take place, it described the events of recent days. The White House counsel, drowsy eyed, slit open the pouch and read its contents as his visitors sank into a sofa. Gonzales smiled, inexplicably serene.

"Don't worry, Jack," he said. "This is all going to work out. Tomorrow's another day."

Goldsmith could not imagine what the man was thinking.

"I am quite sure this is not going to work out," Goldsmith told Gonzales. "I think the whole executive branch is going to melt down."

On Friday morning, Bush began entertaining rare second thoughts. Card and Gonzales may have played a role in the president's pragmatic turn. But Bush placed great value on finality of decision. Having made a choice, he seldom brooked further debate. The president would need new information, not new arguments, to save himself. Somebody, at last, had to tell him something.

It was Condi Rice, largely in the dark herself, who threw Bush a lifeline. Fran Townsend had come to the national security adviser after the awkward encounter with Jim Comey in the West Wing hallway. Like a lot of conversations going on that week—Hayden's with Gordon, Comey's with Townsend—her approach to Rice was chancy. Townsend was talking to her boss about something she was not supposed to know. But that was the point: people at Justice were so agitated, evidently, that hints about the subject were in the air. This was no way to keep a secret.

Rice had a few minutes alone with the president shortly before 7:30 a.m. in the Oval Office. She told him what Townsend had reported. Rice did not know what the problem was, but she respected Comey. If Comey was reaching out to someone who was not read in, it might be serious. "It was a compartmented issue," Rice recalled. "Obviously, there was a security issue here and not just a legal one because you didn't want this sort of bumping around."

Rice made a suggestion.

"He's a reasonable guy," she told the president. "You really need to make sure that you are hearing these folks out."

An hour later, Jim Comey and Bob Mueller arrived at the White House to start their last day in government. There would be no door slamming, but the president had made his choice and they had made theirs. Meanwhile, the 8:30 terror briefing had a lot to cover: bombs aboard Spanish commuter trains had killed 191 people and wounded close to 2,000 in Madrid. Bush and Cheney took their usual seats in matching blue-striped chairs, the Oval Office fireplace behind them. Comey and Mueller joined a rectangle of aides on facing sofas: Condi Rice, Andy Card, Tom Ridge, Fran Townsend, John Gordon, and two briefers from the CIA.

Bush stood as the meeting ended, crossing behind Cheney's chair. Comey moved in the opposite direction, on his way out. He had nearly reached the grandfather clock at the door when the president said, "Jim, can I talk to you for a minute?" Bush nodded toward the private dining room a few steps from his desk, the one he shared with Cheney once a week. This time the vice president was not invited.

"I'll wait for you downstairs," Mueller told Comey.

Notice is taken when the president summons anyone for an unscheduled one-on-one. "If he's calling you back it's because he's going to be 'on transmit'—he's got something he wants to say," said one official who was in the room. By now, around 9:15 Friday morning, Bush knew enough to be nervous about what the acting attorney general might do. That did not mean he looked forward to reversing himself. One high-ranking adviser said there was still an "optimism that maybe you can finesse your way through this."

Afterward, in conversations with aides, the two men described the meeting in similar terms. The president sat with his back to a window. He offered Comey the seat on his right.

"You don't look well," Bush said.

Oldest trick in the book. Establish dominance, put the other guy off his game.

"Well, I feel okay."

"I'm worried about you. You look burdened."

"I am, Mr. President. I feel like there's a tremendous burden on me."

"Let me lift that burden from your shoulders," Bush said.

"Let me take that from you. Let me be the one who makes the decision here."

"Mr. President, I would love to be able to do that."

They spoke at some length about the operations of the program, the disparate legal issues affecting each part. Bush's tone grew crisp.

"I decide what the law is for the executive branch," he said.

"That's absolutely true, sir, you do. But I decide what the Department of Justice can certify to and can't certify to, and despite my absolute best efforts I simply cannot in the circumstances."

Comey had majored in religion, William and Mary class of 1982. He considered himself a man of faith. He might have made a connection with Bush if he had quoted a verse from scripture or a hymn. The line that came to Comey belonged to a sixteenth-century theologian who defied an emperor in the name of conscience.

"As Martin Luther said, 'Here I stand; I can do no other,'" Comey said. "I've got to tell you, Mr. President, that's where I am."

Bush shifted direction, playing for time. Then he said something that floored Comey.

"I just wish that you weren't raising this at the last minute."

The last minute! He didn't know.

The president said a few more words. Not the way it's supposed to work, popping up with news like this. The day before a deadline?

Wednesday. He didn't know until Wednesday. No wonder Card and Gonzales went to the hospital.

"Oh, Mr. President, if you've been told that, you have been very poorly served by your advisers," Comey said. "We have been telling them for months we have a huge problem here that we can't get past. We've been working this and working this, and here I am, and there's no place else for me to go."

"I just need you to certify it. Give me six weeks. If we don't have it fixed in six weeks, we'll shut it down."

"I can't do that," Comey said. "You do say what the law is in the executive branch, I believe that. And people's job, if they're going to stay in the executive branch, is to follow that. But I can't agree, and I'm just sorry."

If they're going to stay.

Comey was edging toward a breach of his rule against resignation threats. You resign or you don't. He had already decided. The problem, he told friends afterward, was that he could no longer assume that the president had made an informed decision.

This man just needs to know what's about to happen.

"I think you should know that Director Mueller is going to resign today," Comey said.

Bush raised both eyebrows. He shifted in his chair. He could not hide it, or did not try. He was gob-smacked.

"Thank you very much for telling me that," he said. "I really appreciate it, Jim. I'll talk to him. I'm going to talk to him."

He shook Comey's hand, showed him out. Their talk resolved nothing. A witness to Comey's departure said he looked stunned. Comey hurried down to Mueller, who sat in the foyer outside the Situation Room. He had just begun to recount his meeting when a Secret Service agent stepped up. The president would like to see you, he told Mueller.

Now it was Comey's turn to wait. He pulled out his BlackBerry. At 9:27 a.m. he sent a note to six Justice Department colleagues:

The president just took me into his private office for a 15 minute one on one talk. Told him he was being misled and poorly served. We had a very full and frank exchange. Don't know that either of us can see a way out. He promised he would shut down 5/6 if Congress didn't fix FISA. Told him Mueller was about to resign. He just pulled Bob into his office.

Bush and Mueller had a warmer bond, but the FBI director was no more tractable than Comey.

This was a rule-of-law question, he told the president, and the answer was in the Department of Justice. The Federal Bureau of Investigation could not participate in operations that Justice held to be in breach of criminal law. If those were his orders, he would respectfully take his leave. As for others at the bureau, they would speak for themselves.

And there it was, unfinessable. Bush was out of running room, all the way out. He had only just figured out the brink was near, and now he stood upon it. Not twenty-four hours earlier, Bush had signed his name to an in-your-face rejection of the attorney general's ruling on the law. Now he had two bad choices. March on, with all the consequences. Or retreat.

The president stepped back from the precipice. He gave Mueller a message for Comey.

"Tell Jim to do what Justice thinks needs to be done," he said.

Mueller and Comey walked out to their armored black Suburban. They spoke a while in the backseat, the driver standing outside, then drove off. One week later, Bush amended his March 11 directive. The legal certification belonged again to the attorney general. Over the next weeks and months, the program changed. It stopped doing some things, and it did other things differently. Colleen Kollar-Kotelly, the chief FISA judge, got a fuller briefing and established new rules to keep warrantless evidence out of her court. Much of the program, not all of it, remained intact.

The story had two epilogues.

One came in a combative memo to the Justice Department. It was signed "Alberto R. Gonzales," but the composition had all the familiar Addington tropes. Comey and his staff called it the "fuck-you memo." It rejected every point in the Thursday-night letter that Goldsmith and Philbin had brought to Gonzales at home. Oddly out of sync with what Bush had told Mueller in person, the document reiterated the president's sole authority to decide the law and reasserted the lawfulness of every element in the program. Any adjustments would come for strictly operational reasons, at the president's own discretion. Comey read it in his fourth-floor office, then looked up at his chief of staff. He summarized: "So, 'You suck. You don't matter. But, by coincidence, as it happens, we're going to make some changes.'" If this was strictly for the record, that was one thing. If the White House was backpedaling on Bush's promise, quite another. Gonzales called Justice and left a message, practically announcing that the memo was not his. "Tell the DAG not to overreact," the message said. "We're going to make the changes."

The second epilogue came when John Ashcroft returned to health. Ashcroft and Comey paid a call on the White House counsel. For once, Addington did not sit in. Gonzales apologized for the hospital visit. "I never should have done that," he told the attorney general. "I'm very sorry." He and Andy Card agreed, he said, that it had been a terrible week—the most difficult of the Bush administration, including September 11.

According to Dan Bartlett, Bush's counselor since Texas days, two things turned the president around. One was the security risk, more or less as Rice identified it. "If the premise of what you're trying to do is you're trying to protect a highly classified program, and you have the top echelon of your Justice Department resign, I think it's going to get out pretty quick as to why," Bartlett said. "So in some respects, it's counterintuitive: (a) you want the program to continue but (b) you don't want it disclosed. I think that's how the president looked at it."

Then there was the perspective of an election year. "I mean, it would be damn near unprecedented for the top echelon of your Justice Department to resign over a position you've taken," Bartlett said.

There might be one precedent, he allowed. He did not want to spell it out.

"Not a good one," he said after a moment.

During the Watergate scandal, the attorney general and deputy attorney general resigned, refusing to carry out Richard Nixon's order to fire the special prosecutor. The next guy in line, Robert Bork, complied. Nixon lost his top two Justice officials, and that was called the Saturday Night Massacre. Bush had come within minutes of losing his FBI director and at least the top five layers at Justice. What would they call that? Suicide, maybe?

"Gee, it probably would have helped to have some of us political thinkers involved, or at least given hypotheticals," said Mark Corallo, who was John Ashcroft's communications director and, during Bush's first race for the White House, chief spokesman for the Republican National Committee. Like others who learned only after the fact, Corallo was appalled at how close the president came to an abyss.

"George Bush is a pretty smart guy," he said. "You don't have to be the smartest guy to figure out that [mass resignations] would be pretty much the most devastating thing that could happen to your administration.

"It's over," he said. "Tell me how your presidency survives." Corallo mapped the road to ruin. "You know, one guy resigns on principle and it can be uncomfortable, it can even be damaging. If six or seven of your top lawyers—and, excuse me, think about this. And this is the truth. If John Ashcroft resigned, the entire political leadership of the Justice Department goes with him. That means the heads of all the divisions, the deputies—every political appointee of the Justice Department would have walked. We would have all walked out the door, because we would have said, 'If this is big enough for Ashcroft to resign over, we're all out of here.' . . . And then you have Bobby Three Sticks. . . . The rush to hearings on the Hill, both in the House and Senate, would be unbelievable. The media frenzy that would have ensued would have been unlike anything we've ever seen. That's when you're getting into Watergate territory."

Because Bush did not walk off the cliff, and because so much of the story stayed quiet, an extraordinary moment in presidential history passed unrecognized. When Comey gave his riveting Senate testimony, three years after the fact, political jousting diverted our eyes from something larger. (Reporter: Did Gonzales try to take advantage of Ashcroft? White House spokesman Tony Snow: "Because he had an appendectomy, his brain didn't work?") Comey and others who came forward in 2007 could not tell most of what had happened, because the Bush administration warned them not to talk about anything privileged or classified. And just about everything in the story was alleged to be one or the other, right down to the constitutional principles at issue.

Long after departing as chief of staff, Andy Card held fast to the proposition that whatever happened was nobody's business, and no big deal anyway. "To me, this is the executive branch doing what they have to do under Article Two of the Constitution, and you're not

Article Two," he said. He added, "I don't know anybody who's claimed the public is part of Article Two."

What chief of staff before the Cheney years would talk like that, wave around the vesting clause like a talisman? (He was referring to the first words of Article II: "The Executive Power shall be vested in a President of the United States of America.") Where was it inscribed that events of state belonged to the president alone?

"I think you're writing about something that's irrelevant," Card said. "Voyeurism."

Because?

"You keep saying, 'Oh, this is critically important,' but . . . nobody resigned over this." It all boiled down to trash talk: "'Oh, I was gonna swing at the pitch but it was too high.'"

That seems unlikely to stand as history's verdict. In the fourth year of his presidency, a man who claimed unbounded power was forced by subordinates to comply with their ruling on the law. Ashcroft, Comey, Goldsmith, Philbin—believers, one and all, in the "unitary executive branch"—obliged the commander in chief to lay down the most important weapon he had, as he saw it, in an ongoing war. For the first time, a president claimed in writing that he alone could say what the law was. A rebellion, in direct response, became so potent a threat that the president reversed himself in a day. Had he not done so, political advisers said, his first term would have been his last, and a Watergate-style backlash, shackling future presidents with new restraints, would have been hard to prevent.

"FDR and Lincoln pushed around their attorneys general, and they got exculpatory decisions," Jack Goldsmith said later, after studying those episodes. "This is the first time when the president of the United States *really* wanted something in wartime, and tried to overrule the Department of Justice, and the law held. The rule of law stopped him from doing something that was the most important thing in the world to him. It just wouldn't have happened in any other era." American law and culture had evolved, he said. "This was the chest-pounding unitary executive administration to end all unitary executive administrations. In theory, the president does have the power to determine the law of the executive branch. In practice, however, this episode shows he doesn't always."

In the aftermath, the White House senior staff asked questions. Was the crisis avoidable? Was the president getting timely information? Had secrecy become an impediment to vetting risky plans? Did Bush relinquish too much control to Cheney?

If any of this was on the president's mind, he did not show it. Another man, so badly blindsided, might have railed against his counsel and chief of staff. Fired somebody, even. Coolness might have descended on relations with his Number Two. None of those things happened. By all outward signs, Bush gave undiminished value to Cheney's advice. The partnership remained secure. Neither did the president adjust the spigot on information that reached his desk. He had made it this far without a traditional "policy process"— without reaching down for other points of view, without inviting shades of gray to the Oval Office. The system suited him. Yet Bush did learn something, something he would not forget. A president could not operate as Cheney did, doctrinally unbending come what may. Bush had barely escaped the consequence, this time, of trying to govern by force of will alone. Cheney was the nearest thing there was to an antipolitician in elected office. A vice president, this vice president, could afford to be. Bush could not. In his second term, his second chance, the president would take greater care to consult his own instincts.

"Cheney was not afraid of giving pure, kind of principled advice," Dan Bartlett said. "He thinks from a policy standpoint, and I think he does this out of pure intentions. He thinks of the national security interest or the prerogatives of the executive. The president has other considerations he has to take into account. The political fallout of certain reactions—he's just going to calculate different than Cheney does.

"He grew accustomed to that," Bartlett said.

Chapter Thirteen

NEMESIS

The White House switchboard passed a call from John Kerry to the Oval Office at 11:06 a.m. on Wednesday, November 3, 2004. Another long election night had passed without decision. Florida looked like a toss-up at first, but this time the donnybrook was Ohio. George Bush and Dick Cheney awoke to news that the Kerry campaign was refusing to concede. John Edwards, the Democrat's running mate, spoke of a lawsuit over provisional ballots. In Boston, a few hours later, Kerry put a stop to the contest. He got the president on the line and congratulated him on winning a second term. Tears filled the president's eyes. Karl Rove, Andy Card, Dan Bartlett, and Mike Gerson had waited with him, along with Blake Gottesman, Bush's personal aide. The president stood and embraced each of them in turn, wrapping his arms around them and squeezing hard. "It was very emotional," Gerson said. "It was a tremendous relief that it wasn't going to be a disputed result again." The president headed out the door, looking for Cheney. They met in a West Wing hallway, the vice president already on his way. Bush reached for his Number Two but kept his upper body to himself. He held out a hand. Cheney did, too. They shook hands firmly, like men. "I know you're not the hugging kind," Bush told him.

Exactly twenty-four hours later, an exultant president appeared before the White House press corps. "When you win," Bush said, "there is a feeling that the people have spoken and embraced your point of view." He had come armed with a metaphor. "Let me put it to you this way: I earned capital in the campaign, political *capital*." Bush raised and lowered the flat of his hand, as though slapping down banknotes. "And now I intend to *spend* it." The president's liquid assets drained quickly. A big investment in Social Security reform went bust. The House defied a veto threat on stem cell research. The Senate tied Bush's nominees in knots. Even the Mod Squad had a brief comeback, blocking a White House attempt to ram controversial judges through confirmation. Cheney had lobbied for a rare invocation of his power to control Senate procedures as presiding officer. The idea was to rule Democrats out of order for refusing to close floor debate on nominees they did not like. Three of the moderates—Susan Collins, Olympia Snowe, and Lincoln Chafee—joined with John McCain to broker a deal that kept the gavel out of Cheney's hands. In Iraq, elections in January 2005 gave way to a spasm of violence that turned Americans decisively against the war. Bush's approval ratings sank below 50 percent and began a steady second-term plunge toward the 30s, the lowest of any president since Nixon. Cheney's ratings led the way down, pacing Bush's decline by 5 to 10 points.

Hurricane Katrina made landfall on August 29, 2005, drowning a great American city and blowing away Bush's prospects of recovery. Press Secretary Scott McClellan later wrote that the blundered White House response would "largely come to define Bush's second term," creating "a narrative of government failure that would be irresistible and, once established, practically indelible." What he did not describe was Cheney's role, or more aptly, his disinclination to play one. Days after the storm had passed, when he finally returned to Washington from Crawford, Bush assembled his senior staff in the Oval Office. He was going to form a cabinet-level task force, he said.

"I asked Dick if he'd be interested in spearheading this," Bush announced. "Let's just say I didn't get the most positive response." Bush nodded ironically toward the vice president, putting on a show for the others: Card, Rove, Bartlett, Condi Rice. His expression, the tone of voice, had a hint of edge. *Can you believe this guy?* Anyone who had face time with Bush said he was smarter than the public believed, and meaner. He spared Cheney the thunderbolts—Rove got the worst of them, when Bush was in a mood to yell—but now and then aides saw the president give Cheney the back of his hand.

"Will you at least go do a fact-finding trip for us?" Bush said.

"That'll probably be the extent of it, Mr. President, unless you order otherwise," Cheney replied. He was the Cheshire Cat inverted, only the smile dissolving, the rest of him still in the chair.

As well as he knew the two of them, Bartlett had to fight an impulse to roll his eyes. Katrina was shaping up as a true catastrophe. New Orleans was four-fifths under water, and the Gulf Coast had suffered grievous losses of life and property. The leisurely pace of federal action was not doing a bit of good for Bush. "Cheney wanted nothing to do with it," Bartlett said. Looking back on that moment, the president's counselor remained of two minds. Cheney was the Master of Disaster, one of the government's most capable emergency managers. "It would send a powerful signal of our level of concern" to put the vice president in charge, Bartlett said. Eventually, though, Bartlett came to see Cheney's demurral "quite frankly as pretty good judgment." Cheney "doesn't do touchy-feely,"

Bartlett said. "Understanding what people's problems are and show-ing compassion—that is an important part of the job of being the representative of the president. . . . He was not going to go down there and hug the babies."

Cheney led his fact-finding mission to Gulfport, New Orleans, and Baton Rouge on September 8, ten days after the storm. Aboard a command ship moored nearby, Cheney met with Michael Brown, director of the Federal Emergency Management Agency. Bush had just told the fellow six days before, "Brownie, you're doing a heck of a job." Cheney sat through an excruciating briefing and concluded that Brown had no idea what his job was. "The incompetence left him wide-eyed," said an aide who accompanied Cheney. The vice president told reporters that day that everyone he met was "positive and upbeat," adding that "the progress we're making is significant." Aboard the helicopter to his next stop, Cheney told Brown's immedi-ate boss, Secretary of Homeland Security Michael Chertoff, that something had to change fast. Brown was stripped of the Katrina assignment the following day, and he resigned a few days after that. Even the vice president's own staff did not know whether Cheney delivered the message to Bush or left the job to Chertoff. "That's the mystery of Cheney," the aide said. "You'll never know."

These were bad-news times at the White House, not least in the vice-presidential suite. David Addington once told Jack Goldsmith, his sparring partner at Justice, "We're going to push and push and push until some larger force makes us stop." The second term brought pushback from all over, including, more often than before, the Oval Office. Newton had a law for it: action and reaction, ever in balance. The Greeks put a goddess in the story, but it ended the same way. Cheney had disturbed the old proportions of things, overleaping customary bounds of nation with nation, branch with branch, office with office. Nemesis arrived to knock him down. Gravity reasserted itself. Cheney thrust onward, but the arc of his vice presidency began its descent.

Aaron Friedberg had posed a question back in the summer of 2003. Was it 1947 or 1967, a time of expanding horizons or contracting hopes? The reply came before Cheney's new adviser finished setting up his desk. On August 19, 2003, an unidentified man drove a flatbed truck as close as he could get to the Canal Hotel in Baghdad. The explosion a moment later tore the face off United Nations headquarters in Iraq, killing twenty-two people and wounding a lot more. One of the dead was Sergio Vieira de Mello, the secretary-general's special envoy. Vieira de Mello embodied White House hopes for international help to rebuild Iraq. It turned out that reconstruction would not pay for itself, as optimists at the Pentagon supposed; the insurgents had squeezed oil revenues to a trickle. Now the UN packed up its staff and withdrew. This was terrorism at its most effective, a strategic blow. "For me the bombing was final confirmation that things were going to be much tougher in Iraq than people had been expecting. I remember having a vertiginous feeling in the pit of my stomach, like being in a dropping elevator," Friedberg recalled. "I used to do a kind of mental experiment: imagine if I took all the paper that flowed over my desk each day, which included all the internal memos on NSC meetings and all the intelligence." If he stacked them, Friedberg wondered, "what would those stacks look like? And increasingly there was this big Iraq stack over here and there was the GWOT stack over here." By now the professor talked like a government guy, saying *gee-watt* for global war on terror. "Some weeks there's a North Korea stack, some weeks there's an Iran stack, some weeks there's a stack on something else. But the biggest stacks are always on Iraq and the war on terror."

Word reached Cheney's office in the fall of 2004 that the Defense Intelligence Agency had a guy who understood Iraq like nobody else. He was fresh from Baghdad, a year and a half as the senior analyst. Colonel Derek J. Harvey was a "foreign area officer," one of the Army's cadre of lifetime regional specialists. He spoke Farsi and some Arabic. In Baghdad, fellow officers said, he was not the kind of "intel weenie" who hid at his desk. Harvey drove all over Iraq, meeting with insurgents and tribal leaders. One day in October, he got an invitation from John Hannah. Harvey made his way to the West Wing for the first of many conversations with the vice president and Scooter Libby.

Over time, Cheney heard some things he liked and a lot of things he did not. Ahmed Chalabi, who had led an Iraqi opposition in exile with strong support from Cheney's office, was a talented leader, Harvey said. But untrustworthy. Fully capable of aligning with Tehran over Washington if that became convenient. Harvey said Saddam's regime had forged extensive ties to terrorist groups, just as Cheney alleged. The M5 division of the Iraqi Intelligence Service gave money and training to recruits from Algeria, Morocco, the Palestinian territories, Egyptian Islamic Jihad. But Harvey saw no link to operations outside Iraq, no evidence of Iraqi intent to harm Americans. Saddam was buying tolerance from Islamists who posed a threat to his own regime.

The vice president asked tough questions but took the journey, following the logic trains. Harvey told him the United States had misjudged the enemy, its strategy and its strength. The bad guys had better intelligence than we did. The U.S. strategy was all about process: constitution, referendum, election. We were punting on the issues of power and status and religious identity that were tearing the country apart. The Sunni elites were used to running things, and they would fight as long as they faced an unrestrained Shia majority. Cheney's was the strongest voice for purging members of the former regime. With the backing of Cheney's office, Chalabi defied attempts by the occupation authority to disband the de-Baathification commission, which rooted out members of Saddam's political party from government jobs. Harvey said it would be wiser to forge ties to displaced Sunnis, including most Baath Party members, protecting them from simple majority rule. Condi Rice leaned that way, too, thinking about her native South. "Actually, it's a classic problem with democracy," she said. "Right? On any given day, a majority can simply slam something through. But let's say that that majority doesn't include, you know, black people, for instance, as was once the case."

Harvey's point was in basic conflict with the strategy that Cheney kept talking about in public. Putting elections before power sharing would inflame the insurgency and the Sunni-Shia divisions, one already violent and the other on the brink. There were people in the Pentagon, Harvey said, who saw Sunni tribal leaders as vestiges of the bad old past, irrelevant to the New Iraq. The Sunnis they were looking for were the secular, urban, democratic ones, a demographic that did not exist in abundance. If you wanted Sunnis, you needed the important people in the tribes and clans.

Briefing Don Rumsfeld, Harvey used to say, was like being cross-examined. Rumsfeld was a prosecutor, picking you apart. Cheney came across as a professor, exploring your ideas without saying much about his own. George Bush was nothing like either. He was not at all a stupid man, but he worked on instinct and viscera. Harvey gave the president indigestion. At Cheney's urging, the DIA colonel had an audience with Bush on December 17, 2004. The room was full: Rice, Card, Colin Powell, Paul Wolfowitz, William Luti from the Office of Special Plans, and the new CIA director, Porter Goss. Harvey told the president as politely as he could that the troops in Baghdad were fighting the wrong war. The insurgency was not about foreigners, not mainly, and not about jihadists, although some of al Qaeda's allies had taken up Bush's challenge to "bring 'em on." The enemy was tough, resilient, and in this fight for the long haul. Harvey was not the most politic of briefers, and he let the V-word slip. At a Fort Leavenworth symposium not long afterward, he offered a version of what he told Bush and Cheney. "We've constantly heard that we've 'reached a tipping point,' or we've 'broken the back of the insurgency,' or we've heard things similar to 'there's light at the end of the tunnel,' which harkens back to Vietnam," he said. "Now when you say problems are contained and that things are going well in 14 out of 18 provinces, that's an absolute fact. But it's like saying things are going well in Arizona, except in Phoenix and Tucson." Harvey urged his audience to look at Iraq from another point of view. "What if your life, your future, the future of your grandchildren and your children, your place in society, your wealth, even your homes, your jobs, your careers were suddenly taken from you?" he asked, referring to the Sunnis and other Iraqis dislodged from privilege. Harvey wasn't lawyering for the enemy. He was saying the war could not be won without driving a wedge between committed adversaries and ordinary "POIs"—"short for Pissed Off Iraqis," he explained.

Bush made it clear that he could not understand what Harvey was doing in his office. How could some colonel possibly know so many things that contradicted what the generals were saying? What were his credentials?

Harvey got no second invitation to the Oval Office, but Cheney kept bringing him back for more. They stayed in touch through Cheney's staff, in e-mails over the classified Sipranet, when Harvey returned to Baghdad. One of the points Harvey hammered home was that official measures of progress did not count what mattered.

MNF-Iraq, the headquarters of the nominally multinational force, reported in mid-2005 that the coalition had killed, wounded, or captured more than fifty thousand insurgents in eighteen months. But go back to January 2004, the start of that period. MNF-Iraq said then there were only five thousand insurgents! Lord preserve us from progress like that. The coalition seized cache after weapons cache, but the black market price of explosives stayed about level. The number of insurgent attacks went up and down, mostly up, but the number did not matter as much as the effects—on investment, police recruitment, freedom of movement. Electricity and oil production would not come back until the people stopped being afraid to "collaborate." Most of the meaningful indicators said the insurgency's impact was growing.

The vice president and the DIA colonel agreed entirely on the war's strategic terrain. "Early on, they said that they could exhaust us," Harvey said in his Leavenworth lecture. "It might take them five, seven years, but they could exhaust us, because we would not have the national will to sustain the course." Cheney had just that on his mind when he asked Victor Davis Hanson to talk about unpopular wars. Libby and other staffers kept in touch with the Hoover fellow by phone, calling for historical perspective, Hanson said, "when things got really bad."

History would say what it liked, but what about the public here and now? Winston Churchill, the hero Libby likened to Cheney on September 11, famously said that "in wartime, truth is so precious that she should always be attended by a bodyguard of lies." What did that imply in a war whose decisive battles—and their secrets—would look nothing like Normandy? What if the hearts and minds of Americans, as much as Iraqis, were the battleground? Eight months after his conversations with Harvey began, Cheney invited Larry King and his CNN cameras to the Naval Observatory. Dick and Lynne Cheney sat together for an interview on a bright spring morning, Friday, May 27, 2005, taping ahead for broadcast on Memorial Day.

"When do we leave?" King asked.

Cheney gave his usual answer. When the job is done, no fixed deadline, depends on conditions.

"You expect it in your administration?"

"I do."

Five, seven years. Derek Harvey said that was how long the insurgents figured it would take to break the American public. Cheney's answer had the war wrapped up by then. Light at the end of the tunnel.

"To be removed?" King asked. "It's not going to be—it's not going to be a ten-year event?"

"No."

And that is when the vice president said something that dropped jaws all over Baghdad and Washington. It was one of those things that made people wonder how a man so smart could manage to be, as one of his top aides put it privately, so "consistently wrong, unyielding and unbending" on Iraq.

"I think they're in the last throes, if you will, of the insurgency," Cheney said.

One theory in Cheney's office was that he believed it, every word. He had been reading *Armageddon,* a history of the last months of World War II.

The Nazis, as Max Hastings recounted the story, fought hardest and wrought greatest carnage just when they came to see they were going to lose. Cheney saw a parallel: this was the storm before the calm in Iraq. He said so to Wolf Blitzer when the "last throes" remark came up again. "If you look at what the dictionary says about 'throes,' it can still be a violent period—the throes of a revolution. . . . When you look back at World War II, the toughest battle, at—the most difficult battles, both in Europe and in the Pacific, occurred just a few months before the end."

There was another theory about Cheney, which doubted his candor. No senior leader knew more about the ground truth of the war. "He wanted Iraq details beyond what even Rumsfeld was interested in, knew more about the depths of the problems we were having," said a four-star officer who briefed him. "By 2005 he clearly knew we were in trouble. The strategy we were executing was failing." How then explain Cheney's remarks? By this account, the vice president was still thinking of the shelf life of American resolve, the problem he had chewed on with Hanson and Harvey. A political leader—a Bush, a Cheney, a Churchill—did not command troops in the field. His role was to marshal the national spirit. Public support in a democracy was an essential source of strength, yet fragile and inconstant. For the war in Iraq, support was falling fast. Cheney fought gravity, trying to slow the descent. Implacable certainty might help stave off consensus against the war, much as the seeds of scientific doubt staved off consensus about endangered Klamath basin fish. Cheney did not have to win either argument, but he had to stop the other side from winning.

Holding the public was Bush's job more than Cheney's, but they had a division of labor. Bush drew on the qualities that won him two terms, still appealing even if diminished. He was a regular guy, asking for trust, visiting the wounded, even acknowledging trouble now and then. "I know that some of my decisions have led to terrible loss, and not one of those decisions has been taken lightly," he said in December. That was not a speech that Cheney would make. In Lynne Cheney's novel *Executive Privilege,* President Jenner is faced with

rioting against the presence of U.S. forces overseas. "They're screaming for us to get out of there, and any sign of weakness or vacillation
in our government is going to make them scream louder," says the
fictional president. Jenner makes up his mind to show "moral force,"
conceding nothing. In present-day Iraq, where Cheney rallied troops
the same day that Bush spoke of loss, the vice president saw only
gains. He said the recent election in Iraq had been "a seminal event,"
that it was "increasingly difficult for the insurgents to be effective,"
that "in fact, the number of attacks has declined." Everything Derek
Harvey disputed, along with a lot of other analysts by now. Cheney
was matter-of-fact, ineluctable, staking a reputation of decades on
his words.

On February 21, 2006, a group of armed Sunnis overpowered the
guards in the al Askari mosque in Samarra, Iraq. They took their
time setting charges overnight. Twin explosions the next morning
collapsed a structural wall and severed the golden dome of one of
Shia Islam's holiest sites. It was an architectural beheading, the insult
all the greater because beheading is the Koranic penalty for deviance.
From that moment, there were two conflicts raging in Iraq: an insurgency against occupation and a sectarian civil war. Three, if you
counted Iran's involvement in the other two.

Four months later, in June 2006, Cheney took a question at the
National Press Club. It had been written on an index card and passed
to the stage. Someone read it aloud. "About a year ago, you said
that the insurgency in Iraq was in its final death throes. Do you
still believe this?" Cheney looked manfully into the crowd and
said, "I do."

Bush threw one of his thunderbolts in the Situation Room in December 2003, a sudden squall about Guantánamo Bay. There was big

trouble coming there in the second term, but the president had no way to know that yet. He was focusing at the moment on the torpor of a system he had put in place for speed. Two years had passed since the detainees—don't call them "prisoners," the lawyers cautioned Bush—began arriving at the naval base in Cuba. *More* than two years since the president signed an order to place the terrorists out of the reach of ordinary courts. He would try them in military tribunals, same as FDR did in World War II. Quick and efficient, Cheney told him. Well, it didn't look quick to Bush. It was coming up on 2004 and not a single charge had been laid against a single terrorist. Now Rumsfeld here was giving a bunch of reasons. He had people on it. They were drafting procedures. Building a system from scratch. Had to find the right defendant for the first case, a lot of considerations to think through. Meanwhile half the lawyers from New York to Sydney had a client, or claimed to have one, at Gitmo. They were scratching at every door into federal court.

The president lost it. Enough excuses. He had told the world he would bring terrorists to justice. Tony Blair, John Howard in Australia, a lot of good friends, were banging on Bush to do something about their nationals at Guantánamo: try them, please, or get them out of there. Bush raised his voice and jammed a finger toward the secretary of defense. "We are *going* to have a trial," he said, "and the proceedings are going to start by the end of January." Condi Rice sat between them, caught in the backwash. The president had given a clear command. As national security adviser, she set about making it happen.

Rumsfeld never wanted to be the "world's jailer," according to Doug Feith, his undersecretary for policy. He was "displeased to have the Defense Department take on the detention mission and protested the idea repeatedly." In the Situation Room that December day, one participant got "the strong sense that Rumsfeld wanted no part of

Gitmo at all, and was kind of passive-aggressive about it." The vice president, according to others, was not in any hurry to see a trial. The objectives of the program, from Guantánamo to the CIA's "black sites" and the new interrogation rules, were already met. The detainees were locked up and disabled. They had no law but the president's to appeal to—not habeas, not Geneva, not the federal Speedy Trial Act. They could be held for life without a charge, assuming the "war on terror" did not end. Their submission to interrogators depended, in part, on isolation from the outside world. Trials would bring lawyers. Rules would bring claims that they had been broken. The vice president, whose counsel David Addington wrote the order of November 2001, was well aware of something that the president maybe forgot. The order said a designated enemy combatant "*shall* be detained" under Pentagon control. A military tribunal would get involved "*if* the individual is to be tried." The politics, at home and abroad, were one thing. But legally, Bush had promised nothing.

Cheney and Rumsfeld would slow-roll the tribunals for many months to come. They were natural partners, picking up cues that were not visible to others. "Watching them at meetings, you could see them reading each other's mind," said Richard Haver, who was Rumsfeld's special adviser for intelligence. "You could tell that Rummy would let the process roll forward—he wouldn't interject if it was going in the direction that the vice president wanted it to go." And vice versa. Sometimes the two of them could steer an outcome without showing up at all.

Rice's staff could not seem to schedule a meeting on the president's order. Rumsfeld was especially hard to pin down. He was famously contemptuous of the NSC staff, slashing lines through any memo that purported to describe an "NSC position" on policy. By law, he said, there was no such thing. The National Security Council consisted of the president, the vice president, and the heads of certain cabinet departments, along with legal, military, and intelligence advisers. The only statutory member of its staff was "a civilian executive secretary." That would be Rice. He did not regard her as an equal, and barely hid it. The opinions of her staff did not interest him, and neither did their scheduling priorities. Weeks passed. Rumsfeld finally said yes to a meeting on January 29, two days before Bush's deadline for tribunal proceedings. "I remember being astonished," said a regular in the detainee gatherings. "The president of the United States has directed that something is going to happen by a date certain. Surely it's going to happen?"

At the appointed hour on the twenty-ninth, Rice took the head of the long mahogany table in the Situation Room. It was Bush's seat when he attended, hers when he did not, the chair a little taller than the rest and the presidential seal on the wall behind. Steve Hadley, Rice's deputy, sat opposite, across the room. Cheney usually took the seat to her right, but Rice did not see him today. Along that side of the table, in black leather swivel chairs, sat Andy Card, John Ashcroft, and George Tenet. To Rice's left were Colin Powell and Air Force General Richard Myers, chairman of the Joint Chiefs of Staff. Between them, looking sheepish in Rumsfeld's seat, was his deputy Paul Wolfowitz.

"Where is the secretary?" Rice asked.

"He's unavailable," Wolfowitz said.

Rice picked up her papers.

"We're not going to have this meeting. We're going to reschedule this for a date in the next week, and the principals *will* be present," she said.

It took two weeks. Same room, same cast. Same question. Same answer. Rumsfeld was unavailable. Rice marched out and sent a memo, not so much an invitation as a demand. The principals would gather on Wednesday, February 25, 2004. They were running a full month now behind Bush's deadline. The day arrived. The group filed in: Hadley, Card, Ashcroft, Powell, Tenet, Myers. Wolfowitz.

"*Where's* the secretary?" Rice demanded.

Wolfowitz looked as though he would rather be in that other place. Or anywhere.

"Unavailable," Wolfowitz said.

Tenet stood up, pushing back his chair a little harder than strictly required. There are several doors to the Situation Room, and one was just behind him.

"This is bullshit," he said. "I'm out of here."

"George, do *not* leave this room," Rice commanded.

"This is *bull*-shit," Tenet pronounced, more emphatic. He took a couple of steps and he was gone.

Something happened to Rice's face, control melting away. Her eyes welled up and her next words caught in her throat. The men in the room did not know where to look. "She started to cry," said one of them. "And she said—I can't remember the exact words because I was so shaken—something like, 'We will talk about this again,' and she turned and walked quickly out the door."

Until now, Bush had not done everything Cheney suggested, not even close, but he did not seem to worry much that the vice president was steering for trouble. The early loss of the Senate, with Jim Jeffords bolting the party, had been recouped in the 2002 midterm election. The rigid secrecy of the energy task force was yesterday's news, and Cheney's position was winning in court. Iraq still looked, from the Oval Office, like a victory. Strong leaders had to pay a price sometimes, but Cheney had not cost Bush anything he could not afford.

There had been one time Bush jumped off the Cheney bus, a big decision on bioterror defense at the end of 2002. Two sensitive intelligence reports set off alarms for the vice president. One said "al Qaeda is interested in acquiring biological weapons, to include smallpox." The other, from the CIA's Weapons Intelligence, Nonproliferation and Arms Control Center, assessed (with confidence ranging from "medium" to "very high") that North Korea, Iraq, France, and Russia had undeclared samples of the smallpox virus, variola, which no longer existed in nature. Cheney and his staff connected the dots and brought the government to the brink of a mass vaccination campaign. Scooter Libby argued so forcefully that colleagues called him Germ Boy behind his back. "You have a threat, not currently treatable, which can be dispersed by terrorists or terrorist states—which can be dispersed, as the textbooks used to call it, anonymously," Libby said at one White House meeting at the peak of the debate. Public health experts said they could control an outbreak with a "ring vaccination" strategy, inoculating the victims and those around them. Cheney said an exercise called "Dark Winter"—his old friend Frank Keating played himself in the role of Oklahoma governor—proved that the ring strategy would not stop the kind of mass outbreak involved in an efficient terrorist attack. When decision time came in the Roosevelt Room, the doctors told Bush the vaccine would kill about one in a million recipients, something like three hundred Americans. Dan Bartlett sat there trying to picture the communications plan for that.

"The vice president set a very—kind of a cold, calculating view of those things," Bartlett said. " 'We'll be harshly judged if ten thousand people die as opposed to a couple hundred.' " Painful, but an easy call, objectively. Not so different from the shootdown order on September 11. Even so, Cheney had thought it through enough to know the choice was not that simple. A smallpox attack was one of those "low-probability, high-consequence" events that Aaron Friedberg described. The right kind of mind, with some dots to connect, could think of a lot of terrible things that might possibly happen. Which ones should we treat as though they were coming for real? Who could calculate the price worth paying right now, in lives and dollars and opportunity costs? How many enemies, exactly, could we afford? "The president understood him, but just couldn't bring himself to go that far," Bartlett said.

More of that started happening in 2004, the bridge year between the two terms. March brought the near-calamitous rebellion at Justice, and Bush veered sharply off the vice president's course. In April the president made another in a series of embarrassing climbdowns from positions Cheney had urged him to take with the 9/11 Commission. Cheney led efforts to stiff the commission on documents, testimony, access to executive secrets in general, but Bush kept discovering that the political costs were too high. He agreed to appear before the commission himself, Cheney alongside. Cheney watchers in the White House said the public suspicions about the joint meeting had it backward: the vice president was not there to guide or speak for Bush; they appeared together so Cheney could defer on each question to the commander in chief. Four people in the room that day said he barely spoke at all. Also in April—the twentieth and twenty-eighth, the latter when CBS News broadcast the ugly images from Abu Ghraib—the Supreme Court heard the first oral arguments about the military detention system. Multiple cases that year asked variations on one big question: Did any law protect alleged terrorists held offshore, or could the president lock them up as long as he liked, and interrogate, try, and execute them under rules he invented himself?

The cases involved British citizen Shafiq Rasul and Americans Jose Padilla and Yaser Hamdi. Justice Department lawyers increasingly found themselves defending what they believed to be losing positions in court. Solicitor General Theodore B. Olson, a conservative stalwart whose wife, Barbara, had died in the September 11 attacks, shared Cheney's robust view of executive authority. But his job was to win cases, and he worried especially about the ones involving American "enemy combatants." Decision time came in a heated meeting with Gonzales. Olson was backed by associate White House counsel Bradford Berenson, a former law clerk to Supreme Court justice Anthony Kennedy. Berenson told Gonzales that the Court's swing voter would never accept absolute presidential discretion to declare a U.S. citizen an enemy and lock him up without a lawyer or a hearing. Two more alumni of Kennedy's chambers, Brett Kavanaugh and Jack Goldsmith, had made the same point. Addington accused Berenson of trying to surrender executive power on a fool's prophecy about an inscrutable Court. Berenson accused Addington of "know-nothingness." This was going to be Gonzales's call. He listened quietly as the Justice Department and his own staff lined up against the lawyer for the vice president. And the winner was: Addington. Olson was ordered to make the most extreme of the available arguments.

On June 28, 2004, the Supreme Court ruled 8–1 in the Hamdi case that detainees must have a lawyer and an opportunity to challenge their status as enemy combatants before a "neutral decision maker." The Rasul decision, the same day, held 6–3 that Guantánamo Bay is not beyond the reach of federal law. Eleven days later, Olson stepped down as solicitor general. His deputy, Paul Clement, moved up. What came next was a message to Nemesis: Even in victory, expect to pay a price. Patrick Philbin, who had helped lead the Justice Department uprising on domestic surveillance, was Ashcroft's choice for deputy solicitor general, a plum among plums in the profession. Addington passed word that the vice president found the choice unsuitable. "OVP plays hardball," said a close observer of the episode. "No one would defend Philbin."

Until the Supreme Court started ruling, critics had huffed and puffed, but the legal house that Cheney built was intact. More change was coming, but the vice president and his allies hunkered down.

David Addington's Triumvirate, so dominant in the first years after September 11, was breaking up by early 2004. One of his fellow Triumvirs, Tim Flanigan, left the White House. The other, Alberto Gonzales, continued to follow Addington's lead, but the personal bond was strained. "David is just permanently stuck on 'loud,'" Gonzales told a friend. Addington still had Jim Haynes, a close ally at the Pentagon, but John Yoo, his invaluable link at Justice, had quit.

Jack Goldsmith, who now ran the Office of Legal Counsel, withdrew the second of Yoo's main torture opinions in June. Repudiating a formal OLC ruling was akin to a reversal of precedent by the Supreme Court, except that the OLC had not done it before. Goldsmith was no liberal, and he was embarrassed, years later, when Bush administration critics adopted him as one of their own. Goldsmith disagreed with Addington on the merits of Yoo's torture memos, but the three of them believed in common that there was no legal ban on cruelty. "The torture convention explicitly distinguishes between torture and cruel, inhuman and degrading treatment," Goldsmith wrote in an e-mail. "Its prohibitions on the former are firmer and more express. And only torture, not CID [cruel, inhuman, and degrading treatment], was made part of the domestic criminal prohibition."

Legal issues aside, detainees had become a big foreign-policy problem. Chronic trouble with allies over Guantánamo became acute after Abu Ghraib and the torture memos. Rice succeeded Powell as secretary of state in January 2005. She made it a top priority to stop the diplomatic bleeding.

In the first half of the year, her counselor Philip Zelikow began working secretly on a plan to reshape the legal landscape. He made common cause with two officials at the Pentagon. Gordon England, a corporate-minded manager who had replaced Paul Wolfowitz as Rumsfeld's deputy, wanted to bring some order to a messy and controversial detention system, and he found a like mind in Matthew Waxman, the deputy assistant secretary for detainee affairs. Waxman had the unhappy task of visiting allies and defending the White House position that no existing legal standards applied in Guantánamo. Agitated e-mails suggested his state of mind. On March 24, 2005, after returning from Geneva and The Hague, Waxman wrote to Sandra Hodgkinson on the NSC staff. "They are starving for info and explanations. . . . Our own embassies are in the dark on key aspects of our policy!" he wrote. "We're both slowly bleeding ourselves and shooting ourselves in the head with our current position."

Zelikow, Waxman, and England hovered together at a keyboard over the weekend of June 11 and 12. Their product, completed in England's E Ring suite in the Pentagon, was a document of nine single-spaced pages, marked "SENSITIVE BUT UNCLASSIFIED." The draftsmanship had a skill that Cheney might have admired, proposing a reversal of course while claiming continuity with the system already in place. The way the memo put it was that the existing rules made perfect sense after September 11, when "the U.S. government quickly devised some initial procedures." Enough time had passed to "learn more from experience" and "refine our approach." The president had an opportunity to offer a "vision of new institutions to sustain our effort for years to come." Working with allies and Congress, the Bush administration could build an "international system for handling captured combatants."

The memo alluded to secret CIA prisons, the "black sites" where the cruelest interrogations took place. At the time, their existence was a highly classified secret. "The policies of government agencies other than DOD cannot be walled off," the memo said. "That wall will inevitably be broken anyway, probably soon. It is better that this administration do it, and do it early in the second term." Zelikow, England, and Waxman made a concession here, proposing to permit "immediate post-capture interrogations on a special basis." In a "small number of selected cases," suspects could be "held temporarily, away from public scrutiny . . . in order to conduct humane but effective questioning and gather information while it is most current." These secret detentions would "last for a defined period—measured in days or weeks, not months or years."

After that, however, even captives like Khalid Sheikh Mohammed, the main planner of September 11, would "move into the regular detention system." The Bush administration "should not assume they can just be secretly detained for the rest of their lives without trial." Instead they should be treated "as if they were civilian detainees under the law of war." Here Zelikow & Co. turned the corner to the international legal standard that Cheney & Co. had squashed: "We thus accept the applicability of the baseline Article 3 that appears in all four of the Geneva Conventions on the Law of War." As a sign of their awareness that this might be a sensitive point, the authors turned on the Caps Lock key:

WE ARE NOT NECESSARILY SAYING THAT THESE DETAINEES ARE NECESSARILY ENTITLED TO THIS STATUS. TO BE CLEAR: WE ARE GIVING THEM A TEMPORARY STATUS THEY DO NOT DESERVE. BUT WE ARE NOT DOING THIS FOR THEM. WE ARE DOING IT FOR US.

Yes, there was "a risk that some intelligence may be lost when enemy captives are ultimately placed in a less coercive" environment. "As in our prior wars, this risk should be recognized, but accepted as necessary to maintain the integrity of the system and our common, fundamental values." One more thing: "As part of this interim system, and as the number of detainees goes down, the U.S. will no longer need to maintain a detention facility in Guantanamo. That facility will close and we expect to transfer remaining detainees to a facility in the United States."

The document was a top-to-bottom assault on the Cheney-Addington legal model. Its authors proposed to seek legislation, negotiate a new agreement with allies, acknowledge secret prisons, give the worst of the terrorists Geneva rights, and bring them back within the full jurisdiction of American courts.

Rice showed the memo to Bush on Monday morning, June 13. The report she brought back said Bush was intrigued and asked for the views of his other top advisers. Shortly after noon, Steve Hadley scheduled a "close-hold Detainee-related PC," or principals committee meeting, for 3:30 the next day. There would be a paper circulated in the meeting, but not ahead of time. Rice and Zelikow were playing by Cheney Rules, trying to game the system and give their adversary the briefest opportunity to object. They were not very good at this sort of thing. England, Rumsfeld's deputy, brought the paper to his boss on Monday, too. Rumsfeld reacted coldly. He had not authorized this. According to one official, Rumsfeld directed that all copies be withdrawn from circulation and shredded. Cheney's office, alerted, made contact with Hadley. Just before 8:00 p.m., Hadley sent out a revised agenda. The principals would confine themselves to "a preliminary 'big picture' discussion," and "no paper would be tabled or advanced," according to notes made that evening by a participant.

The Zelikow paper had been the shining future of U.S. policy for almost eight hours.

A few weeks after the "'big picture' discussion," Harriet Miers took a stab at the problem. It would be helpful, she wrote, to flesh out "a clear and concise and compelling description of the current legal framework under which we are and have been conducting the war on terror." Miers had replaced Alberto Gonzales as White House counsel, and she sent the e-mail on July 17 to her counterparts around government. The State Department, she wrote, seemed to be concerned "that we are loosing [sic] the battle of articulating how we are operating and why it is appropriate." What did everyone think, she asked, about tying U.S. legal policy to "specific international standards previously not used or rejected as inapplicable"? John Bellinger, who followed Rice from the White House and was now the State Department legal adviser, replied to the group the same evening. "Why do we care about international standards?" he wrote. "Because for more than one hundred years, beginning after our own Civil War, the United States has been at the forefront of setting international standards for the conduct of warfare. . . . These are not simply 'diplomatic' or 'foreign policy' issues; the US military and our Defense Department were at the forefront of developing these standards. . . . Surely one of the most basic rights is the right to be treated humanely and in accordance with legal rules."

The distribution list for the e-mail exchange included David Addington and Jim Haynes. Neither of them replied. Miers made no more progress than Zelikow or Rice.

Later that summer, Rumsfeld gathered his senior subordinates. Now it looked as though Congress was going to intercede. The defense secretary warned his staff to steer clear of Senate Republicans

John McCain, John Warner, and Lindsey Graham, who were drafting a bill to govern the handling of terror suspects. "Rumsfeld made clear, emphatically, that the vice president had the lead on this issue," said one of the officials who received that order. Though his fingerprints were not apparent, Cheney had already staked out a categorical position for the president. It came in a last-minute insert to a Statement of Administration Policy by the Office of Management and Budget, where Nancy Dorn, Cheney's former chief of legislative affairs, was deputy director. Without normal staff clearance, David Addington added a paragraph—just before publication on July 21, 2005—to the OMB's authoritative guidance on the 2006 defense spending bill. "The Administration strongly opposes" any amendment to "regulate the detention, treatment or trial of terrorists captured in the war on terror," the statement said. Before most Bush administration officials became aware that the subject was under White House review, Addington wrote that "the President's senior advisers would recommend that he veto" any such bill.

Inside the Defense Department, Gordon England and Matt Waxman made another attempt to bring back Geneva. There need be no grand presidential initiative. Bush had announced more than three years before that captives would be treated according to the "principles" of Geneva. It was the Pentagon's job to write rules to interpret that command. On August 26, 2005, England gathered three dozen Pentagon officials and asked Waxman to present a proposed directive. Waxman said the department should incorporate Common Article 3 directly into the military rules. That would restore the ban on cruelty that Cheney and Addington had spent three years expunging. Jim Haynes and Stephen Cambone, Rumsfeld's general counsel and undersecretary for intelligence, respectively, spoke against the proposal. Haynes, according to contemporary notes, said Waxman's idea was "perilous in terms of unintended consequences" for intelligence gathering. But they were the only dissenters. "Every vice chief came out strongly in favor, as did every JAG," said Alberto Mora, the Navy general counsel. He was referring to the second-ranking uniformed officers of each military service and their judge advocates general. Waxman thought he had Haynes and Cambone boxed in. He circulated a formal draft of DOD Directive 2310.

A few days later, Waxman got a call. Come brief Scooter Libby and David Addington. According to what he told colleagues after returning to the Pentagon, the two men handed Waxman his head, Libby cool and polite about it and Addington not much of either. Libby asked about Geneva's vague terms. What could interrogators do with instructions to respect "personal dignity"? Addington called Waxman's directive "an abomination," dumbest proposal he had ever heard, and a direct affront to a decision the president had already made. He was referring to the February 7, 2002, directive he had written for Bush's signature, which mentioned Geneva "principles" but made them subject to military necessity. Waxman returned to the Pentagon with word that his directive was "unacceptable to the vice president's office." According to Mora, "the impact of that meeting is that Directive 2310 died." Asked later about Addington's use of the word "abomination," Waxman did not want to go into details but said it "very well sums up their perspective, which was about theological visions about presidential powers and about the place of international law, as opposed to really thinking through and grappling with what I thought were the empirical pros and cons of the different approaches."

McCain and Warner and Graham were not deterred by the OMB veto threat. On October 5, 2005, a veto-proof Senate majority of 90–9 passed their Detainee Treatment Act, which included the same Geneva language. It was, by any measure, a rebuke to Cheney. Bush signed the bill into law. "Well, I don't win all the arguments," Cheney told the *Wall Street Journal*. The vice president had lobbied unsuccessfully for the bill to include an exception for interrogations by the CIA. But he and Addington found a roundabout path to their goal. Friends in Congress made little-noticed adjustments to the bill. The final measure spelled out concrete restrictions on Pentagon interrogations, but handled the CIA differently. It sounded good, banning "cruel" or "inhuman" treatment of the Agency's detainees, but at Addington's behest the fine print said those words would be interpreted in light of U.S. constitutional law. The Supreme Court defined cruelty as an act that "shocks the conscience," and that test took account of circumstances. Addington told colleagues that harsh interrogation methods would not be shocking when weighed against the risk of a mass-casualty attack. And just like that, the old interrrogation program—even waterboarding, Addington maintained—was legal again. Cheney went on television and said that "what shocks the conscience" is to some extent "in the eye of the beholder."

McCain, the former Vietnam War POW, had won the moral victory and marched away. Cheney sliced out the only part of the bill he really cared about, and it looked as though McCain did not even know. Addington, in his usual zeal, could not leave well enough alone. It was not enough to win in practice; he had to win in principle as well. The vice president and his lawyer did not accept that Congress could restrict the commander in chief on so fundamental an element of war, and Addington intended to have the president say so. Other advisers were eager to claim victory and put the scandals behind the White House. They spent days composing a statement in which Bush would embrace the new law that Cheney had threatened with veto. Just before the statement reached Bush on December 30, 2005, Addington intercepted it. He just "literally takes his red pen all the way through it," Bellinger recalled. Addington substituted a single sentence. Bush would interpret the law "in a manner consistent with the constitutional authority of the President to supervise the unitary executive branch and as Commander in Chief." Harriet Miers sent Addington's version to Bush. It sounded as though Bush was signing the law but did not feel bound by its terms. The president was blindsided by the outrage that followed. As Bellinger saw it, the vice president's office had "snatched defeat from the jaws of victory" in the battle for public support.

On June 29, 2006, Nemesis reappeared in the guise of Anthony Kennedy, the Supreme Court justice whose pushback his former clerks had predicted. The opinion was even more damaging than they expected. In *Hamdan v. Rumsfeld*, the case of Osama bin Laden's former driver Salim Hamdan, Kennedy concurred in the high court's decision that the president had no lawful power to try alleged terrorists in military commissions. The tribunal order that Cheney brought to Bush's dining room, and the game plan Addington wrote to defend it, were cast aside. If Bush wanted military tribunals, he would have to ask permission from Congress. And if he did not give "enemy combatants" the full protection of Geneva's Common Article 3, they could enforce their Geneva rights in U.S. courts. The decision was, in principle, a calamity for Cheney's war plan against al Qaeda.

No matter what else happened, the highest court had placed new constraints on a White House that chafed against all constraint. Bush and future presidents would have to live with the restrictions. Even if a compliant Congress handed back the authority the Court had taken away, the president was nonetheless beholden to the other branches of government. A Supreme Court majority had established that the legislature and judiciary could limit the president's exercise of inherent wartime power. The vice president steamrolled his litigation plan through the Justice Department, but that tactical victory led to strategic defeat. This was the Supreme Court's third and most important rebuff to his claim of unchecked authority for the commander in chief. "Addington was deeply principled, but he was principled to the point of being stupid," Jack Goldsmith said later. "He held fast to his hard-core views of unilateral executive power even when they led to self-defeatingly adverse political consequences for the presidency." Bruce Fein, who was associate deputy attorney general under President Ronald Reagan, said likewise that "the irony with the Cheney crowd pushing the envelope on presidential power is that the president has now ended up with lesser powers than he would have had if they had made less extravagant, monarchical claims."

Bush rejected Cheney's plan to repair the damage. Addington had drafted a one-page bill, which amounted to asking Congress to reverse the outcome in *Hamdan*. By this proposal, Bush would not ask Congress for authority to hold military tribunals. He would ask Congress to affirm that Bush did not need its permission, and to strip the Court of jurisdiction over the matter. The president's political, diplomatic, and communications advisers were appalled at that idea. Bush himself was tired of losing arguments about detainees, tired of playing defense. He decided on a course, Chief of Staff Josh Bolten said, that "did not come out exactly as the vice president would have wanted."

The president negotiated for months on the law that became the Military Commissions Act of 2006. And all of a sudden he was in the market for a visionary plan. Something a lot like the memo that Zelikow & Co. had drafted the year before. Now they were calling it the Big Bang. After working through the details all summer, Bush acknowledged publicly on September 6, 2006, that the CIA had been holding "high-value detainees" in secret facilities overseas, a subject on which he had held his silence since the *Washington Post* disclosed the black sites a year before. The president announced that he had emptied the secret prisons and transferred fourteen captives to Guantánamo Bay. They would all receive trials under new tribunal rules that more closely resembled the ones in use for military courts-martial. Drafts of Bush's speech were codeword-classified until the president said the words out loud. All through Labor Day weekend, the president's advisers worked through the final details. Jim Haynes and his senior deputies were on vacation. Somehow it fell to Diane Beaver to carry a sealed orange pouch into the Eisenhower Building, keeper of the computer drive that held the secrets. She kept on popping up, the same Diane Beaver who had played host to David Addington at Guantánamo, then heard him make that cryptic remark, years later, about how "great minds think alike." Now she was watching him finesse the details of an announcement that he and his boss had tried to stop. "He had to make sure we did it right to protect whatever program was going to be left for the future," Beaver said. One of the things that Addington did was to keep alive secret authorities to resume the black-site detentions on demand. After a private meeting with Cheney, Bush decided not to promise that the facilities would shut down for good. Seven months later, the White House acknowledged that secret detention had resumed.

That same first week of September, the Pentagon dusted off the Waxman document that Libby and Addington had shelved the year before. DOD Directive 2310.01E, the Department of Defense Detainee Program, included the verbatim text of Geneva's Common Article 3 and described it, just as Waxman had, as "a minimum standard for the care and treatment of all detainees." A new Army field manual, published alongside, said interrogators were forbidden to employ a long list of techniques that had been used against suspected terrorists since September 11, 2001—including stripping, hooding, inflicting pain, and forcing the performance of mock sex acts.

For all the setbacks, Cheney preserved his top-priority tools in the "war on terror." The Military Commissions Act, passed by strong majorities of the Senate and House on September 28 and 29, 2006, exempted CIA officers and other government employees from prosecution for past war crimes or torture. And once again the fine print held great importance for Cheney and his allies. Without repealing the War Crimes Act, which imposed criminal penalties for breaches of Geneva's humane-treatment standards, Congress said the president, not the Supreme Court, had final authority to decide what the standards meant. He would interpret them very narrowly.

Even so, the new rules imposed on military tribunals, by Congress and federal courts, proved to be just the headaches that Cheney and Addington foresaw. Captives at Guantánamo were entitled to "status reviews" and could challenge the results in federal court. The first of those challenges won big. A three-judge panel in the U.S. Court of Appeals for the D.C. Circuit found the government's evidence to be Carrollian, as in Lewis Carroll. The Bush administration gave enemy combatant status to Huzaifa Parhat, a Chinese national from the Uighur minority, because he was "affiliated" with forces that were "associated" with al Qaeda. The judges said the classified files contained mere assertions, not evidence. When the government declared the intelligence reliable because it appeared in three different documents, the judges mocked that reasoning. "The fact that the government has 'said it thrice' does not make an allegation true. See Lewis Carroll, *The Hunting of the Snark* 3 (1876) ('I have said it thrice: What I tell you three times is true.')." The Bush administration "comes perilously close to suggesting that whatever the government says must be treated as true, thus rendering superfluous both the role of the Tribunal and the role that Congress assigned to this court," the court wrote.

And what of Mohammed Qahtani, Detainee 063, the man subjected to forty-nine days of torment at Guantánamo? When his circumstances were made public in 2004, Jim Haynes and his Pentagon deputy said the methods worked—Qahtani's resistance had been broken, and he spilled valuable information on the "dirty bomb" plot of Jose Padilla. A chain retraction followed. The Bush administration abandoned its dirty-bomb charge against Padilla the following year, rescinding his status as an enemy combatant a few days before the deadline for legal briefs in his Supreme Court appeal. On May 11, 2008, the military tribunal at Guantánamo dropped all charges against Qahtani. In an interview with Bob Woodward, tribunal chief Susan Crawford explained why. "His treatment met the legal definition of torture," Crawford said.

As the Supreme Court weighed the future of terror detainees, Cheney weighed the future of the Court, looking for a reversal of his reversals of fortune. Chief Justice William Rehnquist was in failing health in May 2005. It was time to begin choosing a successor. The attorney general, the White House chief of staff, and political adviser Karl Rove gathered to interview candidates, but none of them ran the meetings. The interviews were held at Cheney's residence, and the vice president was the man in charge.

Bush had asked for only one thing: diversity. He wanted a conservative judge, but what animated him, advisers said, was the prospect of appointing a woman or a minority, maybe the first Hispanic justice. Cheney was animated, too, unusually so in front of others. "Some of the few times I can remember the vice president speaking up in an Oval Office meeting was on this subject," Brad Berenson recalled. Cheney's overriding concern was to promote the correct judicial philosophy.

The Cheney-led selection panel had eleven potential nominees when it started work, including women and minorities. The panel culled the list, recommending that the president interview only five. Those were U.S. Court of Appeals judges John G. Roberts Jr., Samuel A. Alito Jr., James Harvie Wilkinson III, J. Michael Luttig, and Edith Brown Clement. All five were white; four were men. What they shared were clear records of support for the positions most important to Cheney. Collectively, the group saw executive power in expansive terms and congressional authority more narrowly. Three of the five ruled for the Bush administration in challenges to its detention policies. Most had records demonstrating that they shared Cheney's view on affirmative action—that it was unconstitutional to take account of race in any way, a position that differed substantially from the president's. One of the judges had sided with a power company in a case involving enforcement of the "new source" pollution rule, which Cheney wanted to abolish.

Cheney's panel questioned the potential nominees for hours. One participant said the vice president probed for information that would shed light on legal philosophy, deftly avoiding improper questions on how a judge might rule in a given case. He had a strong layman's understanding of jurisprudence, asking nuanced questions that went right to the seam between competing schools of thought. The subsequent interviews with Bush were briefer and "far more relaxed," the participant said. The president and the potential justice might speak of personal matters, family, exercise.

Sandra Day O'Connor retired while Cheney still had his eye on Rehnquist's seat. From among the five culled candidates, Bush chose John Roberts as his nominee on July 19, 2005. Cheney assigned Steve

Schmidt, his own communications adviser, to run the confirmation campaign. In September, Rehnquist died, giving Bush his second opportunity for an appointment. Cheney gave Bush the same list, only four people left, and still no minority. (For reasons unknown, Bush did not take to Edith Brown Clement.) Bush began speculating in public about appointing Alberto Gonzales, his longtime lawyer. Conservatives funneled objections to Rove and Cheney, according to Leonard Leo of the Federalist Society. After the backlash against Gonzales, Bush settled unexpectedly on Harriet Miers. He would have his diversity, Cheney or no. The president sent Andy Card to break the news October 2. "Didn't have the nerve to tell me himself," Cheney muttered to an associate in a rare display of pique. When conservatives rebelled against that choice, too, and Miers withdrew, Bush gave up on his freelance efforts to recruit. He made another pick from Cheney's list, and got Alito.

By the time Bush announced Alito's nomination, the vice president had other things on his mind. Three days earlier he had suffered a grievous blow, losing the close friend and alter ego who was a mainstay of Cheney's effectiveness in the White House. The vice president would not recover fully from that loss.

Just after noon on October 28, 2005, six men and thirteen women filed silently into courtroom 4 of the E. Barrett Prettyman Federal Courthouse. For two years they had served on a grand jury under the direction of Special Counsel Patrick J. Fitzgerald. Now the anonymous forewoman, dressed in a black cardigan, carried out a ritual that dated to the Magna Carta. She stepped forward to the magistrate on a raised bench and handed up a sheaf of papers. The twenty-two-page indictment opened the criminal case of *United States of America v. I. Lewis Libby, also known as "Scooter Libby."* Hobbled by a broken foot, Libby left the White House that day on crutches, unable to drive or make further use of a government limousine that no longer belonged to him.

Nemesis came to Cheney this time with long blond hair, the only conspicuous feature of a woman who did what she could to avoid attention. In a career as a clandestine officer of the CIA, Valerie Plame had used an assortment of simple legends. She was a student in Europe, an energy analyst, a diplomat's wife, a mother of twins who did not work outside the home. Her cover was blown in the summer of 2003, collateral damage in political combat that crossed one of Washington's remaining lines of restraint. Scooter Libby was not the first to disclose her identity to a reporter, nor was he even the second source for Robert Novak, the newspaper columnist who ended Plame's operational career. But Libby and Cheney were at the white-hot center of events that put Plame's identity in play. No one outside their office made more extensive efforts to get her name in print.

Joseph Wilson, Plame's husband, was a retired ambassador as flamboyant as she was subdued. He made it his mission to persuade the public that Cheney was a liar, promoting a nonexistent Iraqi nuclear threat. Wilson appeared to believe that Cheney knew he had traveled to Niger and disputed a report that Iraq was trying to buy uranium there. He was enraged when he heard the vice president repeat the Niger story, assuming that Cheney knew it to be false. The particulars of Wilson's charge, ironically, were untrue. The CIA had not passed his report to Cheney. If Cheney lied about Iraq, he did so elsewhere. The vice president and Scooter Libby, meanwhile, took Wilson's campaign as an assault on Cheney's honor. Who was this man? What had he done in Niger, and why had he been chosen for the job?

Grand jury testimony and the trial record made clear that Cheney, as much as Libby, became obsessed with Wilson. As good as Libby was at extracting information from the CIA, Cheney was better. It was the vice president, according to unrebutted evidence from the prosecution, who supplied Libby with the detail "that Wilson's wife worked . . . in the Counterproliferation Division"—an unambiguous declaration that her position was among the case officers of the operations directorate, and therefore very likely to be a secret. And it was Cheney who first alluded to the accusation that would soon be flung against Wilson. He used a small pocketknife to clip Wilson's July 6, 2003, opinion article from the *New York Times,* and in the margin he wrote: "Have they done this sort of thing before? Send an Amb. to answer a question? Do we ordinarily send people out pro bono to work for us? Or did his wife send him on a junket?"

Cheney had established Plame's CIA employment and the political line of attack: Wilson was an unqualified dabbler who got the Niger assignment as a favor from his wife. If that was meant to discredit Wilson, the CIA has a word for operations that go so badly wrong: "blowback." In the Nemesis myth, the term is "vengeful fate." The fictional president in Lynne Cheney's novel describes it this way: "One of the crazy things about this job is the strange sort of ricochet effect there is sometimes," the president says. "You make a decision with one goal in mind and it glances off a hundred complicating factors until the end result is the opposite of what you intended."

At least four people told reporters about Valerie Plame's CIA employment: Karl Rove, Ari Fleischer, Richard Armitage, and Scooter Libby. The first three told enough of the truth under oath, and soon enough, to avoid indictment. Libby, among the most cautious of men, did not. On October 14 and November 26, 2003, he crossed a point of no return. He lied to the FBI about what he knew, how he learned it, and what he told reporters. In two grand jury appearances, March 5 and 24 of the following year, he stuck to his story. If Libby had told the truth, he would have led investigators directly to his boss. Cheney was his source on Plame, Cheney directed him to speak to reporters, and Cheney invented the line about the junket. None of that constituted a crime, but Libby had every reason to fear its disclosure would be—as indeed it became—immensely harmful politically. Nor is it out of the question that Libby had evidence that would expose the vice president to a criminal charge. Under some circumstances it is a felony to disclose the identity of a clandestine officer. Libby's grand jury testimony left open the question whether Cheney asked him to do that.

> *Q. You told the FBI in your first interview, or in one of your two interviews, that it's possible that the Vice President could have told you on Air Force Two that you should tell the press about Wilson's wife, but you do not recall that happening. Correct?*
> *A. Correct.*
> *Q. And does that remain true?*
> *A. It remains true that it was possible, I don't remember it happening.*

Cheney, too, gave an interview to the FBI, and almost certainly was asked whether he directed the leak of Plame's identity. What he said has never been released. Cheney was still resisting congressional demands for the transcript in the final months of the administration.

On March 6, 2007, reporters and spectators began pressing toward the courthouse entrance upon receiving word that the jury had reached its verdict. Just at that moment, shortly before Libby was convicted on four counts of perjury, obstruction of justice, and lying to the FBI, Cheney's motorcade sped past the courthouse on Pennsylvania Avenue. The vice president was headed to his regular Tuesday lunch with the Senate Republican caucus.

Libby's loss deprived Cheney of his most capable and experienced adviser, his regular stand-in and the overseer of meticulous preparations for nearly everything Cheney did in government. Colleagues said Addington, who became chief of staff, was a match for Libby in bureaucratic combat but not in breadth of knowledge or managerial skill. Nor could Addington replace himself as the Bush administration's alpha lawyer. "The most effective team in government," as the State Department's Lawrence Wilkerson called them without affection, was no longer in a league of its own. The voice of the vice president's office became quieter. "OVP just doesn't have the room-clearing effect it used to have," said a high-ranking White House official.

There were other changes of the guard in the second term. Bush fired Don Rumsfeld, over Cheney's strong objection. Ideological allies—Paul Wolfowitz, John Bolton, Douglas Feith—left government, too. Andy Card resigned, and Josh Bolten, a much more independent figure, replaced him as White House chief of staff. Bolten forged alliances with other new faces in high-ranking posts, some of whom brought experience and bureaucratic skill to the jobs that their predecessors had lacked. In a symbolic maneuver, the new treasury secretary, Henry Paulson, moved the weekly lunch of top economic advisers back to the Treasury Building, uprooting it from the White House Ward Room, where Cheney had made a point of sitting in. Fred Fielding, Bush's third White House counsel, had a background to match Addington's and a far more pragmatic style. The vice president's dominance of legal policy softened further. Cheney was by no means exhausted, but he had less lift and more drag as time went on.

Six months after taking the job of chief of staff, on October 18, 2006, Josh Bolten sat down for an on-the-record interview, prepared to talk about the vice president for most of an hour. A lot of his peers regarded that as dangerous territory for a conversation with reporters; some spoke of Cheney anonymously, and others remained carefully anodyne. Bolten had a message to send. His language was measured and full of respect, but the meaning was unmistakable. "The president really took him on as a counselor and not as an alter ego or not even really as a deputy," Bolten said at one point. Later, he said the president oftentimes "takes his advice seriously and says no." Bush, he said, "is more courteous to the vice president than to almost anybody else, but he's not actually any more deferential." When asked about Cheney's history of settling cabinet disputes, such as the battle between Ashcroft and Rumsfeld over military tribunals, Bolten replied bluntly. "In my six months' experience, it would not fall to the vice president to referee that kind of thing," he said. "If it is a presidential decision, the president will make it. If it is not presidential, it is going to be one of the cabinet officers [who] would make it—or me." Bolten added, "I think the vice president appreciates that. That his role is in support of the president, not as a second-tier substitute."

Chapter Fourteen

REGIME CHANGE

On the last Tuesday in June, in his last year in office, Dick Cheney walked down a flight of stairs and through a hall-way past the Situation Room. White wooden doors with six-paned windows led him out of the White House and into the heat of a Washington summer morning. Cheney crossed West Executive Avenue and made his way to the Eisenhower Building. A group of visiting Australian leaders awaited him in a small amphitheater on the fourth floor. Cheney delivered a thirty-minute, off-the-record tour of the global horizon.

Cheney was Cheney, speaking of existential threats: terrorists, rogue regimes, weapons of mass destruction. *Nexus.* On his mind as much as ever. Iraq, the war that consumed his White House years, remained, he said, the center of a global conflict with a dangerous and determined enemy. Prime Minister Nouri al-Maliki had turned a corner in the New Iraq, proving himself a true patriot by confront-ing an Iranian-backed militia in the southern city of Basra. Iran, meanwhile, was actively pursuing nuclear weapons in bald defiance of the international community. One of the Australians raised a hand.

What would the Americans do if Israel carried out a preemptive strike? For some time now, Bush had been tamping down such talk, saying he made "very clear to all parties" that the "first option ought to be solve this problem diplomatically." The vice president did not exactly answer, but the Australians took away a menacing vibe. Israel was an independent democracy that would make its own choices in self-defense, Cheney said. Iranian president Mahmoud Ahmadinejad called openly for Israel's destruction, and it was only a matter of time before Iran reached the point of no return in its quest for nuclear arms.

A matter of time. It was June 24, 2008, and Cheney had his eye on the clock, not even seven months to go. Now, amid all the strong words, he said something that slipped past most of his audience. According to notes made shortly afterward, Cheney said, "If we do not resolve our Iran problem during the days we have left in office, this problem will be among the highest and most important issues on the front end of the next administration." The offhand use of that introductory clause, the "if" that foretold a job unfinished, was something new for Cheney. You had to listen closely with this guy, because the vice president did not wave a white flag in retreat. He adjusted position by small degrees, and over time it was easy to miss that he had moved to a different hill. Until that moment, Cheney had not imagined aloud that he and the president might leave the White House with Iran on an unimpeded path to nuclear arms. George Bush and Dick Cheney often said they were not the kind of leaders who kicked the can down the road. Eight months earlier, Cheney had accused Iran of speeding ahead with uranium enrichment while dragging out talks, practicing "delay and deception in an obvious attempt to buy time." Iran would not be allowed to win at that game. "Our country and the entire international community cannot stand by as a terror-supporting state fulfills its most aggressive ambitions. The Iranian regime needs to know that if it stays on its present course, the international community is prepared to impose serious consequences. . . . We will not allow Iran to have a nuclear weapon." In diplomatic argot, "grave consequences" always means war. "Serious consequences" sometimes means that, too. When the United States and Britain sought UN authority to invade Iraq, the resolution they proposed had the latter formula. In 2007, Cheney alluded often to the possibility of military force. It was never clear he favored such a step, and there were reasons for doubt, but Cheney wanted to keep the threat alive. Advocates of military intervention had a motto: Better to bomb Iran than let Iran get the Bomb. After John McCain made a version of that remark, Cheney responded in a newspaper interview, "I would guess that John McCain and I are pretty close to agreement."

For more than a year, frustrated at the president's disinclination to use force, some Cheney advisers had been floating a scenario in which Israel could mount a largely symbolic strike that would force Bush's hand. David Wurmser, recently departed from Cheney's office, told a private strategy group in the first week of May 2007 that Israel could draw the United States into military conflict with Tehran by firing conventional ballistic missiles at Natanz. Missiles would not do much damage, but Iran would be likely to retaliate against nearby U.S. forces as well as against Israel. The urgency, Wurmser said, was that Cheney believed Iran was close to the point of no return in mastering uranium enrichment to "weapons grade." To build a bomb Iran needed a quantity of 90 percent pure U-235. Once Iran could reach a purity of 15 to 17 percent, though, it would know how to do the rest. That was why a strike would have to come soon, Wurmser said. (In an interview, Wurmser denied categorically that he had outlined such a scenario, but two sets of contemporary notes obtained by the author said otherwise.) Now, in the summer of Cheney's discontent, that kind of talk sounded like bluster. Iran was stronger and the United States weaker, pretty much for the same reason: American forces were mired in Iraq. By just about any measure, the Bush administration had given enormous strategic gifts to the Islamic Republic. The Afghan and Iraqi governments, both hostile to Iran and both right on its border, were gone, courtesy of George W. Bush. Iran no longer had a military competitor in a region of vital interest to every oil-burning economy in the world. Prices of its principal export had also surged by nearly sevenfold. There were other factors at work, but the invasion of Iraq and its aftermath played a large role in driving crude oil prices from the $20 range to a new record of $144 a barrel the week Cheney spoke to the Australians.

Regime change was coming, but not in the axis of evil. In Washington, power had drained from the Bush White House, almost palpably so from the vice president himself. The job had aged and grayed him, thickened him around the middle. He was sixty-seven years old, an athlete once, more than four years the junior of his party's presidential nominee, but he did not look like any of those things. Cheney still carried his big leather briefcase off Air Force Two, but he gripped the railing tightly and looked at his feet as he stepped down the stairs. The "Fuck yourself" Cheney snapped at Democrat Patrick Leahy on the Senate floor may or may not have been one of his demonstration shots, but it came across as a loss of control. In the second term, the big donors who met with him periodically at the Hoover Institution were saying, according to David Brady, the deputy director, that Cheney seemed "pissed off all the time, an increasingly bitter man who doesn't like where he is." Heart specialists, none of whom had access to Cheney's closed records, said the cumulative damage of Cheney's "cardiac events" could account for some of the observed changes of mood and physical condition. Cheney had suffered four episodes of minor to moderate severity in the second term, following a first term that included a (postelection) heart attack, angioplasty, insertion of a coronary stent, and implantation of a defibrillator. "The disease of the arteries of the heart is often not limited to the arteries of the heart, but it also involves the arteries of the brain," said Anthony Komaroff, professor of medicine at Harvard. Typical symptoms include "impairments of memory, impairments of judgment," and "less well-controlled mood swings."

Personal factors aside, geopolitics had grown unkind. No longer was Cheney reshaping "a world that can be changed," as historian Victor Davis Hanson described his frame of mind on the eve of war with Iraq. Initiative did not belong as often to the administration he served, and neither, within the administration, did it belong to Cheney. The vice president spent more of his time fighting gravity, trying to break the fall.

At the very end of his meeting with the Australian American Leadership Dialogue, Cheney's game face slipped. "Last question," he said. He pointed to Steve Clemons, the well-sourced publisher of TheWashingtonNote.com. Clemons had heard some inside dope on a forthcoming policy shift. "Mr. Cheney, thank you so much for your time," Clemons said. "On Wednesday or Thursday we will be delisting North Korea from the terrorist blacklist. Could you set the context for this decision?" The vice president had been speaking fluidly for half an hour. Now he simply stopped. He looked at Clemons for a long time, long enough to make it uncomfortable, nothing but dead air at the microphone. Then even more. Bruce Wolpe, a corporate manager in Australia's largest publishing group, turned to a friend afterward and said the vice president looked like a big fish, smelling suspiciously at bait. Finally, Cheney pointed at his chest. "I'm not going to be the one to announce that decision," he said. "Address your interest to the State Department." Without further pleasantries, Cheney walked out. Peter Costello, deputy leader of the Liberal Party of Australian prime minister John Howard until its recent defeat in the polls, walked up to Clemons. "What was that all about?" he asked.

At minimum, it was about a setback to Cheney's preferred approach to North Korea. That did not seem to explain quite enough. He had cheerfully defended presidential decisions before without hinting at dissent. The question at issue was how to respond, in disarmament talks, to the Pyongyang government's first official nuclear inventory. The document was said to be arriving in Beijing. On Thursday, two days after Cheney's talk, Bush made the announcement, welcoming the North Korean declaration as "one step in a multistep process." Bush struck the government of Kim Jong Il from the U.S. list of state terror sponsors and lifted sanctions based on the Trading with the Enemy Act. In a briefing, National Security Adviser Steve Hadley acknowledged that the North Korean document left plutonium quantities imprecise and made no mention at all of uranium, weapons fabrication, or technology sales to other countries. The U.S. government, it emerged, had not even received the document as yet from China. Hadley said it "was probably unrealistic" to expect Kim Jong Il to "provide a document which on its face would be so compelling that we could say it's complete and correct."

All this turned the old Bush policy, the Cheney version, on its head. Never exchange concrete benefits for the promise of future behavior by a rogue regime, Cheney said. When Colin Powell suggested publicly in early 2001 that Bush would pick up talks where Bill Clinton had left off, he was forced to retract his remarks. "Sometimes you get a little too far forward in your skis," he said. The vice president did not oppose talks in principle, "but he was certainly for applying much more pressure, and getting others to do the same," according to Aaron Friedberg, an Asia policy expert who did strategic planning on his staff. "We used to talk around the office about a 'talk and squeeze' strategy." During interagency meetings, Cheney and his staff said North Korea should begin with "complete, verifiable, irreversible dismantlement" of its nuclear program before the United States made any payments. That standard, said Undersecretary of State John Bolton during the first term, when Cheney's position carried the day, "is 'engagement' like we engaged the Japanese on the deck of the *Missouri* in Tokyo Bay in 1945." Washington need only discuss with Pyongyang, he said, "the terms of its surrender."

When Condi Rice became secretary of state and jockeyed Bolton out of the department, she began advocating a return to small, progressive steps that might lead to something bigger. She and her new counselor, Philip Zelikow, had been partners on the National Security Council staff when Bush's father helped reunify Germany in 1990. Colleagues said she intimated to the younger Bush that there was a chance he could match that accomplishment on the Korean Peninsula—building toward a nuclear deal, a peace agreement to replace the armistice of 1953, and, eventually, unification of North and South. That appealed to Bush's fondness for big, game-changing ideas, and he gave Rice some room to maneuver. He did some maneuvering himself. In April 2006, on a visit to Washington, Chinese president Hu Jintao spoke to Bush about Kim Jong Il's fear of invasion. "How about I give Kim a peace treaty?" Bush replied suddenly at their luncheon in the East Room. Cheney, according to two staff members, was stunned. "I think that's fine if you're willing to sacrifice the North Korean people," Bolton, by then long gone from government, said sarcastically. Kim's decision to test his first nuclear weapon later that year put the talks on hold, but Rice revived them in 2007.

It would be too simple to say Rice began to win and Cheney to lose. The vice president recognized, advisers said, that refusing to negotiate with Pyongyang would harm U.S. interests in China, South Korea, and Japan. "The idea that he doesn't consider pragmatic considerations just because he's principled, I just don't—I don't find that right about him," Rice said. Later she added, "The kind of classic way that people teach public policy, which, by the way, I used to teach public policy that way before I actually was involved in it, is the president gets option A, he gets option B, and the vice president is for option A and maybe the secretary of state is for option B, and the president decides. It just isn't the way that it happens. We will sit around and we'll have a debate, and people will raise the upsides and the downsides, and then we'll decide on a course. And the president is the one who decides on the course, but it's very rare that it is a course that is black and white." There was little doubt, even so, that Rice and Cheney saw upsides and downsides very differently. Bush's approach to North Korea and Iran—after listing them, with Iraq, in an "axis of evil" in 2002—was beginning to look more like the secretary of state's.

Rice had not suddenly become a bureaucratic powerhouse or learned to overmatch the vice president. Her influence grew, if that is the right way to put it, because the president wanted to try a new direction. Bush and Cheney had coincided on the means in Iraq, but not necessarily on the ends. Transformation still had more prominence in Bush's worldview, prevention of emerging threats in Cheney's. The president's hopes were bogged down in Baghdad. "By the time it became clear how problematic Iraq was going to become, nobody was in the mood to say change this or that regime," Friedberg said. That included Cheney. But the vice president's alternative tended toward the kind of grinding, steady pressure that might get nowhere by the time they reached January 2009. With experience, Bush began to trust more in his own instincts. "The president is deeply, deeply, deeply conversant in these issues in a way that he was not when he came into office," Rice said.

Cheney and his advisers believed that the North Korean regime was incapable by nature of honoring an agreement, among other reasons because Kim would have to open the world's most shuttered society to intrusive foreign inspections. Cheney was opposed to "starting down the road of paying off the North Koreans up front for something they haven't done," according to Friedberg. But negotiations tended to take on a life of their own, and Friedberg said the vice president's office adopted a "rope a dope" strategy in the interagency meetings—slowing things down, "playing out the string and not being coerced into making bad agreements." On North Korea policy, he said, "the basic concern is, 'Do no harm, and don't let others do harm by accepting something they shouldn't accept.' "

All those things were in play on June 24, when Cheney had his frozen encounter with Steve Clemons. Could it be that Angler had been angled? A review of the time line afterward made it look as though the North Korea decision was made without him, or before he believed it was final. It was eleven o'clock Tuesday morning in Washington, or eleven the same night in Beijing, when Cheney neared the end of his talk with the visiting Australians. According to China's official Xinhua news agency, North Korean ambassador Choe Jin Su did not deliver his government's nuclear declaration to Beijing until Thursday, which meant Wednesday night in Washington. Somebody was telling Clemons that the document was good enough, and North Korea had not handed it over yet. Cheney would have expected a chance to ask hard questions about the declaration, according to Steve Yates, who was his senior Asia hand until 2005.

Yates asked his old friends in the vice president's office whether Cheney had been sandbagged, but he, too, "was met with total silence," he said. "It's plausible there was a meeting [scheduled] on the subject, given the time line of actions by our negotiator, but no one in OVP would say."

People had wondered if this would happen when Scooter Libby dropped out of the picture. Would the vice president lose a step? Libby was not only Cheney's "gatekeeper, intellectual partner, and personal friend," Yates said. He also had "visibility on everything" in bureaucratic combat because of his exceptional skill and his rank as assistant to the president. John Hannah, who replaced him as Cheney's national security adviser, "is not an assistant to the president," Yates said. "I don't know that it's working out for him as well as it did for Scooter, having the same level of consultation and impact."

Newton's law, or Nemesis, or a bureaucracy's natural impulse toward balance—something was throwing more skillful challengers at Cheney's office. Assistant Secretary of State James Kelly, who had the Korea portfolio in the first term, was replaced by Christopher Hill, a cannier player who once said the truculent North Korean diplomats were no match for Serb negotiators he had wrestled in the Balkans. Some Cheney staff members and their allies, according to John Bolton, called him "Kim Jong Hill" for what they saw as softness toward Pyongyang, but Hill was a worthy adversary in Washington. The new undersecretary of state for political affairs, Nicholas Burns, maintained respectful relations with Cheney, but he, too, understood the use of back channels and proxies. The vice president still kept his office paperwork from leaking out, while seeing everything that went to Bush, but some of his bureaucratic intelligence-gathering slipped. In the first term most White House staff members were unaware that many of their e-mails were blind-copied to Cheney's staff. Anyone who sent a memo to Condi Rice, for example, addressed it to @NSA, and it went not only to the national security adviser, her two executive assistants, and two secretaries, but also to the vice president's office. NSC distribution lists, such as @asia, did the same. Eventually, Yates said, the NSC staff discovered that "all they had to do was right-click and look at Properties and see who was on the list. Over time a lot of them would find creative ways to make new lists where we were not on them." Cheney's aides were called the Watchers by their nervous counterparts in other agencies, for their habit of attending meetings and reporting back without disclosing the vice president's position. As the second term passed its midpoint, there were more things the Watchers did not see.

Cheney and David Addington had better luck maintaining the legal structure of the "war on terror," recouping some of the losses in Congress and courts and continuing to slow-roll plans they did not like in the executive branch. One important success came on July 20, 2007. Bush signed an executive order authorizing the CIA to devise and carry out interrogation plans using any method that the president certified as free of "cruel, inhuman or degrading treatment or punishment." That was the core requirement of Geneva's Common Article 3—which the vice president had expunged from U.S. legal policy until the Supreme Court ordered the president to obey. The new order clarified nothing concrete, because it did not say—and White House spokesman Tony Snow would not say—whether any particular interrogation method was or was not unlawfully cruel. Anyone who had claimed a human-rights victory for the Detainee Treatment Act or the Military Commissions Act was now obliged to think again. Addington, making the most of language that Cheney helped insert in the latter bill, drafted the two essential provisos of Bush's new order. One said the president's interpretation of cruelty "shall be treated as authoritative for all purposes as a matter of United States law, including satisfaction of the international obligations of the United States." All purposes. That was a direct rejoinder to the Supreme Court. The president, according to the president, now had final word on whether the president was complying with his obligation to prevent cruel treatment of captives. Addington had already established the rationale for declaring that waterboarding and other harsh measures stopped short of cruelty. The other new proviso stated that "any individual acting on behalf of the Central Intelligence Agency" in the interrogation program could rely on the president's order as a defense "in a civil, criminal, or administrative proceeding." Exclusive presidential power, and advance immunity, were back on the books—at least for the CIA.

For more than a year, Bush had been on record that "I'd like to close Guantanamo." It stayed open. In Cheney's most productive years, he had made big things happen. Cheney reshaped national security law, expanded the prerogatives of the executive branch, midwifed the birth of domestic espionage, rewrote the president's tax bill, shifted the course of a river out west, shut down negotiations with North Korea, and had a major role in bringing war to Iraq.

Now he played a game of inertia, slowing down initiatives that would disturb the pieces he already had in place. He did not need a powerful engine for that. Mainly, he needed brakes. Cheney had lost allies—Scooter Libby, Don Rumsfeld, John Yoo, Paul Wolfowitz, Doug Feith, John Bolton. But a lot of former antagonists were gone, too: John Ashcroft, Jim Comey, Jack Goldsmith, Patrick Philbin, Colin Powell, Richard Armitage, Paul O'Neill, Christie Whitman. Of the five Mod Squad members, two had departed the scene—Jim Jeffords quitting the Senate, and Lincoln Chafee defeated after a single term. The vice president neatly dispatched a third one, Arlen Specter, humiliating him in the Judiciary Committee he chaired.

When the Pennsylvania Republican asked telecommunications executives to testify about their cooperation with domestic surveillance, Cheney lobbied behind his back to persuade committee Republicans to vote against the chairman. No subpoenas, no classified hearing. Specter sent an angry letter, expressing bafflement that Cheney had "determine[d] the action of the committee without calling me first," or even "calling me at some point." Cheney's "Dear Arlen" reply, a Cheshire grin nearly visible on the page, said his "frequent contacts with senators" had proved "helpful in maintaining good relations between the executive and legislative branches." Specter never got his hearing.

Nearly half a year after the president spoke of closing Guantánamo, former White House counselor and speechwriter Michael Gerson said in an interview that Cheney and his aides were using "a molasses process" to prevent it. Cheney persuaded the president to consider the risks, and there were risks. Some detainees would have to be freed, and the ones brought to U.S. territory might gain more rights. When officials from the attorney general's office joined with Cheney, John Bellinger sometimes erupted, "You're not the Department of Litigation Risk! You're the Department of Justice." Public diplomacy was suffering, many of Bush's advisers believed, harming relationships with allied governments and even more so with publics in the Arab and Islamic worlds. Addington often said there was no point sacrificing presidential power for "public relations," because critics would find something else to complain about. "They didn't circumvent the process," Gerson said, laughing somewhat bitterly. "They were very effective in using the process. . . . The president wanted to solve the problem at Gitmo. It was a major drawback on the public diplomacy front. They'd insist on presidential prerogatives and not establishing any precedents that would limit the president's authority."

John Bellinger, after seven years, finally voiced his frustrations in public as the clock began to run out on the second term. The State Department legal adviser, who had fought and often lost the battles with Addington, said the White House refused to change with changing conditions. At Bellinger's church in Virginia, he said, they sing a nineteenth-century hymn called "Once to Every Man and Nation," which, as it happens, is based on an antiwar poem. He quoted a stanza from memory:

> *New occasions teach new duties, time makes ancient good*
> *uncouth,*
> *They must upward still and onward, who would keep abreast of*
> *truth.*

"And that's been my credo on these detainee issues," he said. "You can make decisions at the time, under the circumstances, but when you see later what the full implications may be, what wasn't really analyzed, then you need to admit mistakes and change. Did I stand up on day one, in December 2001, and say, 'Gee, we shouldn't send these people to Guantánamo, and we should bring them in and put them into federal prisons in the Southern District of New York?' People who were captured by one's soldiers on the battlefield? You know, no. One didn't have perfect clarity of vision. But certainly by 2003 or so—and certainly more as each year has gone by, and Guantánamo has become this incredibly negative symbol—one needs to be able to change. Even if some of the original justification for Guantánamo, which was to have a secure place to hold people, is still valid, it's become a net negative. The failing of this administration, because of a fear of admitting error, has been an unwillingness to evolve."

Condi Rice, Bellinger's boss, sounded resigned to defeat in remarks a month later. "We'd like nothing better than to close Guantanamo," she said in a question-and-answer session with Google employees in May 2008. "We look all the time at whether it's possible. And when and if it's possible, we'd like to do it."

Cheney's motives, his convictions, were the same as ever. The day after Bush signed the new executive order, claiming final word on cruelty "for all purposes as a matter of United States law," the president was sedated for removal of polyps from his colon. He duly notified Congress that he would "transfer temporarily my Constitutional powers and duties to the Vice President." For two hours and five minutes, Dick Cheney was commander in chief. He spent his presidency at his Chesapeake Bay vacation home in St. Michaels, Maryland. Cheney wrote letters to his six grandchildren, the text of each the same. The words were everything we had come to expect of the man, sober and disciplined, an affectionate impulse giving way to a consuming sense of danger and duty:

> *As I write this, our nation is engaged in a war with terrorists of global reach. My principal focus as vice president has been to protect the American people in our way of life. As you grow, you will come to understand the sacrifices that each generation makes to preserve freedom and democracy for future generations. I ask of you as my grandchildren that you always strive in your lives to do what is right.*
>
> *Signed, Acting President of the United States, Grandpa Cheney*

Autumn of 2007 brought a Fox News Special on the vice president. The hour-long program was framed around a series of articles in the *Washington Post* that gave this book its name. The newspaper series, by the author in partnership with Jo Becker, was titled "Angler." That was Cheney's Secret Service code name, until then not widely known, and the articles used it as a metaphor to examine his methods of governing. Neither Cheney nor Fox correspondent Bret Baier mentioned the series on camera, but the questions and answers amounted to the vice president's only public comment. Cheney gave the network unusual access—in the West Wing and the official residence, aboard Air Force Two, and on a fishing trip out west—but he did not say much he had not said before. George Bush, on the other hand, opened a fascinating window on their relationship.

Cheney answered his first question outdoors, after lush introductory footage that showed him wading, casting, and tying flies along a broad, shallow stretch of moving water. He wore a fleece vest over a blue denim shirt and looked relaxed. Baier put an edge on his questions, mixing up the language of the news stories with the partisan accusations of Cheney's political critics. "They say that you grab power, that you run the angles, play the angles, and that you've taken the country in the wrong direction. What do you make of all that?" Baier asked. Cheney frowned and said, "Well, I think it's grossly overdone. I'm there to serve the president. He asked me to come serve as vice president. I have been pleased to do that. That's my job, my responsibility. I do the best I can to give him the best advice I can. Sometimes he takes it, sometimes he doesn't." The Fox correspondent tried again. "You love fishing. *They* say you're the Angler in more ways than one." Cheney laughed this time, looking genuinely amused. "Well, the Secret Service came up with the code name. The code name I had in the Ford administration was 'Backseat.' Maybe I should go back to that one."

The vice president had no more to say on the subject. The president said plenty. Bush was a fascinating subject on camera, his expressions and body language all over the place as he struggled to define the relationship. The president's head tilted back, and his eyes wandered away from Baier as he searched for words. "I would classify our relationship as very comfortable with each other. Dick

Cheney is an easy guy to be around. He is a person who, uh"—he stopped, eyes wandering again—"really—" Bush stopped again, and this time the camera pulled back, Baier beginning a voice-over. Later, Baier asked whether the two of them were more like pals or like business associates. "Yeah," Bush said. "I would describe it as two men who love the same thing, our country, who have been through some amazing times together. You know, I would say friends"—he stopped, head nodding slowly for two or three seconds—"but on the other hand we run in separate circles. He goes home to his family and I go home to mine. I wouldn't call him a very social person. And I'm not a very social person either, so we don't spend a lot of time together socially." Bush shrugged. "But, uh, *friends.*"

Soon Baier came to the money shot, two questions that turned Bush on a dime from affable to something else. "Some critics paint him as pulling the strings," Baier began. Bush cut in with a disparaging laugh. "Others don't go that far," Baier added hastily. "They say he's just managed to figure out the *angles,* and to present you with certain options that limit *your* options when your time to make a decision comes." By this time Bush was impatient, grinning derisively. He cut off Baier's last word with a *"Yeah"* that seemed to mean, it's time for you to quit talking. Bush did not laugh away the question or say the vice president would never try such a thing. The subject was no longer Dick Cheney. The subject was George Bush.

"I think I'm *wiser* than that—than to be pigeonholed or, you know, get cornered by a wily adviser," Bush said. "Look, that's not the way it works. Dick Cheney walks in, I say what's your advice on this subject, and he gives it to me. And I make up my mind based upon a variety of factors, including the advice of key advisers. And he is one of them."

Some say the most powerful vice president ever, Baier observed. There was more than a year left in the second term, but Bush shifted to the past tense. Bush also alluded, it seemed, to something Dan Bartlett observed—a hard-won realization that there were facts of political life that Cheney was unable or unwilling to take into account.

"I would say he was very influential," Bush said, "but he was no more influential than Condi Rice or a Bob Gates or a Steve Hadley. And the thing about Vice President Cheney is his decisionmaking—or his recommendations about my decisionmaking—are based upon a core set of principles that are deeply rooted in his very being. And he is predictable in many ways, because he brings a set of beliefs." Bush stopped, pursed his lips, and made a tight little nod. "And, uh, they're firm beliefs."

And that was all the president had to say.

For the public, Cheney had become a punch line, an inverse Dan Quayle—ridiculed not for vacuity but for dark and all-too-clever scheming. That these were unfair caricatures of both men did not diminish the impact. By the summer of 2007, they were more or less tied as the least-liked vice presidents in the history of modern polling. Later, Cheney took an uncontested first place.

Cartoonist Garry Trudeau featured Cheney in his *Doonesbury* strip, overseeing a "black branch" of government and declaring, "My shirt size is classified." The *Onion* featured headlines such as "Dick Cheney Celebrates Earth Day by Breathing Air" and "New Heart Device Allows Cheney to Experience Love." Manhattan Mini Storage ran a long ad campaign on bus shelters in which a Cheney stand-in wore an "I ♥ Halliburton" pin, and the headline said, "Your closet's so narrow it makes Cheney look liberal." The turning point, the Waterloo for Cheney's pop culture image, was his hunting accident on a Texas ranch on February 11, 2006. Cheney's inadvertent blast of birdshot at his friend Harry Whittington became an irresistible metaphor: watch out for that guy or he'll shoot you in the face. The damage was reinforced by secrecy, Cheney keeping the incident under wraps for a full day, and by the creepy announcement of Whittington's apology for getting in the way of the vice president's shot. An episode of HBO's mob drama *The Sopranos* showed Uncle Junior, who had shot his nephew point-blank in the belly, writing a letter to ask for Cheney's support as a man with "a kindred history of gunplay." The event was dreadful, of course, for Cheney and Whittington alike. The vice president's old friend Alan Simpson said Cheney told him it was "one of the worst times in my life."

Writing in the *Washington Post* about Cheney's secrecy, the author and his reporting partner mentioned a collection of "man-size Mosler safes" in the vice president's office. The reference was to testimony by John Hannah in the Scooter Libby trial. Hannah said Libby had kept "several, I would say, person-size safes filled with—multiple safes; I don't know if it was two, three, four safes filled with—top to bottom with materials." It became another tile in the Cheney mosaic, a viral hit on the Internet. Jon Stewart demanded to know whom Cheney kept locked in such a safe and speculated that it was Cheney's doppelganger from 1994, the one who had warned against invading Iraq. Ben Allison, a New York composer, formed a new band, Man Size Safe. Some people were prepared to believe almost anything about Cheney, not least the Iranian government. When someone posted a fake Maureen Dowd "interview" with Cheney on the Web, the official Iran Press TV service sent it out as a news bulletin. Speaking of an attack on Iran, the fictitious Cheney said: "We are not going to get hung up on democracy this time. It's time for squash."

The vice president was more and more isolated, with occasional speeches and interviews on conservative talk radio but almost no public appearance in which he risked exposure to an unscreened audience. The fact-finding visit to Gulfport after Hurricane Katrina brought him close enough to hear one man shout, "Fuck yourself, Mr. Cheney," returning the vice president's salute to Pat Leahy. Even a hospital visit, to check on a potentially threatening blood clot in his leg, exposed him to "scattered boos" from passersby. Cheney's public calendar seldom had any entries at all for more than a few days a month. Even on days with listings, it was not uncommon for all of them to be "CLOSED PRESS" except for photo opportunities at the arrival and departure of Air Force Two.

For a while the White House communications staff did not worry. "This overriding driving feeling was that he personally didn't have to worry about politics," Dan Bartlett said. "There was a strategic premise that maybe early on was accurate but later became flawed—that as long as he was taking the arrows or taking on water, the president wasn't. But I think there was a tipping point where it did hurt the president. Some of it was out of his control—the whole year in which Iraq turns really bad, the investigation that put the focus on Scooter. Different people would say different points, but at some point during the early part of the second term, you could not only look at it [and say], 'At least it's not the president.' "

One of Cheney's last forays into the American wild came in the spring of 2007, a commencement address at Brigham Young University—quite possibly the most decorous campus in the United States, heavily Republican, with a long tradition of sending graduates into the military and intelligence services. There were minor protests in advance, but nothing to speak of. Cheney gave advice that would profit any graduate. He was uncommonly personal, reflective. He mentioned that he had "dropped out" of Yale, then circled back to say, "asked to leave would be more like it. Twice." He turned serious: "You, too, may face some disappointing turns of your own— times when you fall short, knowing you could have done better.

And when that happens, don't give up or let your doubts get the best of you. I have met some very successful people in my day— men and women of talent and character who have risen to the very top of their fields. And it's the rare one who hasn't had a taste of failure, or a false start along the way. Setbacks in life can stop you dead in your tracks, or they can inspire you forward. Either way, you'll look back on them as turning points. They are crucial days in your life, when you see the starkest kind of choice, and know that it belongs to you alone."

Were these disappointing days for the vice president? He did not say. In the 2008 election, Republicans had to make a choice when asked about Cheney and the Cheney Model. Even in those crowds, Cheney was the subject of criticism and mirth. At a debate in Iowa, John McCain was asked, "What authority would you delegate to the office of vice president?" McCain said, "The vice president really only has two duties. One is to cast a tie-breaking vote in the case of a tied vote in the Senate. And the other is to inquire daily as to the health of the president." Having earned his laugh, McCain found an applause line: "Look, I would be very careful that everybody understood that there's only one president." Sam Brownback, in the same debate, said, "Cheney came in with a lot of experience. . . . And I think the president overrelied on that." At another one, Brownback was asked, "Would you grant your vice president as much as authority and as much independence as President Bush has granted to Vice President Cheney?" Brownback got only as far into his answer as "No," when the crowd started laughing. The question kept coming up, debate after Republican debate. In one of them, a cartoon version of Cheney on screen was the one who asked it. Of all the candidates—including Fred Thompson and Mitt Romney, for whom Liz Cheney worked in succession—only Rudy Giuliani was openly interested in associating himself with the vice president.

John McCain, who had clashed with Cheney over torture and executive power, came out one day and said the vice president was responsible for the "witch's brew" of a "terribly mishandled" war in which U.S. forces were on the verge of defeat. "The president listened too much to the vice president," he said. This was the guy, the one and only Republican Liz Cheney described on television as "bad for the country," who became the party's nominee.

Who supposed that Dan Quayle would play the sage? He warned Cheney, one vice president to another, that the job evolves, that the president decides the vice president's role and the president can reconsider. Cheney began with "a different understanding," a brief so wide-ranging and autonomous that he was the nearest thing we have had to a deputy president. Until the Bush-Cheney years, it would have been laughable to worry about a vice president's unaccountable power. Cheney inspired a search for instruments that might hold the man in check. Even so, the confluence of personalities, talents, and events that defined his relationship with Bush was unique. No successor is likely to match his influence soon. Candidates of both parties in 2008 alluded to the Cheney vice presidency as a cautionary tale. Bush, too, came to see disadvantages in the arrangement, and over time it changed.

The history of the Bush administration cannot be written without close attention to the moments when Cheney took the helm— sometimes at Bush's direction, sometimes with his tacit consent, and sometimes without the president's apparent awareness. In those moments, especially in the early years, Cheney had lasting impact on the nation's course. Cheney was the UNODIR vice president, following his own stars "unless otherwise directed." But it is just as important to note the times when Bush stepped in, grabbed the wheel, and veered from Cheney's heading. The substantive differences between the two men were seldom apparent during their White House years. But this was decidedly not a Cheney administration. Had there been such a thing, it would have looked very different. Almost certainly it would have self-destructed, as Bush's very nearly did at the cliff's edge with Justice in March 2004. Many of those who worked for Cheney called him the "ultimate staffer," and that said more than most of them intended. Cheney had prodigious talents and appetite for work and, above all, force of will. He knew what he wanted. In previous roles—chief of staff, minority whip, defense secretary—he had learned finesse and compromise. After September 11, most of the battles he fought involved core principles on which he was disinclined to look for middle ground. A staffer can afford to be unbending; the principal cannot. Cheney Unbound was unsuited for the top job. He had no regulator on his engine. Bush discovered that belatedly but never forgot. At the peak of his power, Cheney did what Marx forecast (wrongly) for capitalism and the conservative scholar Martin Malia (rightly) for the Soviet state: he created the conditions that brought about his defeat.

Cheney served his country with devotion, at some cost to himself. The stresses of the job did not improve his health. After more than a decade without incident, Cheney suffered eight cardiac events in eight years. He relinquished millions of dollars in stock options and income forgone. The author found no evidence of self-dealing behavior in office, involving Halliburton or anything else. There were times when Cheney stretched the truth, times he may have snapped it clean in half, but he was fundamentally honest about his objectives. Cheney believed that the country was in mortal danger and that he knew better than others how to avert it. That raised intriguing questions about his future. He had defined himself as the man who would not run for office again, but what would he do when January came and the dangers still remained? In Lynne Cheney's touchstone novel,

an immense boon to those who study her husband, the fictional president's closest aide says that "challenging work—the kind of work
that can fill up your life entirely—is essential to mental health for
many people."

Cheney's most troubling quality was a sense of mission so acute
that it drove him to seek power without limit. His indifference to
public opinion, an important constraint on most office holders, verged
on contempt. He spoke most openly in disdain of the news media and
self-appointed elites, but he had a way of saying "polls"—the kind
that measure public opinion—that made the word sound dirty.
Cheney would not put it this plainly, but the fact was he did not much
admire the way his fellow Americans made decisions. Our fickle loy-
alties, our emotional swings, our uneven grasp of facts, our failure to
see the main point, our logical errors—all the things that made our
collective conversation so unlike Dick Cheney's conversation with
himself—brought the vice president close to saying he need not
bother listening. The most striking display of that attitude came in a
televised interview in March 2008 with Martha Raddatz of ABC
News. The vice president and the correspondent faced each other in
matching brocade wing chairs in the Barr Al Jissah Resort and Spa
in Muscat, Oman. They spoke of Iraq.

"Two-thirds of Americans say it's not worth fighting, and they're
looking at the value gain versus the cost in American lives, certainly,
and Iraqi lives," Raddatz said. The vice president flicked his head a
few degrees. He leaned forward. He looked Raddatz straight in the
eye, brows raised, lips compressed in a mirthless half smile. For two-
thirds of Americans, he had a one-word answer.

"*So?*"

Cheney kept his eyes locked on Raddatz, a challenge.

"So—you don't care what the American people think?"

"No, I think you cannot be blown off course by the fluctuations in the public opinion polls. Think about what would have happened if Abraham Lincoln had paid attention to polls, if they had had polls during the Civil War. He never would have succeeded if he hadn't had a clear objective, a vision for where he wanted to go, and he was willing to withstand the slings and arrows of the political wars in order to get there."

Well, yes. Lincoln plowed ahead with the war, intent on preserving the Union, even when doing so imperiled his reelection. But he did not press on for years after the people turned against him. He did not refuse to be blown off course by a shortsighted public. He *rallied* the people and won them over, offering results that inspired confidence. It was not mere force of will that distinguished Lincoln, but successful leadership of a public nearing despair.

Cheney, by contrast, wore his low ratings like a medal. To withstand public scorn was a virtue. He willingly made that sacrifice. The whole transaction, start to end, was about Cheney—a measure of his character and place in posterity. Did he see no other stakes for a democracy? When "We the People" elected him, was that our final chance to give him direction? Could he do anything at all on our behalf, regardless of what we thought? Short of impeachment or sedition, did we relinquish all influence on his conduct for the next four years? Cheney said in one of his late-term speeches, the clock winding down, that "with an economy to strengthen and a war to fight, we'll stay focused on the business of the people." He did not say, "whether they like it or not." He said, "without regard to polls or elite opinion."

Bowing to no master but history had a certain convenience. Cheney was pretty sure about history's verdict, and that freed him to do as he thought best. He and Bush had all the authority they needed from the electorate. "You get to vote every four years on who gets to be president," Cheney said. Go to the polls, he said, "and then entrust those you've elected to govern." There are many theories of representation in a democracy. The "trustee" model that Cheney described was an eighteenth-century British construct. Its most influential advocate was Edmund Burke, the Old Whig philosopher, who believed in the virtues of a governing class remote from the passions of the crowd. Cheney used "elite opinion" as an insult, meaning newspaper columnists and professors he didn't like, but his own concept of democracy was at the far elite extreme.

Even if only history mattered, Cheney did not show it as much respect as he might. Pervasive efforts to shield his work made no more concession to posterity than to the electorate here and now. It was Cheney's lawyer who wrote Executive Order 13233, stifling the release of old White House records to historians. Presidents—and, for the first time, vice presidents—now had wide new discretion to conceal from the national memory any records "reflecting military, diplomatic, or national security secrets, Presidential communications, legal advice, legal work, or the deliberative processes of the President and the President's advisers." Cheney, Libby, and Addington invented an extralegal classification for their notes and memos. They called it "Treated As: SECRET/SCI" and made up official-looking stamps. Even "press guidance"—instructing Cheney's spokesmen about what to tell reporters—was sometimes stamped that way. The workaday business of Cheney's office, that is, would be protected as though it were "sensitive compartmented information," comparable to the innermost secrets of national security. The stamps added no short-term security to documents already locked in safes. Their greatest impact was likely to be on historians, because they threw the status of clearly releasable documents into doubt. "I don't know what the motivation is, but I can very well foresee the consequence of it," said J. William Leonard, who directed the Information Security Oversight Office of the National Archives until 2008. "I cannot imagine a future archivist finding a mark like that and saying, 'Oh, well, I'll release it anyway.' It'll go in a queue [for special screening] that takes years and years and years to get to the public." Leonard clashed with Cheney on another matter: the vice president's refusal, a first by any federal official, to permit an audit of his classified documents. When Leonard would not back down, Addington tried to abolish his entire operation. It was a fine example of the Addington method. He composed a few lines of technical-looking language and sent it to the Office of Management and Budget: "Strike 'director of the Information Security Oversight Office' each place it appears . . . in sections 1.3(e), 1.6(c), 1.7(c)(3). . . ."

Dick Armey, who for all his cowboy manner was once a professor, said he has a theory about Cheney and history. "My guess is, you know there is a notion that Schumpeter gave us," Armey said. "You know, Joseph Schumpeter? He had a great notion called auto-therapeutic rationalizations. I love that expression, auto-therapeutic rationalizations. You never heard a beautiful person say beauty's only skin deep, right? And so if I were Dick Cheney right now, I'd be much content to make the argument that I find my solace in that history will vindicate me. I do not believe that history is going to be very kind to this president. I think that most of the time history is about a presidency, and a president. And the vice president is almost always merely a footnote in that story. But I believe that in this case the history is going to treat both the president and vice president unkindly almost in equal part."

Political reputations shift with time. That does not seem to be nearly so true of wars. When voters, generals, and the political class reach consensus on a strategic mistake, they do not tend to change their minds. Rehabilitation has not come for the southern war of secession or MacArthur's drive toward the Yalu River, which brought China into the Korean War. Nor has the nation's verdict wavered on Vietnam. The Bush-Cheney strategy after September 11, with its claims of White House supremacy and its sharp tilt from civil liberty to state command, estranged even proponents of a unitary executive and a strong national security state. The invasion of Iraq may have passed a point of no return when Dick Armey—the majority leader of the president's party, from the president's home state—said it was "very likely the biggest foreign policy blunder of modern times." Today cannot speak for tomorrow, and Cheney may turn out to be right that the pendulum will swing back. Nothing is likelier to bring that about than Cheney's worst nightmare made flesh. If *Nexus* comes, loosing a plague or igniting a mushroom cloud, posterity may decide we should have stayed the vice president's course. This made for a paradox as Cheney neared the end of his second term. His best hope of vindication appeared to lie in a future no one could want, a future in which all his efforts failed.

A man could not do much with thoughts like that. Cheney had defended the nation and the powers of its commander in chief. He fought the fight and never bent and did what had to be done. As he neared the end of public life, Cheney found ways to reinforce that message. On the Fourth of July 2008, he spent his afternoon aboard a ship named *Constitution*. She had put to sea in 1797, a decade after the Founders completed her namesake. Back then the USS *Constitution* was the scourge of Tunis and Tripoli, projecting the might of a young democracy against a barbaric foe. Old Ironsides, they called her, the thickest-skinned warship of her day, twenty-four inches of layered oak plank absorbing shot after shot. Battered but undefeated, she had grown old now, the last of her kind afloat. Richard Bruce Cheney, unsinkable, paid a call on Independence Day to perform a rite of renewal. Eight bells rang, and the bosun of the watch piped him aboard, and Lieutenant Commander Erik Neal called out, "United States, arriving!" A group of young sailors on the spar deck stood at stiff attention in a light rain. Cheney had come to reenlist them, replenishing the Navy to carry on the fight. The sailors raised their right hands and repeated after the vice president of the United States: . . . *support and defend the Constitution . . . bear true faith and allegiance . . . obey the orders of the President.* . . . Cheney's credo, exactly. He may have said a few words afterward. Usually he did. If so, they were lost to history. This event, like nearly all the rest in Cheney's White House years, was closed to the public and the press.

AFTERWORD

Dick Cheney proposed an epitaph in his final days at the White House. His, he said, had been "a consequential vice presidency." An aptly chosen adjective, enigmatic as the man himself. "Consequential" might describe Lincoln or Lenin, Gandhi or Genghis Khan. Cheney was speaking of power, and for once he acknowledged his own. He had impact. He made a difference. He mattered. On the merits, this was hardly an extravagant claim. Cheney set the nation's course as no vice president, and not every president, had done before. From a man of so few words the display of pride was akin to a dance in the end zone. Cheney had long dismissed what he called "the notion" that he had command of events. During two terms in office, he professed to be no more than a quiet adviser, one among many servants of George Bush's will. On his way out the door, he spoke in the first person singular. "I think a prime motivation for me and much of what I've done was 9/11," he told ABC News, adding: "I said at that point, 'That's not going to happen again on my watch.'"

Cheney's heading diverged from the president's more openly in their final year. Aware of appearances, they joked awkwardly about the challenges of a vice president at the helm. As John McCain vetted running mates, Bush counseled him "to be careful about who he names to be the head of the selection committee." When Rahm Emanuel, the incoming chief of staff for Barack Obama, convened his predecessors for advice, Cheney deadpanned: "Above all else, control your vice president."

Captain and first mate had grown apart. The president abandoned attempts at strict isolation of Iran and North Korea, opting for the kind of diplomatic engagement that Cheney disdained with governments he thought incapable of change. The president also drew back from his farthest-reaching claims of executive supremacy, asking permission from Congress and courts to carry on with domestic surveillance. Cheney mounted no direct public challenge here, but he sought to limit the reach of policies he disliked.

On other subjects, Cheney not only broadcast dissent but acted on it. After so many breaches of precedent, Cheney came up with a fresh one in his final year. When a Washington, D.C., resident mounted a challenge to the District's ban on private handgun possession, Cheney saw an opportunity. The Supreme Court had never decided squarely whether the "right to keep and bear arms" belonged to individuals or state militias. Cheney urged the Justice Department to press the view that gun ownership was a basic constitutional right and the D.C. law breached the Second Amendment. As usual, Cheney made the most uncompromising argument. He did not rule out exceptions, but neither did he affirm any. Solicitor General Paul Clement and other top leaders at Justice persuaded Bush to take a more nuanced view. The Bush administration's brief said "the Second Amendment's protection of individual rights does not render all laws limiting gun ownership automatically invalid." Speaking for the president, Clement argued in favor of "numerous laws governing the sale, transportation, and possession of various categories of firearms." He asked the Supreme Court to send the case back to lower courts to weigh the proper balance. Cheney sought no balance. As president of the Senate, he joined a competing brief that asked the court to declare the D.C. law "unreasonable per se," or flatly unconstitutional. "No purpose would be served by remanding this case for further fact finding or other proceedings," the brief said. The vice president calculated correctly. With a 5–4 conservative majority on the high court, Cheney's argument, not the president's, prevailed.

Cheney granted about twice as many exit interviews as Bush did, and he spoke plainly for the first time about the core themes of this book. In the past he had made Darth Vader jokes, but the role play helped him sidestep true disclosure. "Am I the evil genius in the corner that nobody ever sees come out of his hole?" he asked a group of newspaper reporters in the first term. He gave a reply beyond parody, illuminating nothing: "It's a nice way to operate, actually." In his last weeks in power he stopped cracking wise. About the Justice Department's torture memoranda of 2002, repudiated by the president and without a defender left in Washington, he said: "We spent a great deal of time and effort getting legal advice. . . . I thought the legal opinions that were rendered were sound." Waterboarding? "I'd do exactly the same thing." Public opinion? "If we had responded to polls . . . Saddam Hussein would still be in power." The wartime prerogatives of Congress? Here Cheney offered a classic non sequitur in defense of the proposition that Congress "has the ability to write statutes" but the president need not obey. The greatest power of all, command of the nuclear arsenal, is solely under presidential control, he said; therefore, as a "general proposition," any use of power short of that by the commander in chief must be lawful. "He could launch a kind of devastating attack the world's never seen," Cheney said. "He doesn't have to check with anybody. He doesn't have to call the Congress. He doesn't have to check with the courts." Cheney's respect for presidential prerogative, even so, had its limits. When asked about Bush's declared goal of closing the prison at Guantánamo Bay, Cheney replied as though the president had voiced a naive dream. "I think everybody can say we wished there were no necessity for Guantánamo," he said, but closing it would have to await "the end of the war on terror." In these final weeks in office, Cheney parted the curtain on his views and deeds as never before.

Not long after the book's debut, Cheney spoke at a closed-press gathering of young business leaders in Washington. One of those present said the vice president asked for a show of hands: How many of you have seen *Angler*? Then—and I am unsure how to interpret this—he recommended that they read it. Didn't agree with a lot of things, he said. He took particular issue with the charge that congressional leaders were kept in the dark about warrantless domestic surveillance. But Cheney said the author "did his homework," and several top advisers have since made contact to say the narrative captured the Cheney they knew. Not long after that, the vice president allowed a photograph to be displayed outside the Situation Room that showed him reading *Angler* aboard Air Force Two. The picture, a copy of which made its way to me, was date-stamped September 18, 2008, two days after the book went on sale. Cheney, pen in hand, looks to be halfway through the book, and a scrap of paper marks the chapter notes at the end.

There was something for everyone to dislike in *Angler*, I found. The received view in the *Weekly Standard*, authored by a former deputy spokesman in Donald Rumsfeld's Pentagon, described the book as a transparent effort to assemble evidence against "the quarry." In letters, telephone calls, and conversations with Cheney critics from San Francisco to London, I found a parallel impatience with any story that hinted at honorable motives or even basic norms of human kindness. Many of them did not like to hear that Cheney followed his principles and believed he was serving his country. An audience at Princeton's Woodrow Wilson School of Public and International Affairs was likewise taken aback by my observation that Cheney was loyal and generous to his staff. I told a story, not in the book, of a fly-fishing expedition on which Cheney invited his personal aide, Brian McCormack. The young man, who had not fished before, fumbled his cast and hooked the vice president of the United States. The barb pierced the back of Cheney's neck, drawing blood. Bush, by the accounts of aides, might have lashed McCormack to an anchor. Cheney told him not to worry, and when they got back to shore the vice president taught McCormack how to snap his wrist as he let fly. As it happened, McCormack's parents were in my Princeton audience that evening, and to my astonishment they produced a photograph of the very moment I described, the vice president wincing and swatting at his neck. A souvenir, they said, from Cheney.

In his exit interviews Cheney said he will write a book of his own. What he might say, if he goes through with it, is awfully hard to predict. How, exactly, does a Sphinx find his voice? In her roman à clef of White House life, Lynne Cheney long ago summed up her husband's contempt for "kiss-and-tell books." A president, she wrote in her hero's voice, "deserved at least one person around him whose silence he could depend upon." I look forward as much as anyone to the prospect of the vice president's change of heart.

With time to reflect, I have found a few things I might do differently. This revised edition corrects all the factual errors I could find. They are listed on my

Web site, bartongellman.com. Since the book's release, I have profited from the thoughtful engagement of scholars and critics on subtler matters. One benefit of the new media age was the remarkable experience of conversing in an online roundtable with five of the book's published critics. That dialogue and others—in the Web communities of washingtonpost.com, *Harper's*, *Macleans*, the *American Prospect*, and Firedoglake—drew out my thinking and raised questions I had not addressed. (The transcripts are archived on my Web site.) I tried and failed to arrange similar exchanges in conservative political forums. One happy exception came when Paul Mirengoff, cofounder of the right-leaning Power-Line blog, agreed to join a weeklong conversation about the book on the left-leaning TPMCafé. It is sadly telling of an overpolarized public debate that he regarded the experience as exotic, reflecting on it afterward in a posting titled "Across the Great Divide."

The dominance of ideology in the blogosphere left me wishing, at times, that commentators devoted as much energy to the substance of the book as to guessing my politics. Anyone may judge my success or failure, but *Angler* was not intended as a "pro-" or "anti-" Cheney brief. It aimed, very simply, to describe a history we did not know. I offered personal views in the final chapter, chiefly on the virtues of transparent public debate, but there was no other agenda there or elsewhere.

Even so, I see merit in some of the published critiques. As I reread my words of a year ago, I accept that the focus on one central figure gave insufficient weight, at times, to other players. I remain confident in my evidence and in the narrative as written, but I might bring Bush into the story more often if I were reporting and writing afresh. Though I had considerable access to witnesses and contemporary documents—including, for example, the e-mail that James B. Comey sent colleagues immediately upon leaving the president's private study—the written record was far from complete. There were unavoidable risks in relying upon flawed or selective memories. I have no doubt that future historians will offer corrections and a fuller picture of events. The Obama administration's reversal of Cheney-authored restrictions on White House archives may speed that day, but I suspect it will not come soon.

Another point of context has been raised. *Angler* describes maneuvering by senior figures other than Cheney, but it seemed to some readers that I claimed the vice president's use and abuse of process was unique. It is not true, in fact, that Cheney's opponents made no attempt at stealth or misdirection. Those tools are basic to bureaucratic combat, here and elsewhere. What the evidence suggests, however, is that Cheney's secrecy, guile, and willingness to circumvent White House procedure overwhelmed those of his rivals.

Bush's gradual disenchantment with his Number Two, beginning with the events in chapter 12, became more evident toward the end of the second term. In his final news conference, the president acknowledged many contributors to his work, but left out Cheney, a reflection perhaps of disgruntlement or pride but not of the reality of his eight White House years. Cheney worked mightily to persuade Bush to grant a full pardon to Scooter Libby, convicted in the Valerie Plame affair, but the president refused to budge. Still later, shortly after transition, Cheney broke with traditional niceties and threw himself into rhetorical combat with Obama and Vice President Joe Biden. Bush did not do that, and aides passed word that he thought Cheney's conduct untoward.

My overriding claim in this book is that the Bush years cannot be understood without a central focus on the vice president. *Angler*, most broadly, is a study of power. Recent American history offers few peers to Cheney as an operator. Those who played at his level—James A. Baker III, perhaps, and Henry Kissinger—tended to be pragmatists and deal-makers. It has been the rare leader anywhere who combined radical principles with tactical brilliance and uncompromising will. Men and women like that, like Cheney, change history. The absence of strong counterweights in the first term, and above all Bush's tacit consent, made the vice president all but unstoppable before he overreached his grasp. In the end, Cheney brought a backlash—"consequences"—upon himself. Even so, it will be a long time before we can assess how much of his legacy, institutional and substantive, remains. Leaders, vice presidents included, do not often toss away the prerogatives of those who came before. One small illustration: Biden, following Cheney's lead, has joined the Principals Committee of foreign policy advisers.

Had there been one last chapter of *Angler*, the temptation would have been to title it "The Wheelchair and the Shoe." George Bush and Dick Cheney suffered ignominious exits from public life, with Democrats sweeping the 2009 election, the global economy in collapse, and the Iraq war—despite slowing U.S. casualties—unpopular as ever. The president, seeking affirmation at a valedictory stop in Baghdad, barely ducked a pair of shoes flung hard and true toward his head. It was a sorry mirror image of the U.S. entry into Iraq, six years before, when celebrants in Baghdad shouted "Bush! Bush! Bush!" and aimed their shoes at a statue of their fallen tyrant. This time, mocking crowds roared approval of the insult to Bush. On Inauguration Day, one month later, Angler gave way to Renegade and Celtic, the Secret Service code names for Obama and Biden. The vice president donned a wide-brimmed black hat, a hint of Old West in the uniform, but he rode in on a wheelchair and slung no more than a cane across his saddle. An expressionless aide pushed from behind, and the old cowboy-warrior, powers spent, was carried off the range.

ACKNOWLEDGMENTS

I first met Dick Cheney as a military correspondent in late 1990, just before the war with Iraq that defined his tenure as secretary of defense. In those days he took reporters along on most of his trips, called us forward to chat in his cabin, and joined us for a glass of stout on refueling stops in Shannon, Ireland. (Friends say he is a good beer drinker, but you couldn't prove it on those working trips. Cheney ordered a half-pint and left most of it in the glass.) After his aircraft came close to crashing in a Saudi sandstorm—a sudden gust dipped our wing sharply, seconds before touchdown—he wandered back to steerage, where the reporters sat. He made gentle fun of his military assistant, who had reached the rank of two-star admiral (and went on to fleet command) despite a fear of flying. Some of my regular interlocutors in Cheney's Pentagon—Scooter Libby, Paul Wolfowitz, Mike Hayden, David Petraeus—would take up important positions in Cheney's orbit a decade later.

As vice president, Cheney withdrew from most of the traditional media. He gave the bulk of his interviews to politically friendly radio and television hosts, opinion columnists, and magazines. When he had a message for a broader audience, he chose a live, unedited broadcast such as NBC's *Meet the Press*. Cheney declined to be interviewed for this book. When the vice president allowed me to accompany him on a trip to Fort Hood, Texas, he never came near the press section. (He summoned my seatmate, Bill Sammon of the conservative *Washington Examiner*, for a one-on-one interview.) I wish to thank the vice president, nonetheless, for allowing his office to cooperate with *Angler*. There were many subjects and people held off-limits—I was on my own to find sources on national security, intelligence, legal issues, and Cheney's relationship with George Bush—but on domestic policy the vice president's office encouraged former staff members to grant interviews. I am obliged to Lea Anne McBride and Mary Matalin for their parts in that.

Angler began its life as a newspaper series in the *Washington Post*. Not long after I began reporting for those stories, my editors suggested a partnership with Jo Becker. We had not worked together before, but I quickly discovered that Jo is a force of nature—a tireless digger and thoughtful analyst who became a friend as well as coauthor of the four-part series in the *Post*. Jo's reporting and insights accounted for much of the best material in those stories, and this book would be far less complete without the body of research we accumulated together. Chapter 7 of this book, on early detainee policy, and chapters 8 and 10, on the environment and the economy, are especially indebted to Jo's reporting. Jeff Leen and Larry Roberts, the leaders of the *Post*'s investigative team, posed some of the most important questions and helped develop the strategies to answer them. Any errors of fact or interpretation, of course, are mine alone. My views on Cheney and his tenure evolved as I continued my research after publication of the series. In this book, I speak only for myself.

I have tried to be as transparent as possible, in the main text and in the endnotes, about how I know what I claim to know in the book. My primary sources were hundreds of interviews with people in direct contact with the vice president or his staff—present and former Cheney advisers, senior officials in federal agencies, judges, senators, congressmen and -women, members of foreign diplomatic and military services, and academics. Scores of people agreed to speak on the record, many of them for the first time. Some of those who spoke to me took substantial risks, personal and professional, and some required anonymity to tell what they knew. Overuse of anonymous sources is rightly criticized in contemporary reporting. But some stories, important ones, cannot be told without them. Central events in our recent history would have remained unknown to the public if reporters could not protect their sources. Wherever possible I have supplemented interviews with original government documents, contemporary notes, calendars, and e-mails of participants in the events described.

Portions of this book that touch on Cheney's handling of intelligence on weapons of mass destruction draw on reporting I did in partnership with Dafna Linzer and Walter Pincus in the *Post*.

Julie Tate provided indispensable research for the newspaper stories on Cheney, and she fact-checked the embargoed manuscript with discretion. It is unlikely I would have found some of my most important sources without her. In New York, I had the benefit of research assistance from a pair of New York University graduate students whose names you will hear again: Meredith Angelson, a second-year law student, and Justin Jouvenal, an accomplished young journalist who came back for an advanced degree. Abra Bron and Daniel Ades wrote me valuable memos as well, on the 2008 campaign and the energy task force, respectively.

Karen Greenberg and her lively policy salon at NYU, the Center on Law and Security, offered me a fellowship and good company as I researched and wrote this book. I extend warm thanks to Nicole Bruno, Maggie McQuade, David Tucker, and the whole crew at CLS who kept me sane and well provisioned. I also thank Michael Sheehan, my predecessor in the fellow's office, who left behind some really cool souvenirs.

It was my great fortune to be represented by the literary agents Andrew Wylie and Scott Moyers. Wylie had a lot to teach me about the art of framing a book around compelling events and characters. Moyers, who was among the best of the best as a book editor before joining the Wylie agency, became an important critical reader and source of encouragement, long after the publishing deal was done. My lifelong friend Robin Davis Miller of the Authors Guild helped me navigate a new world of publishing.

Ann Godoff and her team at The Penguin Press have been everything an author could want—enthusiastic, devoted to the book, and exceptionally competent at their work. Godoff & Co. made all the right moves in shepherding this project to completion, and they stretched themselves to permit the latest possible completion of the manuscript before production. Particular thanks go to Lindsay Whalen, Bruce Giffords, Tracy Locke, Abigail Cleaves, and Adam Goldberger.

The *Washington Post* has been my professional home for twenty years, and it remains among the very few newsrooms, old or new, with the resources and commitment to do original reporting on the unknown. I grew up there under a succession of remarkable leaders. Three generations of one extraordinary family—the late Katharine Graham, her son Don Graham, and now her granddaughter Katharine Weymouth—have led the company as if it were an invaluable public trust. Which is exactly, in my estimate, what it is. I cannot put it better than my friend Tom Ricks, who said he considers their stewardship an act of patriotism. Ben Bradlee hired me; Len Downie ran the paper for most of my career; each of his three managing editors—Bob Kaiser, Steve Coll, and Phil Bennett—became an important mentor. I doubt there is a match in American journalism for that team. As I write this, the *Post* has named a new executive editor, Marcus Brauchli. I expect great things.

Above all I am blessed by family. My late mother, Marcia Jacobs, is still the reader I have in mind when I ask whether my words are clear to a smart nonspecialist. My father, Stuart Gellman, is the family's first newspaperman and author. My teenagers—Lily, Michael, and Abigail—are well launched on a journey to adulthood that fills me with pride. My son Benjamin offers daily joys and took his first steps as I wrote the final chapters of *Angler*. To his mother, Dafna Linzer, my best friend and the love of my life, I dedicate this book and everything I have in me to give.

NOTES

The arrival of President Barack Obama in January 2009 brought a new team and new content to the White House Web site. The resulting changes broke many links to Bush administration documents. At this writing, the George W. Bush Presidential Library has stored a snapshot of the Bush White House Web site. On the following pages, the chapter notes cite the original Web addresses. In many cases, the cited document may be found by substituting http://georgewbush-whitehouse.archives.gov for http://www.whitehouse.gov in the address.

CHAPTER ONE: A VERY SHORT LIST

1 **Frank Keating reached for the telephone:** For Keating's political biography, see http://www.odl.state.ok.us/oar/governors/bios/keating.pdf. For the Capitol Dome project, see http://www.oklahomadome.com/images/success.pdf.

1 **A form letter, Keating knew:** Glen Johnson, "Bush Sends Letters Seeking Advice on Running Mate," Associated Press, May 19, 2000.

1 **And yet . . . Keating could not help:** Interviews with Frank Keating, Jan. 14, 2008, and Jan. 22, 2008. For Bush's attitude toward Keating, interviews with two senior officials who followed Bush from Texas to the White House. Oklahoma under Keating was second only to Texas under Bush in the number of prisoners executed, 54 as compared with 141, with only one-seventh of the population. See Bureau of Statistics, Department of Justice, at http://www.ojp.usdoj.gov/bjs/cp.htm, and U.S. Census data at http://www.census.gov/population/www/projections/stproj.html.

3 **"My relationship with Cheney was a good one":** Keating interview, Jan. 14, 2008. In preparation for the interview, Keating reviewed notes and files on his interactions with Cheney.

3 **Cheney served as producer:** The choice of running mate, who becomes next in the

constitutional line of succession, is commonly described as a nominee's first presidential decision. The first recorded use of the term on the day of Cheney's selection came from Mary Matalin, then cohost of CNN's *Crossfire* and soon to become the vice president's communications director. "This is not really about Dick Cheney," she said. "It's about George W. Bush, how does he make decisions, and this is the first presidential decision. And in our same poll that we took yesterday, respondents said that they thought this reflected on Bush's ability to make decisions favorably by 64 percent." CNN transcript, *Crossfire,* July 25, 2000.

4   **"You're hard to reach":** Interviews with Lamar Alexander, Jan. 16, 2008, and Jan. 24, 2008. Alexander took handwritten notes as he spoke with Cheney and typed out a fuller version shortly afterward. He has given truncated descriptions of this conversation elsewhere; this account is drawn verbatim from the notes he read aloud in recorded interviews with the author.

4   **His 2000 campaign did not last out 1999:** Iowa straw poll results are at http://www.cnn .com/ALLPOLITICS/stories/1999/08/14/iowa.saturday.02/.

6   **Alexander and Keating and the rest:** Interviews with two confidential sources, senior participants in the Bush-Cheney campaign.

6   **"The only thing was":** Alexander interview, Jan. 16, 2008.

7   **"Cheney was pushing on an open door":** Interviews with Dan Bartlett, Dec. 17, 2007, and Jan. 15, 2008.

7   **Not even Bush's closest aides:** For the paucity of information flowing to Bush's inner circle, interviews with Bartlett, Jan. 15, 2008, David J. Gribbin III, Jan. 10, 2008, and a confidential campaign source, as well as Karen Hughes, *Ten Minutes from Normal* (New York: Viking, 2004), p. 142. For the Quayle letter and Rove's reaction, interviews with Dan Quayle, Feb. 7, 2007, and Lamar Alexander, Jan. 16, 2008.

7   **Only three people were privy to the dossiers:** For the list of three people privy to the dossiers, interview with Gribbin, Jan. 10, 2008. See also Stephen F. Hayes, *Cheney: The Untold Story of America's Most Powerful and Controversial Vice President* (New York: Harper Collins, 2007), p. 278. For Gribbin's roots with Cheney, from high school and graduate school onward, interview with Gribbin, Sept. 15, 2006.

8   **For a Top Secret clearance in the U.S. government:** For the definition of "Top Secret," see Executive Order 12958, "Classified National Security Information," Apr. 17, 1995, available at http://www.usdoj.gov/oip/foia__updates/Vol__XVI__2/page5.htm. For security clearance investigations, see Standard Form 86, "Questionnaire for National Security Positions," OMB 3206-0007, available at http://www.opm.gov/forms/pdf__fill/SF86.pdf.

8   **"By definition, this is a process":** Gribbin interview, Jan. 10, 2008. The author obtained the questions, which have not been made public before, from one of the candidates who answered them.

9   **"marital, family, or grief counseling":** Standard Form 86, question 21.

9   **the Cheney team also sought details:** Cheney questionnaire, heading 48.

9   **A catchall question near the end:** Cheney questionnaire, heading 78.

10   **"Dear Dick," he wrote:** Keating made his application file and all attachments available to the author.

12   **What brought him low:** Keating file, vol. 2.

12 Dilantin, which is government approved: The FDA-approved labeling for Dilantin says it can help in "control of grand mal and psychomotor seizures." See http://www.fda.gov/cder/foi/nda/pre96/084427.pdf, at p. 7.

12 Dreyfus had no known financial interest: The Dreyfus story from his own perspective is at http://www.remarkablemedicine.com/.

13 a man who had built his career: Many early stories on Keating's race for governor described him as a model of openness. See, for example, Editorial, "(Un)Common Sense," *Daily Oklahoman,* March 6, 1994.

13 Gary Davis, general counsel of the Office of Government Ethics: Correspondence with Gary Davis and memorandum for the record, May 25, 1990, provided by Frank Keating and on file with the author.

13 "What did you do that for?": Keating interview, Jan. 14, 2008.

14 He sought a trustworthy adviser: For Bush's depiction of advice he received from Cheney, confidential interviews with Bush campaign advisers. Cheney told his authorized biographer much the same story he gave to Bush, calling Ford's time as vice president "the worst nine months of his life." See Hayes, *Cheney,* p. 2. For the analogy to Laura Bush, see Jacob Weisberg, *The Bush Tragedy* (New York: Random House, 2008), p. 147.

15 Federal Reserve chairman Alan Greenspan: Interview with a confidential source who heard Greenspan's account of the conversation and another source closely familiar with Greenspan's admiring assessment of Cheney. For his gradual disenchantment, see Alan Greenspan, *The Age of Turbulence: Adventures in a New World* (New York: Penguin Press, 2007), pp. 210–12, 216–17.

15 "It was a firm no": For Cheney's "firm no" and Bush on Washington experience, see Hayes, *Cheney,* p. 277. For Bush on loyalty, see Robert Draper, *Dead Certain: The Presidency of George W. Bush* (New York: Free Press, 2007), p. 89. On July 25, when Bush announced his choice of Cheney, he said in his news conference: "Before I asked Dick Cheney to chair the selection process, I had asked him whether he would consider being a candidate himself. At the time he said no. . . . But I kept the thought of him joining me in the back of my mind."

16 "And plus, *he didn't want it*": Draper, *Dead Certain,* p. 89. Emphasis in original. In Draper's words, "Cheney was done with politics. And Bush loved that about Dick Cheney."

16 Former vice presidents accounted: Of the first forty-four vice presidents, fourteen became president. (There were forty-two presidents in the same period, ending with Clinton.) See Mark O. Hatfield, Senate Historical Office, *Vice Presidents of the United States, 1789–1993* (Washington, D.C.: Government Printing Office, 1997), pp. xiii–xxiii, excerpts available at http://www.senate.gov/artandhistory/history/common/briefing/Vice__President.html.

16 Most of them, unlike Cheney: After Cheney took office, his lack of ambition became a regular talking point for aides explaining his loyalty and closeness to Bush. Mary Matalin, his communications director, said in an interview with the author on June 29, 2006: "The huge, major organizing principle that's different in all modern presidential history is Cheney had no personal agenda. . . . The difference between a vice president who himself psychologically is not running . . . allowed us to be integrated [into the White House staff] and allowed us to contribute not as an add-on, because he had no personal agenda."

17 The official story, in accounts the two men gave in 2000: For the "thorny" Twelfth

Amendment challenge and other reasons for Cheney's demurral, Draper, *Dead Certain,* p. 89, and Hayes, *Cheney,* p. 277.

18   When asked whether his heart: Hughes, *Ten Minutes from Normal,* pp. 142ff. Karl Rove echoed Cheney's language in public as Bush prepared to announce the choice, saying the "heart attacks occurred in the '70s and '80s," after which Cheney oversaw the Persian Gulf War from the Pentagon. "I don't know of a more stressful situation than serving as secretary of defense during an armed conflict," Rove said. *Face the Nation,* CBS, July 23, 2000.

19   According to both men: Hayes, *Cheney,* p. 278.

20   "We can see it going on right now": Alexander interview, Jan. 16, 2008, and Hayes, *Cheney,* p. 279.

21   July 3 was the decisive day: Interviews with senior campaign officials, January and February 2008. See also Hayes, *Cheney,* pp. 281–82, and Draper, *Dead Certain,* p. 90.

21   For the next three weeks, campaign spinners: See Dana Milbank, "Bush Addresses a Big Decision, Sort Of," *Washington Post,* July 14, 2000; Dan Balz, "Bush Quietly Considers Running Mate; Candidate, Adviser Meet but Tell Little," *Washington Post,* July 4, 2000 (touting Keating). *Time* continued to place Danforth in the lead, harking back to its story "John Danforth, a Minister, Tops Veep List," available at http://archives.cnn.com/2000/ALLPOLITICS/stories/05/28/danforth5__27.a.tm/index.html. Ridge's appearance on CNN was July 9, 2000, transcript at http://transcripts.cnn.com/ TRANSCRIPTS/0007/09/sun.09.html.

21   On his public agenda was a meeting with Frist: See Adam Nagourney and Frank Bruni, "The Selection: Gatekeeper to Running Mate: Cheney's Road to Candidacy," *New York Times,* July 28, 2000.

21   Campaign officials said Pataki: Marc Humbert, "New York's Pataki in the Mix as Possible Bush Running Mate," Associated Press, July 17, 2000.

22   Bush "never brought up the issue of the vice presidency": Interview with David Catalfamo, Feb. 21, 2008.

22   Back in Texas the next day: Interviews with two senior campaign officials, January and February 2008. See also Hughes, *Ten Minutes from Normal,* pp. 142–43, Draper, *Dead Certain,* p. 90, and Hayes, *Cheney,* p. 282.

22   Bush scheduled his second and last interview: Campaign officials continued to portray Danforth as the last finalist in contention. See, e.g., "Cheney, Danforth Emerge as Bush's Top Choices," CNN, July 22, 2000, available at http://archives.cnn.com/2000/ALLPOLITICS/stories/07/22/bush.veepstakes/.

22   "Here's one for you. This guy's great": Interview with Alan Simpson by Jo Becker, Sept. 8, 2006.

22   The same day . . . he notified the board: For the Halliburton notice, see Carl P. Leubsdorf and David Jackson, "VP Speculation Still Centers on Cheney; Recent Moves Seem to Show He'd Take Job," *Dallas Morning News,* July 24, 2000.

22   Some campaign officials disputed that: Ronald G. Shafer, "A Special Weekly Report from *The Wall Street Journal*'s Capital Bureau," *Wall Street Journal,* June 30, 2000. Interview with John Engler, Feb. 22, 2008. A spokesman for Kasich confirmed that the congressman filled out a questionnaire but had no interview. E-mail from Ben Kanzeg, Feb. 21, 2008.

23 **"And everybody has negatives":** Interview with Dan Quayle, Feb. 7, 2007.

23 **Hughes said Allbaugh scrutinized:** See for example Adam Nagourney and Frank Bruni, "Gatekeeper to Running Mate: Cheney's Road to Candidacy," *New York Times,* July 28, 2000.

24 **"we were on our heels":** Bartlett interview, Jan. 15, 2008.

25 **According to the Bush campaign:** See Guy Gugliotta, "Heart Experts Say Cheney's Past Problems Need Not Be Present Ones," *Washington Post,* July 25, 2000, which cited a campaign statement that Cooley "had reviewed Cheney's cardiac record at the request of former president George Bush" and declared that "Mr. Cheney is in good health with normal cardiac function."

25 **"It wasn't a real surprise at all":** Interview with Denton A. Cooley by Meredith Angelson, the author's research assistant, Jan. 9, 2008.

26 **"was on the supershort veep list":** Michael Hirsh and John Barry, "Leader of the Pack," *Newsweek,* Dec. 25, 2000, p. 38. As for the barbecue, Bush was actually serving Oklahoma fans after losing his bet on the 1997 game between Oklahoma and the University of Texas. http://www.state.ok.us/osfdocs/nr21397a.html.

27 **Keating wanted the job:** He told one newspaper, "If I was asked to be attorney general, I would be intrigued. Anything else, I wouldn't be interested." See Arnold Hamilton, "Oklahoma Wonders: What If Keating Goes to D.C.?" *Dallas Morning News,* Dec. 18, 2000.

27 **"Most of the conservatives were backing":** Interview with Leonard Leo, Apr. 11, 2008.

27 **"Frank Keating is a straight shooter":** E-mail from Leonard Leo, Apr. 11, 2008.

27 **"Maybe that's not what they were looking for":** Interview with conservative legal activist, spring 2008.

27 **"No," Keating replied, smiling:** Interview with senior GOP elected official, who was present, January 2008. Keating confirmed the report.

28 **"My close association with the President":** Vice President's Remarks at the Conservative Political Action Conference, Feb. 7, 2008, transcribed at http://www.whitehouse.gov/news/releases/2008/02/print/20080207-11.html.

28 **"I'd tell him to":** Statement by the President with Senator John McCain, Rose Garden, Mar. 5, 2008.

28 **"I was told that my friends":** E-mail from Frank Keating, Feb. 25, 2008. Certain old friends of Cheney gave themselves license to tease him about the choice, but only in private. "I said, 'Jeez, you run around the country and it's you. That's the most Machiavellian thing I've ever seen,'" recalled Republican operative Stuart Spencer. "He just laughed." Interview with Stuart Spencer by Jo Becker, Oct. 25, 2006.

29 **The Oklahoma governor, *Newsweek* wrote:** Michael Isikoff, "Why Keating Didn't Cut It," *Newsweek,* Jan. 15, 2001.

29 **By the time reporters examined:** Cheney aides disclaimed any knowledge of the leak in interviews with the author. The *Newsweek* writer did not dispute Keating's account of the conversation. He said he could not confirm or deny that his source was linked to Cheney: "That is ancient history. To the extent that I can remember, I don't think there is anything I can say for all the obvious reasons." E-mail to author from Michael Isikoff, Jan. 16, 2008.

29 Liz Cheney, in an e-mail, denied the charge: In the family's only direct response to this book, the vice president's older daughter wrote: "There were a lot of things you got right, but also a lot wrong (including, by the way, most of the chapter on VP selection and the suggestion that my dad leaked anything out of that process)." She declined to elaborate. After agreeing by phone to meet for a discussion of other errors she had collected, she changed her mind. E-mail from Liz Cheney to author, May 15, 2009.

29–30 "There's only one way that": Engler interview, Feb. 22, 2008.

30 "Dick Cheney knows more about me": Terry M. Neal and Dan Balz, "GOP Hails Cheney's Inclusion on Ticket," *Washington Post,* July 26, 2000.

Chapter Two: A Different Understanding

31 Dick Cheney picked himself up: The election-night scene is drawn from interviews with James A. Baker III, Nov. 10, 2006, and another person in the room, who did not wish to be named. See also Hayes, *Cheney,* pp. 296–97.

31 537 votes out of more than 5.9 million: The official federal vote count is at http://www .fec.gov/pubrec/2000presgeresults.htm. The very first tally had Bush up by 1,784.

32 There will be thousands of jobs to fill: Interview with Brian McCormack, Dec. 8, 2006. The official inventory said Bush had 6,722 presidential appointments to decide. Government Printing Office, *The Plum Book (United States Government Policy and Supporting Positions): 2000 Edition,* appendix 1, available at http://www.gpoaccess.gov/plumbook/2000/p321-323 .pdf. By the end of his first term, Bush would expand the number of political appointments to more than 9,000. Ibid., 2004 edition, at http://www.gpoaccess.gov/plumbook/2004/ p213__215__appendix1.pdf.

32 Somebody had to start assembling a team: Interview with Dan Bartlett, Jan. 15, 2008; McCormack interview, Dec. 8, 2006.

32 6613 Madison McLean Drive: Property records show the Cheneys bought the town house for $450,000 on June 11, 1987, and kept it as a Washington outpost during the Halliburton years in Texas. Soon after moving into the vice president's residence at the Naval Observatory, the Cheneys sold the house, at a quarter-million-dollar profit, to Joe Allbaugh, Bush's Texas chief of staff and the incoming chief of the Federal Emergency Management Agency. An aerial photo can be found at http://maps.google.com/maps?q=6613+Madison+ McLean+Dr,+McLean,+VA+22101,+USA&sa=X&oi=map&ct=title.

33 Cheney's view was that "we need to prepare": This and other McCormack quotes on following pages are from McCormack interview, Dec. 8, 2006.

33 Cheney "had a calming effect": Interview with Juleanna Glover by Jo Becker, Sept. 5, 2006.

33 "The problem when you try": Herbert J. Storing, *The Ford White House: A Miller Center Conference* (Lanham, Md.: University Press of America, 1986), p. 90. Todd Purdum dug out this gem for his profile on Cheney in the June 2006 *Vanity Fair.*

34 "major concern, one of them was": Interview with John Marsh by Jo Becker, Oct. 17, 2006.

34 It is true that Cheney does not speak: The closest he came was in an exchange on CBS's *Face the Nation* on Dec. 17, 2000, shortly after the Supreme Court settled the election. While emphasizing the preeminent role of the president, Cheney did not dispute Bob Schieffer's hypothesis that he would be "chief operating officer" of the incoming administration:

> SCHIEFFER: It seems to me that—from what I've seen so far, that you're going to be the chief operating officer of this administration with George W. Bush as sort of a chairman of the board. Is that a fair way to put it?
>
> CHENEY: Well, if he's chairman of the board, he's also the chief executive officer, without question. . . . There is no contract between us, there really can't be. But he's been very good at asking me to get heavily involved in the—the work of the administration to be, to take charge of the transition. And it's been a great experience for me. He's a great boss. He gives you an objective and then turns you loose on it, holds you accountable for your performance. I think it'll make him a very effective executive.

34 **"He knew exactly what he was doing":** The conference was the Washington Forum on the Role of the White House Chief of Staff, and Cheney made time for it as a favor to his old friend Baker. An edited transcript was later published in Terry Sullivan, ed., *The Nerve Center: Lessons in Governing from the White House Chiefs of Staff* (Texas A&M University Press, 2004). See http://www.tamu.edu/upress/BOOKS/2004/sullivan.htm.

34 **"Once he's taken a position, I think that's it":** Interview with James A. Baker III, Nov. 10, 2006.

35 **"He said from the outset":** Bartlett interview, Jan. 15, 2008.

35 **Al Gore sponsored Les Aspin:** Interview with William Wise, former deputy national security adviser to Vice President Gore, June 21, 2006.

35 **"personnel is policy":** See for example David Frum, " 'Personnel Is Policy'—Sadly, True," *National Review,* Oct. 24, 2005, available at http://www.aei.org/publications/pubID.23427/pub__detail.asp.

35 **It started before Reagan:** See Lynne Cheney, *Executive Privilege* (New York: Simon & Schuster, 1979), p. 238.

37 **third-most-admired man in America:** The Gallup poll released Dec. 29, 2000, placed Powell just behind Bill Clinton and Pope John Paul II. See http://www.adherents.com/misc/poll__GallupAdmired.html.

37 **"You could help yourself a lot":** Karen DeYoung, *Soldier* (New York: Knopf, 2006), p. 320.

37 **"All I'm going to say to you is":** Baker interview, Nov. 10, 2006. See also Draper, *Dead Certain,* p. 282.

38 **"the aggressive establishment of another philosophy":** Interview with Bob Smith by Jo Becker, Jan. 19, 2007.

38 **"market-oriented, property rights–based":** Norton made that statement as chair of the Council of Republicans for Environmental Advocacy. See *Chemical Market Reporter,* Aug. 17, 1998.

39 **"Cheney somehow intimidates me":** For Hadley's anxiety about Cheney, interview with David Gribbin, Aug. 30, 2006.

40 **"What he knows as well as anyone":** Interview with Paul Hoffman by Jo Becker, Sept. 11, 2006.

40 all of them were touted as top prospects: One well-connected reporter, in a summary of expectations in mid-December, wrote this lead: "There are three givens in President-elect Bush's cabinet—Colin Powell, a lot of governors and as many Democrats as Bush can entice." Thomas M. DeFrank, "Gen. Powell Is First in Line: GOP Govs Likely Candidates for Other Cabinet Posts," *New York Daily News,* Dec. 14, 2000.

41 "Cheney's Cheney": Interview with Mary Matalin, Oct. 10, 2006. Addington has also been called Cheney's Cheney, a role that perhaps no one man can fill.

41 incongruous nickname, "Scooter": During Libby's 2007 trial for perjury and obstruction of justice, his lawyer Ted Wells gave a folksy explanation to the jury: "He has been 'Scooter' since he was a little baby because he would scoot around, and his parents nicknamed him 'Scooter,' and it stuck." *United States v. Libby,* CR 05-394, opening statement by the defense, Jan. 23, 2007. Transcript on file with the author.

42 "My name is Scooter": Interview with Pete Williams, Nov. 9, 2006. On the other hand, Libby once told a profiler that "it's pretty hard to take yourself seriously when your name is Scooter." Elisabeth Bumiller, "White House Letter; Novelist in Chief of Staff's Clothing," *New York Times,* Feb. 18, 2002.

42 vice president of the campus Democrats: This and the *Star Trek* reference are in Jack Mirkinson, "Libby '72 Leaned Left Before Serving as Cheney's Chief of Staff," *Yale Daily News,* Nov. 5, 2005, available at http://www.yaledailynews.com/articles/view/15491. For a *Star Trek* episode list, see TREKGUIDE, http://www.gateworld.net/startrek/tos/index.shtml.

42 among the few to dissent: The author covered Wolfowitz and Libby for the *Washington Post* during and after the Gulf War, interviewing them periodically and speaking frequently to senior members of the policy staff. Their views on war aims in Iraq were described in on-the-record and background interviews in 1991.

42 In *The Apprentice*, a nameless youth: Lewis Libby, *The Apprentice* (New York: Graywolf, 1996). After Libby's indictment in 2005, the small print run became a collectible, fetching close to $1,000 a copy on eBay. Aside from all the intrigues of state, the book features voyeurism, bathtub sex, and a disturbingly vivid subplot involving a child in a brothel, caged with a bear "trained to couple with young girls." (The bear in a cage begins on p. 81; the closing speech, on p. 230 of the paperback edition.) The book is "sprinkled with sex to keep the reader awake," Libby once said. Bumiller, "White House Letter," *New York Times,* Feb. 18, 2002.

43 happened to be reading *A Man Called Intrepid*: Libby described his reaction to the book in James Mann, *Rise of the Vulcans* (New York: Penguin Books, 2004), p. 112. Mann's chapter note says the interview took place on May 7, 2002. Two members of Libby's staff and a family friend, none of whom was willing to be quoted by name, said they had made similar observations about him.

44 Libby proposed to hold two jobs: Cheney described the meeting in an interview with his official biographer. Hayes, *Cheney,* pp. 298–99.

45 there was "a very slight heart attack": See for example the campaign's statements on CNN, at http://archives.cnn.com/2000/ALLPOLITICS/stories/11/22/cheney.hospitalized .01/. Cheney later denied any intent to deceive the country: "They didn't say there was no heart attack; they said, 'There's been an elevation in the enzyme levels,' which is the technical term." NBC, *Meet the Press,* Dec. 3, 2000.

47 **"my job is to get an organization stood up":** CNN, "Vice Presidential Candidate Dick Cheney Holds News Briefing on Transition," Nov. 29, 2000, available at http://transcripts .cnn.com/TRANSCRIPTS/0011/29/se.04.html.

48 **"I have asked President Bush to withdraw my name":** Text of Linda Chavez news conference, Jan. 9, 2001, available at http://transcripts.cnn.com/TRANSCRIPTS/0101/09/ bn.02.html.

48 **"that isn't a great signal either":** Linda Chavez interview with Wolf Blitzer, CNN, Jan. 9, 2001, available at http://edition.cnn.com/2001/ALLPOLITICS/stories/01/09/chavez .transcript/index.html.

48 **"Right answer," Cheney said:** Interview with Ron Christie by Jo Becker, Aug. 2, 2006.

49 **"integrated with the West Wing":** Matalin interview, June 29, 2006.

49 **"tending the gardens of politics":** John Carney and James F. Dickerson, " 'Big Time' Punches In," *Time,* Feb. 12, 2001, available at http://www.time.com/time/magazine/ article/0,9171,999185,00.html.

49 **his favorite movie was** *Red River:* Todd Purdum, "A Face Only a President Could Love," *Vanity Fair,* June 2006.

49 **"gave himself permission not to run for president":** Gribbin interview, Aug. 30, 2006.

50 **"Everyone is up a step from my day":** E-mail from William Kristol, Mar. 1, 2008.

51 **"The vice president," Bolten said:** Interview with Joshua Bolten, Oct. 18, 2006.

52 **Lynne Cheney once wrote a novel "celebrating lesbian lifestyles":** Interview with Jan LaRue by Jo Becker, June 13, 2006. Her reference was to *Sisters: The Novel of a Strong and Beautiful Woman Who Broke All the Rules of the Frontier* (New York: Signet, 1981). Now a collector's item, the novel said on its back cover that "women were forced to band together for the strength they needed and at times for the love they wanted." The heroine, Sophie Dymond, leaves her job as publisher of a New York women's magazine to search for her lost sister in Wyoming. The sister, Helen, is the one who has a steamy affair with her school-teacher.

52 **"The iron issues":** Matalin interview, June 29, 2006.

52 **"guiding the ship of state":** Interview with Bradford Berenson by Jo Becker, June 5, 2006.

54 **"That doesn't sound like you to me":** Interview with Stephen J. Hadley, Jan. 3, 2007.

55 **Cheney drew what he called "staffing loops":** Untitled notes on Cheney's advice for a White House chief of staff, Nov. 19, 1980, James A. Baker III Papers, Seeley G. Mudd Manuscript Library, Princeton University, series 6H, box 66, folder 9.

55 **There was a regular Wednesday lunch:** Bolten interview, Oct. 18, 2006; interviews by Jo Becker with Rob Nichols, Aug. 2006; Ed Lazear, Dec. 1, 2006; and Lawrence Lindsey, Sept. 14, 2006.

57 **"He's very pointed in his defense":** Interview with Senator Arlen Specter by Jo Becker, June 27, 2006. After his first such lunch, Cheney told waiting reporters it was "a great way to stay involved and aware of developments in the Senate." He denied "redefining the role" of the vice president, saying, "I clearly have a constitutional responsibility—it's the only one actually—as the president of the Senate. . . . And the president has asked me to devote a portion of my time to working with the Congress." White House transcript, Press Availability of the Vice President, Jan. 23, 2001.

57 **"It's not always easy to speak directly":** Interview with Jon Kyl by Jo Becker, Aug. 8, 2006.

59 **Cheney "thought the vice president had overstepped his bounds":** Interview with Dan Quayle, Feb. 7, 2007. My account of the Cheney-Quayle contretemps during the Philippines coup attempt draws also on an interview with Quayle's former chief of staff, William Kristol, on Aug. 24, 2006; an interview with historian Tim Naftali, Aug. 23, 2006; and accounts of the episode in Dan Quayle, *Standing Firm: A Vice-Presidential Memoir* (New York: Harper-Collins, 1994), pp. 136–38, and George Bush and Brent Scowcroft, *A World Transformed* (New York: Knopf, 1998), p. 160. Among many other fascinating premonitions of her husband's career, Lynne Cheney imagined such a coup attempt and the likelihood of a U.S. military response eleven years before it happened. See Lynne Cheney, *Executive Privilege* (New York: Simon & Schuster, 1979), p. 233.

CHAPTER THREE: PIVOT POINTS

61 **half a million fewer votes than his opponent:** Gore's national margin over Bush was 543,816 votes out of some 101 million cast, or 48.4 to 47.9 percent. Ralph Nader won most of the rest, or 2.7 percent. (Gore's popular victory, therefore, was by plurality.) The results in 1888 were remarkably similar, with president-elect Benjamin Harrison winning 47.8 percent of the popular vote to Grover Cleveland's 48.6 percent. The spoiler in that election was the Prohibition Party's Clinton Bowen Fisk, with 2.2 percent. David Leip, online reference, *Atlas of U.S. Presidential Elections,* available at http://uselectionatlas.org/RESULTS/index.html.

62 **appointed electors:** Article II, Section 1, Clause 2, of the Constitution directs that "Each State shall appoint, in such Manner as the Legislature thereof may direct, a Number of Electors, equal to the whole Number of Senators and Representatives to which the State may be entitled in the Congress." One reason for the relative lack of scandal in 1888 was that Harrison, the Electoral College victor, also won the popular vote in far more states than Cleveland did. Cleveland's slim national margin came from big wins in six southern states, based on a narrow appeal to the regional interest on tariffs. See William C. Kimberling's monograph, "The Electoral College," available on the Federal Election Commission Web site at http://www.fec.gov/pdf/eleccoll.pdf. Kimberling, writing in 1992, noted that the last of the "historical curiosities" in which the college and the popular vote diverged took place "over a century ago." The college therefore provided stability, he argued, "without endangering the legitimacy of the sitting president" (pp. 9–10). The implication, of course, was that a "curiosity" in contemporary times might pose that danger.

62 **"We don't negotiate with ourselves":** Interviews with White House officials, 2007. Bush, the officials said, loved that expression. He started using it two months later, in reply to a reporter's question about compromise on his tax cut plans. Bush said: "Well, I'm certainly not willing to negotiate with myself." White House transcript, Bush Press Availability, Jan. 24, 2001. Bush made no recorded use of the expression before that. Years later, looking back, Cheney attributed his own advice to Bush: "He never wanted to allow, correctly, the closeness of our election to in any way diminish the power of the presidency, lead him to make a decision that he needed to somehow trim his sails, and be less than a fully authorized, if you will, commander in chief, leader of our government, president of the United States." Broadcast on *Inside the Presidency,* History Channel, Jan. 20, 2005.

63 nameless little caucus of five: In an inventory of caucuses that year, one magazine listed Specter's bunch as Unnamed Republican Moderate Group. See "Congressional Centrists," *National Journal,* Dec. 16, 2000.

63 "to sell us rather than tell us": For Cheney's meeting with the five Republican moderates, interview with Lincoln Chafee, Nov. 17, 2006, and interview with another participant who declined to be named. Chafee sat for the interview on one of his last days as a senator. He had been defeated for reelection ten days before.

64 "a humble nation" that won friends with self-restraint: Transcript, Second Gore-Bush Presidential Debate, Commission on Presidential Debates, Oct. 11, 2000, available at http://www.debates.org/pages/trans2000b.html.

64 an accidental senator whose seat: Lincoln Chafee was appointed to the Senate on Nov. 2, 1999, to fill the remaining term of his father, John H. Chafee, who died in office. See http://projects.washingtonpost.com/congress/members/c001040/. He won reelection in November 2000.

65 Two would quit the party: The Jeffords defection and Chafee's kneecapping on Rhode Island radio are discussed later in this chapter. Chafee quit the GOP after his reelection defeat in 2006. For Cheney's machinations against Specter on the Judiciary Committee, see chapter 14. In Chafee's memoir, he writes that there was no talk of rebellion at the December lunch with Cheney. His interjection about the need for centrist voters was not joined by the other four senators, he writes. Lincoln Chafee, *Against the Tide: How a Compliant Congress Empowered a Reckless President* (New York: Thomas Dunne/St. Martin's Press, 2008).

65 Two days after the hideaway lunch: Letter from Lincoln Chafee to Richard Cheney, Dec. 15, 2000, provided by Chafee and on file with the author.

66 Cheney drew a line in cement: Compare White House transcript, George Bush Press Availability, Austin, Texas, Dec. 17, 2000, and Dick Cheney, *Face the Nation,* CBS News, Dec. 17, 2000.

67 "If you had interviewed Bush candidly": Interview with David Frum by Jo Becker, Sept. 11, 2006.

67 Analyze its "center of gravity": The term dates to the nineteenth-century Prussian general Carl von Clausewitz, who described it in his nineteenth-century treatise *On War.* Today's U.S. military defines it as the principal source of an enemy's strength or will to fight. Clausewitz wrote most famously that "war is only a continuation of state policy by other means," an insight that works almost as well in the other direction for Cheney.

68 "mission, enemy, troops, terrain and time available": The Army's keystone planning document is Field Manual 100-5, *Operations.* Major revisions were under way as Cheney completed his service as defense secretary, and top generals briefed him on it. The resulting 1993 edition is available at http://www.fprado.com/armorsite/US-Field-Manuals/FM-100-5-Operations.pdf. The quoted portions are on p. 18.

68 Education reform held little interest: Close to half of candidate Bush's substantive speeches were devoted to education. See *Renewing America's Purpose: Policy Addresses of George W. Bush, July 1999 to July 2000* (Republican National Committee, 2000), available at http://campus.murraystate.edu/academic/faculty/mark.wattier/Purpose.pdf. Among the best-remembered was this refrain: "Some say it is unfair to hold disadvantaged children to rigorous standards. I say it is discrimination to require anything less—the soft bigotry of low expectations." Speech to Latin Business Association Luncheon, Sept. 2, 1999. Ari Fleischer, the incoming White House press secretary, called education Bush's "top legislative priority." White House transcript, News Briefing, Jan. 4, 2001.

68 **"had given most of that to the president":** Interview with Nina Shokraii Rees by Jo Becker, Sept. 25, 2006.

68 **"Dick once told me that our president":** Interview with Phil Gramm by Jo Becker, Aug. 10, 2006. A spokeswoman for Cheney, Lea Anne McBride, denied that Cheney said this.

69 **a fast-track review of Bill Clinton's:** Interviews with two members of Cheney's staff, 2006. The vice president mentioned the review on television later that week. "Interview with Dick Cheney," *Hannity & Colmes,* Fox News, Jan. 24, 2001.

69 **"Focus on the economy":** Interview with Cesar Conda by Jo Becker, June 24, 2006.

70 **"He understands Article I, Section 7":** Interview with Bill Thomas by Jo Becker, Sept. 26, 2006. For the text see http://www.law.cornell.edu/constitution/constitution.articlei.html #section7: "All bills for raising revenue shall originate in the House of Representatives. . . ."

70 **Cheney was far too sophisticated:** The description of the Cheney-Greenspan meetings comes from a confidential source with close knowledge of Greenspan's perspective, and from two domestic advisers to Cheney.

71 **"a golden opportunity to advance the ideals":** Greenspan, *The Age of Turbulence,* pp. 210–22. Greenspan goes on to describe his gradual disillusionment with the "literal" approach the White House took to the transition from campaigning to governing. "Their stance was 'This is what we promised; this is what we'll deliver,'" he wrote (p. 217; see also p. 212).

71 **Greenspan acknowledged a place:** A recording of this portion of Greenspan's testimony is at http://money.cnn.com/2001/01/25/economy/greenspan/green02.wav.

71 **Greenspan later wrote that he thought:** Greenspan, *The Age of Turbulence,* ibid.

72 **He felt the pain of the waitress:** Radio Address by the President to the Nation, Feb. 3, 2001, http://www.whitehouse.gov/news/radio/20010203.html.

75 **"I'm surprised that Senator Chafee":** John E. Mulligan, "The Pressure Is Mounting on Chafee," *Providence Journal-Bulletin,* Apr. 5, 2001.

75 **"How would you like the vice president?":** Interview with Steve Kass, Apr. 1, 2008.

76 **"Linc is of course new to the Senate," Cheney said:** A digital recording of *The Steve Kass Show* of Apr. 4, 2001, was kindly made available by Steve Kass and is on file with the author.

78 **The Jeffords threat placed the White House:** This account of the White House debate draws on interviews with Dan Bartlett, January 2008; interviews with two White House officials who declined to be named, 2007 and 2008; and an interview with Sean O'Keefe by Jo Becker, Sept. 18, 2006. See also Trent Lott, *Herding Cats: A Life in Politics* (New York: HarperCollins, 2005), pp. 214–16.

78 **"It was about both the money":** Gramm interview, Aug. 10, 2006.

79 **"He likes to have strong people":** Press conference with transition spokesman Ari Fleischer, Jan. 4, 2000.

79 **"Once he's made up his mind":** Interview with Charles E. Walcott by Jo Becker, Oct. 20, 2006.

80 **"He spent an hour-plus, overtime":** Interview with Aaron Friedberg, Dec. 13, 2006.

CHAPTER FOUR: ENERGY IN THE EXECUTIVE

81 **Cheney chaired the first meeting:** http://www.whitehouse.gov/news/releases/20010129-1.html. The task force was formally known as the National Energy Policy Development Group.

82 **"restore the powers of the presidency":** See Hayes, *Cheney,* p. 313.

83 **"I would strongly recommend":** Interview with Christine Todd Whitman by Jo Becker, Sept. 12, 2006. See also the account in Christine Todd Whitman, *It's My Party Too: The Battle for the Heart of the GOP and the Future of America* (New York: Penguin Press, 2005).

83 **"eco-extremism":** Haley Barbour, memorandum to Vice President Dick Cheney, Mar. 1, 2001, obtained by Judicial Watch in a Freedom of Information Act lawsuit relating to the energy task force. Available at http://www.judicialwatch.org/cases/67/barbour.gif.

84 **Four Republican senators wrote to Bush:** Paul O'Neill, then treasury secretary, suspected that Cheney orchestrated the letter himself. See Ron Suskind, *The Price of Loyalty* (New York: Simon & Schuster, 2004), pp. 118–25. Whitman said Cheney simply took advantage of an opportunity. "I don't think they needed any prompting," she said of Senators Chuck Hagel, Pat Roberts, Jesse Helms, and Larry Craig. Whitman interview, Dec. 12, 2006. The letter from the senators is at http://www.lavoisier.com.au/papers/articles/Hagelletter.html.

84 **"the current state of scientific knowledge":** Memorandum to John Bridgeland Re CO_2 Policy, Mar. 8, 2001, full text on file with the author. Italics in the quoted portion correspond to underscores in the original. As far as I know, the memo was first mentioned in Andrew C. Revkin, "Bush vs. the Laureates: How Science Became a Partisan Issue," *New York Times,* Oct. 19, 2004. Portions were first quoted in Tim Dickinson, "The Secret Campaign of President Bush's Administration to Deny Global Warming," *Rolling Stone,* June 28, 2007, available at http://www.rollingstone.com/politics/story/15148655/the__secret__campaign__of__president__bushs__administration__to__deny__global__warming/print.

85 **the U.S. government's own National Assessment:** National Assessment Synthesis Team, U.S. Global Change Research Program, Climate Change Impacts on the United States, November 2000, available at http://www.usgcrp.gov/usgcrp/Library/nationalassessment/overview.htm.

85 **"as close to a global scientific consensus":** Briefing memo for Christine Todd Whitman by EPA staff, Mar. 6, 2001. Copy on file with the author.

86 **"BE AN HONEST BROKER":** Notes, "11/19 Cheney," James A. Baker III Papers, Seeley G. Mudd Manuscript Library, Princeton University, Series 6H, box 66, folder 9.

86 **"If you don't trust the process":** Interview with Richard B. Cheney by historian Martha Joynt Kumar, July 27, 1999, quoted in Martha Joynt Kumar and Terry Sullivan, eds., *The White House World: Transitions, Organization, and Office Operations* (Austin: Texas A&M University Press, 2003), p. 10.

87 **"I'm not a staffer":** Hayes, *Cheney,* p. 305. Emphasis added.

87 **"Ford was someone who":** Interview with Terry O'Donnell by Jo Becker, Dec. 22, 2006.

87 **"his staff gave him a bicycle wheel":** Interview with confidential White House source, August 2006.

87 **"he could disagree with you":** Interview with Stuart Spencer by Jo Becker, Oct. 25, 2006.

88 **"I think he's been fairly consistent":** Interview with Nelson Polsby by Jo Becker, Dec. 12, 2006. Polsby died in 2007.

88–89 **Condi Rice . . . placed a hasty phone call:** Interviews with aides to Rice and Powell, 2006 and 2007.

89 **Cheney's letter for Bush skated:** Cheney brought the letter on global warming to Bush before the White House staff secretary received approval from aides with "assistant to the president" rank, and before some key cabinet officials saw it at all. Among those bypassed, along with Whitman, was her ally Paul O'Neill, the treasury secretary. Interviews with senior White House officials; Whitman interview, Dec. 12, 2006. See also Suskind, *The Price of Loyalty.* The text of Bush's letter is at http://www.c-span.org/executive/bush__letter .asp?Cat=Current__Event&Code=Bush__Admin. The Supreme Court later ruled that carbon dioxide is, in fact, a pollutant subject to regulation under the Clean Air Act, as candidate Bush had acknowledged.

89 **"on the whole, U.S. energy markets":** This memo, portions of which were read aloud to the author by a confidential source, was first reported in Judy Pasternak, "Bush's Energy Plan Bares Industry Clout," *Los Angeles Times,* Aug. 26, 2001. The final task force report, "Reliable, Affordable, and Environmentally Sound Energy for America's Future," May 2001, is available at http://www.whitehouse.gov/energy/National-Energy-Policy.pdf. The quoted passage is on p. viii.

90 **"Do you have it?":** Whitman interview, Dec. 12, 2006.

90 **president . . . had aligned himself with fringe-group claims:** Nonpartisan science journals compare "denialist" advocacy groups, which are funded by the fossil fuel industry, to the Tobacco Institute and its years of deception about cigarettes and cancer. The fundamental claim—that the link is unproved and requires more study—is essentially similar. See, e.g., Editorial, "Oil Giants' Money Fuels a Climate of Suspicion," *New Scientist,* Jan. 13, 2007.

90 **"They all got together . . . and said to hell":** Powell made that statement in an interview for DeYoung, *Soldier,* pp. 327–28.

90 **"encourage conservation on the one hand":** Remarks by the President in Question and Answer Session with the Press, Oval Office, Jan. 29, 2001, available at http://www.whitehouse .gov/news/releases/20010129-7.html.

90 **a speech describing conservation as "a sign of personal virtue":** Remarks of the Vice President at the Annual Meeting of the Associated Press, Toronto, Canada, Apr. 30, 2001, available at http://www.whitehouse.gov/vicepresident/news-speeches/speeches/print/vp20010430 .html.

90 **"whether it serves a purpose":** Interview with former aide to the vice president, September 2006.

91 **"Markets would take care of":** Interview with Michael Gerson by Jo Becker, Nov. 1, 2006.

91 **Bush loved to hear . . . Cheney "was in a different place":** Interview with senior White House official, October 2006. Interview with Karen Knutson by Jo Becker, Jan. 18, 2007.

91 **he directed David Addington:** Interview with Michael Malbin by Jo Becker, June 19, 2006. See also Hayes, *Cheney,* pp. 314–15.

92 **One of the first . . . was James J. Rouse:** The *Washington Post,* relying on confidential sources, first obtained a partial list of experts consulted by the task force in late 2005. Another two years passed before the newspaper managed to piece together the whole roster. See Dana Milbank and Justin Blum, "Document Says Oil Chiefs Met with Cheney Task Force," *Washington Post,* Nov. 16, 2005, at http://www.washingtonpost.com/wp-dyn/content/article/ 2005/11/15/AR2005111501842.html, and Michael Abramowitz and Steven Mufson, "Papers Detail Industry's Role in Cheney's Energy Report," *Washington Post,* July 18, 2007, at http:// www.washingtonpost.com/wp-dyn/content/article/2007/07/17/AR2007071701987.html.

92 **Environmental groups—more than a dozen of them:** Abramowitz and Mufson, "Papers Detail."

92 **"the president and vice president would have fired me":** Interview with Andrew Lundquist by Stephen Hayes, cited in Hayes, *Cheney,* p. 315.

92 **Cheney made clear to those who attended:** Scooter Libby, Cheney's chief of staff, would later claim otherwise: "What we're talking about are those Americans who came to talk to us, who have on their own chosen not to go out and say who they were. We encourage anyone who comes to meet with us to go out and say, here I am." Participants in the task force, in and out of government, said they had heard only the reverse. See "Interview with Lewis 'Scooter' Libby," *Larry King Weekend,* CNN, Feb. 16, 2002.

93 **"That must be inaccurate":** Milbank and Blum, "Document Says Oil Chiefs Met."

93 **"Don't ever suggest that to me again":** Lundquist recounts that exchange in Hayes, *Cheney,* p. 324.

93 **"We were hiding something":** Bartlett interview, Dec. 17, 2007.

94 **"he didn't give a rat's ass":** Interview with senior White House adviser, 2008.

94 **Nor did Cheney stand to gain financially:** The Annenberg Center's study analyzed John Kerry's accusation in 2004 that Cheney took money from Halliburton "as vice president" and Kerry's intimation that Cheney stood to gain from Halliburton's government contracts. For that purpose it obtained and posted previously unreleased documents from Cheney's personal attorney. See http://www.factcheck.org/kerry__ad__falsely__accuses__cheney__ on__halliburton.html. A copy of the nine-page "Gift Administration Agreement," dated Jan. 18, 2001, is on file with the author. It shows that Dick Cheney divested himself of stock options from Halliburton, EDS, AT&T, AT&T Wireless, Comcast, and Procter & Gamble. Lynne Cheney divested herself of options from Lockheed Martin. Dick Cheney's public denial of a financial interest in Halliburton was made on NBC's *Meet the Press* on Sept. 14, 2003. At George Washington University, the medical faculty used its $2.7 million share of the Cheney gift to endow the Richard B. and Lynne V. Cheney Cardiovascular Institute, http://www.cheneycardioinstitute.org/.

95 **"I really got under his skin":** Interview with Rob Portman, Sept. 21, 2006.

96 **"He firmly believes":** In a television interview, Libby explained why Cheney would not disclose the names of energy task force advisers: "When he walks through the House, through the—or through the Senate chamber, he can tell you stories about every nook and cranny. He loves that institution. And I think he would rather chew off his right arm than do anything to violate the prerogatives of that place. But he also feels strongly about the White House and constitutional rights and obligations and duties of the presidency, and protecting those. And this is a case where he firmly believes—believes to the point where,

when he talks about it, his eyes get a little bluer—that for the presidency to operate properly, it needs to be able to have confidential communications. And that's part of what our forefathers set up when they set up two coequal branches of government. The courts have looked at issues like this, and they have decided that there are certain communications and certain roles that are distinct and that should be protected. Reporters claim a privilege to protect their sources, not just what they said, but who said it. Why? Because we, in everyday common sense, believe that there are some people who won't come forward and tell you exactly what they think if either their identity or the content would be known." See "Interview with Lewis 'Scooter' Libby," *Larry King Weekend,* CNN, Feb. 16, 2002.

97 **"Energy in the Executive":** Alexander Hamilton, *Federalist* No. 70, first published in the *New York Packet,* Mar. 18, 1788, available at http://thomas.loc.gov/home/histdox/fed__70.html.

97 **"a collective, deliberative body":** Dick Cheney, "Congressional Overreaching in Foreign Policy," in Robert A. Goldwin and Robert A. Licht, eds., *Foreign Policy and the Constitution* (Washington, D.C.: AEI Press, 1989), pp. 102, 116.

98 **In No. 69, Hamilton weighed:** Alexander Hamilton, *Federalist* No. 69, first published in the *New York Packet,* Mar. 14, 1788, available at http://thomas.loc.gov/home/histdox/fed__69.html. I owe a debt in this discussion of the two *Federalist* papers to Charlie Savage, who compared them in *Takeover: The Return of the Imperial Presidency and the Subversion of American Democracy* (New York: Little, Brown, 2007), pp. 125–27. His work, in turn, drew on interviews with New York University professor David Golove and University of Chicago professor Richard Epstein.

99 **"ignores the selfsame Hamilton's admonition":** See Andrew C. McCarthy, "Idée Fixe," *National Review,* Jan. 28, 2008. McCarthy wrote in criticism of Savage, *Takeover,* accusing him of "a typical omission" in failing to cite *Federalist* No. 73. As I note below, No. 73 actually tends to strengthen Savage's point more than undermine it. McCarthy might better have looked for support in *Federalist* No. 74, in which Hamilton wrote, "Of all the cares or concerns of government, the direction of war most peculiarly demands those qualities which distinguish the exercise of power by a single hand." But again, in context, Hamilton emphasized the interlinked responsibilities of the executive and legislative branches. The commander in chief commanded nothing until Congress chose an enemy and declared war. Quoting Article II, Section 2, of the Constitution, Hamilton emphasized the legislative role with all capital letters. The president is commander in chief of the Army and Navy "WHEN CALLED INTO THE ACTUAL SERVICE of the United States," he wrote. Alexander Hamilton, *Federalist* No. 74, first published in the *New York Packet,* Mar. 25, 1788, available at http://thomas.loc.gov/home/histdox/fed__74.html.

99 **Hamilton's case for restraining Congress:** Alexander Hamilton, *Federalist* No. 73, first published in the *New York Packet,* Mar. 21, 1788, available at http://thomas.loc.gov/home/histdox/fed__73.html.

99 **That imperative—to protect and expand:** In interviews, speechwriter Michael Gerson, associate White House counsel Bradford Berenson, counselor Dan Bartlett, and three senior officials who declined to be named said that Cheney had impressed the idea on Bush during the transition, and that Addington then took it up with Gonzales.

99–100 a governor's post that, by constitutional structure: University of North Carolina professor Thad Beyle, who has compared the constitutional strength of state governors annually since 1985, ranked the Texas chief executive the nation's tenth weakest in 2000. See http://www.unc.edu/depts/polisci/faculty__pages/beyle.html.

100 Bush's lieutenant governor, Robert Bullock: For example, Bullock cochaired the Budget Board, orchestrated the flow of legislation, and appointed the members and chairs of Senate committees. A helpful "explainer" on this subject, drawing on Thad Beyle's work, may be found in Chris Suellentrop, "Is George W. Bush a 'Weak' Governor?" *Slate,* Jan. 5, 2000, available at http://www.slate.com/id/1004307.

100 "You had the nadir of the modern presidency": Vice President's Remarks to the Traveling Press, Air Force Two, En route Muscat, Oman, Dec. 20, 2005, available at http://www.whitehouse.gov/news/releases/2005/12/20051220-9.html.

101 "All these things were marginalizing": Interview with Bruce Fein by Jo Becker, June 29, 2006.

101 "Pres. seriously weakened in recent yrs.": See "Cheney 11/19," James A. Baker III Papers, Seeley G. Mudd Manuscript Library, Princeton University, series 6H, box 66, folder 9.

101 "what had become known as the imperial presidency": Interview with David Gergen by Jo Becker, Dec. 5, 2006. Historian Arthur Schlesinger Jr. popularized the term in his book *The Imperial Presidency* (New York: Houghton Mifflin, 1973).

101 "should not have to reveal": Cheney aboard Air Force Two, Dec. 20, 2005, http://www.whitehouse.gov/news/releases/2005/12/20051220-9.html. Two White House officials said in 2006 and 2007 that the vice president used much the same formula during the transition and again in the debate over release of energy task force records.

102 his wife wrote a roman à clef: Lynne Cheney, *Executive Privilege*. The cited passages are on pp. 43, 48, 63, 70, 74, 84, 87, 123, 182, 218, 228, 259, 269, and 277.

104 Whitefeather Indians, a fictional tribe: The film *White Feather* depicts a nineteenth-century peace mission by U.S. Army cavalry to the Cheyenne tribe in Wyoming. Westerns of the 1950s are the vice president's genre of choice. See http://www.imdb.com/title/tt0048805/.

104 On April 19, 2001, the ranking Democrats: Letter from John Dingell and Henry Waxman to Andrew Lundquist, Apr. 19, 2001, available at http://energycommerce.house.gov/press/107ltr42.shtml.

104 they enlisted the help of the General Accounting Office: Letter to Comptroller General David Walker, Apr. 19, 2001, available at http://energycommerce.house.gov/press/gao.ltr.pdf. In 2004, the GAO changed its name to the Government Accountability Office.

104 could not "intrude into the heart of Executive deliberations": David Addington to Anthony Gamboa, May 16, 2001, http://energycommerce.house.gov/press/vp.ltr.pdf.

104 Walker issued a rare "demand letter": David Walker to the Vice President of the United States, July 18, 2001, http://energycommerce.house.gov/press/gao.demand.ltr.pdf.

104 "would unconstitutionally interfere": The Cheney letter is available at http://energycommerce.house.gov/press/cheney.rsp.802.pdf.

105 a lawsuit, the GAO's first: That fact was noted later in Dana Milbank, "GAO Ends

Fight with Cheney over Files; Weakening of Hill's Oversight Decried," *Washington Post,* Feb. 8, 2003.

105 "We decided to stiff the Comptroller General": Berenson interview, June 5, 2006.

105 Congress had no enforceable right: Cheney's brief said, among other things, that "the Comptroller General's access does not extend beyond what is allowed under FOIA," the Freedom of Information Act used by members of the public to request government data. See Memorandum of Points and Authorities in Support of Defendant's Motion to Dismiss, May 21, 2002, *Walker v. Cheney,* Civil Action No. 1:02CV00340, pp. 21–23.

105 Congress had no option: See Memorandum of Points and Authorities at pp. 10, 15, and 39. Cheney's brief also quoted *Federalist* No. 70.

106 "seeks to work a revolution": Plaintiff's Consolidated Reply in Support of his Motion for Summary Judgment and Opposition to Defendant's Motion to Dismiss, *Walker v. Cheney,* Civil Action No. 1:02CV00340, p. 13. For the court's decision to avoid a ruling on the merits, see 230 F.Supp. 2d 51.

106 Cheney's energy task force had been studying: The documents are online at http://www .judicialwatch.org/iraqi-oil-maps.shtml.

106 Cheney refused to comply: *Cheney v. U.S. Dist. Court for Dist. of Columbia,* 542 U.S. 367 (2004).

107 The high court declined to issue the writ: *Cheney v. U.S. Dist. Court for Dist. of Columbia,* 542 U.S. 367 (2004).

107 "literally devastating to the General Accounting Office's": Dana Milbank, "GAO Ends Fight with Cheney over Files; Weakening of Hill's Oversight Decried," *Washington Post,* Feb. 8, 2003.

107 "You should not underestimate": Bartlett interview, Dec. 17, 2007.

CHAPTER FIVE: VERY HARD AND VERY QUICK

109 On a closed patch of desert: Interviews with Richard Clarke, Roger Cressey, Stephen J. Hadley, Air Force general John Jumper, and confidential U.S. government sources in December 2001 and January 2002. This initiative was first disclosed in Barton Gellman, "A Strategy's Cautious Evolution: Before Sept. 11, the Bush Anti-Terror Effort Was Mostly Ambition," *Washington Post,* Jan. 20, 2002. The 9/11 Commission disclosed the "Afghan Eyes" code name. See National Commission on Terrorist Attacks Upon the United States, *The 9/11 Commission Report,* July 22, 2004, p. 187, available at http://www.gpoaccess.gov/911/ Index.html. A valuable resource for searching the report is the cross-indexed version at http://www.vivisimo.com/911.

109 A modified Predator, on a test flight: The missile was a redesigned Hellfire, which normally carries an antitank warhead. This was a new antipersonnel variant. John Jumper interview and interviews with confidential national security sources, December 2001 and January 2002.

110 "Any would-be terrorist out there": See, e.g., "Cheney: Swift Retaliation Needed," Associated Press, Oct. 13, 2000. Bush hedged his own remarks that day, vowing to "take the necessary action" if he received "enough intelligence to figure out who did the act." *Ahead of the Curve,* CNN, Oct. 13, 2000.

110 "I don't recall it cropping up": Hayes, *Cheney,* pp. 322–23.

110 At 4 p.m. on February 9, 2001: Interviews with two participants in the briefing, Jan. 16, 2002. The quotation of the slide is from verbatim notes. The 9/11 Commission, which cited subsequent communications to the vice president and other Bush advisers, did not appear to be aware of this one.

111 "definitively conclude that *al-Q'ida* was responsible": NSC Memo, Richard Clarke to Vice President Cheney, Feb. 15, 2001. Years later, when Clarke went public with his frustrations, the White House political team portrayed him as a disgruntled partisan. Contemporary records backed his factual assertions, not the denials. *The 9/11 Commission Report* describes the Feb. 15 memo on p. 526 n. 179. Note 180, on the same page, lists additional communications on the subject on March 2, 22, and 24; and two dates in June 2001, the same month the armed Predator became available. The Bush administration dropped any pretense of doubt about the *Cole* after the Sept. 11 attacks. In his address to a joint session of Congress the following week, for example, Bush said "the same murderers" in al Qaeda who attacked the twin towers and the Pentagon were "responsible for the bombing of the USS *Cole.*" Text of President Bush's Speech to a Joint Session of Congress, Sept. 20, 2001.

111 George Tenet said for three years running: Tenet's public testimony three weeks after Bush and Cheney took office began this way: "For me, the highest priority must invariably be on those things that threaten the lives of Americans or the physical security of the United States. With that in mind, let me turn first to the challenges posed by international terrorism. . . . Usama bin Ladin and his global network of lieutenants and associates remain the most immediate and serious threat. Since 1998, Bin Ladin has declared all US citizens legitimate targets of attack. As shown by the bombing of our Embassies in Africa in 1998 and his Millennium plots last year, he is capable of planning multiple attacks with little or no warning." See "DCI's Worldwide Threat Briefing," Feb. 7, 2001, at https://www.cia.gov/news-information/speeches-testimony/2001/UNCLASWWT_02072001.html. See also "DCI Statement: Current and Projected National Security Threats," Feb. 2, 1999, at https://www.cia.gov/news-information/speeches-testimony/1999/ps020299.html; "DCI Statement: The Worldwide Threat," Feb. 2, 2000, at https://www.cia.gov/news-information/speeches-testimony/2000/dci_speech_020200.html.

111 "had their hair on fire": Interviews with high-ranking CIA and White House officials, December 2001 and January 2002. *The 9/11 Commission Report* cites many classified memos, e-mails, and cables in support of this description.

111 On August 6, Bush and Cheney received: *The 9/11 Commission Report* reproduces the PDB on pp. 260–61.

111 John McLaughlin, Tenet's deputy, expressed frustration: See CIA Senior Executive Intelligence Briefing, "Bin Ladin Threats Are Real," June 30, 2001, cited in *The 9/11 Commission Report,* p. 534 n. 16. For McLaughlin's frustration, see "Staff Briefing for the 9/11 Commissioners," Mar. 24, 2004.

111 Cheney later downplayed the summer warnings: Hayes, *Cheney,* pp. 322–23.

112 "candidly speaking I didn't detect any": Interview with Lieutenant General Donald L. Kerrick, Jan. 15, 2002. Kerrick has since retired.

112 "We question whether it is advisable to": *The 9/11 Commission Report* at pp. 210ff and 530 describes the financial dispute over the Predator. John McLaughlin's handwritten comments, emphasis in original, were made Aug. 3, 2001.

112 Fearing embarrassment, the White House cut a deal: Interview with Richard Clarke, Jan. 24, 2007.

113 "Nobody gave a crap about this": Interview with confidential source, Jan. 2, 2007. The second of five reports from the Gilmore Commission had recently been published. See http://rand.org/nsrd/terrpanel/terror2.pdf.

113 president mentioned the word "terrorism": Remarks by President George W. Bush, Aug. 21, 2001.

113 Cheney and Defense Secretary Don Rumsfeld cared: Rumsfeld had chaired a missile defense commission, the final report of which made no mention of terrorism or terrorists. It cited instead "developing threats in North Korea, Iran and Iraq . . . in addition to those still posed by the existing ballistic missile arsenals of Russia and China." See *Report of the Commission to Assess the Ballistic Missile Threat to the United States,* July 15, 1998, Section IIA, available at http://www.fas.org/irp/threat/bm-threat.htm.

113 "Are we serious about dealing": NSC Memo, Clarke to Rice, Sept. 4, 2001, cited in *The 9/11 Commission Report,* p. 212, p. 513 n. 247 (emphasis in original).

114 "I can tell you the strategy": Interview with Stephen J. Hadley, Jan. 16, 2002.

114 *"Turn on the TV":* The account of the scene in Cheney's West Wing office on the morning of Sept. 11 is drawn from interviews with Brian McCormack, Dec. 7, 2006, and Mary Matalin, June 29, 2006; *The 9/11 Commission Report* (minute-by-minute chronologies of flights AA 11, UA 175, and AA 77 are on pp. 32–33); and published or broadcast interviews noted below with Dick and Lynne Cheney. Cheney's biographer adds some nice details, including the name of the Secret Service agent who first moved Cheney, in Hayes, *Cheney,* pp. 331ff.

114 "How in hell could a plane hit the World Trade Center?": White House Transcript of Vice President Cheney Interview with *Newsweek,* Nov. 19, 2001, quoted in *The 9/11 Commission Report,* p. 35.

114 "The cabinet is going to need direction": McCormack interview, Dec. 7, 2006.

115 Like the firefighters in Manhattan: I was at the scene of the World Trade Center on the morning of Sept. 11. In my story that day, I wrote: "By the thousands, emergency workers converged from Nassau and Westchester counties, northern New Jersey, the Bronx. Many carried hand tools, oddly poignant amid the apocalypse: a spade, an axe, a halligan—the firefighter's medieval tool, like a cross between a crowbar and a pike. They carried these implements to Vesey and West Streets, and stopped." Barton Gellman, "'I Saw Bodies Falling Out—Oh, God, Jumping, Falling,'" *Washington Post,* Sept. 12, 2001. For the mass of the two towers, see Steven Ashley, "When the Twin Towers Fell," *Scientific American,* Oct. 11, 2001.

115 Scott grasped Cheney's shoulder: Cheney described it in an interview not long afterward: "They practice this. You move. Whether you want to be moved or not, you're going. They don't exactly pick you up and carry you. It's more like they propel you forward." See Evan Thomas, "The Day That Changed America," *Newsweek,* Dec. 31, 2001.

115 Official accounts do not mention it: *The 9/11 Commission Report* did not address this question directly, but comparison of separate chronologies for the aircraft, pp. 1–13 and 33, and for Cheney's movements, on pp. 39–40, permit no other conclusion. After turning around their Dulles–Los Angeles flight, the hijackers took a heading that was more or less directly toward the White House. Three government analysts I interviewed in 2001 and 2002 were convinced that the White House was the intended target and the terrorist pilot overshot. Before diverting to the Pentagon, the aircraft banked through another broad half circle and turned around again. Without the additional maneuvering, they could have reached the White House—the target presumed by Cheney's Secret Service detail—long before the vice president reached relative safety at 9:37 a.m. News accounts often describe the Presidential Emergency Operations Center as invulnerable to nuclear attack, but two sources I interviewed said it is only two floors down. Specifications are highly classified, so it is impossible for outsiders to judge whether it could have withstood the impact and fire inflicted on the Pentagon.

116 "the intensity of the situation": McCormack interview, Dec. 7, 2006.

116 Once through the first vaulted door: There are several published descriptions of the Presidential Emergency Operations Center. This one is based on photographs and on interviews with Richard Clarke and a military aide to the president who made multiple visits to the bunker during the Bush administration.

116 "I urged him not to return": See Hayes, *Cheney,* pp. 335–36, which cites an interview with Cheney on Aug. 9, 2006. Cheney told his biographer that this was the sole reason for his call to Bush. He gave a strikingly different account, discussed below, to *Newsweek* two months after the attack.

116 "There was a groan in the room": The witness recounted events in the bunker and shared pages of notes during three days of interviews in January 2007. He declined to be identified by name.

117 Cheney said nothing: Witness account, January 2007. On the first anniversary of the attack, Cheney called the first tower's collapse "a very emotional moment for everybody." In the same broadcast, an interviewer asked Mary Matalin, "And the vice president said nothing?" She replied, "No, but he emoted in a way that he emotes, which was to stop." Transcript, "America Remembers: Sunset Ceremony Commemorates Lighting of Eternal Flame," CNN, Sept. 11, 2002.

118 "Who's the asshole who keeps answering": Interview with Richard Clarke, Jan. 24, 2002.

118 surprisingly little contact between them: Interviews with two staff members present, 2002 and 2006.

119 One staff member's notebook: Untitled notes of confidential source, Sept. 11, 2001.

119 The transcript of an "air threat conference call": *The 9/11 Commission Report,* p. 38.

119 Two jetliners were reported down: Untitled notes of confidential source, Sept. 11, 2001.

119 Cheney paused for "about the time": See Evan Thomas, "The Day That Changed America," *Newsweek,* Dec. 31, 2001.

119 Cheney used the vocabulary: Note the words "I" and "me." Dan Balz and Bob Woodward, "America's Chaotic Road to War: Bush's Global Strategy Began to Take Shape in First Frantic Hours After Attack," *Washington Post,* Jan. 27, 2002, available at http://www.washingtonpost.com/wp-dyn/content/article/2006/07/18/AR2006071801175.html.

120 "Aircraft 60 miles out": Libby's notes are quoted in *The 9/11 Commission Report,* p. 465 n. 220.

120 "Take it out": This quotation came from Lynne Cheney's notes, which she made available to *Newsweek* and the 9/11 Commission. See Evan Thomas, "The Day That Changed America," *Newsweek,* Dec. 31, 2001, and *The 9/11 Commission Report,* p. 41 and p. 465 n. 223.

120 Twelve years earlier: See chapter 2.

120 Cheney and Bush insisted: Cheney gave this account, among other places, in interviews with NBC's *Meet the Press,* Sept. 16, 2001; with Evan Thomas, "The Day That Changed America," *Newsweek,* Dec. 31, 2001; and with 9/11 commissioners on Apr. 29, 2004. For the latter, see *The 9/11 Commission Report,* pp. 40–41 and 464.

120 "there is no documentary evidence": *The 9/11 Commission Report,* p. 41.

120 "They said one thing": Interview with Slade Gorton, Apr. 21, 2008.

121 According to John Farmer: Interview with John Farmer, June 2, 2008.

121 "It was quite clear that the staff": Interview with Jamie Gorelick by Jo Becker, Dec. 14, 2006.

122 "Fleischer's 10:20 note": *The 9/11 Commission Report,* p. 465 n. 221.

123 "I recommended that we authorize": Evan Thomas, "The Day That Changed America," *Newsweek,* Dec. 31, 2001.

123 There was no record: White House logs record the content of conversations between the president and foreign leaders but not, since the Nixon administration, the content of conversations between the president and his advisers.

123 When the conversation began, Rumsfeld: NORAD ordered fighters to battle stations at 9:49. This part of the chronology is described in *The 9/11 Commission Report,* p. 38.

123 According to White House records: The date of the interview is disclosed in *The 9/11 Commission Report,* p. 462 n. 185. The commission staff did not take note of the important discrepancy between Cheney's *Newsweek* account and the ones he gave after that.

123 By December, Democrats were pressing: Contemporary news stories described the Democratic call for investigations. A more recent account describes a January 2002 phone call in which Cheney warned Senate majority leader Tom Daschle that the Democratic Party would suffer politically if it insisted on public hearings. See Philip Shenon, *The Commission* (New York: Hachette Book Group, 2008), p. 29.

124 When Cheney recommended the shootdown order: Balz and Woodward, "America's Chaotic Road to War," *Washington Post,* Jan. 27, 2002. From then on, Bush and Cheney stood by their story of an unlogged telephone call.

124 That is the lawful procedure: See the Goldwater-Nichols Department of Defense Reorganization Act of 1986, Pub. L. 99-433.

124 When Bush spoke to Rumsfeld: *The 9/11 Commission Report,* p. 43.

124 At 10:33, by which time: DOD Transcript, Air Threat Conference Call, Sept. 11, 2001, cited in *The 9/11 Commission Report,* p. 465 n. 223.

124 At 10:39 a.m.: DOD Transcript, Air Threat Conference Call, Sept. 11, 2001, as quoted in *The 9/11 Commission Report,* p. 43.

125 A suicide pilot is inbound: In his interview with the commissioners, "the President told us he was frustrated with the poor communications that morning. . . . The line to the White House shelter conference room—and the Vice President—kept cutting off." *The 9/11 Commission Report,* p. 40.

125 But the busy Capitol Building: Until recently, more attention has been paid to "continuity of government" in the executive branch than in its legislative and judicial counterparts. Their vulnerabilities, in some ways, are potentially greater. The Constitution defines a "quorum to do business" as a majority of each house of Congress, which means that mass casualties could bar the legislative branch from even convening until special elections were held. Six justices, likewise, must be present before the Supreme Court may hear a case. Cheney was well aware of these issues, having studied them since the Ford administration. After Sept. 11, the U.S. government created a new Continuity of Government Commission. See http://www.continuityofgovernment.org/.

125 Likewise the Supreme Court: See "Judges Evacuate Supreme Court," UPI, Sept. 11, 2001.

126 Bush and Cheney . . . did not mount a necessity defense: Jack Goldsmith, a high-ranking Bush administration lawyer who broke with the White House, compared Bush unfavorably with Lincoln because Bush failed to ask the public for the "wide latitude" required to meet an urgent threat. "Lincoln often invoked public necessity during the Civil War as a justification to stretch the Constitution and laws to meet the crisis," and both the public and Congress gave their assent, he wrote. See Jack Goldsmith, *The Terror Presidency* (New York: Norton, 2007), pp. 191–92.

126 "I was sitting outside the classroom": White House transcript, President Meets with Displaced Workers in Town Hall Meeting, Dec. 4, 2001, available at http://www.whitehouse.gov/news/releases/2001/12/20011204-17.html. One month later, Bush told a similar story: "Well, I was sitting in a schoolhouse in Florida . . . when we walked into the classroom, I had seen this plane fly into the first building. There was a TV set on. And you know, I thought it was pilot error and I was amazed that anybody could make such a terrible mistake." White House transcript, President Holds Town Hall Forum on Economy in California, Jan. 5, 2002, available at http://www.whitehouse.gov/news/releases/2002/01/20020105-3.html.

127 It is possible that the president watched a *replay:* There are several inconsistent accounts of Bush's movements that morning, but the 9/11 Commission placed him in a holding room in the elementary school at about 9:15, and said he "saw television coverage" there. The World Trade Center towers were struck at 8:46 and 9:03. *The 9/11 Commission Report,* pp. 33, 39.

127 If so, he confused both the sequence: It would be strange for Bush to have mused about a "terrible pilot" after two successive aircraft hit the World Trade Center. Yet the only video Bush could have seen that morning was of the second strike. By the time Bush reached a television, White House chief of staff Andrew Card had already whispered in his ear, "America is under attack." See *The 9/11 Commission Report,* p. 38.

Perhaps the likeliest possibility is that Bush conflated a memory of what he heard (various accounts suggest that aides mentioned the first collision during Bush's drive to the elementary school) with what he later saw. Behavioral psychologists describe this kind of false "constructive memory" as commonplace, the result of after-the-fact suggestion and assembly. See, e.g., Deborah Davis and Elizabeth F. Loftus, "Internal and External Sources of Misinformation in Adult Witness Memory," in D. F. Ross and R. C. L. Lindsay, eds., *Handbook of Eyewitness Psychology* (Mahwah, N.J.: Erlbaum, 2007), vol. 1, pp. 195–237, excerpts at https://webfiles.uci.edu/eloftus/Davis__Loftus__Misinformation__Handbook ChapScan07.pdf?uniq=e418yu.

It is plausible, though hardly provable, that Bush similarly came to believe, after endorsing Cheney's shootdown order ex post facto, that he had authorized it in advance.

127 "this crusade, this war on terrorism": These two terms made their debut in the same sentence, five days after the 9/11 attacks. Bush spoke without a text: "This is a new kind of—a new kind of evil. And we understand. And the American people are beginning to understand. This crusade, this war on terrorism, is going to take a while. And the American people must be patient." Remarks by the President on Arrival, the South Lawn, Sept. 16, 2001, available at http://www.whitehouse.gov/news/releases/2001/09/20010916-2.html. The global reaction to the word "crusade," regarding a war with a self-described Islamic enemy, discouraged Bush from repeating that part of the formula.

127 UNODIR: See Joint Publication 1-02, *Department of Defense Dictionary of Military and Associated Terms,* updated Mar. 4, 2008, available at http://www.dtic.mil/doctrine/jel/new__ pubs/jp1__02.pdf.

127 As a division commander in 2003, Petraeus: I had dinner with Petraeus at the al-Rasheed Hotel in Baghdad when he commanded the 101st Infantry Division (Air Assault). Petraeus smiled and explained the term "UNODIR," describing its importance as he tried to solve problems that were "above my pay grade" as a two-star general but festering for lack of initiative in the capital. The details were off the record. Interview with Major General David Petraeus, Dec. 10, 2003.

128 There were casualty reports: These casualty estimates are taken verbatim from the reports briefed to Cheney. They do not match the confirmed final counts.

129 A jam-packed agenda awaited: The list described here is a close paraphrase of the handwritten agenda for the National Security Council meeting Bush convened that evening in the PEOC after his return to Washington. Agenda made available to the author by a participant.

130 *Turn around. The vice president needs you:* The account of Addington's evacuation, return to the White House, and initial consultations with Cheney comes from a Bush administration official with direct knowledge.

CHAPTER SIX: ENEMIES, FOREIGN AND DOMESTIC

131 "I don't want to get too poetic about this": Interview with Jack Kemp by Jo Becker, Aug. 14, 2006. Kemp was Bob Dole's running mate in the 1996 presidential election. They lost to Bill Clinton and Al Gore. Since I tease him for channeling Winston Churchill, I suppose I should note that "used to be a future vice president" borrows from Al Gore's post-2000 joke: "I used to be the next president of the United States."

131 Scooter Libby quoted that line, too: In an interview with James Mann in December 2001, Libby said he looked at Cheney on Sept. 11 and thought of this passage from Churchill's memoir: "I felt as if I were walking with destiny, and that all my past life had been but a preparation for this hour and for this trial." Mann, *Rise of the Vulcans,* p. 294. Libby was quoting from Winston Churchill, *The Gathering Storm* (Boston: Houghton Mifflin, 1948), p. 601.

131 The three of them simply knew: Brad Berenson, a White House lawyer, explained Cheney's and Addington's influence this way in an interview with producers of "Cheney's Law," a documentary for PBS's *Frontline:* "In government, as in other fields of endeavor, it's far more typical for people to be unsure of what the right thing to do is and unsure of what they think than it is for them to be sure of what the right thing to do is and to be sure of what they think. And so, the people who are sure and confident and are capable of expressing their certainty and their confidence in a persuasive way to others, to those who are unsure, often have an outsize influence on events." Unbroadcast portion of interview with Bradford A. Berenson, November 2007, transcript courtesy James Gilmore and Michael Wiser of Kirk Documentary Group, on file with author.

131 Churchill was prime minister: Libby knew that. In his interview with James Mann, Libby cited not only the famous line but its context: the moment when Churchill finally realized his ambition to become head of government, just before the outbreak of war with Nazi Germany. Mann, *Rise of the Vulcans,* p. 294.

132 Cheney made no-notice deployments: Three teams typically deployed simultaneously from Andrews Air Force Base, each with a different destination, such as a National Guard air base in Michigan. Donald Rumsfeld, then in the private sector, was another of the faux chiefs of staff. Interviews with Rand Beers, May 6, 2008, and Richard Clarke, May 3, 2008. Beers and Clarke participated in the exercises. James Mann disclosed them, using anonymous sources, in *Rise of the Vulcans,* pp. 138ff.

132 But if "everything changed": It would be unkind to single out one or two commentators. A Google search in mid-2008 produced more than twenty-nine thousand hits for the combination of "September 11" and "everything changed."

132 a 44 percent spike: National Center for Health Statistics, "Deaths from Each Cause, by 5-Year Age Groups, Race, and Sex: United States, 2001," available at http://www.cdc.gov/ nchs/data/statab/mortfinal2001__workI.pdf. There were 2,416,425 deaths from all causes in 2001, averaging 6,620 per day. For statistics on terrorism and pedestrian deaths, see pp. 1959, 1964. In comparison to the 2,922 terrorism deaths, there were 17,386 lives lost to ordinary homicide and 101,537 to accidents. See *National Vital Statistics Reports* 52, no. 9 (Nov. 7, 2003), Table E, "Deaths and Percentage of Total Deaths for the 10 Leading Causes of Death, by Race: United States, 2001," at http://www.cdc.gov/nchs/data/dvs/nvsr52__09p9.pdf. In the first quarter of 2008, the number of U.S. troops killed in Iraq, a war of choice launched after Sept. 11, exceeded 4,000. See www.defenselink.mil.

132 The economic damage was extensive: See Mark L. Burton and Michael J. Hicks, "Hurricane Katrina: Preliminary Estimates of Commercial and Public Sector Damages," Center for Business and Economic Research, Marshall University, September 2005; and the report of the Senate's Joint Economic Committee, *The Subprime Lending Crisis: The Economic Impact on Wealth, Property Values, and Tax Revenues, and How We Got Here*, October 2007, at http://jec.senate.gov/Documents/Reports/10.25.07OctoberSubprimeReport.pdf.

132 He gave them legal cover: See chapter 7.

133 Gonzales, was stranded in Norfolk: See Remarks of Alberto R. Gonzales at Georgetown University Law Center, Jan. 24, 2006, at http://www.usdoj.gov/archive/ag/speeches/2006 ag__speech__0601241.html.

134 In the *Godfather* movies: Michael Corleone, who took over from his father, said in *The Godfather, Part II:* "Fredo? Well, he's got a good heart but he's weak, and he's stupid." I first saw this reference in a blog maintained by Eric Muller, of the University of North Carolina Law School, at http://www.isthatlegal.org/archives/2007/07/alberto__fredo__g.html. Excerpts from the movie script are at http://www.filmsite.org/godf2B.html. Nora Ephron offered an alternative theory, not much friendlier: "I've always believed that the reason the President called Gonzales Fredo was that when they first met, Bush incorrectly believed that Gonzales' first name was Alfredo, and Gonzales was too much of a toady to correct him." *Huffington Post,* Aug. 27, 2007, at http://www.huffingtonpost.com/nora-ephron/it-was-you -fredo__b__61985.html. Bill Minutaglio, Gonzales's biographer, reached a conclusion more or less like Ephron's, but politer. Bush "didn't linger with people's . . . names in any exact way," Minutaglio wrote, and used Fredo "because it sounded like a shortened version of 'Alberto.' " (Bush called Minutaglio "Mononucleosis.") Bill Minutaglio, *The President's Counselor* (New York: Rayo, 2006), pp. 111, 341.

134 Raised in Humble, Texas: Biographical details from Minutaglio, *President's Counselor.* In interviews with Minutaglio, Gonzales spoke candidly about his late father's alcoholism. See, for example, p. 12. Through the Justice Department press office, and later through personal spokesman Bob Bork on June 30, 2008, Gonzales declined to be interviewed on any subject for this book.

135 "sole organ of the nation": John C. Yoo, "Laws as Treaties? The Constitutionality of Congressional-Executive Agreements," 99 *Michigan Law Review*, 757, 811 (February 2001).

135 "plenary authority" to . . . "almost absolute deference" . . . "violate international law and treaties": John C. Yoo, "Politics as Law? The Anti-ballistic Missile Treaty, the Separation of Powers, and Treaty Interpretation," 89 *California Law Review*, 851, 874 (May 2001).

135 "can place any limits": John C. Yoo, Memorandum Opinion for the Deputy Counsel to the President, "The President's Constitutional Authority to Conduct Military Operations Against Terrorists and Nations Supporting Them," Sept. 25, 2001, at http://www.usdoj .gov/olc/warpowers925.htm. Though Yoo addressed only statutory restrictions directly, the second sentence, which concludes the memo, entails that courts are equally precluded from limiting the president.

135 "differs, at times sharply": John C. Yoo, *The Powers of War and Peace* (Chicago: University of Chicago Press, 2005), p. vii.

135 Yoo's impact: Jack L. Goldsmith, who clashed with Addington after becoming head of the Office of Legal Counsel (see chapter 11), later testified:

In order to ensure that it provides the President with the high-quality advice that he needs, OLC has over the years developed powerful internal norms of detachment and professionalism. It has also developed a number of practices to help it avoid errors, and to compensate for the fact that its opinions are not subject to the same critical scrutiny of adversary process and dissent that characterize the judiciary. These practices include (1) insisting that agencies seeking OLC's advice request OLC opinions in writing, setting forth their view of the law and facts; (2) seeking the written legal and factual views of all agencies with expertise or that may be affected by the opinion; (3) subjecting draft opinions to multiple levels of scrutiny and review inside OLC; (4) writing narrowly tailored opinions; and (5) publishing non-classified opinions when possible. OLC has not always followed these norms and practices during the past six years, or even during the period before that.

Prepared testimony of Jack L. Goldsmith, Senate Judiciary Committee, Oct. 2, 2007.

136 "was not a law of war expert": Interview with John Yoo by Jo Becker, Aug. 23, 2006.

137 In a prolific run of opinions: David J. Barron and Martin S. Lederman, "The Commander in Chief at the Lowest Ebb—a Constitutional History," *Harvard Law Review* 121 (2008), pp. 944, 1094ff., available at http://www.harvardlawreview.org/issues/121/feb08/barron__lederman2.pdf. The authors referred to the Torture Act, the Habeas Act of 1867, the Foreign Intelligence Surveillance Act, and the War Crimes Act. Some of Yoo's opinions are discussed below.

137 The breadth of his language: It is not controversial that a president may decline to enforce a statute under some circumstances. Yoo did not mention the leading Supreme Court case on the subject, which qualifies that answer. Justice Robert H. Jackson's concurring opinion in *Youngstown Sheet & Tube Co. v. Sawyer*, 343 U.S. 579 (1952), which has become the standard framework of analysis, said a president's power "is at its lowest ebb" when he acts against the expressed or implied will of Congress. Jackson added: "Presidential claim to a power at once so conclusive and preclusive must be scrutinized with caution, for what is at stake is the equilibrium established by our constitutional system." Bill Clinton's OLC chief, Walter Dellinger, in an opinion that still stands as the Justice Department's guidance on the subject, emphasized the "special role" of the judicial branch in deciding whether a president may flout a statute: "If . . . the President, exercising his independent judgment, determines *both* that a provision would violate the Constitution *and* that it is probable that the Court would agree with him, the President has the authority to decline to execute the statute" (emphasis added). Dellinger suggested that exercise of that authority should be sparing, as narrow as possible, and announced to the public. See Walter Dellinger, "Presidential Authority to Decline to Execute Unconstitutional Statutes," Nov. 2, 1994, available at http://www.justice.gov/olc/nonexcut.htm. Dellinger did not always take his own advice, on the other hand; he told Clinton that he could disobey a law forbidding U.S. troops to be placed under UN command without going through the *Youngstown* case analysis.

137 Cheney and Addington found Yoo's analysis congenial: See also the discussion of executive supremacy, and Cheney's use and misuse of *Federalist* No. 70, in chapter 4.

137 "We have appropriated the funds": Transcript, "War Powers and the Constitution," a conference held at the American Enterprise Institute, Dec. 6, 1983, on file with author.

138 Gerald Ford, the former president: Ford's Dec. 7, 1983, commentary on the conference came in videotaped remarks, published as an appendix to the conference report. He agreed with Cheney that the War Powers Resolution was unconstitutional, but differed with Cheney's broadly stated claims of exclusive presidential authority over war. Ibid.

138 striking new claims: Barron and Lederman, "Commander in Chief at the Lowest Ebb," pp. 1083ff.

138 "I would say he was a perfect agent": Interviews with Jack Goldsmith, April 2008. For the story of their clashes, see chapters 11 and 12. Berenson, in his PBS *Frontline* interview, agreed: "It was always my impression that there wasn't a sliver of daylight between the two of them on these issues, that the Vice President himself had thought about these things and that he had come to a set of views that were essentially identical to those that David Addington held. The two of them, at times, seemed to meet, to really share a brain on these important legal and structural issues."

138 even the law itself . . . was classified: A leading U.S. treatise famously stated that "secret law is an abomination." See Kenneth Culp Davis, *Administrative Law Treatise* (New York: Aspen Publishers, 1970 supp.), § 3A. There had been occasions before for secret legal opinions, or portions of legal opinions, when they touched on classified information. In the Bush-Cheney years, the existence and constitutional reasoning of important opinions were routinely withheld, not only from the public but from other government lawyers with classified clearances.

138 Cheney's committed views: In the AEI transcript, Cheney cited his strong disagreement with Jimmy Carter's handling of foreign policy, including the botched attempt to rescue U.S. hostages in Iran, but said those things were for the president to decide.

139 "I don't think you can ignore the idea of time on task": Interview with John Ashcroft, Sept. 21, 2006.

139 a federation of fourteen other agencies and offices: Congress later removed that coordinating role from the CIA director and created a new director of national intelligence. It also added a sixteenth member of the "intelligence community," the Office of Intelligence and Analysis in the new Department of Homeland Security.

141 Abuses exposed by the Church Committee: Frank Church, an Idaho Democrat, chaired the Senate Select Committee to Study Governmental Operations with Respect to Intelligence Activities. One important set of hearings, "The National Security Agency and Fourth Amendment Rights," held Oct. 29 and Nov. 6, 1975, is available in digital form at http://cryptome.org/nsa-4th.htm.

141 "were to turn its awesome technology": *Meet the Press,* NBC, Oct. 29, 1975.

141 If their communications were scooped up inadvertently: The governing rules are implemented in the NSA's *United States Signals Intelligence Directive 18: Legal Compliance and Minimization Procedures.* More recent editions are classified, but the declassified 1993 version is available at http://cryptome.org/nsa-ussid18.htm.

141 Cheney asked George Tenet: George Tenet, *At the Center of the Storm: My Years at the CIA,* with Bill Harlow (New York: HarperCollins, 2007), p. 237.

141 **He brought a Venn diagram:** Testimony of Michael V. Hayden, Hearing of the Senate Select Committee on Intelligence, May 18, 2006.

142 **"After September the 11th":** President Discusses War on Terror and Operation Iraqi Freedom, March 20, 2006, at http://www.whitehouse.gov/news/releases/2006/03/print/20060320-7.html.

142 **Bush got it wrong:** Interviews with U.S. national security officials, 2005–8. See also Tenet, *At the Center of the Storm,* p. 137.

142 **Set aside the third one:** Interviews with two government officials who heard Hayden's account of his conversation with Cheney.

142 **al Qaeda "sleeper cells":** Interviews with the NSC officials Richard Clarke, Daniel Benjamin, Roger Cressey, Wayne Downing, and John A. Gordon and FBI assistant director for counterterrorism Larry Mefford, 2001 and 2002. See also Tenet, *At the Center of the Storm,* p. 239.

142 **"The database is being built":** Interview with Condoleezza Rice, December 2002.

142 **750 to 1,000 warrants a year:** For a summary of the Justice Department's annual reports, see "Foreign Intelligence Surveillance Act Orders 1979–2007," Electronic Privacy Information Center, at http://epic.org/privacy/wiretap/stats/fisa__stats.html.

143 **the first Presidential Authorization:** Shannen Coffin, counsel to Vice President Cheney, to Senator Patrick Leahy, Aug. 20, 2007.

143 **The program went operational:** Hayden testimony.

144 **"I'm not going to tell you":** Bellinger's encounter with Addington was described by an official with contemporary knowledge and confirmed by Bellinger's deputy. Interview with Bryan Cunningham, May 23, 2008.

145 **In the damage-control effort:** James Risen and Eric Lichtblau, "Bush Lets U.S. Spy on Callers Without Courts," *New York Times,* Dec. 16, 2005. Bush used the new public relations name five weeks later. Transcript, "President Bush Holds a Media Availability Following a Tour of the National Security Agency," Jan. 25, 2006.

145 **"It seems like to me":** President Bush Delivers Remarks on Terrorism, Louisville, Ky., Jan. 11, 2006.

145 **Content was reviewed:** Interviews with three U.S. government sources, 2005, 2006, and 2007. See Barton Gellman, Dafna Linzer, and Carol D. Leonnig, "Surveillance Net Yields Few Suspects: NSA's Hunt for Terrorists Scrutinizes Thousands of Americans, but Most Are Later Cleared," *Washington Post,* Feb. 6, 2006.

145 **A valuable clue was no less so:** See Gellman, Linzer, and Leonnig, "Surveillance Net Yields Few Suspects." This helped explain Cheney's reluctance to work through the FISA court. In order to find that the NSA's screening algorithms met the "probable cause" requirement for a warrant, the judges would have to find that the grounds for suspicion were reliable. A washout rate of close to 100 percent could hardly meet that standard. Interviews with two government lawyers with experience in the FISA court, 2006.

145 **The program branched out:** When the Bush administration decided to seek legislative authority for the program in 2007, FBI director Robert Mueller confirmed his bureau's participation. He testified that "we received pieces of information from the NSA" and that there was "activity we undertook as a result of the information we received." A new law,

Mueller said, "would help not just the FBI, but operating together with NSA, the CIA, the DIA, all of whom—all of us share the same responsibility to protect the homeland." Hearing of the House Judiciary Committee, July 26, 2007.

146 "It's all chicken and egg": Interview with Joseph Billy Jr., Oct. 13, 2005.

146 After his second secret briefing: Jay Rockefeller to Dick Cheney, July 17, 2003, on file with author.

147 In a memoir of his government service: John Yoo, *War by Other Means: An Insider's Account of the War on Terror* (New York: Atlantic Monthly Press, 2006), pp. 105–7. One official who was briefed on the program expressed surprise that government vetters, who screen the publications of former employees for classified information, permitted Yoo to include those details.

147 Hayden gave a bravura performance: Michael V. Hayden, National Press Club, Jan. 23, 2006.

148 "At key points": Confirmation Hearing of Michael V. Hayden, Senate Select Committee on Intelligence, May 18, 2006.

149 "The fact of the matter": Interview with Vice President Richard Cheney, CNN, Dec. 20, 2005. Cheney used that formula, or a similar one, many times in his career. Defending the secrecy of Ronald Reagan's invasion of Grenada, an island nation with fifteen hundred men under arms, Cheney said it "might have cost hundreds of lives" had Reagan waited for "the usual dialog and debate about whether Congress would authorize action." AEI conference transcript.

149 "This may not be important now": Interview with a participant in that meeting, 2007.

149 "doesn't agree with Cheney": Interview with U.S. national security official, 2007.

149 There were places Hayden refused to go with the program: For Hayden's insistence on congressional notification, interviews with two knowledgeable officials. For his fears of future congressional investigation, see chapters 11 and 12. Beginning about three weeks after the NSA surveillance began, Cheney and Hayden briefed the chairmen and vice chairmen of the House and Senate intelligence committees.

150 "Legal but stupid": Interview with U.S. government official, 2007.

150 "I've taken literally hundreds of domestic flights": Hayden at National Press Club.

151 At the Justice Department: Baker declined to discuss the program or any connection between the program and the surveillance court, on or off the record. He did grant a brief interview about his decision not to resign in a subsequent controversy. See chapter 11.

151 chief judge of the FISA court: For a full listing of the FISA judges, see http://cryptome.org/fisc-members.htm.

151 "He forced it": Interview with Royce C. Lamberth, May 28, 2008.

152 The young lawyer told him that FISA: Most of Yoo's surveillance opinion remains classified. That one sentence was declassified in 2008 at the Senate's request.

152 Even if Congress forbade the surveillance: About a year later, the FISA appeals court gave some support to Yoo's analysis in its first published decision. The court's remark was "dicta," meaning it was extraneous to the case at issue and therefore not binding law. The unsigned opinion for the three-judge court, which was drafted by senior judge Laurence Silberman, said: "[A]ll the . . . courts to have decided the issue, held that the President did have inherent authority to conduct warrantless searches to obtain foreign intelligence information. . . . We take for granted that the President does have that authority and, assuming that is so, FISA could not encroach on the President's constitutional power." *In re: Sealed Case No. 02-001,* United States Foreign Intelligence Surveillance Court of Review, Nov. 18, 2002, available at http://epic.org/privacy/terrorism/fisa/FISCR__opinion.pdf.

154 "You're trying to say": Interview with Andy Card, May 4, 2008.

154 "One of the possible functions": Interview with William J. Haynes II, Apr. 13, 2007.

155 Congress made its last major rewrite in 1947: Presidential Succession Act of 1947 (3 U.S.C. § 19). In the Patriot Act renewal of 2006, Congress added the secretary of homeland security to the line of succession. See § 503 of Public Law 109-177.

155 qualify as a constitutional "officer": Interviews with three U.S. government lawyers, 2008. There is mainstream legal debate on this question. See Akhil Reed Amar and Vikram David Amar, "Is the Presidential Succession Law Constitutional?" *Stanford Law Review* 48 (1995), p. 113, and the reply by John F. Manning in the same issue.

155 "We had discussions": Interview with senior Bush administration lawyer, 2008. Thurmond relinquished the post of president pro tempore to Senator Robert Byrd in 2001.

155 "threats to the continuity of our government": George Bush, Radio Address to the Nation, Dec. 17, 2005. If there was persuasive evidence of such threats, it might be relevant to legal arguments that the program was based on "necessity" or "self-defense." Thomas Jefferson, Abraham Lincoln, and a line of judicial opinions since 1949 have been cited as authority that the Constitution does not require national suicide. Jefferson justified the Louisiana Purchase, which he believed to violate the Constitution, with the observation: "To lose our country by a scrupulous adherence to the written law, would be to lose the law itself, with life, liberty, property and all those who are enjoying them with us; thus absurdly sacrificing the ends to the means." Thomas Jefferson to John B. Colvin, Sept. 20, 1810, available at http://press-pubs.uchicago.edu/founders/documents/a2__3s8.html. "Are all the laws, but one, to go unexecuted, and the government itself go to pieces, lest that one be violated?" Lincoln asked after suspending the right of habeas corpus in the Civil War. First Message to Congress, 1861. Justice Robert H. Jackson's dissent in *Terminiello v. Chicago,* 337 U.S. 1 (1949), famously warned against converting the "Bill of Rights into a suicide pact." A subsequent case adopted that phrase for the majority, saying that "while the Constitution protects against invasions of individual rights, it is not a suicide pact." *Kennedy v. Mendoza-Martinez,* 372 U.S. 144 (1963). It is notable, however, that the holding in *Kennedy* did not justify a departure from the Constitution; it struck down a law stripping draft evaders of their citizenship, despite the acknowledged need to enforce conscription.

156 worked on a parallel team: Interview with Rand Beers, May 6, 2008.

156 disperse its leaders to hardened locations: See Barton Gellman and Susan Schmidt, "Shadow Government Is at Work in Secret," *Washington Post,* March 1, 2002.

156 "The whole premise was": Interview with White House official, Nov. 25, 2002.

157 rotating cadre of 70 to 150 senior managers: Interview with Joseph Hagin, Feb. 26, 2002. See also Gellman and Schmidt, "Shadow Government." The *Washington Post* agreed to withhold the location of the bunker.

157 **"They never included":** Interview with Norman Ornstein, Apr. 18, 2008.

157 **"One of the biggest problems":** Interview with Wayne Downing, Dec. 17, 2002. Downing died of meningitis in 2007.

157 **"I think it would be a reasonable issue":** Libby's reply was conveyed by a person with firsthand knowledge, interviewed Dec. 18, 2002.

157 **Six months later, Cheney hosted:** Chaired by Lloyd Cutler and Cheney's friend Alan Simpson, the commission brought the vice president the findings of its first report, available at http://www.continuityofgovernment.org/report/report.html.

CHAPTER SEVEN: DARK SIDE

159 **Before, the vice president's motorcade:** Interview with Cheney staff member, 2007.

159 **Unable to attend meetings in person:** Interview with a senior official who took part in meetings with the vice president by SVTS, the Secure Video Teleconferencing System 2006.

159 **Cheney's car, already armored:** The equipment uses filters and a pressurized interior to prevent the intrusion of chemical or biological pathogens. Interviews with two confidential sources, 2008.

159 **A large hump:** Todd Purdum, "A Face Only a President Could Love," *Vanity Fair,* June 2006. It is possible that Cheney was only teasing his friend. Here is the story, as Robin West recounted it to Purdum: "And then there was this big duffel bag in the middle of the backseat, and I said, 'What's that? It's not very roomy in here.' And he said, 'No, because it's a chemical biological suit,' and he looked at it and said, 'Robin, there's only one. You lose.' "

159 **The Secret Service gave special lapel pins:** White House transcript, Radio Interview of the Vice President, *Chaz and AJ in the Morning Show,* June 12, 2008.

160 **"one of the things":** Interview with Wayne Downing, Dec. 22, 2002.

160 **"We're working as hard as we can":** Interviews with members of Cheney's staff, 2006.

160 *"We also have to work": Meet the Press,* NBC, Sept. 16, 2001.

160 **"Dark side" came to define him:** For Bush's use of the Veep as a nickname, interview with Bradford Berenson by Jo Becker. For Big Time, interviews with two White House officials who had no interest in being named. The reference was to an inadvertently broadcast dialogue on Sept. 4, 2000. Bush called the *New York Times* reporter Adam Clymer a "major league asshole," and Cheney replied, "Oh yeah, he is, big time." For Management, interviews with three White House officials. (For the denial, interview with Karl Rove, Nov. 20, 2006.) For Deadly Dick, Bartlett interview, Dec. 17, 2007.

161 **Jokes about the Dark Side:** Sometimes Gore was cast as Darth Vader, as in Deborah Orin, "Speech Ties Bill Around Al's Neck," *New York Post,* Aug. 4, 2000. Sometimes it was Bush, as in David M. Shribman, "Bush, McCain Need Each Other," *Boston Globe,* Apr. 4, 2000. Sometimes it was political hit men doing those negative TV spots, as in Steve Kraske, "It's Time for Deluge of Political Ads," *Kansas City Star,* July 28, 2000. Now and then someone got to be Luke Skywalker. See Bill Adair, "McCain Puts His Lightsaber Away," *St. Petersburg Times,* July 30, 2000.

161 **"We need to be able":** Interview with the vice president by John King, CNN, June 22, 2006, at http://www.whitehouse.gov/news/releases/2006/06/print/20060622-8.html.

161 Cheney was dressing his dog as Lord of the Sith: He lost few opportunities to bring up Darth Vader in his final year, usually claiming that Hillary Clinton stuck him with the nickname. On a conservative radio talk show, for example, he had this exchange:

> Q: Is your nickname "Big Time"?
>
> THE VICE PRESIDENT: It was for a while there.
>
> Q: What is it now?
>
> THE VICE PRESIDENT: What is it now? Darth Vader, I think. [Laughter]
>
> Q: Well, that's original.
>
> THE VICE PRESIDENT: That's what Senator Clinton dubbed [me] a while ago. So
>   I ask my wife about it, I said, doesn't that make you angry when they call me
>   Darth Vader? She said, no, it humanizes you. [Laughter]

White House transcript, Radio Interview of the Vice President, *Chaz and AJ in the Morning Show,* June 12, 2008.

161 Here the vice president: Interview with Aaron Friedberg, Dec. 13, 2006. Interviews with Bradford Berenson, Michael Gerson, Tom Foley, Anthony Fauci, and Juleanna Glover by Jo Becker, 2006 and 2007. Emphasis added to the quotations from Foley and Fauci.

163 "Once you start diving into it": Interview with Pierre Prosper, Sept. 29, 2006.

163 "the interagency was just constipated": Haynes interview, Apr. 13, 2007. Informally, he went by Jim, after his middle name.

163 By relying on Roosevelt's model: The case was *Ex parte Quirin,* 317 U.S. 1 (1942). In it the Court upheld the president's right to try and execute alleged Nazi saboteurs caught in the United States by means of a special military tribunal, giving the defendants no recourse to civilian courts.

163 Universal Declaration of Human Rights: UN General Assembly, Universal Declaration of Human Rights, Dec. 10, 1948, available at http://www.un.org/Overview/rights .html.

163–64 John Yoo and his colleague Patrick Philbin: Philbin's memo, never released publicly, was cited as authority in Yoo's. Patrick F. Philbin to Alberto R. Gonzales, "Legality of the Use of Military Commissions to Try Terrorists," Nov. 6, 2001. The second memo, not officially released but on file with author, is John Yoo to William J. Haynes II. General Counsel, Department of Defense, "Application of Treaties and Laws to al Qaeda and Taliban Detainees," Jan. 9, 2002.

164 Over Veterans Day weekend: The account of this meeting is from interviews with participants, by the author and by Jo Becker, in 2006, 2007, and 2008.

165 "I'm just not prepared": Interview with John Ashcroft, Sept. 21, 2006.

165 "the president's most precious commodity": Interviews by Jo Becker with Ron Christie, Aug. 2, 2006, and Jack Marsh, Oct. 17, 2006.

166 "who is going to bring that to the president?": Interviews with Ron Klain by Jo Becker, June and Sept. 1, 2006.

166 "was very closely held": Haynes interview, Apr. 13, 2007.

166 "I was astonished": Interview with Tim Flanigan by Jo Becker, Dec. 21, 2006.

166 gave its words the power of command: Military Order, "Detention, Treatment, and Trial of Certain Non-citizens in the War Against Terrorism," Nov. 13, 2001, available at http://www.whitehouse.gov/news/releases/2001/11/20011113-27.html.

167 "orderly paper flow": See discussion of Cheney's management style as chief of staff, and his advice to James Baker on how to run the White House, in chapter 4.

167 "This has to be staffed": The Berenson-Bowen interchange is reconstructed from an interview with Stuart Bowen, May 30, 2008; interviews with two White House officials, June 2007; interview with Brad Berenson by Jo Becker, June 2007.

168 Bush pulled out a Sharpie: For the Oval Office scene, Bowen interview, May 30, 2008. A sample of Bush's signature may be found at http://www.nea.gov/news/news03/images/bush_sig.jpg.

168 Condi Rice, furious: Interview with a senior adviser to Rice, 2007.

168 "What the hell just happened?": Interview with a witness to Powell's call, Sept. 29, 2006.

168 "deserve to be treated as a prisoner of war": Remarks by Vice President Dick Cheney to the U.S. Chamber of Commerce, Nov. 14, 2001, available at http://www.whitehouse.gov/vicepresident/news-speeches/speeches/vp20011114-1.html.

169 the United States had refused to ratify: William R. Levi, "Identifying and Explaining Change: Development of U.S. Interrogation Policy, 1949–2006," unpublished thesis for Stanford University's Interschool Honors Program in International Security Studies, spring 2006, p. 146. According to Levi, there were suggestive changes in an Army interrogation manual after that, intimating that Geneva's requirement of "humane" treatment might not apply to terrorists and insurgents, but the Reagan administration never said that openly.

169 The American government had never been in the business: Levi's thesis, ibid., offers a helpful summary of Geneva's structure (see pp. 31–32):

> There are four Geneva Conventions. Two of the Conventions, the Geneva Convention Relative to the Treatment of Prisoners of War (Geneva III or GPW) and the Geneva Convention Relative to the Protection of Civilian Persons in Time of War (Geneva IV or GC), contain provisions that are most relevant to interrogation. These Conventions, applicable in instances of international armed conflict that involve a High Contracting Party, protect different classifications of persons—as their titles indicate. Both, however, share a uniform Article 3 that establishes a basic standard of humane treatment. Referred to as "Common Article 3," this "convention in miniature" was drafted to provide a minimum level of protection in "armed conflict not of an international character occurring in the territory of one of the High Contracting Parties" for persons "taking no active part in the hostilities, including members of armed forces who have laid down their arms and those placed hors de combat by sickness, wounds, detention, or any other cause." Common Article 3 proscribes "cruel treatment and torture" as well as "outrages upon personal dignity, in particular humiliating and degrading treatment. . . ."

169 "Protect your client": Alberto Mora, "Memorandum for Inspector General, Department of the Navy," July 7, 2004, p. 13, recounting a meeting between Mora and Pentagon general counsel Jim Haynes on Jan. 9, 2003.

170 Gonzales signed his name to a memo: Alberto R. Gonzales, Memorandum for the President, "Decision Re Application of the Geneva Convention on Prisoners of War to the Conflict with Al Qaeda and the Taliban," Jan. 25, 2002, draft time-stamped 3:30 p.m. Available at http://www.washingtonpost.com/wp-srv/politics/documents/cheney/gonzales_adding ton_memo_jan252002.pdf.

170 Addington, in fact, had written the text: Interview with a White House lawyer with firsthand knowledge, 2006.

170 Powell did not argue that al Qaeda and Taliban forces: Interview with David Bowker, July 17, 2006.

172 Jane Harman, a hawkish Democrat: Interview with Jane Harman, Dec. 17, 2007.

172 Legal historians, in fact, are divided on the question: See Aaron D. Simowitz, "The Original Understandings of the Capture Clause," Social Science Research Network, Mar. 12, 2008, available at http://ssrn.com/abstract=1105417. Simowitz argues that the contrary view is based almost entirely on a statement by a justice who *dissented* in the leading Supreme Court case. In an e-mail to the author, Simowitz said there is much debate about the subject, but "any statement that the Capture Clause is only 'about piracy' is a serious misreading of the historical record." E-mail from Aaron Simowitz, June 16, 2008.

173 "in full Nurse Ratched mode": Interview with a witness, 2007.

174 "He was kidnapped and tortured": Interview with Tom Smeeton by Jo Becker, July 19, 2006.

175 "You have also asked": Memorandum for William J. Haynes II from John C. Yoo, "Re: Military Interrogation of Alien Unlawful Combatants Held Outside the United States," March 14, 2003, p. 48, n. 53. Originally classified SECRET/NOFORN, it was declassified on March 31, 2008, and is available at http://www.fas.org/irp/agency/doj/olc-interrogation .pdf.

175 The War Crimes Act of 1996: See 18 U.S.C. 2441, at http://www.law.cornell.edu/uscode/ html/uscode18/usc_sec_18_00002441----000-.html.

176 He was completely off the map: The existence of the "black sites" was disclosed by Dana Priest, "CIA Holds Terror Suspects in Secret Prisons," *Washington Post,* Nov. 2, 2005.

177 The CIA could not have been blunter: Declaration of Ralph S. DiMaio, Information Review Officer, National Clandestine Service, Central Intelligence Agency, Apr. 21, 2008, filed in *Amnesty International v. Central Intelligence Agency,* Southern District of New York, Case No. 07 Civ. 5435, available at http://www.ccrjustice.org/files/2008-2-21%20Declaration %20of%20Ralph%20Dimaio%20-%20CIA.pdf.

177 Yoo gave interim authority: Interview with a participant, 2008.

178 to decide which torments: Interview with national security official with firsthand knowledge. It took six years for this story to get out. The participation of cabinet members in interrogation decisions was first reported by ABC News on Apr. 9, 2008.

178 When ABC News revealed: Bush defended waterboarding specifically. "We had legal opinions that enabled us to do it," he said. "And no, I didn't have any problem at all trying to find out what Khalid Sheikh Mohammed knew." He added: "I think it's very important for the American people to understand who Khalid Sheikh Mohammed was. He was the person who ordered the suicide attack—I mean, the 9/11 attacks." Interview with ABC News, Apr. 11, 2008.

179 The U.S. government held war crimes trials: For an account of the first such court-martial, see Paul Kramer, "The Water Cure," *New Yorker,* Feb. 25, 2008, available at http://www.newyorker.com/reporting/2008/02/25/080225fa_fact_kramer?printable=true. In another example, the U.S. Army court-martialed a soldier who was shown in a published photograph supervising the waterboarding of a captured North Vietnamese soldier. See front-page photograph, *Washington Post,* Jan. 21, 1968.

179 approved waterboarding for at least three men: They were captured, respectively, in March and November 2002 and March 2003. The administration has stated that no other detainees were waterboarded. Testimony of Michael V. Hayden before Senate Intelligence Committee, Feb. 5, 2008. Bush administration officials made clear the same day that they continue to regard waterboarding as a lawful technique. If employed in the future, they said, it would require a request from the CIA director and approval of the attorney general and the president personally.

179 In that form of waterboarding: Admiral Mike McConnell, the director of national intelligence, described it this way in early 2008: "You know what waterboarding is?" he asked. "You lay somebody on this table, or put them in an inclined position, and put a washcloth over their face, and you just drip water right here." He pointed to his nostrils. "Try it! What happens is, water will go up your nose. And so you will get the sensation of potentially drowning. That's all waterboarding is." Referring to his teenage days as a lifeguard, he said, "I know one thing. I'm a water-safety instructor, but I cannot swim without covering my nose. I don't know if it's some deviated septum or mucus membrane, but water just rushes in." For him, "waterboarding would be excruciating. If I had water draining into my nose, oh God, I just can't imagine how painful! Whether it's torture by anybody else's definition, for me it would be torture." See Lawrence Wright, "The Spymaster," Jan. 21, 2008, at http://www.newyorker.com/reporting/2008/01/21/080121fa_fact_wright?currentPage=all.

179 The reliability of information: Since 2004, military and FBI interrogators have stepped forward to argue that a detainee will "confess" to anything under enough duress and that softer psychological methods are more reliable. Tenet and others have insisted that only the harshest measures were effective on resistant suspects.

In confidential interviews with the author, national security officials said it is foolish to claim that harsh methods never work. They said detainees have provided names, places, telephone numbers, electronic passwords, and other details that could be verified as facts, and some led to further discoveries. Abu Zubaida's waterboarding, the government said, produced a chain of information that led to Khalid Sheikh Mohammed.

The earliest public discussion of this subject was in Dana Priest and Barton Gellman, "U.S. Decries Abuse but Defends Interrogations: 'Stress and Duress' Tactics Used on Terrorism Suspects Held in Secret Overseas Facilities," *Washington Post,* Dec. 26, 2002. The story quoted several officials defending the use of violence against terror suspects. "If you don't violate someone's human rights some of the time, you probably aren't doing your job," one of them said. "I don't think we want to be promoting a view of zero tolerance on this. That was the whole problem for a long time with the CIA."

180 "When we asked the CIA, 'Were there alternatives?'": A year before the cabinet discussions were revealed, Tenet gave a similar account of his views on interrogation to the television correspondent Scott Pelley:

> PELLEY: Water boarding?
>
> TENET: We do not—I don't talk about techniques.
>
> PELLEY: It's torture.
>
> TENET: And we don't torture people. Now, listen to me. Now, listen to me. I want you to listen to me. The context is it's post-9/11. I've got reports of nuclear weapons in New York City, apartment buildings that are gonna be blown up, planes that are gonna fly into airports all over again. Plot lines that I don't know—I don't know what's going on inside the United States. And I'm struggling to find out where the next disaster is going to occur. Everybody forgets one central context of what we lived through. The palpable fear that we felt on the basis of the fact that there was so much we did not know. I know that this program has saved lives. I know we've disrupted plots.
>
> PELLEY: But what you're essentially saying is some people need to be tortured.
>
> TENET: No, I did not say that. I did not say that.

60 Minutes, CBS, Apr. 29, 2007, excerpts available at http://www.cbsnews.com/stories/2007/04/25/60minutes/printable2728375.shtml.

180 Rice declined to discuss those meetings: Secretary Condoleezza Rice, Policy Talks@ Google, Google Headquarters, Mountain View, California, May 22, 2008.

181 to reconsider the Venn diagram he once showed Cheney: See chapter 6.

181 "'OK, that's our work space, right in there'": Unpublished transcript of interview with Michael V. Hayden by Joby Warrick of the *Washington Post,* May 27, 2008. Warrick kindly made the transcript and Hayden's drawing available to author.

182 "We remain worried": For the newspaper story on Hayden's interview, see Joby Warrick, "U.S. Cites Big Gains Against Al-Qaeda: Group Is Facing Setbacks Globally, CIA Chief Says," *Washington Post,* May 30, 2008.

182 "standards of conduct for interrogation": Jay S. Bybee to Alberto R. Gonzales, "Standards of Conduct for Interrogation Under 18 USC 2340-2340A," Aug. 1, 2002. Yoo has acknowledged that he wrote the memo for Bybee's signature. The text is at http://www.washingtonpost.com/wp-srv/politics/documents/cheney/torture_memo_aug2002.pdf. It was disclosed in Dana Priest and R. Jeffrey Smith, "Memo Offered Justification for Use of Torture," *Washington Post,* June 8, 2004, available at http://www.washingtonpost.com/wp-dyn/articles/A23373-2004Jun7.html.

182 Another one, substantially similar: The Yoo memo was declassified on March 31, 2008, and is available at http://www.fas.org/irp/agency/doj/olc-interrogation.pdf.

183 Yoo delved instead into the Torture Act: The Torture Act was enacted as 18 U.S.C. 2340.

The Convention Against Torture and Other Cruel, Inhuman, or Degrading Treatment or Punishment is available at http://www.unhchr.ch/html/menu3/b/h_cat39.htm.

184 "I always thought that only the CIA": Interview with John Yoo by Jo Becker, Aug. 23, 2006. Confirmation of Yoo's account came from an interview by the author with a high-ranking Bush administration lawyer, 2007.

184 Into the tropical Cuban heat: Accounts vary on the White House counsel's presence. Lieutenant Army Colonel Diane Beaver, who greeted and briefed the traveling party, said Alberto Gonzales was there. Interview with Diane Beaver, May 27, 2008. In an e-mail from Beaver to the author, June 12, 2008, she said she specifically recalled giving Gonzales an Army coin commemorating the judge advocate general corps. In his memoir of service in the Bush administration, Jack Goldsmith writes that he was present as well, along with Patrick Philbin and Alice Fisher from Justice. Jack Goldsmith, *The Terror Presidency* (New York: W. W. Norton & Co., 2007), pp. 99-100. In an interview, he said he did not recall the presence of Gonzales. Interview with Jack Goldsmith, June 12, 2008. Another member of the delegation expressed confidence that Gonzales was not present.

Doubt has also been raised about the date of the trip. The British international lawyer Philippe Sands, in a recent book and magazine article, describes the visit as taking place variously on Sept. 25 or "toward the end of the month." In her interview, Beaver was uncertain of the date. Goldsmith said the trip took place on Sept. 26, his birthday. See Philippe Sands, "The Green Light," *Vanity Fair,* May 2008; and Philippe Sands, *Torture Team: Rumsfeld's Memo and the Betrayal of American Values* (New York: Palgrave Macmillan, 2008).

184 "It was definitely the jacket-and-tie brigade": Beaver interview, May 27, 2008.

186 "They wanted to know what we were doing": In an e-mail exchange, Dunlavey said, "Mr. Sands's article was the product of a very imaginative imagination trying to establish something that didn't occur." He declined to specify any inaccuracy or to be interviewed further. E-mail from Michael E. Dunlavey to author, May 27, 2008. See also Sands, "Green Light" and Sands, *Torture Team*.

186 "It should never have happened that way": Interview with the retired general James T. Hill, May 28, 2008. Hill said his first notice of the visit came from Philippe Sands, the British lawyer.

187 four days to analyze the proposal: Dunlavey's proposal and Beaver's analysis are available at http://news.findlaw.com/hdocs/docs/dod/dunlavey101102mem.pdf.

187 According to disputed minutes of a meeting: Counter Resistance Strategy Meeting minutes, Oct. 2, 2002, held at Guantánamo Bay, made public by Senate Armed Services Committee, June 17, 2008. The Senate committee's final report also quoted the CIA lawyer, Jonathan Fredman, as having said that "if the detainee dies, you're doing it wrong." Fredman strongly disputed the quotation, and it later became clear that the unsigned minutes were far from verbatim. See *Inquiry Into the Treatment of Detainees in U.S. Custody,* Senate Armed Services Committee Report, Nov. 20, 2008, declassified Apr. 22, 2009, at p. xvii.

187 In logs recording the subsequent handling: First reported by *Time* magazine in 2005, the document, classified SECRET/ORCON (which meant it was intended to remain within the organization that produced it), was titled "Interrogation Log: Detainee 063." It is available at http://ccrjustice.org/files/Publication_AlQahtaniLog.pdf.

187 There were reports: SERE (Survival, Evasion, Resistance, and Escape) training for U.S. pilots involves capture and rough handling by U.S. special forces playing the bad guys. The first extensive story on the connections between SERE and Guantánamo was Jane Mayer, "The Experiment," *New Yorker,* July 11, 2005.

188 "The basic KGB technique": Interview with Tom Malinowski, Dec. 7, 2006.

188 Mora threatened to file: Mora told Haynes he would sign his memorandum on Jan. 15, 2003, unless authority for those methods was withdrawn. Haynes notified him "that Secretary Rumsfeld would be suspending the authority to apply the techniques that same day." See Alberto Mora, "Memorandum for Inspector General," July 7, 2004, p. 15.

190 a pair of stories: Jess Braver, "Pentagon Report Set Framework for Use of Torture," *Wall Street Journal,* June 7, 2004; Dana Priest and R. Jeffrey Smith, "Memo Offered Justification for Use of Torture," *Washington Post,* June 8, 2004, available at http://www.washington post.com/wp-dyn/articles/A23373-2004Jun7.html.

190 "abstract . . . legal theory": News briefing by Alberto Gonzales and William J. Haynes II, June 22, 2004.

191 The most brutal interrogations ever sanctioned: The Levi thesis, "Identifying and Explaining Change," offers a fascinating account of the ebbs and flows of coercive interrogation policy after World War II and includes strong evidence that the CIA permitted highly aggressive methods at times, especially by foreign liaison partners working on the CIA's behalf. But waterboarding was never an approved technique in any circumstances, and there was no precedent for cabinet-rank advisers' ordering treatment of that sort.

191 In an interview after leaving government: Interview with John Yoo by Jo Becker, Aug. 23, 2006.

192 "If I had it to do all over again": Beaver interview, May 27, 2008.

192 "I still think you were right": Ibid. Philippe Sands first quoted the "great minds" line, but Beaver did not tell him that Addington explicitly said her torture opinion had been correct. In her interview with this author, Beaver said Addington seemed sincere. "I don't know if he felt sorry for me," she said. "Mr. Haynes put my legal opinion out there, and I was getting a lot of flak. I took it as he was trying to make me feel better, or at least pay me a compliment."

193 It was a syllogism: Dahlia Lithwick critiqued the Bush administration's use of false legal syllogisms in other contexts, but the author has not seen the point made in this one. See Dahlia Lithwick, "When Less Is More: The Nutty Legal Syllogism That Powers the Bush Administration," *Slate,* March 21, 2007, at http://www.slate.com/id/2162374/.

193 "Torture" was *defined:* In his remarks that day, Bush said: "We do not condone torture. I have never ordered torture. I will never order torture. The values of this country are such that torture is not a part of our soul and our being." Statement of the President, June 22, 2004. The Gonzales remark is from his briefing for reporters the same day.

Chapter Eight: Matching the Science

195 "This is Dick Cheney": Interview with Sue Ellen Wooldridge, June 2, 2006. The author also draws upon an interview with Wooldridge by Jo Becker, Jan. 5, 2007.

195 the nineteenth-ranking official: Wooldridge, at the time, was deputy chief of staff to interior secretary Gale Norton. After the secretary, in order of precedence, were a deputy secretary, five assistant secretaries, eight bureau directors, and two more Senate-confirmed appointees, the inspector general and the chairman of the Indian Gaming Commission. Norton's chief of staff would make eighteenth on the list, and assuming no other official came next, the deputy chief of staff would rank nineteenth. See the department's leadership team at http://www.doi.gov/secretary/officials.html.

196 There are three miles of corridors: The building's history and architecture are described on the Interior Department Web site at http://www.doi.gov/interiormuseum/about/history .html.

196 "consummate staffer": Interview with Ron Christie by Jo Becker, Jan. 9, 2007.

196 Drought had struck hard: See Drought Monitor archive at http://www.drought.unl .edu/dm/archive.html.

196 Growers were counting on a century-old complex: See http://www.usbr.gov/dataweb/ html/klamath.html.

197 survival was at stake: The Bureau of Reclamation announced its decision on Apr. 7, based on two scientific assessments. The Fish and Wildlife Service rendered its formal Biological Opinion on Apr. 1, 2001, about two sucker species. The National Marine Fisheries Service did the same for coho salmon. The *Chasmistes brevirostris,* or shortnose sucker, and *Deltistes luxatus,* or Lost River sucker, were declared "endangered" in 53 Fed. Reg. 27130 (1988); *Oncorhynchus kisutch,* or coho salmon, were declared "threatened" in 62 Fed. Reg. 24588 (1997). The Endangered Species Act of 1973 is at 16 U.S.C. 1531–1543.

197 Bad enough that the federal government: The Council of State Governments, Western Region, puts the figure at 51.9 percent. See http://www.csgwest.org/committees/Exec/ resolutions/02_01.pdf.

197 "They swim upstream": Interview with Roger Marzulla by Jo Becker, Aug. 14, 2006. The ocean, for what it's worth, is downstream.

197 Yellowstone Park, the nation's oldest: Interview with John Varley by Jo Becker, Sept. 5, 2006.

198 Still later, a smart reporter noticed: Juliet Eilperin, "Utilities Apply to Construct Power Plants Near Parks; Officials Concerned About Air Quality, *Washington Post,* Oct. 29, 2004.

198 "the magic man": Scott McClellan, *What Happened* (New York: Public Affairs, 2008), p. 247.

198 There is a fascinating artifact: The easiest way to see how the vice president slipped offstage, excising all references to his role, is in the concordance published by OMB Watch among the three relevant executive orders: EO 12866 of Sept. 30, 1993; EO 13258 of Feb. 26, 2002; and EO 13422 of Jan. 18, 2007. See http://www.ombwatch.org/regs/PDFs/ EOchangeshighlighted.pdf.

199 Bush changed one other thing: For Cheney's initiative in the matter, interviews with two U.S. government officials, 2008. For the changes themselves, see previous note.

199 an endangered minnow now playing hell: A federal court ruled in 2003 that the endangered Rio Grande silvery minnow, under the Endangered Species Act, had a higher priority for water than farmers, ranchers, and the Albuquerque municipal water system.

200 scarce government resource: An excellent guide to the issues is available in a CRS report for Congress, RL33098, "Klamath River Basin Issues and Activities: An Overview," Sept. 22, 2005, available at http://www.nationalaglawcenter.org/assets/crs/RL33098.pdf.

200 "There's a saying": Interview with Paul Hoffman by Jo Becker, Sept. 11, 2001.

201 When economic claims came into play: See CRS report, "Klamath River Basin Issues and Activities," p. 7.

201 "at first blush": Interview with Dylan Glenn by Jo Becker, Aug. 17, 2006.

202 "This wasn't about fish": Interview with Mike Thompson by Jo Becker, Aug. 10, 2006.

202 "Hello, it's Dick": Christie interview, Jan. 9, 2007.

203 "If we're going to put a bunch of farmers": Wooldridge interview, June 2, 2008.

203 a symbolic bucket brigade: See "A History of the Klamath Bucket Brigade," at http://www.klamathbucketbrigade.org/a_history_of_KBB.htm. For the chain saw and blow-torches, see "Conflict in Klamath," *SPLC Intelligence Report,* at http://www.splcenter.org/intelinterreport/article.jsp?sid=112.

204 Whitman's cell phone rang: Interview with Christine Todd Whitman by Jo Becker, Sept. 12, 2006.

205 one of the touchstone achievements: Among the laws were the Clean Air Act, the Clean Water Act, the Federal Water Pollution Control Act, the National Environmental Protection Act, the Endangered Species Act, and the General Authorities Act of 1970, which expanded upon the National Park Service Organic Act of 1916. The "unimpaired" standard originated in the 1916 law.

205 Dick Cheney was one of the complainers: National Petroleum Council, *U.S. Petroleum Refining—Assuring the Adequacy and Affordability of Cleaner Fuels,* June 20, 2000, p. 8, on file with author. Executive summary at http://www.npc.org/reports/RefExSum.pdf. Cheney was a member of the study panel.

205 "to encourage the development": *Report of the National Energy Policy Development Group,* May 2001, p. 108.

208 "emit an incredible 5 million tons": Resignation letter of Eric V. Schaeffer, Feb. 27, 2002, available at http://www.grist.org/news/muck/2002/03/01/.

208 "Every day you can postpone": Interview with Eric Schaeffer by Jo Becker, Aug. 29, 2006.

209 A panel of seven cabinet officials: The committee has very seldom been used. See CRS report, "Klamath River Basin Issues and Activities," p. 3.

210 Two federal agencies had already issued: See discussion of the Apr. 1, 2001, opinions by the Fish and Wildlife Service and the National Marine Fisheries Service, in note for p. 197.

210 "as far as I know": Interview with William Kearney, June 27, 2007.

211 "We had four documents to review": Interview with Suzanne Van Drunick by Jo Becker, Apr. 24, 2007.

211 "was produced very quickly": Interview with William Lewis by Jo Becker, Apr. 2, 2007.

212 "The protocol is": Interview with Stuart Pimm by Jo Becker, Aug. 14, 2007. Lewis defended the report: "The farmers were grateful for our decision, but we made the decision based on the scientific outcome," he said. "It just so happened the outcome favored the farmers."

212 **not "supported by our recommendations":** Interview with J. B. Ruhl by Jo Becker, Aug. 14, 2007.

213 **"that can be controlled to any degree":** The sixty-seven-page analysis by California's Department of Fish and Game, dated January 2003, is available at http://www.krisweb .com/biblio/klamath_cdfg_ncncr_2003_kill.pdf.

CHAPTER NINE: DEMONSTRATION EFFECT

216 **"I want to share with you some things":** Interview with Dick Armey, June 19, 2008. Lea Anne McBride, a spokeswoman for Cheney, said the vice president's office would not comment on classified matters or on Cheney's private discussions, but that in general his assertions about Iraq relied on intelligence thought to be valid at the time. Armey has discussed this meeting before, but he made important new revelations in his interview with the author. For previous accounts, see Michael Isikoff and David Corn, *Hubris: The Inside Story of Spin, Scandal, and the Selling of the Iraq War* (New York: Crown, 2006), and Draper, *Dead Certain*.

216 **The vice president had been beating war drums:** At the time, the return of UN inspectors was Bush's declared objective. Cheney said the inspection debate would do little more than abet an effort by Saddam Hussein "to obfuscate and delay and avoid having to live up to the accords that he signed up to at the end of the Gulf War." Vice President Discusses the President's Economic Security Agenda, Aug. 7, 2002, at http://www.whitehouse.gov/news/ releases/2002/08/20020807-4.html.

216 **"I don't believe that America":** Mike Glover, "Armey Warns Against Unprovoked Attack on Iraq," Associated Press, Aug. 8, 2002.

216 **a lifetime rating of 97 percent:** See http://www.freerepublic.com/focus/news/853282/ posts.

217 **The vice president by then had dialed up:** *Meet the Press,* NBC, Sept. 8, 2002.

217 **Two of them crossed so far beyond:** There is a bookshelf by now of lengthy studies on U.S. intelligence about Iraqi weapons of mass destruction, before and after the war, and on the conformity of the Bush administration's public claims to the intelligence. None of them have addressed the claims Cheney made to Armey in private, because Armey has not disclosed them before. The voluminous information available in those reports—from David Kay, Charles Duelfer, the Silberman-Robb Commission, the 9/11 Commission, the Senate Select Committee on Intelligence, and the Butler Commission in the United Kingdom—includes much discussion of the state of knowledge of the Iraqi nuclear program and the connections between Saddam and al Qaeda. What Armey said Cheney told him broke the bounds of even the most forward-leaning and disputed estimates.

217 **Iraq produced partial schematics:** Interview with U.S. nuclear weapons physicist, July 30, 2003.

218 **"no firm evidence":** This was a significant concession because the DIA was among the strongest voices for a resurgent Iraqi nuclear program. DIA, "Iraq: Nuclear Program Handbook" (DI-1610-81-01), Defense Intelligence Assessment, May 2002, cited in "Report on Whether Public Statements Regarding Iraq by U.S. Government Officials Were Substantiated by Intelligence Information," Senate Committee on Intelligence, June 2008.

218 **Cheney unrolled a full-scale photograph:** More precisely, the tubes were 910 millimeters

long and 81 millimeters in diameter, with walls that were 3.3 millimeters thick. These dimensions became significant in subsequent analysis.

218 Cheney told Armey they were centrifuge rotors: The tubes became a major talking point for White House officials in the public campaign to portray Iraq as a "grave and gathering danger." On Sept. 8, 2002, Cheney, Powell, Rice, and Rumsfeld discussed the tubes in television interviews after administration officials leaked the news to the *New York Times.* Cheney went into more technical detail with Armey.

219 Houston G. Wood III: Interview with Houston G. Wood III, Aug. 1, 2003. His assessment, he said, came in August 2001, more than a year before Cheney briefed Armey.

219 An alternative explanation for the tubes: Interviews with U.S. and allied members of inspection teams for the International Atomic Energy Agency and the UN Special Commission, or UNSCOM, 2003.

219 The idea that Saddam wanted the tubes: See Barton Gellman and Walter Pincus, "Depiction of Threat Outgrew Supporting Evidence," *Washington Post,* Aug. 10, 2003.

220 Cheney had asked to see them on September 3: The account of the meeting with the Gang of Four—Trent Lott, Tom Daschle, Dennis Hastert, and Richard Gephardt—draws on confidential interviews with two participants in July and August 2003, and simultaneous reporting by my colleague Walter Pincus at the *Washington Post.* See also Isikoff and Corn, *Hubris,* p. 23.

220 a Los Alamos employee named Frank Pabian: The account of Pabian's presence and his back-channel reports to Washington is based on interviews with two senior participants in the U.S. intelligence debate about the Iraqi nuclear program. For the dates of inspections at the Nasr plant (spelled Nassr in some reports) and nuclear facilities at Tuwaitha and Ash Shaykhili, see the time lines available from the International Atomic Energy Agency at http://www.iaea.org/NewsCenter/Focus/IaeaIraq/index.shtml. A helpful compilation of IAEA data is at http://www.fourthfreedom.org/pdf/inspections__chart1.pdf.

220 Sure enough, the inspectors found: In debate with the small community of analysts who knew about the Nasr artillery rockets, Joe Turner said the production lines were part of an elaborate cover story, which still did not disprove a covert program to divert some of the tubes for nuclear use. But in public, and even inside the U.S. government, the Iraqi rocket program was still portrayed as fiction. Working from a draft prepared by Cheney's office, Colin Powell made the tubes a centerpiece of his speech in the UN Security Council on Feb. 5, 2003, ridiculing the notion that anyone would use precision-machined special alloys to build a rocket. The Bush administration did not disclose to the public or to Congress that Iraq and Italy did exactly that.

221 No forbidden program: The author visited all the main nuclear sites during two months of reporting in April and December 2003, obtaining and confirming the unreleased government findings that Iraq's scientific infrastructure had crumbled after more than a decade of economic sanctions. For the most extensive account, see Barton Gellman, "Iraq's Arsenal Was Only on Paper; Since Gulf War, Nonconventional Weapons Never Got Past the Planning Stage," *Washington Post,* Jan. 7, 2004.

222 David Wurmser ... was connecting dots: Interview with David Wurmser, Dec. 14, 2007.

223 "Link analysis" . . . is a burgeoning field: See for example Michael Wolverton et al., "Issues in Algorithm Characterization for Link Analysis," American Association for Artificial Intelligence, 2006, at http://www.ai.sri.com/pubs/files/1452.pdf.

223 Wurmser worked on *Hydra of Carnage:* Uri Ra'anan, Robert L. Pfaltzgraff Jr., Richard H. Shultz, Ernst Halperin, and Igor Lukes, eds., *Hydra of Carnage: International Linkages of Terrorism and Low-Intensity Operations* (Lexington, Mass.: Lexington Books, 1985).

223 Kennan, the severe and brilliant diplomat: The full text of the Long Telegram is at http://www.gwu.edu/~nsarchiv/coldwar/documents/episode-1/kennan.htm. The story of its genesis is in George F. Kennan, *Memoirs, 1925–1950* (New York: Little, Brown, 1967). See also Barton Gellman, *Contending with Kennan: Toward a Philosophy of American Power* (New York: Praeger, 1985).

223 In National Security Council Report 68: NSC-68, United States Objectives and Programs for National Security, Apr. 14, 1950, is available at http://www.mtholyoke.edu/acad/intrel/nsc-68/nsc68-1.htm.

224 Wilkerson called Cheney every angry name: Interview with Lawrence Wilkerson, Sept. 13, 2006.

225 Luti interrupted an early staff meeting: Interview with Karen Kwiatkowski, Oct. 5, 2006.

226 "Cheney and Rumsfeld hammered on this idea": Interview with Douglas Feith, Dec. 14, 2007.

226 Before September 11, Feith said: Feith was quoting a well-known terrorism analyst, who made that widely repeated observation in 1975. See Brian Jenkins, "International Terrorism: A Balance Sheet," *Survival* 17, no. 4 (July 1975).

226 "Our greatest fear is that terrorists": George W. Bush, Address to the United Nations General Assembly, Sept. 12, 2002.

226 "after September 11 he took very, very seriously": Interview with Aaron Friedberg, Dec. 13, 2006.

227 As Wurmser noted, the State Department: The State Department's annual survey for 2003 is available at http://www.state.gov/documents/organization/31944.pdf.

228 American officials blamed it: See Louis J. Freeh, "Khobar Towers: The Clinton Administration Left Many Stones Unturned," *Wall Street Journal,* June 25, 2006. Freeh was FBI director when the bombing took place. In this op-ed article, he wrote: "the bombers admitted they had been trained by the Iranian external security service (IRGC) in Lebanon's Bekaa Valley and received their passports at the Iranian Embassy in Damascus, Syria, along with $250,000 cash for the operation from IRGC Gen. Ahmad Sharifi. We later learned that senior members of the Iranian government, including Ministry of Defense, Ministry of Intelligence and Security and the Spiritual Leader's office had selected Khobar as their target and commissioned the Saudi Hezbollah to carry out the operation."

228 There was fresh evidence of clandestine nuclear programs: For a more extensive treatment of these nuclear developments see Barton Gellman and Dafna Linzer, "Unprecedented Peril Forces Tough Calls; President Faces a Multi-Front Battle Against Threats Known, Unknown," *Washington Post,* Oct. 26, 2004.

228 **"That intel was very, very sensitive":** Interview with Stephen Yates, Jan. 25, 2007.

229 **When a French official proposed:** Interview with participant in the October 2002 meeting, September 2004.

230 **On the Korean Peninsula:** For the 1990s military balance, interviews with Air Force Col. Robert Gaskin and Air Force Gen. Merrill McPeak, December 1993. The author gave a more extensive treatment in Barton Gellman, "Trepidation at Root of U.S. Korea Policy; Conventional War Seen Catastrophic for South," *Washington Post,* Dec. 12, 1993. For an updated study in the journal of the U.S. Army War College, see Homer T. Hodge, "North Korea's Military Strategy," *Parameters,* Spring 2003, pp. 68–81, available at http://www.carlisle .army.mil/usawc/Parameters/03spring/hodge.pdf.

230 **Iran's Quds Force, intelligence ministry, and Hezbollah clients:** Interviews with Richard Clarke, Roger Cressey, Daniel Benjamin, and Steve Simon, 2001 and 2002.

230 **"Anytime the question would come up":** Interview with Aaron Friedberg, Dec. 20, 2006.

231 **"the image which we should avoid":** Interview with Bernard Lewis by Jo Becker, Jan. 9, 2007.

232 **as Voltaire explained about a public execution in** *Candide:* In Voltaire's eighteenth-century classic, the title character, a naive Frenchman, asks why a British officer has been put to death. Martin, his interlocutor, replies, "In this country it is found requisite, now and then, to put an admiral to death, in order to encourage the others to fight." One translation of this exchange, which begins chapter 23, is available at http://www.literature.org/authors/ voltaire/candide/chapter-23.html.

233–34 **the intelligence suggested plans for a spectacular attack:** Interviews with Joseph Billy Jr., the FBI's second-ranking counterterrorism official; Valerie Caproni, general counsel of the FBI; and confidential national security sources, 2005.

235 **"Policymakers are allowed to argue with the intel":** Interview with Mark Lowenthal, Sept. 18, 2006.

237 **He saw himself as Iran's rightful monarch:** See http://www.rezapahlavi.org/. For a recent profile, see Connie Bruck, "Exiles: How Iran's Expatriates Are Gaming the Nuclear Threat," *New Yorker,* Mar. 6, 2006.

238 **"need freedom now, and if they can only achieve it":** Jamie Wilson, "Make Iran Next, Says Ayatollah's Grandson: Khomeini Calls US Freedom the Best in the World from Base in Occupied Baghdad," *New York Observer,* Aug. 10, 2003.

238 **Khomeini told the audience:** A transcript of the event is at http://www.aei.org/events/ filter.all,eventID.630/transcript.asp.

239 **A top-ranking adviser, who would not speak:** Interview with high-ranking member of the Cheney national security team, Mar. 23, 2007.

239 **"Regime change starts with a diagnosis":** Interview with Aaron Friedberg, Dec. 20, 2006. Even in Iraq, "regime change does not necessarily equal war," according to a Pentagon memo produced the summer before war began. See Office of the Undersecretary for Policy, "Amnesty and Regime Change," Aug. 23, 2002, reproduced in Douglas J. Feith, *War and Decision* (New York: Harper, 2008), p. 539.

240 **"What evidence do we have":** Yates interview.

241 **"Our model was something Martin Malia wrote":** Martin Malia, "To the Stalin Mausoleum," *Daedalus,* January 1990.

241 **"If for instance there will be a strike":** Interview with Uri Lubrani, Sept. 28, 2004.

242 **Marine General Anthony Zinni:** Interview with Anthony Zinni, Apr. 7, 2006.

242 **"How dare he? This is illegal!":** Interviews with a witness, 2006. Through a spokeswoman, Edelman declined to be interviewed. E-mail from Lt. Col. Karen Finn to author, Feb. 24, 2007.

243 **John R. Bolton, a Cheney ally:** See Dafna Linzer, "Lugar Predicts Bolton's Approval; White House Depicts Nomination Battle as Fight over U.N.'s Future," *Washington Post,* Apr. 28, 2005.

243 **"I had conversations with UAE officials":** Interview with Richard Haass, Sept. 25, 2006.

245 **" 'Mr. President, I went out to the agency yesterday' ":** Interview with Stephen J. Hadley, Jan. 3, 2007.

246 **Miller was profoundly skeptical of Chalabi:** After the invasion of Iraq, U.S. intelligence was made public that accused Chalabi of funneling classified American communications to Tehran.

246 **The president had decided not to install:** The Defense Department, with Cheney's backing, proposed to install a provisional government of six exile organizations, dominated by Chalabi. Interviews with U.S. officials, 2003, 2004, 2005. See also Assistant Secretary of Defense Peter W. Rodman to Secretary of Defense, "Who Will Govern Iraq," Aug. 15, 2002, declassified February 2005, reproduced in Feith, *War and Decision,* appendix 7. Cheney later expressed regret that the president had not chosen to take this course. See Hayes. *Cheney.*

247 **The principal consumers of his intelligence:** Entifadah Qanbar, Memo to Senate Appropriations Staff, "Iraqi National Congress—Information Collection Program," June 26, 2002. *Newsweek* first disclosed the memo and kindly provided a copy, on file with the author.

248 **"My men have only just found these":** Interview with Ahmed Chalabi in Baghdad, Dec. 15, 2003.

248 **Back in April, Judith Miller:** Judith Miller, "Aftereffects: Germ Weapons; Leading Iraqi Scientist Says He Lied to U.N. Inspectors," *New York Times,* Apr. 27, 2003.

249 **"The search is going to go on":** Interview with Lester Holt, MSNBC, The Vice President's Ceremonial Office, March 2, 2004, available at http://www.whitehouse.gov/news/releases/2004/03/20040302-8.html.

249 **Armey had cast his reluctant vote:** From an account that day: "Mr. Armey, 62, who is retiring at the end of this session, cried as he spoke of the troops who might be sent to war. 'Mr. President,' he said, 'we trust to you the best we have to give. Use them well so they can come home and say to our grandchildren, 'Sleep soundly, my baby.' He choked up and walked out of the House chamber." See Jim VandeHei and Juliet Eilperin, "Congress Passes Iraq Resolution: Overwhelming Approval Gives Bush Authority to Attack Unilaterally," *Washington Post,* Oct. 11, 2002.

249 That evening at One Observatory Circle: The account of the dinner party comes from an interview with Victor Davis Hanson by Jo Becker, Dec. 6, 2006, and an interview by the author with another participant who did not wish to be named. Some descriptions of the setting are based on photographs and a video tour of the residence at http://www .whitehouse.gov/history/life/vpresidence.html.

249 Cheney had been reading *An Autumn of War*: See Victor Davis Hanson, *An Autumn of War: What America Learned from September 11 and the War on Terrorism* (Anchor, 2002). For Cheney's remarks to his staff, see Glenn Kessler and Peter Slevin, "Cheney Is Fulcrum of Foreign Policy; In Interagency Fights, His Views Often Prevail," *Washington Post,* Oct. 13, 2002.

251 Three years later, in remarks: The interview took place on April 15, 1994, and was broadcast on C-Span. YouTube returns several dozen versions with a search for "Cheney," "Iraq," and "1994." The two most popular had been viewed a combined three million times by mid-2008.

Chapter Ten: Supply Side

255 Air Force Two touched down: E-mail from Cheney spokeswoman Lea Ann McBride to author, May 24, 2007: "The records maintained by the scheduling office indicate the VP attended the mtgs at the Greenbrier on February 6, 2003. . . . He took AFII and drove from local airport. Flight from Andrews to Greenbrier Valley Airport was approx 50 mins, followed by a short drive to the Greenbrier for the meetings which appear to have started around 7pm." U.S. Naval Observatory data recorded sunset at 5:50 p.m. that day in White Sulphur Springs. See http://aa.usno.navy.mil/data/docs/RS__OneDay.php.

255 The historic hotel had been equipped: The secret was blown in 1992, after the fall of the Soviet Union, and President Clinton decommissioned the facility three years later. See Ted Gup, "The Ultimate Congressional Hideaway," *Washington Post,* May 31, 1992, at http:// www.washingtonpost.com/wp-srv/local/daily/july/25/brierl.htm.

255 Its cavernous underground bunker: See Bunker Tour schedule, http://www.greenbrier .com/site/activities-detail.aspx?cid/2035.

256 He had spent the morning, February 6, 2003: Remarks by the Vice President at Ceremony Dedicated to the Crew of the Space Shuttle *Columbia,* the National Cathedral, Feb. 6, 2003, 10:48 a.m., http://www.whitehouse.gov/news/releases/2003/02/20030206-8.html.

256 Glenn Hubbard, then chairman: E-mail from Glenn Hubbard to author, June 3, 2008, and interview with Glenn Hubbard by Jo Becker, Aug. 23, 2006.

256 "The president's attention and energy": Interview with Michael Gerson by Jo Becker, Nov. 1, 2006.

257 "For the whole first campaign": See chapter 3 for more on the waitress, and the difference between Bush's approach and Cheney's.

257 "There was a question of priorities": Interview with Karl Rove, Nov. 20, 2006.

257 The story became well known: Jude Wanniski, *The Way the World Works* (New York: Basic Books, 1978). In the Gateway paperback edition of 1998, the story comes on p. 299.

257 Ford had just given a speech: Speech by President Gerald Ford, "Whip Inflation Now," Oct. 8, 1974, at http://millercenter.org/scripps/archive/speeches/detail/3283.

258 He picked up a pen and a napkin: An image of the curve may be seen at http://www
.qando.net/blog/images/laffer.gif.

258 "They got it," Laffer said: Interview with Arthur Laffer by Jo Becker, July 21, 2006.

258 In 1983, when supply-side conservatives: *The MacNeil/Lehrer Report,* PBS, June 14, 1983.

259 "I'm not convinced": Interviews with Cesar Conda and Lawrence Kudlow by Jo Becker,
2006 and 2007.

259 "He was a late convert": Conda interview, June 24, 2007.

259 In Bush's first year: There are very few written references to the review board's existence. One of them is a memo for heads of departments and agencies prepared by Joshua B.
Bolten, then director of the Office of Management and Budget. See "Budget Discipline for
Agency Administrative Actions," May 23, 2005, p. 2, at http://media.washingtonpost.com/
wp-srv/politics/documents/cheney/boloton__omb__m05-13.pdf.

260 "In the three budgets": Interview with Mitch Daniels by Jo Becker, Sept. 6, 2006.

261 In the second half of 2002: The description of Cheney's consultations in this section is
based on interview with Brian V. McCormack by author and interviews with Rob Nichols,
Lawrence Kudlow, Michael Boskin, Arthur Laffer, Martin Feldstein, Cesar Conda, and
John Makin by Jo Becker, 2006 and 2007.

262 Kudlow had once advised Ronald Reagan: See Sylvia Nasar, "Economist Is Said to
Enter a Six-Month Drug Program," *New York Times,* July 4, 1995. Kudlow acknowledged
the problem. See, e.g., this blog entry: "Please take it from my experience—alcohol and drug
addiction wrecked my life. Completely. Nowadays, if I get a little blue, I work harder in my
twelve-step group, pray more frequently, and stay close to my family and friends. With
God's grace, I have nine and a half years sober and clean." Kudlow's Money Politics, Nov.
29, 2004, at http://lkmp.blogspot.com/2004/11/high-for-holidays__29.html.

262 The new "chained" consumer price index: The Chained Consumer Price Index for All
Urban Consumers, designated C-CPI-U, was introduced by the Bureau of Labor Statistics on
August 16, 2002. See http://findarticles.com/p/articles/mi__m1153/is__9__125/ai__96306436.

262–63 Aaron Friedberg, a senior staff member: Interview with Aaron Friedberg, Dec. 13,
2006.

263 Cheney's script was compressed: Some of Cheney's handwritten notes were introduced
as evidence in Scooter Libby's perjury trial. See, for example, Government Exhibit GX53201.
The writing at the top of the page is Libby's print. At the bottom is Cheney's script. Available
at http://www.usdoj.gov/usao/iln/osc/exhibits/0130/GX53201.PDF.

264 Cheney no longer worried: E-mail from Glenn Hubbard to author, June 3, 2008, and
interviews by Jo Becker with Wayne Angell, Jack Kemp, and Cesar Conda, 2006. See also
Nina Easton, "Why Is Dick Cheney Smiling?" *Fortune,* Nov. 25, 2007.

264 The Laffer Curve was back: Years later, when Representative Charlie Rangel proposed
to roll back the 2001 and 2003 tax cuts, Cheney asserted that the rate cuts *increased* tax revenues. Speaking of Rangel's plan, he said, "I think it's bad in several respects. It raises the
rate on capital gains. It raises the rate on dividends. It raises the top rate on the income tax.
Those are terrible ideas. Those are all rates we reduced when we came in, in 2001 and 2003.
They've been absolutely crucial to driving this economy and to creating the incentives out
there for businesses to invest and to create more jobs and more wealth. They're the prime

reason we've seen an increase in tax revenues." *Kudlow & Company,* CNBC, Oct. 26, 2007. That assertion is not widely accepted among nonpartisan analysts. Revenues grew for a variety of reasons, but they remained well below the growth projected by the Congressional Budget Office just before the two big Bush-Cheney tax cuts in 2001 and 2003.

264 O'Neill and Alan Greenspan: Interviews with confidential White House source and a source who had contemporary knowledge of Greenspan's views, 2006. See also Suskind, *The Price of Loyalty,* pp. 274–82.

265 According to author Ron Suskind: Suskind, *The Price of Loyalty,* p. 284. O'Neill proved correct about the budget: in fiscal year 2004, after the 2003 tax cuts and the launch of war in Iraq, the deficit reached a record $413 billion.

266 War with Iraq, he said: "Bush Economic Aide Says Cost of Iraq War May Top $100 Billion," *Wall Street Journal,* Sept. 16, 2002. Lindsey said it would be between 1 and 2 percent of gross domestic product, which in 2002 would have meant $105 billion to $210 billion. By mid-2008 the Congressional Budget Office said the war cost had surpassed $500 billion.

266 Bush told his press secretary: See McClellan, *What Happened.*

266 "Reagan proved deficits don't matter": Suskind, *The Price of Loyalty,* p. 290. Years later the vice president appeared to confirm that. "The conversation, as I recall, was in a political context," he said. See Nina Easton, "Why Is Dick Cheney Smiling?" *Fortune,* Nov. 25, 2007.

267 He no longer had inside knowledge: Angell was also more inclined to supply-side theory than Greenspan was, which made him a natural ally for Cheney. No less an authority than Larry Kudlow touted Angell for treasury secretary, describing him as a "brave free-enterprise warrior" who backed "supply-side tax cuts to promote economic growth." Larry Kudlow, "An Angell in Waiting: The Right Guy for Treasury," *National Review Online,* Dec. 9, 2000.

267 "The vice president was certainly aware": Interview with Wayne Angell by Jo Becker, Oct. 9, 2006.

268 Not until years later did Greenspan learn: Greenspan learned about it from questions conveyed to him by the author and Jo Becker in September 2006. He declined to make any public comment.

268 Conda had years of experience: Conda, now at the lobby firm Navigators LLC, describes his résumé at http://www.navigatorsllc.com/CesarConda/26/default.aspx.

268 The paper Conda reviewed: Cheney got an advance copy. The Fed later published it. See Thomas Laubach, Board of Governors of the Federal Reserve System, "New Evidence on the Interest Rate Effects of Budget Deficits and Debt," May 2003, at www.federalreserve .gov/Pubs/feds/2003/200312/200312pap.pdf. Laubach, who has since taken a post at the University of Frankfurt, did not reply to inquiries by the author.

269 Josh Bolten, Paul O'Neill, and Mitch Daniels: The account of this meeting is from interviews with Daniels, Hubbard, and Conda, and from Suskind, *The Price of Loyalty,* pp. 295ff.

269 When Bush unveiled his tax package: The Bush administration proposal came in the initial version of HR 2, the "Jobs and Growth Tax Act of 2003," available at http://media .washingtonpost.com/wp-srv/politics/documents/cheney/2003__taxbill__HR2__House Version.pdf.

271 **"Yes, sir?" Paul O'Neill said:** O'Neill provided his account of the conversation, and his notes, in Suskind, *The Price of Loyalty,* p. 309.

271 **"I was a big advocate of his, without question":** Transcript of interview with Vice President Cheney by *USA Today* and the *Los Angeles Times,* Jan. 18, 2004.

271 **When George Bush came to the Greenbrier:** Remarks at the Congress of Tomorrow Republican Retreat Reception in White Sulphur Springs, West Virginia, Feb. 9, 2003, available at http://findarticles.com/p/articles/mi__m2889/is__7__39/ai__99377590/print.

274 **Glenn Hubbard, who chaired:** Glenn Hubbard, e-mail to author, June 3, 2008.

CHAPTER ELEVEN: OFF THE TRACKS

277 *The president doesn't want this:* The account of this meeting is based on interviews with Jack Goldsmith, who was in attendance, and another government official who had access to a contemporary report of what transpired. The two accounts agree that the language in italics is a close paraphrase of Addington's. Goldsmith's memoir of his service in the Bush administration alludes to the episode in one sentence. See Goldsmith, *The Terror Presidency,* pp. 181–82. Through spokesmen, Potenza, Brenner, and Addington declined to be interviewed. Patrick Philbin, who was also present, declined to discuss the meeting.

A broad note on sourcing for this chapter: In interviews, people with classified knowledge of the NSA surveillance program were careful to stay well clear of its operations and legal problems. No official who was "read in" to the program would speak to me, on or off the record, about those things.

At a hearing of the Senate Judiciary Committee on Oct. 2, 2007, Goldsmith explained his constraints in an exchange with Senator Arlen Specter:

> GOLDSMITH: The government has forbidden me from talking about the legal analysis.
>
> SPECTER: Now, wait a minute. You might not be able to tell us about classified material. You might not be able to tell us about what you told the President or his subordinates. But I think you can tell us what constitutional law principle was violated.
>
> GOLDSMITH: Well, that's—unfortunately the executive branch has taken the view, and unfortunately I'm bound by this by contract and law.
>
> SPECTER: That you can't even say what constitutional law principle was violated?
>
> GOLDSMITH: They've told me that I'm not allowed to talk about the legal analysis.

278 **Cheney would come close to leading them off a cliff:** This story is told throughout chapters 11 and 12.

278 **Their subject was codeword-classified:** Letter from Shannen Coffin to Senator Patrick Leahy, Aug. 20, 2007, p. 2, refers to the documents as "Top Secret/Codeword." That means that they are handled as "sensitive compartmented information," with special procedures. See Director of Central Intelligence Directive 1/19, "Security Policy for Sensitive Compart-

mented Information and Security Policy Manual," Mar. 1, 1995, available at http://www.fas
.org/irp/offdocs/dcid1-19.html, which states: "The primary security principle in safeguard-
ing SCI is to ensure that it is accessible only by those persons with appropriate clearance,
access approval, clearly identified need-to-know, and an appropriate indoctrination."

278 In spy parlance it was a SCIF: In the NBC series *Get Smart,* a spy farce broadcast in the
1960s, the (comically defective) Cone of Silence descended from the ceiling to muffle the
hero's secret conversations. In the U.S. government, those communications take place in a
SCIF, pronounced "skiff," which is described in Director of Central Intelligence Directive
6/9, "Physical Security Standards for Sensitive Compartmented Information Facilities,"
Nov. 18, 2002, available at http://www.fas.org/irp/offdocs/dcid6-9.htm.

278 They already knew the really secret stuff: Brenner was the in-house watchdog over "all
aspects of NSA's signals intelligence," according to the official job description. Potenza had
been the agency's first- or second-ranking lawyer for a decade.

278 The program, a hybrid: Interviews with confidential sources, 2006 through 2008.
Hayden and White House counsel Alberto Gonzales acknowledged almost from the beginning, in elliptical comments, that there was more to the program than Bush confirmed
publicly in late 2005. In a letter to Senator Arlen Specter, Director of National Intelligence
Mike McConnell made the clearest public statement that the Presidential Authorizations
covered "various intelligence activities." The "details of these activities changed in certain respects over time and I understand from the Department of Justice these activities
rested on different legal bases." McConnell to Specter, July 31, 2007, available at http://www
.washingtonpost.com/wp-srv/politics/documents/NID__Specter073107.pdf.

278 spread its tentacles to the FBI, the CIA: FBI director Robert Mueller confirmed his
bureau's connection to the program the same month: "I . . . understand the Department of
Justice had some concerns about the legality of an NSA program. That affected the FBI in
the sense that we received pieces of information from the NSA. . . . So my concern was to
assure that whatever activity we undertook as a result of the information we received was
done appropriately and legally." New legislative authority for the program, Mueller said,
"would help not just the FBI, but operating together with NSA, the CIA, the DIA, all of
whom—all of us share the same responsibility to protect the homeland." Hearing of the
House Judiciary Committee, July 26, 2007.

279 Hayden, a reassuring uniformed presence: Interviews with Senator Bob Graham, Senator Pat Roberts, and Representative Jane Harman, December 2005 and January 2006.
Hayden used identical language at a news conference after portions of the surveillance program became public. See "Remarks by General Michael V. Hayden," National Press Club,
Washington, D.C., Jan. 23, 2006. There was another lawyer involved in the NSA discussions,
then–general counsel Robert Deitz, but he was detailed soon after that for a lengthy assignment at the Pentagon.

279 "I was concerned about the legality": President Discusses War on Terror and Operation
Iraqi Freedom, Mar. 20, 2006, available at http://www.whitehouse.gov/news/releases/2006/03/
print/20060320-7.html.

279 Brenner and Potenza had told Hayden: This account is based on interviews with confidential sources familiar with their analysis. In an exchange with Senator Dianne Feinstein, Hayden confirmed that his lawyers gave only oral, not written, advice, and that they based it on the president's commander-in-chief powers under Article II of the Constitution:

> HAYDEN: I then brought the question to NSA lawyers. . . .
>
> FEINSTEIN: Did they put anything in writing?
>
> HAYDEN: No, and I did not ask for it. I asked them just to look at the authoriza-
> tion, and then come back and tell me. . . . Although they didn't rule out other
> underpinnings for the president's authorization, they talked to me about Ar-
> ticle II.

Hayden said the lawyers noted that there were other issues involved and did "not rule out" that the program could be supported with other legal arguments, but they rendered no such opinion. "Confirmation Hearing of Michael Hayden to Be Director of the Central Intelligence Agency," Senate Select Committee on Intelligence, May 18, 2006.

279 When the program began: Interviews with two confidential sources, 2008, both of whom read Yoo's first memorandum. They declined to discuss its contents, other than to say that Yoo made no reference to an actual surveillance program. One of the officials, who knew when Yoo was "read in," said it was not before November. The date of the program's inception is provided in Coffin letter to Leahy, Aug. 20, 2007.

280 "Yoo wrote a broad but generic memorandum": John C. Yoo and Robert J. Delahunty, Authority for Use of Military Force to Combat Terrorist Activities Within the United States, Oct. 23, 2001. The opinion did not become public until the Obama administration released it, shortly after taking office in January 2009. See http://www.usdoj.gov/opa/documents/olc-memos.htm.

280 Brenner and Potenza figured: Those memoranda, which have never been made public, were dated Oct. 4 and Nov. 2, 2001; Jan. 9, May 17, and Oct. 11, 2002; and Feb. 25, 2003. See Coffin letter to Leahy, Aug. 20, 2007.

280 Without the program, they said: Interviews with confidential sources from the legislative and executive branches who were present for Cheney's and Addington's comments.

280 *Did no one else care?:* Three White House lawyers, in interviews, said Addington asked this question often, exasperated that colleagues did not take the pains he took to protect executive prerogatives.

280–81 "Hayden is a very accomplished": Interview, 2008.

281 The technical, operational, and legal issues: Here is what Brenner wrote about NSA operations in general, without reference to the "Terrorist Surveillance Program," just a few months after the meeting with Addington: "You must know where to dip the bucket. Gathering all the bits of data floating around in the hope that you can sort through it all—in effect, swallowing the sea—is a fatuous idea. No organization, and no technology, can do it. Doing SIGINT for foreign intelligence purposes therefore implies electronic filtering, sorting, and dissemination systems of amazing sophistication, but that are imperfect. Nor does the problem end here. Once you gather data, you must decrypt it, translate it, analyze it to make sense of it, sanitize it to protect the sources and methods of collection, and route it—or parts of it—to the people who need to know it. Routing, or dissemination, is itself an enormously complex problem." See Joel F. Brenner, "Information Oversight: Practical Lessons from Foreign Intelligence," Heritage Lecture #851, Sept. 30, 2004, available at http://www .heritage.org/research/NationalSecurity/h1851.cfm.

281 Brenner and Potenza understood the NSA machinery: For a thorough survey of the legal infrastructure, see David S. Kris and J. Douglas Wilson, *National Security Investigations and Prosecutions* (Eagan, Minn.: Thomson/West, 2007).

281 No novice could master all that quickly: Yoo claimed, for example, that Congress had not intended to restrict the president from conducting warrantless surveillance for "national security" purposes when it said that FISA would be the "exclusive" legal means of domestic surveillance for intelligence and counterterrorism. When disclosed publicly, this assertion attracted no support from any legal scholar and was widely described as preposterous. See chapter 6 for Yoo's language.

281 If that were not enough, Potenza: Potenza's party registration in Maryland is a public record. I do not know for a fact that Addington was aware of that, but three Bush administration officials said Addington checked routinely on the party memberships and political contributions of lawyers he encountered, and he talked about his findings in White House conversations. Two officials said, for example, that Addington made dismissive references to Bryan Cunningham, the deputy to National Security Council legal counsel John Bellinger, as a Clinton Democrat.

282 Its controlling documents, which gave strategic direction: Interviews with confidential sources. The official and rather grand name for the roadway between the West Wing and the EEOB is West Executive Avenue, but "alley" or "driveway" is a better fit for the short, dead-end stretch of asphalt used for automobile access by high-ranking officials and their visitors.

282 Each authorization package included a fresh assessment: In his memoir, Tenet called it "a comprehensive assessment of the value of continuing the program." George Tenet with Bill Harlow, *At the Center of the Storm: My Years at the CIA* (New York: HarperCollins, 2007), p. 238.

282 There was also a brief testament: Interviews with two confidential government sources, 2007. James B. Comey testified after leaving his post as Ashcroft's deputy: "I'm quite certain that there wasn't a statute or regulation that required it, but that it was the way in which this matter had operated since the beginning. I don't—I think the administration had sought the Department of Justice, the attorney general's certification as to form and legality." Hearing of the Senate Judiciary Committee, May 15, 2007.

282 Addington typed on a Tempest-shielded computer: The layout of Addington's office was described by a confidential source. All classified documents must be written and stored on a computer with Tempest shielding, which prevents the inadvertent emanation of signals, such as from a display monitor, that might be intercepted by others. A good introduction is at http://www.fas.org/irp/program/security/tempest.htm.

282 Back in 2001, it had been Cheney: See chapter 6.

283 "I would consider him *a* drafter, not *the* drafter": Interview with Andrew Card, May 4, 2008.

283 Addington pulled out a folder: It is true by definition that the classification markings were new to Goldsmith, because the program was codeword-classified. Until an official is "read in," he does not know there is a special access program with that codeword. If a hypothetical program was called "Banana," the document would be marked at the top and bottom of each page with TOP SECRET / BANANA.

283 "David Addington was doing all the legal work": Interview with Jack Goldsmith, December 2007.

284 "Bellinger didn't know," said Bryan Cunningham: Interview with Bryan Cunningham, June 27, 2006.

284 Hayden had to brief close to a hundred employees: He told senators later that he briefed "80, 90 people" in his biggest conference room. Hayden confirmation hearing, May 18, 2006.

284 Attorney General John Ashcroft balked: Yoo acknowledged cutting out members of his chain of command, citing the pressures of time and orders from the White House, but he denied doing anything without Ashcroft's knowledge. Five high-ranking departmental officials said otherwise in confidential interviews, stating that Ashcroft sometimes learned of Yoo's opinions after the fact from others. "There was a huge problem with John Yoo giving advice to the White House without running it through the proper channels," one of the officials said. "OLC is an extension of the attorney general's authority. It doesn't have any independent authority. It is absolutely improper for anyone in OLC to give advice or issue opinions without it being run through the proper channels. Our view was that John Yoo was a frequent violator of that rule." In Yoo's defense, one White House lawyer said that if Ashcroft was unaware of Yoo's work "the reason was speed. They wanted to reach right down to the substantive policy person" because "things were happening so fast. Policy was being made in real time. Things that normally take eight to ten months were getting done in eight to ten days." Interview with Bradford Berenson by Jo Becker, Sept. 14, 2006.

285 He urged the government to fight: The memo to Rumsfeld is quoted in Goldsmith, *The Terror Presidency,* p. 60. See also pp. 21, 59. For an example of his academic scholarship see Jack L. Goldsmith and Eric A. Posner, *The Limits of International Law* (New York: Oxford University Press, 2005).

285 emerging from Yale Law School as a conservative: Goldsmith, *The Terror Presidency,* pp. 19–20.

285 "The only thing I could think of": Goldsmith's account of his interview for the OLC job is on pp. 25–30 of *The Terror Presidency.*

285 But they did not discuss the subjects: Goldsmith later wrote that Addington did not appear to know he had other opposing views: "While I believed the government could detain enemy combatants, I thought it needed more elaborate procedures for identifying and detaining them, and had been working on this issue since I arrived at the Pentagon. I had long argued to Haynes that the administration should embrace rather than resist judicial review of its wartime legal policy decisions. I could not understand why the administration failed to work with a Congress controlled by its own party to put all of its antiterrorism policies on a sounder legal footing. And I had been critical, again only to Haynes, of what I viewed as unnecessarily broad assertions of presidential power in an obscure draft OLC opinion by John Yoo." Goldsmith, *The Terror Presidency,* p. 29.

286 He had lettered in football, baseball, and soccer: Interview with Jack Goldsmith, Apr. 26, 2008. Other biographical details come from Goldsmith, *The Terror Presidency,* pp. 19–21.

286 The son of a Miss Teenage Arkansas: Goldsmith, *The Terror Presidency,* p. 20, called his stepfather "a mob-connected Teamsters executive named Chuck O'Brien who was Jimmy Hoffa's right-hand man and for decades a leading suspect in Hoffa's disappearance." For one among many news accounts of O'Brien's expulsion from the Teamsters for ties to organized crime, see http://www.cbc.ca/news/background/hoffa/.

287 He cited a 1995 case: Interview with confidential source who read the e-mail. At issue was "federalism," the division of power between state governments and Washington. Addington cited *United States v. Lopez,* 514 U.S. 549 (1995).

287 With Yoo, he had written muscular memos: Patrick F. Philbin and John Yoo to William J. Haynes II, "Possible Habeas Jurisdiction over Aliens Held in Guantanamo Bay, Cuba," Dec. 28, 2001, available in Karen J. Greenberg and Joshua L. Dratel, *The Torture Papers* (New York: Cambridge University Press, 2005), p. 29. Philbin also wrote the opinion that gave a green light to military commissions: Patrick F. Philbin to Alberto R. Gonzales, "Legality of the Use of Military Commissions to Try Terrorists," Nov. 6, 2001. See chapter 6.

288 Some of the things the program did: Philbin declined to be interviewed. The description of his overall conclusion comes from others familiar with his work. Corroboration comes from subsequent decisions by the Bush administration, cited below, to seek authority from Congress and the Foreign Intelligence Surveillance Court. In the internal 2004 debates, the White House claimed not to need that external authority.

288 On its face, the program violated: In general, a judicial warrant, either from a criminal court or a special intelligence court, is "the exclusive means" for "any person" to intercept domestic wire, oral, or electronic communications. Violation of those statutes is a felony punishable by five years in jail. See "Interception and Disclosure of Wire, Oral, or Electronic Communications Prohibited," 18 U.S.C. 2511(1) and (4), and the Foreign Intelligence Surveillance Act, 50 U.S.C. 1809. There is a provision for emergency surveillance without a warrant, but it has its own strict limits that the program did not respect. See Kris and Wilson, *National Security Investigations and Prosecution.*

The legal issues identified in this chapter are drawn from a review of reference works, law journals, and interviews with more than two dozen government experts on electronic surveillance and its legal rules, none of whom were cleared for access to the program when we spoke. It is likely that Philbin's concerns covered some of these issues, because all of them were addressed by the Bush administration in subsequent years. (See following notes.) No one with specific knowledge of Philbin's legal analysis agreed to discuss it for this book.

288 It was possible to argue that Congress: See interview with chief FISA judge Royce Lamberth in chapter 6. After portions of the program were disclosed, the Justice Department claimed authority in the Authorization for Use of Military Force of Sept. 18, 2001, 115 Stat. 224 (2001), because intelligence gathering "is a fundamental incident" of the use of force. See "Legal Authority for the Recently Disclosed NSA Activities," Department of Justice, Dec. 22, 2005. That resolution specified that its authority covered only those who aided or abetted the September 11 attacks. It could not be used, therefore, to justify a broad sweep for information about potential attacks from any quarter—for example, from Hezbollah or Iran. Many scholars said the AUMF supplied no valid exception to surveillance laws at all because the standard practice in construing apparent conflicts among statutes is to give priority to the specific (no warrantless surveillance) over the general (military force permitted in response to 9/11). In negotiations with Congress over the USA Patriot Act in October 2001, the Bush administration specifically declined invitations to propose new statutory authority for warrantless surveillance.

288 Lawyers could debate which of two: The two alternatives are the full memberships of two congressional committees, or eight specified senior leaders of Congress. For two and a half years, until the Justice Department refused to certify the program's legality, the Bush administration notified only four of the specified leaders. Letter of John Negroponte to Dennis Hastert, May 17, 2006, on file with author. For U.S. intelligence activities in general, including any "significant anticipated intelligence activity," the president is obliged by statute to keep the entire House and Senate Intelligence committees "fully and currently informed." Intelligence Authorization Act of 1991, PL 102-88. See also National Security Act of 1947, 50 U.S.C. 413–413(2b). In special cases involving "covert action," in which the president determines that additional secrecy is required "to meet extraordinary circumstances affecting vital interests of the United States," the president is authorized to limit reporting to the so-called Gang of Eight—the chairmen and ranking members of the congressional intelligence committees and the House and Senate majority and minority leaders. See National Security Act of 1947, 50 U.S.C. 413b. For a detailed analysis of the notification requirements, see Alfred Cumming, "Statutory Procedures Under Which Congress Is to Be Informed of U.S. Intelligence Activities, Including Covert Actions," Congressional Research Service, Jan. 18, 2006, available at http://epic.org/privacy/terrorism/fisa/crs11806.pdf.

288 There was a case to be made: Interviews with confidential U.S. government sources, 2006 and 2007. Verizon's terms of service in mid-2006, for example, promised customers privacy but stated: "However, we do release customer information without involving you if disclosure is required by law *or to protect the safety* of customers, employees or property." (Emphasis added.) See http://www22.verizon.com/about/privacy/customer/. The weakness of this argument became clear in 2007 and 2008, when the Bush administration campaigned relentlessly for retroactive liability protection for telecommunications companies that assisted the government in its surveillance.

In a 2006 news release, an attorney for Joseph Nacchio, the former chairman of Qwest Communications, said that in the fall of 2001 the company "was approached to permit the Government access to the private telephone records of Qwest customers. Mr. Nacchio made inquiry as to whether a warrant or other legal process had been secured in support of that request. When he learned that no such authority had been granted and that there was a disinclination on the part of the authorities to use any legal process, including the Special Court which had been established to handle such matters, Mr. Nacchio concluded that these requests violated the privacy requirements of the Telecommunications Act." Statement by Herbert Stern, May 12, 2006.

289 Unless the program rejected surveillance laws altogether: The Foreign Intelligence Surveillance Act of 1978, 50 U.S.C. 1801(f), offers four different definitions of "electronic surveillance." If the interception takes place "in the United States . . . other than from a wire or radio communication," then the government must have a warrant even if the person doing the communicating is neither an American nor on American soil. That is much stricter than the standard for eavesdropping on telephone calls.

289 Another problem for e-mail surveillance: Kenneth Wainstein, chief of the Justice Department's national security division, made a public allusion to this problem at an American Bar Association breakfast on March 3, 2008. He was explaining the need for changes in surveillance law. At the time of the 2004 legal review the Bush administration sought no authority from Congress to solve the problem Wainstein described: "The concern is . . . especially with e-mail, at the time of interception you don't know where the recipient is going to be. So carving the world of surveillance up between foreign-to-foreign and everything else is good in certain areas of surveillance, but for instance in e-mail it doesn't get you where you need to be, because at the time of surveillance you're not going to know if it's foreign-to-foreign or foreign-to-domestic and that's our—that's the dilemma." The remark comes shortly after the one-hour mark on this audio recording: http://www.abanet.org/natsecurity/multimedia/FISA__reform__panel__March__3__2008__WS__30144.mp3.

289 Advocates of the program found it absurd: Confidential interview with U.S. government official. This point was also made in public after the Bush administration decided to seek a change in surveillance laws, but during the legal battle over the special surveillance program in 2004 the White House insisted it needed no authority from Congress. Robert L. Deitz of the NSA later testified: "We think the most significant factor in determining whether or not a court order is required ought to be the location of the target of the surveillance, and that other factors such as where the surveillance takes place and the mode of communication surveilled should not play a role in this determination." Statement for the Record, House Judiciary Committee, Sept. 6, 2006, on file with author.

290 "He reserved his comments for a time": Interview with John Ashcroft, Sept. 21, 2006.

290 He asked for . . . Jim Comey: Goldsmith, *The Terror Presidency,* p. 159.

290 "He always invoked the president, not the vice president": Later, when asked to attend a congressional hearing after he replaced Scooter Libby as Cheney's chief of staff, Addington would assert through his lawyer: "The Chief of Staff to the Vice President is an employee of the Vice President, and not the President, and therefore is not in a position to speak on behalf of the President." Letter from Kathryn L. Wheelbarger, counsel to the vice president, to Perry Apelbaum, chief of staff and counsel to the House Judiciary Committee, Apr. 18, 2008. Even as a strictly literal matter, this did not seem to be true: Addington had inherited Libby's additional title of "assistant to the president." It certainly bore no resemblance to reports from at least two dozen witnesses that Addington spoke with absolute confidence, during internal debates, for the Bush administration as a whole.

291 People around the president began calling him "Cuomey": Two officials said in interviews they heard the pejorative used by members of the White House staff. The account of Bush's garble at the Iowa rally comes from Comey, who heard it from his mother-in-law, Maurene Failor. Her political contribution is noted in Federal Election Commission records. The first report of the nickname came in Daniel Klaidman, Stuart Taylor Jr., and Evan Thomas, "Palace Revolt," *Newsweek,* Feb. 6, 2006.

291 "You're the head of the Office of Legal Counsel": According to Goldsmith, Addington and Gonzales delivered variations on this message four or five times. Interviews with Jack Goldsmith, 2007 and 2008.

292 "worried very, very much": Testimony of Jack L. Goldsmith, Senate Judiciary Committee, Oct. 2, 2007. In his memoir, Goldsmith explained, "I first encountered the program in 2003–2004, long after it had been integrated into the post-9/11 counterterrorism architecture. Putting it legally aright at that point, without destroying some of the government's most important counterterrorism tools, was by far the hardest challenge I faced in government." Goldsmith, *The Terror Presidency,* p. 182.

292 "I'm so glad you're getting read in": Interview with James B. Comey, May 16, 2008. When Comey and Hayden met, Kerry's main rivals for the Democratic nomination, Howard Dean and John Edwards, were on the verge of dropping out.

292 "Holy shit, what is the head of the NSA": For the staff conversation after Comey's meeting with Hayden, interview with participant.

293 "agreed on a course of action": Comey testimony before Senate Judiciary Committee, May 15, 2007.

294 "If you rule that way, the blood": In his memoir, Goldsmith quoted the outburst but did not quite name the subject. Goldsmith, *The Terror Presidency,* p. 71. In an interview in April 2008, he said the bad news he delivered that day involved the NSA surveillance program. Though Addington was shouting, Goldsmith did not interpret him to be indulging in hyperbole. "Addington didn't have to tell me the blood of a hundred thousand people could be on my hands," Goldsmith said. "Those are stakes we all understood."

295 Bush was across the river in Arlington: Bush's schedule showed this 11:00 a.m. appearance: President Commends Recipients of Malcolm Baldrige Awards, Crystal Gateway Marriott, Arlington, Virginia.

295 "How can you possibly be reversing course": This account of the meeting draws on interviews with two officials who had contemporary knowledge of and access to unclassified notes of what transpired. They did not describe the substance of the program. The times of and participants in the two meetings in Card's office were recorded in notes from Mueller released by the Justice Department. "RSM Program Log," accompanying letter from Richard C. Powers to Representative John Conyers, Aug. 14, 2007.

296 "No *good* lawyer," Comey said: Comey's jab about "no good lawyer" was first reported in Scott Shane, David Johnston, and James Risen, "Secret U.S. Endorsement of Severe Interrogations," *New York Times,* Oct. 4, 2007.

296 "I don't think it would be appropriate": Card interview, May 4, 2008. Card explained the reasons for delay but declined to say exactly when he notified Bush of the legal crisis. Three sources said Bush got his first word on Wednesday and did not know the breadth of the Justice Department problem until at least late Thursday.

297 They huddled in the West Wing lobby: Intervie w with eyewitness, 2008.

298 "The program's classified code name": The code name "Stellar Wind" was first disclosed in Michael Isikoff, "The Fed Who Blew the Whistle," *Newsweek,* Dec. 22, 2008.

298 "I think this is something I am not a part of": The account of this conversation comes from confidential sources with contemporary knowledge.

298 **Like Steve Hadley and John Gordon and Secretary of Homeland Security Tom Ridge:** Interviews with senior national security officials, 2006, 2007, and 2008. One White House aide recounted a telephone call from Ridge when the NSA story broke in the *New York Times* in December 2005. "I sort of knew something was up," the aide said. "You can't be around there that long and in the thick of things and not know something is up. But when Tom asked me was I involved, I said, 'Absolutely not.' He was the secretary of homeland security, and this was domestic surveillance, and he didn't know about it!"

CHAPTER TWELVE: U-TURN ON CONSTITUTION AVENUE

299 **"They probably thought there was a palace coup":** Goldsmith interview.

300 **Bush, even now, was nowhere in the picture:** President's Daily Schedule, Mar. 10, 2004, 12:15 p.m., President Discusses Jobs & Trade at Women's Entrepreneurship Forum, Cleveland Convention Center, Cleveland, Ohio.

300 **Some of them, Cheney said:** The account of this meeting is from interviews with two participants, and with two others with subsequent knowledge of what transpired. It also draws, below, on the testimony of Alberto Gonzales. Until this day, Cheney had briefed only the Intelligence chairmen and vice chairmen and—once, when the program needed secret funds—the chairman and ranking member of the Senate Defense Appropriations Subcommittee. Speaker of the House Dennis Hastert, Senate Majority Leader Bill Frist, and Senate Minority Leader Tom Daschle had never heard of the program before. House Minority Leader Nancy Pelosi knew about it because she served previously as the ranking Democrat on the Intelligence Committee. The full list of congressional briefings is in the Negroponte letter to Hastert, May 17, 2006.

300 **not one photon or one electron more:** This was another regular briefing point for Hayden, who eventually made it in public. Testimony of Michael V. Hayden, Senate Select Committee on Intelligence, May 18, 2006.

300 **"'Despite the recommendation of the deputy attorney general'":** Testimony of Alberto Gonzales, Senate Judiciary Committee, July 24, 2007.

301 **Tom Daschle . . . said the Gonzales story:** E-mail from Tom Daschle, May 6, 2008.

301 **"We were briefed on the operational details, period":** Interview with Jane Harman, Dec. 17, 2007.

302 **"Enough people have been briefed," Cheney said:** Harman interview.

302 **That evening, the FBI logged a call:** Interviews with two U.S. government sources. For reasons that remain unclear, the White House has never acknowledged that the call came from Bush. At a Senate hearing, Gonzales made heroic efforts to dodge the question:

> SEN. SCHUMER: Okay. Let me ask you this. Who sent you to the hospital?
> ATTY. GEN. GONZALES: Senator, what I can say is we'd had a very important meeting at the White House over one of the most—
> SEN. SCHUMER: I didn't ask that. I didn't ask for . . .
> ATTY. GEN. GONZALES: I'm answering your question, Senator—

SEN. SCHUMER: Who sent you? . . .

ATTY. GEN. GONZALES: It was one of the most important programs for the United States. It was important—it had been authorized by the president. I'll just say that the chief of staff of the president of the United States and the counsel of the president of the United States went to the hospital on behalf of the president of the United States.

SEN. SCHUMER: Did the president ask you to go?

ATTY. GEN. GONZALES: We were there on behalf of the president of the United States.

SEN. SCHUMER: I didn't ask you that. . . . Did the president ask you to go?

ATTY. GEN. GONZALES: Senator, we were there on behalf of the president of the United States.

SEN. SCHUMER: Why can't you answer that question?

ATTY. GEN. GONZALES: That's the answer that I can give you, Senator. . . .

SEN. SCHUMER: Did the vice president send you?

ATTY. GEN. GONZALES: Again, Senator, we were there on behalf of the president.

Testimony of Alberto Gonzales, Senate Judiciary Committee, July 24, 2007.

302 The next hour or two of the story: The hospital visit was first disclosed in Eric Lichtblau and James Risen, "Justice Deputy Resisted Parts of Spy Program," *New York Times,* Jan. 1, 2006. In the summer and fall of 2007, Comey, Goldsmith, and Gonzales gave riveting testimony about the visit. Ashcroft has never said a word.

303 men in their forties and fifties: Comey and Mueller testified about their hasty trips to the hospital. Goldsmith described his dash to Ashcroft's room, including the double-parking and the sprint upstairs, in an interview.

303 "How are you, general?": This exchange was quoted in Comey's written reply to questions for the record submitted by Senator Pat Leahy after the May 22, 2007, hearing.

303 "I remember thinking, what the *hell* does that mean?": Comey interview. The Gonzales formula seemed to make no legal sense because members of the Gang of Eight could not speak for Congress or notify their fellow legislators of the program. A true consensus among those leaders might add a sense of legitimacy, but it could not cure a conflict with legislation already on the books.

304 The White House counsel testified later: Senate Judiciary Committee hearing, July 24, 2007. Here is his exchange with Senator Arlen Specter.

ATTY. GEN. GONZALES: Senator, obviously there was concern about General Ashcroft's condition, and we would not have sought, nor did we intend to get any approval from General Ashcroft if in fact he wasn't fully competent to make that decision. But General—there are no rules governing whether or not General Ashcroft can decide "I'm feeling well enough to make this decision."

SEN. SPECTER: But Attorney General Gonzales, he had already given up his authority as attorney general. . . .

ATTY. GEN. GONZALES: And he could always reclaim it. There are no rules about—

SEN. SPECTER: While he was in the hospital under sedation? (Laughter.)

304 The showdown with the vice president: Comey interview.

304 Ashcroft said he never should have certified the program: Contemporary notes from Mueller, the FBI director, made cryptic reference to Ashcroft's complaint that he was "barred from obtaining the advice he needed by the strict compartmentalization rules of the WH." See "RSM Program Log," Aug. 14, 2007. The meaning of that line was much debated in commentary when the log was released. The FBI declined to elaborate. According to Comey, who gave a more detailed description of the exchange in an interview, Ashcroft specified a list of facts, and a list of legal concerns, that the secrecy rules had prevented him from discovering. Had he known them, he said, he would have withheld his signature before.

304 Janet Ashcroft "shook her head and stuck her tongue out": Interview with Jack Goldsmith, April 2008. Goldsmith first mentioned Mrs. Ashcroft's silent protest in Jeffrey Rosen, "Conscience of a Conservative," *New York Times Magazine,* Sept. 9, 2007.

305 Later, Card said privately: Interview with confidential source, 2008. Asked about his expression of regret, Card said he would not comment without knowing who told me about it. "It could be someone who doesn't know anything. . . . I don't think I talked about this with very many people, period. It's a pretty exclusive group. . . . You could be making it up to try to get me to confirm it." Card interview, May 4, 2008.

305 "After what I just witnessed": Comey testimony, May 15, 2007.

306 "I knew zilch": E-mail from Ed Whelan to author, May 5, 2008.

307 Card was "concerned," Comey said later: Comey testimony, May 15, 2007.

307 "I don't think people should try": Comey interview.

307 Trouble was still spreading: Interviews with three officials with firsthand knowledge of what Caproni and Muller said, 2008.

307 Asked that question in 2008, Tenet denied: Tenet's statement was made through a longtime spokesman and co-author of his memoir. Interview with William Harlow, May 5, 2008.

307 James A. Baker, the counselor for intelligence: Baker gave the author a brief interview, but would not discuss his dispute with the White House or any aspect of the program and its relationship to the FISA court, on or off the record. This account comes from other officials familiar with his work, and also benefits from stories by the best-sourced reporter covering the surveillance court. See Carol D. Leonnig, "Secret Court's Judges Were Warned About NSA Spy Data; Program May Have Led Improperly to Warrants," *Washington Post,* Feb. 9, 2006.

308 "she concluded they weren't being forthcoming": Lamberth interview, May 28, 2008.

308 "I was determined to stay there and fight": Interview with James A. Baker, May 13, 2008.

308 "Jim, we have a lot riding on your relationship": Baker declined to discuss the meeting with Addington or say whether there was any relationship between the program and the FISA court. This account comes from another participant. In Goldsmith's memoir, he quotes the "one bomb away" line without mentioning Baker's presence or the context of the conversation. Goldsmith, *Terror Presidency,* p. 181.

309 Bush gave a speech to evangelicals: From the president's published schedule:

> 10:42 a.m. Remarks Via Satellite by the President to the National Association of Evangelicals Convention, the Map Room.

11:51 a.m. President Makes Remarks Condemning the Madrid Bombings.

1:32 p.m. Remarks by the President in a Conversation on the Economy, USA Industries, Bay Shore, New York.

6:15 p.m. Remarks by the President at Bush-Cheney 2004 Reception, the Carltun East Meadow, New York City.

309 "My job was to communicate": Card interview, May 4, 2008.

310 The FBI director's daily log: The notes begin: "Meeting at Card's office with him at his request." See "RSM Program Log."

310 "His behavior makes no sense to me if he knew": Interview with former senior White House staff adviser, May 2008.

311 It has been widely reported: Even the legal correspondent who co-authored pathbreaking stories on the NSA program for the *New York Times* reported that the "line for the attorney general's signature remained blank." See Eric Lichtblau, *Bush's Law: The Remaking of American Justice* (New York: Pantheon, 2008). That report may have originated with a misreading of Comey's remark, in his 2007 Senate testimony, that "the program was reauthorized without us, without a signature from the Department of Justice attesting as to its legality."

312 Addington's words remain classified: As noted earlier in this chapter, constitutional scholars generally construe the "take care" clause of Article II to give the president authority to interpret the law; he cannot execute the law without deciding what it means. It is generally uncontroversial, as well, that a president may decline to enforce a statute, under some circumstances, if he believes in good faith that the Supreme Court would hold it to be unconstitutional. Bill Clinton's OLC chief, in an opinion that still stands as the Justice Department's guidance on the subject, emphasized the "special role" of the judicial branch in this analysis: "If . . . the President, exercising his independent judgment, determines *both* that a provision would violate the Constitution *and* that it is probable that the Court would agree with him, the President has the authority to decline to execute the statute." (Emphasis added.) See Walter Dellinger, "Presidential Authority to Decline to Execute Unconstitutional Statutes," Nov. 2, 1994, available at http://www.justice.gov/olc/nonexcut.htm. Some scholars maintain that the president may even disobey an order of the high court itself, if he believes the order encroaches on his fundamental constitutional powers. The general presumption in arguments for presidential disobedience is that the president must state his position openly, allowing the resulting struggle to be resolved by the tools of political combat and public opinion. See Dellinger, which says the president "may properly *announce* [emphasis in original] to Congress and to the public that he will not enforce a provision" of the law. George Bush's March 11, 2004, directive on the program, which included his declaration of authority to override the law, was highly classified and not shared with any member of Congress, even the Gang of Eight. Another extraordinary feature of the Addington draft was its sweep. Those who justify presidential disobedience have generally held that it must be as brief, as specific, and as narrowly framed as possible.

313 Addington's formula may have been: Richard Nixon made a version of this claim, years after the fact, in a television interview: "When the president does it, that means that it is not illegal." Interview with David Frost, May 19, 1977. One scholar described that as "the apo-

gee of presidential arrogance." Even so, Nixon is not known to have signed a formal directive that went nearly so far while in office. Nixon's warrantless wiretapping of antiwar
activists, to which he referred in his remark, formed the basis of one of the articles of impeachment voted against him. See David D. Cole, "Reviving the Nixon Doctrine: NSA
Spying, the Commander-in-Chief, and Executive Power in the War on Terror," *Washington
and Lee Journal of Civil Rights and Social Justice* 13 (2006).

313 Andy Card . . . spoke to at least one member: Interview with an official who received a
contemporary report from a witness to one of the calls, who was troubled by Card's language
and reprised it verbatim.

313 Dear Mr. President: Unsent resignation letter, dated March 16, 2004, on file with author.
This version is identical to the one Comey drafted on March 11, except for a single sentence
I have deleted at the ellipses. The day after drafting this letter, Comey met privately with
Bush. The meeting is described below. Comey then added a penultimate line to his
March 11 resignation letter: "I would give much not to be in this position. But, as I told you
during our private meeting last week, here I stand; I can do no other."

315 David Ayres, Ashcroft's chief of staff: Comey testimony.

316 "It was a compartmented issue," Rice recalled: Interview with Condoleezza Rice at the
State Department, May 20, 2008.

317 He had nearly reached the grandfather clock: The Oval Office briefing and Bush's
comment at the end were described by two participants.

317 "You don't look well": Quotations from the Bush-Comey conversation are taken verbatim from unclassified notes describing Comey's report of the meeting shortly afterward.
Two other depictions of the meeting, one from an aide to Bush, the other from an aide to
Comey, were similar but less detailed. Comey's e-mail, below, immediately after the meeting,
gives the same summary.

319 *The president just took me:* Contents of Comey's e-mail were provided verbatim by an
official who retained a copy. The reference to 5/6 is the date, May 6, 2004.

320 This was a rule-of-law question: Interview with a confidant of Mueller's who had contemporary knowledge of the exchange with Bush.

321 "Tell the DAG not to overreact": The Gonzales phone message was recounted by an
official with firsthand knowledge.

323 "Because he had an appendectomy, his brain didn't work?": Ashcroft lost his gallbladder, not his appendix. Press Briefing by Tony Snow, May 15, 2007, available at http://www
.whitehouse.gov/news/releases/2007/05/20070515-3.html.

324 What chief of staff before the Cheney years: Card absorbed an atmospheric view in the
White House of the Constitution and its meaning for executive authority. He did not sound
as though he had pondered it at length. When he told the author, "You're not Article Two,"
his next words were "You're Article One." Article I established Congress. Presumably Card
referred to the First Amendment. For the record, the author would place himself among
his readers, in the Preamble. The Constitution's opening words establish the government's
source of authority: "We the People of the United States . . ." All powers granted within the
text are delegated.

CHAPTER THIRTEEN: NEMESIS

327 "It was very emotional," Gerson said: Interview with Michael Gerson by Jo Becker, Sept. 5, 2006.

328 "I earned capital in the campaign": President Holds Press Conference, Nov. 4, 2004, 11:17 a.m. EST, video available at http://www.whitehouse.gov/news/releases/2004/11/20041104-5.v.html.

328 The president's liquid assets drained quickly: See Peter Baker and Jim VandeHei, "Bush's Political Capital Spent, Voices in Both Parties Suggest: Poll Numbers Sag as Setbacks Mount at Home and Abroad," *Washington Post,* May 31, 2005.

328 Even the Mod Squad had a brief comeback: Former majority leader Trent Lott called the Cheney-backed proposal the "nuclear option" because it would have removed the minority's traditional right to filibuster, or keep on talking long enough to prevent a floor vote. Collins, Snowe, Chafee, and McCain announced they would not support a vote to ask Cheney for a ruling. They helped broker a compromise involving fourteen senators in all, who promised to give most nominees an up-or-down vote while preserving the filibuster for "extraordinary circumstances."

328 Bush's approval ratings sank: A helpful compilation graph, which looks like a bad year in the stock market, is available at http://politicalarithmetik.blogspot.com/2005/11/approval-of-president-bush-2001.html.

328 "largely come to define Bush's second term": McClellan, *What Happened,* pp. 280, 290.

329 "I asked Dick if he'd be interested": Interview with Dan Bartlett, Dec. 17, 2007. Two officials on Cheney's staff confirmed his reluctance to take on the Katrina assignment, though they emphasized that he would have complied with an order from the president.

329 New Orleans was four-fifths underwater: Katrina was the costliest hurricane in American history, and the fifth deadliest. See Richard D. Knabb et al., *Tropical Cyclone Report: Hurricane Katrina: 23–30 August 2005* (National Hurricane Center), updated Aug. 10, 2006, available at http://www.nhc.noaa.gov/pdf/TCR-AL122005__Katrina.pdf.

330 "Brownie, you're doing a heck of a job": Variations became popular comic fodder, but these were Bush's words. As of mid-2008 they were viewable on YouTube at http://www.youtube.com/watch?v=RO2xiOuLnj8.

330 "We're going to push and push and push": Goldsmith, *The Terror Presidency,* p. 126.

330 Newton had a law for it: Newton's third law of motion: To every action there is always opposed an equal reaction: or the mutual actions of two bodies upon each other are always equal, and directed to contrary parts.

331 The explosion a moment later: The United Nations posted a photo gallery of the attack at http://www.un.org/av/photo/subjects/unhqbombing.htm.

331 "For me the bombing was final confirmation": E-mail from Aaron Friedberg, July 1, 2008.

331 "I used to do a kind of mental experiment": Friedberg interview, Dec. 13, 2006.

332 Word reached Cheney's office: The description of Derek Harvey's views and ongoing relationship with Cheney comes from three people with contemporary knowledge and the author's examination of Harvey's unclassified published work.

332 The M5 division of the Iraqi Intelligence Service: For more on this entity see *Compre-*

hensive Report of the Special Adviser to the DCI on Iraq's WMD, Sept. 30, 2004, annex B, available at https://www.cia.gov/library/reports/general-reports-1/iraq__wmd__2004/index.html.

333 "Actually, it's a classic problem with democracy": Interview with Condoleezza Rice, May 20, 2008.

333 At Cheney's urging, the DIA colonel: Interviews with a participant and another official with contemporary knowledge. This account tracks in part with the one in Ricks, *Fiasco,* pp. 408–9, where the meeting was first disclosed.

334 "bring 'em on": The official White House transcript had it as "bring them on," but reporters in the room heard the jaunty vernacular. Presidential News Conference, July 2, 2003, available at http://www.whitehouse.gov/news/releases/2003/07/20030702-3.html.

334 At a Fort Leavenworth symposium: The symposium was transcribed in John J. McGrath, ed., *An Army at War: Change in the Midst of Conflict* (Fort Leavenworth, Kans.: Combat Studies Institute Press, 2005). Harvey's presentation and question-and-answer session begin on p. 191. Copy on file with the author.

335 Libby and other staffers kept in touch: Hanson interview, Dec. 6, 2006.

336 "When do we leave?" King asked: *Larry King Live,* CNN, May 30, 2005.

336 He had been reading *Armageddon:* Max Hastings, *Armageddon: The Battle for Germany, 1944–1945* (New York: Knopf, 2004).

337 "If you look at what the dictionary says": Interview with Wolf Blitzer on CNN, June 23, 2005, excerpts at http://www.cnn.com/2005/US/06/23/cheney.interview/.

337 "I know that some of my decisions": President's Address to the Nation from the Oval Office, Dec. 18, 2005, at http://www.whitehouse.gov/news/releases/2005/12/20051218-2.html.

338 "They're screaming for us to get out of there": Lynne Cheney, *Executive Privilege,* pp. 48–49.

338 "a seminal event": Interview of the Vice President by ABC News, Al-Asad Air Base, Iraq, Dec. 18, 2005.

338 Four months later ... Cheney took a question: Vice President's Remarks at the Gerald R. Ford Journalism Prize Luncheon Followed by Q&A, June 19, 2006.

339 "We are *going* to have a trial": Interview with a participant in the meeting, who reviewed contemporary notes.

339 Rumsfeld never wanted to be the "world's jailer": Feith, *War and Decision,* p. 160. It is worth noting that in a book of 530 pages, packed with concrete details from his contemporary notes, the undersecretary of defense for policy does not mention military commissions at all. His only mention of detainees or Guantánamo Bay involves the first presidential decision in February 2002 that the Geneva Conventions would not apply as a matter of law to al Qaeda or Taliban fighters captured in Afghanistan.

340 "*shall* be detained . . . *if* the individual is to be tried": Emphasis added. Military Order, "Detention, Treatment, and Trial of Certain Non-Citizens in the War Against Terrorism," Nov. 13, 2001. For more on the order, see chapter 7.

340 reading each other's mind: Interview with Richard Haver by Jo Becker, Jan. 29, 2007.

340 He was famously contemptuous of the NSC staff: For Rumsfeld's attitude toward the NSC staff, interviews with four members of the staff and two Pentagon officials, 2005, 2006. For the legal status of the NSC, see National Security Act of 1947, 50 U.S. 401.

342 "Something happened to Rice's face": After the first edition of *Angler* was published, a British journalist asked Rice about this scene. She deflected the question. "Do I look like the sort to burst into tears?" she asked. BBC "Newsnight," Sept. 26, 2008, available at http://news.bbc.co.uk/1/hi/programmes/newsnight/politics/7637719.stm.

342 "She started to cry": Interview with a participant, 2008.

343 "al Qaeda is interested in acquiring": Interviews with national security and intelligence officials, October and November 2002. For more detail see Barton Gellman, "4 Nations Thought to Possess Smallpox; Iraq, N. Korea Named, Two Officials Say," *Washington Post,* Nov. 5, 2002.

343 "You have a threat, not currently treatable": Notes from a participant in the Oct. 25, 2002, meeting.

343 "The vice president set a very": Bartlett interview, Jan. 15, 2008.

344 "Which ones should we treat": Ron Suskind put a name to the idea that the government should act as though a risk were a certainty if the consequences were high enough. He attributed this "one percent doctrine" to the vice president. Friedberg and some other aides did not agree entirely with Suskind but said the phrase did seem to capture something about Cheney's thinking. See Ron Suskind, *The One Percent Doctrine* (New York: Simon & Schuster, 2006).

346 Jack Goldsmith, who now ran the Office of Legal Counsel: See chapter 7.

346 "The torture convention explicitly distinguishes": Goldsmith's reference was to the Convention Against Torture and Other Cruel, Inhuman or Degrading Treatment or Punishment, available at http://www.hrweb.org/legal/cat.html. E-mail from Jack Goldsmith, Apr. 24, 2008.

346 "only torture, not CID . . . was made part of the domestic criminal prohibition": E-mail from Jack Goldsmith, Apr. 24, 2008. Goldsmith's reference was to the War Crimes Act of 1996, 18 USC 118 sec. 2441, http://www.law.cornell.edu/uscode/18/usc_sed_18_00002441----000-.html.

347 "They are starving for info": The author obtained the Waxman-Hodgkinson e-mail exchange from another official, one of several who received it by cc: or by forwarding.

347 Their product . . . was a document of nine single-spaced pages: Unsigned memorandum, "Elements of a Possible Initiative," June 12, 2005. The Zelikow-England-Waxman proposal has been mentioned before in news accounts but not quoted substantially. The full text was obtained by the author.

349 Shortly after noon, Steve Hadley scheduled: Notice to cabinet principals, examined by author.

351 David Addington added a paragraph: Interviews with two officials directly involved. A copy of the Statement of Administration Policy is available at http://www.washingtonpost.com/wp-srv/politics/documents/cheney/statement__of__admin__policy__july212005.pdf.

352 He was referring to the February 7, 2002, directive: See chapter 7.

352 On October 5, 2005, a veto-proof Senate majority: The text of the act may be found at http://jurist.law.pitt.edu/gazette/2005/12/detainee-treatment-act-of-2005-white.php.

353 Cheney went on television and said that "what shocks the conscience": *Nightline,* ABC, Dec. 18, 2005.

354 In *Hamdan v. Rumsfeld:* For the text of *Hamdan v. Rumsfeld,* see http://supremecourtus .gov/opinions/05pdf05-184.pdf.

355 "Addington was deeply principled, but": Interview with Jack Goldsmith, May 2008.

355 The president negotiated for months: For the text of the act see http://www.washington post.com/wp-srv/politics/documents/cheney/military__commissions__act.pdf.

356 "He had to make sure we did it right": Beaver interview.

356 One of the things that Addington did: See Dafna Linzer, "CIA Held Al-Qaeda Suspect Secretly: Officials Disclose That Use of Overseas Prisons Resumed," *Washington Post,* Apr. 28, 2007.

356 DOD Directive 2310.01E: The full text is available at http://www.washingtonpost .com/wp-srv/politics/documents/cheney/dod__directive__2310__01E.pdf.

357 A three-judge panel in the U.S. Court of Appeals: See *Huzaifa Parhat v. Robert M. Gates,* U.S. Court of Appeals for the D.C. Circuit, a classified opinion that was partially declassified on June 30, 2008, available at http://www.fas.org/sgp/jud/parhat.pdf.

358 "Some of the few times I can remember": Interview with Bradford Berenson by Jo Becker, June 5, 2006.

358 "His treatment met the legal definition": Bob Woodward, "Detainee Tortured, says U.S. Official," *Washington Post*, Jan. 14, 2009.

360 Conservatives funneled objections to Rove and Cheney: Interview with Leonard Leo by Jo Becker, Nov. 7, 2006.

360 "Didn't have the nerve to tell me himself": Interview with eyewitness by Jo Becker. Cheney's office disputed the account. "The vice president did not say that," said his spokeswoman, Lea Anne McBride.

362 "One of the crazy things about this job": Lynne Cheney, *Executive Privilege,* p. 236.

362 On October 14 and November 26, 2003: The dates are provided in Indictment, *United States v. I. Lewis Libby,* Case No. 1:2005-cr-00394-RBW, Count Two, pp. 15–16, Oct. 28, 2005. On Mar. 6, 2007, a federal jury convicted Libby of perjury, false statement, and obstruction of justice.

364 Bush fired Don Rumsfeld, over Cheney's strong objection: Cheney's spokeswoman asserted at the time that "the vice president is right in line with" Bush's decision. Interview with Lea Anne McBride by Jo Becker, Nov. 9, 2006. Cheney dropped that pretense when asked himself. "Uh, I did not. I think he served very well and very ably," Cheney said."Don was the right guy to continue to lead the Department of Defense." Fox News special report, *Dick Cheney: No Retreat,* Oct. 13, 2007.

CHAPTER FOURTEEN: REGIME CHANGE

367 Cheney was Cheney, speaking of existential threats: The scene and Cheney's remarks are from interviews with two participants in the meeting.

368 "If we do not resolve our Iran problem": Interview with a participant in the meeting, who declined to be named while recounting off-the-record remarks, June 26, 2008. Cheney spoke to the American Australian Leadership Dialogue on June 24, 2008. His spokeswoman said she could not provide information "from a closed press event." E-mail from Lea Anne McBride to the author, June 27, 2008.

368 "Our country and the entire international community": White House transcript, Remarks by the Vice President to the Washington Institute for Near East Policy, Lansdowne, Virginia, Oct. 21, 2007.

369 When the United States and Britain sought UN authority: See Carol Castiel, "The Bush Preemption Doctrine: The Case of Iraq," Voice of America, Feb. 26, 2003, available at http://www.globalsecurity.org/military/library/news/2003/02/mil-030226-24187d9d.htm.

369 It was never clear he favored such a step: For Cheney's concerns about the risks of war with Iran, see chapter 9.

369 "I would guess that John McCain and I": Greg Sheridan, "Cheney Hints at Iran Strike," *Weekend Australian,* Feb. 24, 2007, available at http://www.news.com.au/heraldsun/story/0,21985,21279082-5005961,00.html.

369 Wurmser denied categorically: Wurmser interview, Dec. 14, 2007.

369 two sets of contemporary notes: The notes recorded two closely similar versions of Wurmser's remarks by people who heard him describe the scenario in early May 2007.

369–70 Now, in the summer of Cheney's discontent: Except, perhaps, in the political campaigns and in overheated media speculation. Some Democrats and commentators predicted an October Surprise, but Bush said firmly that the United States was on a diplomatic track with Iran, and Admiral Michael Mullen, chairman of the Joint Chiefs of Staff, made clear that U.S. forces were overstretched in Iraq and Afghanistan alone. For an entertaining sketch of the rhetoric and reality, see Dana Milbank, "Not So Quiet on the Third Front," *Washington Post,* July 3, 2008.

370 a new record of $144 a barrel: Associated Press, "Oil Passes $144 to Set Yet Another Record," July 2, 2008. For trends and context see "Oil Price History and Analysis," WTRG Economics (updated frequently), at http://www.wtrg.com/prices.htm.

370 he gripped the railing tightly: The author made the observation in person while accompanying the vice president in Texas and back to Andrews Air Force Base on Oct. 4, 2006.

370 The "Fuck yourself": One adviser said that Cheney, upon hearing that his staff opposed an apology, replied, "Good. Because I'm not going to." For coverage of the episode see Helen Dewar and Dana Milbank, "Cheney Dismisses Critic with Obscenity," *Washington Post,* June 25, 2004.

370 "pissed off all the time": E-mail from David Brady to author, June 27, 2008.

371 "The disease of the arteries": Interview with Anthony L. Komaroff by the author's research assistant, Justin Jouvenal, Jan. 10, 2007.

371 "a world that can be changed": See chapter 9.

371 "Last question," he said: The first account of Steve Clemons's question and Cheney's delayed reply was in Helene Cooper, "Bush Rebuffs Hard-Liners to Ease North Korean Curbs," *New York Times,* June 27, 2008.

372 Bush struck the government of Kim Jong Il: White House Transcript, Statement by the President on North Korea, June 26, 2008.

372 The U.S. government, it emerged: Press Briefing by National Security Adviser Stephen Hadley, June 26, 2008.

372 "Sometimes you get a little too far forward": Doug Struck, "N. Korean Leader to Continue Sale of Missiles," *Washington Post,* May 5, 2001.

372–73 "but he was certainly for applying": E-mail from Aaron Friedberg, July 1, 2008.

373 "is 'engagement' like we engaged the Japanese": Interview with John R. Bolton, Sept. 22, 2004.

373 jockeyed Bolton out of the department: After Bush's reelection, Bolton overplayed his hand. Gunning for deputy secretary of state, he told Rice he did not regard his undersecretary's post as sufficient. She replied, according to State Department officials at the time, that she sadly had nothing suitable and set a date for his departure from the job he had "resigned."

373 "How about I give Kim a peace treaty?": Interviews with two White House officials and a State Department official, 2006 and 2007. See also Glenn Kessler, *The Confidante: Condoleezza Rice and the Creation of the Bush Legacy* (New York: St. Martin's Press, 2007), p. 86.

373 "I think that's fine": Interview with John R. Bolton, Mar. 29, 2007.

374 "The idea that he doesn't consider": Interview with Condoleezza Rice, May 20, 2008.

374 listing them, with Iraq, in an "axis of evil": White House Transcript, President Delivers the State of the Union Address, Jan. 29, 2002, available at http://www.whitehouse.gov/news/releases/2002/01/20020129-11.html.

374 "By the time it became clear": Friedberg interview, Dec. 20, 2006.

375 "The president is deeply, deeply, deeply conversant": State Department transcript, Interview with the NBC Editorial Board, May 6, 2006, available at www.state.gov/secretary/rm/2006/66020.htm. Rice quickly added, " . . . and nobody could have been when he came into office."

375 North Korean ambassador Choe Jin Su: See "DPRK Nuclear Declaration a Step Toward Solution of Korean Peninsula Nuclear Issue," Xinhua, available at http://news.xinhua net.com/english/2008-06/27/content__8449838.htm.

376 he, too, "was met with total silence": E-mail from Steve Yates to author, July 3, 2008.

376 Cheney's "gatekeeper, intellectual partner, and personal friend": Interview with Steve Yates, Jan. 25, 2007.

376 Christopher Hill . . . once said the truculent North Korean diplomats: Interview with a witness, 2007.

376 "Kim Jong Hill": Bolton interview, Mar. 29, 2007.

377 "all they had to do was right-click": Yates interview, Jan. 25, 2007.

377 Bush signed an executive order: "Executive Order: Interpretation of the Geneva Conventions Common Article 3 as Applied to a Program of Detention and Interrogation Operated by the Central Intelligence Agency," July 20, 2007, available at http://www.whitehouse.gov/news/releases/2007/07/20070720-4.html.

377 Addington, making the most of language: For a discussion of the fine print in the Military Commissions Act, see chapter 13.

378 Addington had already established the rationale: See chapter 13.

378 "I'd like to close Guantanamo": Press Conference of the President, June 14, 2006, at http://www.whitehouse.gov/news/releases/2006/06/20060614.html.

379 Specter sent an angry letter: Senator Arlen Specter to Vice President Dick Cheney, June 7, 2008, on file with author.

379 **Cheney's "Dear Arlen" reply:** Vice President Dick Cheney to Senator Arlen Specter, June 8, 2006, on file with author.

379 **"You're not the Department of Litigation Risk!":** Interview with a witness to one such eruption.

379 **"They didn't circumvent the process":** Interview with Michael Gerson by Jo Becker, Nov. 13, 2006.

380 **Bellinger, after seven years, finally voiced his frustrations:** Interview with John B. Bellinger III, Apr. 27, 2008.

380 **"Once to Every Man and Nation":** James R. Lowell published the words in the *Boston Courier,* Dec. 11, 1845, in protest of the war with Mexico. Full text available at http://www .cyberhymnal.org/htm/o/n/oncetoev.htm.

380–81 **"We'd like nothing better than to close Guantanamo":** State Department Transcript, Secretary Condoleezza Rice, Remarks Following a Question-and-Answer Session at Google Headquarters, Mountain View, California, May 22, 2008, available at http://www.state.gov/ secretary/rm/2008/05/105177.htm.

381 **"transfer temporarily my Constitutional powers":** Text of a Letter from the President to the Speaker of the House of Representatives and the President Pro Tempore of the Senate, July 21, 2007.

381 **The words were everything we had come to expect:** He disclosed by the end of the month that he had written letters, but not until months later, in a television broadcast, did he release the text. See *Dick Cheney: No Retreat,* a Fox News Special Report, Oct. 13, 2007, available online at http://www.hulu.com/watch/18605/fox-news-specials-dick-cheney-no -retreat.

381 **Autumn of 2007 brought a Fox News Special:** *Dick Cheney: No Retreat,* ibid.

381 **The newspaper series, by the author in partnership with Jo Becker:** The "Angler" series ran in four parts beginning June 24, 2007, and is available at http://blog.washingtonpost .com/Cheney.

384 **Bush also alluded . . . to something Dan Bartlett observed:** See the discussion, late in chapter 12, of the lesson Bush learned from Cheney's handling of the Justice Department uprising.

384 **And that was all the president had to say:** Baier gave his own closing argument for the jury at home, standing in front of the White House: "You've heard how Dick Cheney's political opponents try to paint him as someone who played the angles, grabbed power, and maneuvered the president into taking the country in the wrong direction. You've also heard both Cheney and President Bush say that's [pause for emphasis, spread hands] *simply not true.*"

384 **as the least-liked vice presidents in the history of modern polling:** See Megan Thee, "Polls: Cheney Nears Quayle as Least Popular Veep," *New York Times,* July 9, 2007, blogged on the Web at http://thecaucus.blogs.nytimes.com/2007/07/09/polls-cheney-nears-quayle-as -least-popular-veep.

385 **"one of the worst times in my life":** Interview with Alan Simpson by Jo Becker.

385 **"several, I would say, person-size safes":** Testimony of John Hannah, Feb. 13, 2007.

385 Jon Stewart demanded to know: "You Don't Know Dick—Safe," part of a series that week on *The Daily Show with Jon Stewart,* June 27, 2007, at http://www.comedycentral.com/videos/index.jhtml?videoId=89163.

385 official Iran Press TV service sent it: Iran Press TV, Oct. 28, 2007. The item was withdrawn and is no longer available.

386 "scattered boos" from passersby: "Reliable Source," *Washington Post,* Apr. 25, 2007.

386 commencement address at Brigham Young University: White House Transcript, Vice President Delivers Commencement Address at Brigham Young University, Apr. 26, 2007, http://www.whitehouse.gov/news/releases/2007/04/20070426-12.html.

387 "What authority would you delegate": Republican Presidential Debate, Aug. 5, 2007, Des Moines, Iowa.

387 "Would you grant your vice president": Republican Presidential Debate, Sept. 5, 2007, Durham, New Hampshire.

388 "The president listened too much to the vice president": Roger Simon, "McCain Bashes Cheney over Iraq Policy," *Politico,* Jan. 24, 2007.

390 "challenging work": Lynne Cheney, *Executive Privilege,* p. 57.

390 televised interview in March 2008 with Martha Raddatz: Interview of the Vice President by Martha Raddatz, ABC News, Mar. 19, 2008. The spa is here: http://www.shangri-la.com/en/property/muscat/barraljissahresort.

392 Executive Order 13233: President George W. Bush, Executive Order 13233, Nov. 1, 2001.

392 They called it "Treated As: SECRET/SCI": One example came to light in the Libby trial, in Government Exhibit 528B, titled "Uranium, 7/12/03."

392 "I don't know what the motivation is": Interview with J. William Leonard, Jan. 4, 2008.

393 When Leonard would not back down: E-mail, David S. Addington to Karen Evans, Office of Management and Budget, March 1, 2007, copy obtained and kept on file by author.

393 "there is a notion that Schumpeter gave us": Armey interview, June 19, 2008. The reference was to Schumpeter's observation about Karl Marx, whose success lay in "formulating with unsurpassed force that feeling of being thwarted and ill treated which is the auto-therapeutic attitude of the unsuccessful many." Joseph A. Schumpeter, *Capitalism, Socialism, and Democracy* (New York: Harper, 1942), p. 6.

394 "very likely the biggest foreign policy blunder": Armey interview, June 19, 2008.

394 Cheney may turn out to be right: One author speculates that Bush (and by implication Cheney) could benefit "from the American tendency to overvalue activist leaders. So a bad president like Wilson is preferred, in our rankings and our hearts, to a good but undistinguished manager like Calvin Coolidge. A sometimes impressive, oft-erratic president like Truman is lionized, while the more even-keeled greatness of Dwight D. Eisenhower is persistently undervalued. John F. Kennedy is hailed for escaping the Cuban missile crisis, which his own misjudgments set in motion, while George H. W. Bush, who steered the U.S. through the fraught final moments of the Cold War with admirable caution, is caricatured as a ditherer." Ross Douthat, "Redeeming Dubya," *Atlantic,* June 2008, available at http://www.theatlantic.com/doc/200806/bush.

394 On the Fourth of July: For the setting and events aboard ship, interviews with Petty Officer Eric Brown, July 3 and July 4, 2008, and the Visitors Brochure available at http://www.ussconstitution.navy.mil/.

395 repeated after the vice president: The full text is available at http://www.navy.com/about/before/meps/#oathofenlistement.

395 This event, like nearly all the rest: Here is the full "Press Schedule of the Vice President for July 4, 2008," distributed by White House e-mail on July 2, 2008, with only credentialing procedures and technical details for television omitted:
FRIDAY, JULY 4, 2008
10:40 A.M. (Eastern)—OPEN PRESS: The Vice President and Mrs. Cheney arrive at Logan International Airport-FBO
11:15 A.M. (Eastern)—CLOSED PRESS: The Vice President participates in a reenlistment ceremony aboard the USS *Constitution*
1:25 P.M. (Eastern)—OPEN PRESS: The Vice President and Mrs. Cheney depart Logan International Airport-FBO

AFTERWORD

396 Dick Cheney proposed an epitaph: See for example "Interview of the Vice President by Wolf Blitzer," *Late Edition,* CNN, Jan. 9, 2009. Among his many exit interviews, more than twice the number George Bush granted, were those with Jonathan Karl on ABC News on Dec. 16, 2008, Jon Ward and John Solomon in the *Washington Times* on Dec. 17, 2008, Bob Schieffer on CBS's *Face the Nation* on Jan. 4, 2009, Mark Knoller on CBS Radio on Jan. 7, 2009, Mike Emanuel on Fox News on Jan. 12, 2009, Bill Bennett on his webcast "Morning in America" on Jan. 13, 2009, Jim Lehrer on PBS *News Hour* on Jan. 14, 2009, and Stephen F. Hayes in the *Weekly Standard* on Jan. 22, 2009.

396 "That's not going to happen again on my watch": ABC News, ibid, Dec. 16, 2008.

396 As John McCain vetted running mates: Statement by the president with Senator John McCain, Rose Garden, Mar. 5, 2008.

397 "Above all else, control your vice president": A senior Obama administration official described the meeting for the author. It was first reported in Michael Duffy, "As Dick Cheney Prepares to Depart, His Mystery Lingers," *Time,* Jan. 19, 2009, at http://www.time.com/time/printout/0,8816,1872531,00.html.

397 The Bush administration's brief: Brief for the United States as Amicus Curiae, *District of Columbia v. Dick Anthony Heller*, 554 U.S. 290 (2008), at pp. 1–2, 8.

397 he joined a competing brief that asked the court to declare the D.C. law "unreasonable per se": Brief For Amici Curiae 55 Members Of United States Senate, The President Of The United States Senate, And 250 Members Of United States House Of Representatives In Support Of Respondent, *District of Columbia v. Heller,* ibid, pp. 1, 5.

398 "Am I the evil genius": Transcript, "Interview with Vice President Cheney," *USA Today,* Jan. 18, 2004. See http://www.usatoday.com/news/washington/2004-01-18-cheney-transcript_x.htm?loc=interstitialskip.

398 "We spent a great deal of time and effort getting legal advice": *Washington Times,* Dec. 17, 2008, ibid.

398 "**He doesn't have to check with anybody**": Interview of the Vice President by Chris Wallace, Fox News Sunday, Dec. 22, 2008, available at http://www.foxnews.com/story /0,2933,470706,00.html.

398 **The received view in the *Weekly Standard*:** Christopher Willcox, "Veep Hunting," *Weekly Standard*, Dec. 29, 2008. I respond to Willcox on the comments tab of my Web site, www.bartongellman.com.

399 **In her roman à clef of White House life:** See discussion of Lynne Cheney's novel *Executive Privilege*, in chapter 4.

399 **One benefit of the new media age:** The roundtable, on TPMCafé Book Club, brought together Jacob Heilbrunn (who reviewed *Angler* for the *New York Times Book Review*), David Greenberg (*Slate*), Steve Clemons (*American Conservative*), Spencer Ackerman (the Attackerman blog), and Paul Mirengoff (PowerLine). It is archived at http://tpmcafe .talkingpointsmemo.com/tpmcafe-book-club/2008/11/16-week/.

400 **The e-mail that James B. Comey sent colleagues:** See chapter 12.

400 **The Obama administration's reversal of Cheney-authored restrictions:** See "Executive Order—Presidential Records," Jan. 21, 2009, available at http://www.whitehouse.gov /the_press_office/ExecutiveOrderPresidentialRecords/, and Alexis Simendinger, "A Quiet Coup on Presidential Records," *National Journal*, April 4, 2009. For comparison to the Cheney-drafted Executive Order 13233, see the text of the order at http://www.fas.org/irp /offdocs/eo/eo-13233.htm and my discussion on pp. 137, 392 of *Angler* and accompanying chapter notes.

400 **Angler describes maneuvering by senior figures other than Cheney:** See, for example, the accounts throughout of efforts by Condoleezza Rice, John B. Bellinger, James B. Comey, Philip Zelikow, Gordon England, and Matthew Waxman to bypass opposition from Cheney on matters of foreign policy, the treatment of detainees, and domestic surveillance. Among those who accuse me of treating Cheney, out of context, as uniquely culpable in such maneuvers are two cofounders of the PowerLine blog. See for example Paul Mirengoff, "Across the Great Divide, A Recap," Nov. 21, 2008, at http://www.powerlineblog.com/archives /2008/11/022125.php, and Scott Johnson, "Across the Great Divide: A Salute," Nov. 22, 2008, at http://www.powerlineblog.com/archives/2008/11/022131.php.

402 **barely ducked a pair of shoes:** In Arab culture, striking a person with a shoe, or even pointing one, is an even greater insult than in the West. A video of the Dec. 14, 2008, shoe-throwing incident is available at http://www.youtube.com/watch?v=uNhzTN0Japc. It was Apr. 9, 2003, when U.S. Marines helped Iraqis pull down a twenty-foot statue of Saddam Hussein on Firdos Square and local residents made a show, for foreign television crews, of beating the statue with the soles of their shoes. Several days later, the author witnessed pick-up truckloads of Iraqi men shouting "Bush! Bush! Bush!" to the tune of a common soccer anthem.

402 **crowds roared approval of the insult to Bush:** See for example BBC News, "Iraq Rally for Bush Shoe Attacker," Dec. 15, 2008, at http://news.bbc.co.uk/2/hi/middle_east/7783608 .stm.

402 **Renegade and Celtic:** See Anne E. Kornblut, "'Renegade' Joins Race For White House: Obama Is Given Code Name by Secret Service," *Washington Post*, June 17, 2007, at http://www .washingtonpost.com/wp-dyn/content/article/2007/06/16/AR2007061601079.html.

402 he rode in on a wheelchair: A White House statement said he injured himself lifting boxes as he departed the Naval Observatory, adding: "Under his physician's recommendation, the Vice President will be in a wheelchair for the next couple of days, including for tomorrow's inauguration." Statement by White House Press Secretary Dana Perino, Jan. 19, 2009.

INDEX

481

Index

Index

Cheney, Dick *(cont.)*
   detainee policy and, 168–70, 173, 177, 190, 193, 351, 377
   doctrinaire approach of, 325–26
   DUI arrests of, 18
   economic policies of, 38, 53, 55–56, 69, 70–71, 72–74, 255–75
   e-mails secretly copied to, 189, 376–77
   energy task force of, 81–82, 89, 90, 91–94, 104–7, 205–6
   as enforcer, 64
   environmental issues and, 82–85, 88–90, 195–213, 378
   favorite movie of, 49
   "first principles" and, 55–56
   in Ford administration, 14, 16, 19, 33, 55, 59–60, 87–88, 100, 138, 177, 257–58
   Fox News Special on, 381–84
   global warming and, 82–85, 88–90
   at GOP caucus, 255–56, 272–73
   Greenspan's relationship with, 70–71, 266, 267–68
   growing isolation of, 385–86, 389
   Halliburton divestiture of, 21, 22, 94–95
   Hamilton admired by, 98
   heart disease of, 18, 24–25, 44–46, 370–71, 389
   House office of, 69–70, 215, 301
   hunting accident of, 385
   Hurricane Katrina role of, 329–30, 386
   as indifferent to public opinion, 50, 386, 389, 390–91
   intellect of, 15
   intelligence community and, 110, 139–40, 160
   Iran and, 235, 242, 243, 245, 367–70, 385
   on Iraqi elections, 338
   Iraqi insurgency and, 249–53
   on Iraqi nuclear threat, 229
   Iraq War and, 229, 232–33, 250, 337–38, 378, 386, 388, 394
   Jeffords controversy and, 78–80
   Justice Department revolt and, 277–78, 294–96, 299, 309–11
   Keating's relationship with, 3
   King's interview with, 336
   "last throes" comment of, 336–38
   legal advice cherrypicked by, 287
   loyalty of, 270
   in meeting with Australians, 367–68, 370, 371–72, 375
   in meeting with moderate Republicans, 62–65
   military approach to government of, 67–68
   military commissions and, 162, 164–65, 166–67
   as monetarist, 258
   Newsweek interview of, 122–24
   in 9/11 response, 114–30, 227
   9/11 shootdown order of, 119–27
   North Korea and, 230, 371–73, 374, 375, 378
   NSA and, 140–43
   O'Neill fired by, 271

   President's Daily Briefs previewed by, 244–45
   "personnel is policy" motto of, 35
   in Philippines crisis, 59
   Plame case and, 361–64, 386
   on policy surprises, 86–87
   Powell's authority limited by, 37
   power accumulated by, 34–35, 53–54, 244, 325
   preordained policy portfolio of, 52
   and presidential authority, 82, 93, 96–99, 100, 101–2, 104–7, 130, 301, 378, 388, 394
   and presidential succession, 157–58
   "president of foreign affairs" myth and, 54
   Principals Committee involvement of, 53–54
   and public opinion on Iraq War, 337–38
   Quayle's meeting with, 57–60, 388
   Raddatz's interview with, 390–91
   "reaching down" policy of, 55, 196
   realism of, 162, 252, 374
   Realpolitik of, 232–33
   regime change views of, 238–41
   at Republican congressional retreat, 255–56
   in Republican Senate caucus, 56–57
   on retreating from Bush campaign agenda, 64–67
   on role of vice president, 33–35, 51–52, 87
   on Saddam–al Qaeda link, 226
   secrecy of, 6–7, 92, 93–94, 95–96, 138, 159, 198, 199, 210, 287, 376, 385, 392–93, 395
   Senate office of, 69, 74
   sense of humor of, 19, 27–28
   smallpox vaccination campaign discussion and, 343–44
   staff hires of, 40–44
   staff memo on global warming of, 84–85
   status of aides to, 49–50
   steel tariff and, 270
   on *Steve Kass Show,* 76
   supply-side economics of, 257–58, 264–65
   Supreme Court nominees and, 358–60
   tax cuts and, 53, 256–57, 269–70, 378
   terrorist threats discounted by, 111–13
   torture as viewed by, 171, 174–75
   transition headed by, 32–40, 47–48
   and 2003 New Year's alert, 234–35
   2004 elections and, 327–28
   unannounced phone calls of, 2
   vetting process avoided by, 23–25
   in vice-presidential search, 1–4, 6–10, 14–19, 20–21, 23–25
   vindictiveness of, alleged, 30
   warrantless surveillance program and, 143, 149, 150, 153–54, 277–78, 282–83, 290, 300–302, 378
   web of contacts of, 40
   WMD search and, 249
   worst-case scenarios as preoccupation of, 53
   Wyoming registration of, 17, 22
Cheney, Liz, 7, 8, 29, 32, 37, 242, 387–88
Cheney, Lynne, 32, 35, 52, 94, 102–4, 116, 117, 121, 250, 336, 337–38, 362, 389–90

Index

Index